Routledge History of Philosophy
Volume VI

The turn of the nineteenth century marked a rich and exciting explosion of philosophical energy and talent. The enormity of the revolution set off in philosophy by Immanuel Kant was comparable, by Kant's own estimation, with the Copernican Revolution that ended the middle ages. The movement he set in motion, the fast-moving and often cantankerous dialectic of "German Idealism," inspired some of the most creative philosophers in modern times: including G.W.F. Hegel and Arthur Schopenhauer as well as those who reacted against them – Marx and Kierkegaard, for example.

This volume traces the emergence of German Idealism from Kant and his predecessors through the first half of the nineteenth century, ending with the "irrationalism" of Kierkegaard. Each chapter has been written by a distinguished scholar in the field, and contributors include Lewis White Beck (on the German background), Daniel Bonevac, Don Becker, Patrick Gardiner (on Kant), Daniel Breazeale (on Fichte and Schelling), Robert C. Solomon, Willem deVries and Leo Rauch (on Hegel), Kathleen M. Higgins (on Schopenhauer), Robert Nola (on the Young Hegelians, including Marx) and Judith Butler (on Kierkegaard).

The Age of German Idealism provides a broad, scholarly introduction to the period for students of philosophy and related disciplines, as well as some original interpretations of these authors. It includes a glossary of technical terms and a chronological table of philosophical, scientific and other important cultural events.

Robert C. Solomon is Quincey Lee Centennial Professor of Philosophy at the University of Texas at Austin. **Kathleen M. Higgins** is Associate Professor of Philosophy at the University of Texas at Austin.

Routledge History of Philosophy
General editors – G.H.R. Parkinson and S.G. Shanker

The *Routledge History of Philosophy* provides a chronological survey of the history of Western philosophy, from its beginnings in the sixth century BC to the present time. It discusses all major philosophical developments in depth. Most space is allocated to those individuals who, by common consent, are regarded as great philosophers. But lesser figures have not been neglected, and together the ten volumes of the *History* include basic and critical information about every significant philosopher of the past and present. These philosophers are clearly situated within the cultural and, in particular, the scientific context of their time.

The *History* is intended not only for the specialist, but also for the student and the general reader. Each chapter is by an acknowledged authority in the field. The chapters are written in an accessible style and a glossary of technical terms is provided in each volume.

Routledge History of Philosophy
Volume VI

The Age of German Idealism

EDITED BY

Robert C. Solomon
and
Kathleen M. Higgins

London and New York

First published 1993
by Routledge
11 New Fetter Lane, London EC4P 4EE

Simultaneously published in the USA and Canada
by Routledge
29 West 35th Street, New York, NY 10001

Reprinted 1998

Set in 10½/12 pt Garamond by Intype, London
Printed and bound in Great Britain by
TJ International Ltd, Padstow Cornwall

British Library Cataloguing in Publication Data
Age of German Idealism – (Routledge History of Philosophy Series; Vol. 6)
I. Solomon, Robert C.
II. Higgins, Kathleen M.   III. Series 190.9

Library of Congress Cataloging in Publication Data
The Age of German idealism / ed. Robert C. Solomon and Kathleen M. Higgins
p.   cm. – (Routledge history of philosophy; v. 6)
Includes bibliographical references and index.
1. Philosophy, German – 18th century.   2. Philosophy, German – 19th
century.   3. Idealism – History – 18th century.   4. Idealism –
History – 19th century. I. Solomon, Robert C.   II. Higgins,
Kathleen Marie. III. Series.
B2615.A35   1993
141'.0943–dc20   92-32040
ISBN 0-415-05604-7

Contents

CONTENTS

General editors' preface

The history of philosophy, as its name implies, represents a union of two very different disciplines, each of which imposes severe constraints upon the other. As an exercise in the history of ideas, it demands that one acquire a "period eye": a thorough understanding of how the thinkers whom it studies viewed the problems which they sought to resolve, the conceptual frameworks in which they addressed these issues, their assumptions and objectives, their blind spots and miscues. But as an exercise in philosophy, we are engaged in much more than simply a descriptive task. There is a crucial critical aspect to our efforts: we are looking for the cogency as much as the development of an argument, for its bearing on questions which continue to preoccupy us as much as the impact which it may have had on the evolution of philosophical thought.

The history of philosophy thus requires a delicate balancing act from its practitioners. We read these writings with the full benefit of historical hindsight. We can see why the minor contributions remained minor and where the grand systems broke down: sometimes as a result of internal pressures, sometimes because of a failure to overcome an insuperable obstacle, sometimes because of a dramatic technological or sociological change, and, quite often, because of nothing more than a shift in intellectual fashion or interests. Yet, because of our continuing philosophical concern with many of the same problems, we cannot afford to look dispassionately at these works. We want to know what lessons are to be learned from the inconsequential or the glorious failures; many times we want to plead for a contemporary relevance in the overlooked theory or to reconsider whether the "glorious failure" was indeed such or simply ahead of its time: perhaps even ahead of its author.

We find ourselves, therefore, much like the mythical "radical translator" who has so fascinated modern philosophers, trying to understand an author's ideas in his and his culture's eyes, and, at the same time, in our own. It can be a formidable task. Many times we fail in the historical undertaking because our philosophical interests are so strong, or lose sight of the latter because we are so enthralled by the former. But the nature of philosophy is such that we are compelled to master both techniques. For learning about the history of philosophy is not just a challenging and engaging pastime: it is an essential element in learning about the nature of philosophy – in grasping how philosophy is intimately connected with and yet distinct from both history and science.

The *Routledge History of Philosophy* provides a chronological survey of the history of Western philosophy, from its beginnings up to the present time. Its aim is to discuss all major philosophical developments in depth, and, with this in mind, most space has been allocated to those individuals who, by common consent, are regarded as great philosophers. But lesser figures have not been neglected, and it is hoped that the reader will be able to find, in the ten volumes of the *History*, at least basic information about any significant philosopher of the past or present.

Philosophical thinking does not occur in isolation from other human activities, and this *History* tries to situate philosophers within the cultural, and in particular the scientific, context of their time. Some philosophers, indeed, would regard philosophy as merely ancillary to the natural sciences; but even if this view is rejected, it can hardly be denied that the sciences have had a great influence on what is now regarded as philosophy, and it is important that this influence should be set forth clearly. Not that these volumes are intended to provide a mere record of the factors that influenced philosophical thinking; philosophy is a discipline with its own standards of argument, and the presentation of the ways in which these arguments have developed is the main concern of this *History*.

In speaking of "what is now regarded as philosophy", we may have given the impression that there now exists a single view of what philosophy is. This is certainly not the case; on the contrary, there exist serious differences of opinion, among those who call themselves philosophers, about the nature of their subject. These differences are reflected in the existence at the present time of two main schools of thought, usually described as "analytic" and "continental" philosophy. It is not our intention, as general editors of this *History*, to take sides in this dispute. Our attitude is one of tolerance, and our hope is that these volumes will contribute to an understanding of how philosophers have reached the positions which they now occupy.

One final comment. Philosophy has long been a highly technical subject, with its own specialized vocabulary. This *History* is intended not only for the specialist but also for the general reader. To this end, we have tried to ensure that each chapter is written in an accessible style; and since technicalities are unavoidable, a glossary of technical terms is provided in each volume. In this way these volumes will, we hope, contribute to a wider understanding of a subject which is of the highest importance to all thinking people.

G.H.R. Parkinson
S.G. Shanker

Notes on contributors

Lewis White Beck is Burbank Professor Emeritus of Philosophy at the University of Rochester. His works include *A Commentary on Kant's Critique of Practical Reason* (1961), *Studies in the Philosophy of Kant* (1965), *Early German Philosophy: Kant and his Predecessors* (1969), *The Actor and the Spectator* (1975), *Critique of Practical Reason and Other Writings in Moral Philosophy* (1976), and *Essays on Kant and Hume* (1978).

Daniel Bonevac (Ph.D. Pittsburgh, 1980) is Professor and Chair of the Department of Philosophy at the University of Texas at Austin. He is the author of *Reduction in the Abstract Sciences* (1982), *Deduction* (1987), and *The Art and Science of Logic* (1990); the editor of *Today's Moral Issues* (1991); and a co-editor of *Beyond the Western Tradition* (1992). He has published articles on Kant, metaphysics, semantics, and philosophical logic.

Donald Becker is Assistant Professor of Philosophy at the University of Texas at Austin.

Patrick Gardiner is an Emeritus Fellow of Magdalen College, Oxford, and a Fellow of the British Academy. His publications include *The Nature of Historical Explanation* (1952), *Schopenhauer* (1963), and *Kierkegaard* (1988). He has edited *Theories of History* (1959), *Nineteenth-Century Philosophy* (1969), and *The Philosophy of History* (1974).

Daniel Breazeale is Professor of Philosophy at the University of Kentucky. His publications include *Philosophy and Truth: Selections from Nietzsche's Notebooks of the Early 1870s* (1979), and *Fichte, Early Philosophical Writings* (1988).

Robert C. Solomon is Quincy Lee Centennial Professor of Philosophy at the University of Texas at Austin. His publications include *In the*

Spirit of Hegel (1983), *From Hegel to Existentialism* (1987), *Continental Philosophy since 1750* (1988), and *A Passion for Justice* (1990).

Willem deVries is Associate Professor of Philosophy at the University of New Hampshire. He is author of *Hegel's Theory of Mental Activity: An Introduction to Theoretical Spirit* (1988).

Leo Rauch is Professor of Philosophy at Babson College. His publications include *The Political Animal: Studies in Political Philosophy from Machiavelli to Marx* (1981), *Hegel and the Human Spirit: A Translation of the Jena Lectures on the Philosophy of Spirit (1805–6) with Commentary* (1983), and *Introduction to the Philosophy of History, with Selections from The Philosophy of Right* (1988).

Robert Nola teaches philosophy at the University of Auckland. Most of his published work is in the philosophy of science. He has also published several papers on Plato, Marx, Nietzsche, and the sociology of scientific knowledge.

Kathleen M. Higgins is Associate Professor at the University of Texas at Austin. She is author of *Nietzsche's Zarathustra* (1987) and *The Music of our Lives* (1991). She is also co-editor of *Reading Nietzsche* (1988), *The Philosophy of (Erotic) Love* (1991), and *Thirteen Questions in Ethics* (1992).

Judith Butler is Professsor of Humanities at Johns Hopkins University and the author of *Subjects of Desire: Hegelian Reflections in Twentieth-Century France* (1987), and *Gender Trouble: Feminism and the Subversion of Identity* (1990).

Chronology

Unless otherwise specified, the dates assigned to books or articles are the dates of publication, and the dates assigned to musical or stage works are those of first performance. The titles of works not written in English have been translated, unless they are better known in their original form.

	Politics and religion	The arts
1712		
1713		
1714		
1715	Louis XIV d.	
1716		
1717		Watteau, *Embarquement pour Cythère*
1719		Defoe, *Robinson Crusoe*
1720		
1723		Bach, *St John Passion*
1724		
1725	Peter the Great d.	
1726		Swift, *Gulliver's Travels*
1727		
1728	William Law, *A Serious Call*	Gay, *The Beggar's Opera*
1729		Bach, *St Matthew Passion* Lessing b.
1732		
1733		1733–4 Pope, *An Essay on Man* 1733–5 Hogarth, *A Rake's Progress*
1734		
1735		
1736	Butler, *The Analogy of Religion*	
1738	Conversion of John Wesley	
1739		
1740	Frederick the Great becomes King of Prussia	
1742		Handel, *The Messiah*
1743		
1744		
1745		
1747		

Science and technology	Philosophy	
	Rousseau b.	1712
Newton, *Principia* (revised edn)	Wolff, *Rational Thoughts on the Powers of the Human Understanding*	1713
	Baumgarten b. Leibniz, *Monadology*	1714
	Crusius b.	1715
	Leibniz d.	1716
		1717
		1719
	Wolff, *German Metaphysics*	1720
Wren d.		1723
Foundation of the Academy of Sciences, St Petersburg	Kant b.	1724
	Vico, *The New Science*	1725
		1726
Newton d. Hales, *Vegetable Staticks* (on plant physiology)		1727
	Wolff, *Philosophia rationalis sive Logica*	1728
	Wolff, *Philosophia prima sive Ontologia* Moses Mendelssohn b.	1729
	Wolff, *Psychologia empirica*	1732
Saccheri attempts to prove Euclid's parallel postulate		1733
	Wolff, *Psychologia rationalis*	1734
Linnaeus, *System of Nature*		1735
	c. 1736 Tetens b. 1736–7 Wolff, *Theologica naturalis* (2 vols)	1736
		1738
	Baumgarten, *Metaphysica*	1739
		1740
		1742
	Crusius, *On the Use and Limits of the Principle of Determining Reason* Jacobi b.	1743
	Vico d.	1744
	Crusius, *A Sketch of the Necessary Truths of Reason*	1745
	Crusius, *The Way to the Certainty and Reliability of Human Knowledge*	1747

	Politics and religion	The arts
1748		Smollett, *Roderick Random*
1749		Fielding, *Tom Jones*
1750		Bach d.
1751		
1753		
1754		
1755		
1757		
1758		
1759		Voltaire, *Candide* Handel d.
1760		Sterne, *Tristram Shandy*, Books I and II
1761		
1762		
1763		
1764		
1765	Stamp Act begins quarrel between Britain and American colonies	
1766		Lessing, *Laocoon*
1767		Sterne, *Tristram Shandy* completed
1768	Schleiermacher b.	
1769	Napoleon b.	
1770		Beethoven b. Hölderlin b. Wordsworth b.
1771		Smollett, *Humphrey Clinker*
1772		
1774		Goethe, *The Sorrows of Young Werther*
1775	War of American Independence begins	
1776	American Declaration of Independence	
1777		

Science and technology	Philosophy	
La Mettrie, *L'Homme machine*	Montesquieu, *L'Esprit des lois*	1748
Hartley, *Observations on Man* First volume of Buffon's *Natural History* (44 vols)		1749
	Baumgarten, *Aesthetica*, Vol. I	1750
1751–80 *L'Encyclopédie*		1751
Linnaeus, *Species of Plants*		1753
	Wolff d. Condillac, *Traité des sensations*	1754
Kant, *General Natural History and Theory of the Heavens*	Rousseau, *Discourse on the Origin of Inequality* Mendelssohn, *On Feelings*	1755
	Burke, *The Sublime and the Beautiful*	1757
Boscovich, *Theoria Philosophiae Naturalis*	Baumgarten, *Aesthetica*, Vol. II Helvetius, *De l'ésprit*	1758
		1759
		1760
Lambert, *Cosmological Letters*		1761
	Rousseau, *Social Contract* Rousseau, *Emile* Fichte b.	1762
	Mendelssohn, *Philosophical Conversations*	1763
James Hargreaves introduces the spinning jenny	Kant, *Only Possible Premise for a Demonstration of the Existence of God* Lambert, *Neues Organon*	1764
Lambert, *Theory of Parallel Lines*	Leibniz, *New Essays*	1765
Cavendish, *On Factitious Airs*		1766
		1767
Lambert proves the irrationality of Π		1768
Watt's steam engine patented		1769
	Kant, Inaugural Dissertation Holbach, *Système de la nature* Hegel b.	1770
		1771
	Herder, *Treatise on the Origin of Language*	1772
		1774
	Tetens, *On Universal Speculative Philosophy* Crusius d.	1775
Adam Smith, *The Wealth of Nations*		1776
	Tetens, *Philosophical Essays*	1777

	Politics and religion	The arts
1778		Voltaire d.
1779		Lessing, *Nathan der Weise*
1781		Lessing d.
1783	War of American Independence ends	
1784		
1785		
1786		Mozart, *The Marriage of Figaro*
1787		Mozart, *Don Giovanni*
1788		
1789	French Revolution begins George Washington first President of the USA	
1790	Burke, *Reflections on the Revolution in France*	
1791		Mozart, *The Magic Flute*
1792		
1793	Louis XVI guillotined Reign of Terror begins	
1794	Lavoisier guillotined Robespierre guillotined Reign of Terror ends	
1795	Kant, *Perpetual Peace*	1795–6 Goethe, *Wilhelm Meister's Apprenticeship*
1796		

Science and technology	Philosophy	
	Rousseau d.	1778
First cast-iron bridge built, Coalbrookdale, England		1779
	Kant, *Critique of Pure Reason* (1st edn)	1781
Ascent of Montgolfier balloon, Annonay	Kant, *Prolegomena to Any Future Metaphysics*	1783
	Kant, "Idea for a universal history" 1784–91 Herder, *Ideas toward the Philosophy of the History of Mankind* (4 vols)	1784
James Hutton, *Theory of the Earth*	Kant, *Foundations of the Metaphysics of Morals* Jacobi, *On the Doctrine of Spinoza* Mendelssohn, *Morning Lessons*	1785
	Mendelssohn, *To the Friends of Lessing* Jacobi, *Against Mendelssohn's Accusations* 1786–7 Reinhold, *Letters on the Kantian Philosophy*	1786
	Kant, *Critique of Pure Reason* (2nd edn) Jacobi, *David Hume on Belief* Herder, *God: Some Conversations*	1787
	Kant, *Critique of Practical Reason* Schopenhauer b.	1788
Lavoisier, *Traité élémentaire de chimie*		1789
	Kant, *Critique of Judgment* Maimon, *Examination of Transcendental Philosophy*	1790
Metric system proposed in France		1791
	Fichte, *Attempt at a Critique of All Revelation* Schulze, *Aenesidemus* Mary Wollstonecraft, *Vindication of the Rights of Woman*	1792
	Kant, *Religion within the Limits of Reason Alone*	1793
1794–6 Erasmus Darwin, *Zoonomia*	1794–9 Fichte, Jena *Wissenschaftslehre*	1794
	Schiller, *On the Aesthetic Education of Mankind* Schelling, *Philosophical Letters on Dogmatism and Criticism*	1795
Laplace, *Système du monde*		1796

	Politics and religion	The arts
1797		
1798		Wordsworth and Coleridge, *Lyrical Ballads* Haydn, *The Creation*
1799	French Revolution ended by Napoleon's coup d'état of 18 Brumaire (9 Nov.)	
1800		Beethoven, First Symphony
1803		
1804	Napoleon proclaimed Emperor	Beethoven, *Eroica* Symphony
1805		Diderot, *Le Neveu de Rameau*
1807		Beethoven, Fourth Symphony
1808	Fichte, *Addresses to the German Nation*	Goethe, *Faust*, Part I
1809		Goethe, *Elective Affinities*
1810		
1811		
1812	Napoleon retreats from Moscow	
1813		
1814	Napoleon abdicates	Scott, *Waverley*
1815	Return and final defeat of Napoleon	
1817		
1818		
1819		
1820		
1821	Napoleon d.	Constable, *The Haywain*
1824		
1825		

Science and technology	Philosophy	
	Kant, *Metaphysics of Morals* Schelling, *Ideas for a Philosophy of Nature* (1st edn)	1797
Rumford, *Enquiry concerning the Source of Heat* Malthus, *Essay on the Principle of Population* (1st edn)	Comte b.	1798
Volta constructs first electric battery		1799
	Fichte, *The Vocation of Man* Schelling, *System of Transcendental Idealism*	1800
Malthus, *Essay on the Principle of Population* (2nd edn)	Schelling, *On University Studies* Schelling, *Ideas for a Philosophy of Nature* (2nd edn)	1803
	Kant d.	1804
		1805
Robert Fulton constructs first practicable steamboat	Hegel, *Phenomenology of Spirit* Tetens d.	1807
Dalton, *A New System of Chemical Philosophy*		1808
	Schelling, *Philosophical Inquiries into the Nature, of Human Freedom*	1809
Goethe, *Farbenlehre*		1810
Avogadro's hypothesis about the molecular composition of gases		1811
	1812–16 Hegel, *Science of Logic* (3 vols)	1812
	Schopenhauer, *On the Fourfold Root of the Principle of Sufficient Reason* Kierkegaard b.	1813
Laplace, *A Philosophical Essay on Probabilities* Stephenson's first steam locomotive	Fichte d.	1814
	Schopenhauer, *On Vision and Colors*	1815
	Hegel, *Encyclopedia of the Philosophical Sciences* (1st edn)	1817
	Schopenhauer, *The World as Will and Representation*	1818
	Jacobi d.	1819
Oersted announces discovery of electromagnetism		1820
	Hegel, *Philosophy of Right*	1821
Carnot, *Puissance motrice du feu*		1824
Opening of Stockton–Darlington railway		1825

	Politics and religion	The arts
1827		Heine, *Das Buch der Lieder* Beethoven d.
1829		
1830		Stendhal, *Le Rouge et le noir*
1831		Hugo, *Notre Dame de Paris*
1832	Great Reform Bill, Britain	Goethe, *Faust*, Part II
1833		
1834	Schleiermacher d.	
1835	1835–6 D.F. Strauss, *The Life of Jesus Critically Examined*	
1836		1836–7 Dickens, *Pickwick Papers*
1837	Victoria becomes Queen of Britain	1837–43 Balzac, *Les Illusions perdues* (3 parts)
1838	People's Charter, Britain	
1839		
1841	Feuerbach, *The Essence of Christianity*	
1842		
1843		Hölderlin d.
1844		Turner, *Rain, Steam and Speed*
1845		
1846		

Science and technology	Philosophy	
		1827
Lobachevski, *On the Foundations of Geometry*		1829
1830–3 Lyell, *Principles of Geology* (3 vols)	Feuerbach, *Thoughts concerning Death and Immortality* 1830–42 Comte, *Philosophie positive* (6 vols)	1830
Independent discovery of electromagnetic induction by Faraday and Henry	Hegel d.	1831
		1832
	Dilthey b.	1833
		1834
		1835
		1836
	Bolzano, *Wissenschaftslehre*	1837
		1838
	Feuerbach, *Towards a Critique of Hegelian Philosophy*	1839
	Schopenhauer, *The Two Fundamental Problems of Ethics* Bruno Bauer, *The Trumpet of the Last Judgment over Hegel* Kierkegaard, *The Concept of Irony*	1841
"Doppler effect" discovered	Ruge, "Hegel's *Philosophy of Right* and the Politics of our Times"	1842
	Feuerbach, *Provisional Theses* Feuerbach, *Principles of the Philosophy of the Future* Marx writes his *Critique of Hegel's "Philosophy of Right"* Kierkegaard, *Fear and Trembling* Kierkegaard, *Either/Or* Kierkegaard, *Repetition*	1843
Robert Chambers, *Vestiges of Creation*	Marx writes his *Economic and Philosophic Manuscripts* Stirner, *The Ego and its Own* Kierkegaard, *Philosophical Fragments* Nietzsche b.	1844
	Marx and Engels, *The Holy Family* Marx writes his *Theses on Feuerbach* 1845–6 Marx and Engels write *The German Ideology*	1845
Planet Neptune discovered close to predicted position	Kierkegaard, *Concluding Unscientific Postscript*	1846

	Politics and religion	The arts
1847		
1848	Revolutions in France, Germany, Italy, and Austria Marx and Engels, *The Communist Manifesto*	Pre-Rapaelite Brotherhood founded
1849	Revolution in Hungary	
1850		Wordsworth d.
1851	Coup d'état of Louis Napoleon	
1854		
1855		
1856		Flaubert, *Madame Bovary*
1857		
1859		
1860		

Science and technology	Philosophy	
Boole, *The Mathematical Analysis of Logic* Helmholtz, *On the Conservation of Energy*		1847
		1848
	Kierkegaard, *Sickness unto Death*	1849
Clausius states second law of thermodynamics		1850
Great Exhibition, London	Schopenhauer, *Parerga and Paralipomena*	1851
Boole, *The Laws of Thought*		1854
	Kierkegaard d.	1855
Bessemer invents process for making steel		1856
	Comte d. 1857–8 Marx's *Grundrisse* (a draft of *Capital*) written	1857
Darwin, *The Origin of Species*		1859
	Schopenhauer d.	1860

Introduction

Robert C. Solomon and Kathleen M. Higgins

The turn of the nineteenth century marked one of the richest and most exciting explosions of philosophical energy and talent, perhaps even comparable to the generation that gave birth to Socrates, Plato, and Aristotle. The enormity of the revolution set off in philosophy by Immanuel Kant was comparable, by Kant's own estimation, to the Copernican revolution that ended the Middle Ages. The movement he set in motion, the fast-moving and often cantankerous dialectic of "German Idealism," inspired some of the most creative philosophers in modern times, including G. W. F. Hegel and Arthur Schopenhauer, not to mention the philosophers he inspired in opposition to him (Kierkegaard and Marx, for example) and virtually every major movement in the twentieth century, including analytic philosophy and idealism in Britain and America, phenomenology and existentialism in France and Germany, and much of the recent philosophy in Japan. Kant is often depicted as appearing virtually out of nowhere (in the far East Prussian town of Königsberg) to resolve several long-standing disputes in French and British philosophy, embracing the competing traditions of rationalism and empiricism. But the philosophical climate in German-speaking Europe was as vibrant with conversation and controversy as the more cosmopolitan centers of London and Paris, and one can fully understand the excitement and the brilliance of the birth of German Idealism by first appreciating the intellectual fervor surrounding and preceding Kant. The chapter that opens this volume, by the distinguished Kant scholar Lewis White Beck, explains that fervor and the philosophers who were part of it. It is in that context, too, that one can appreciate the continuing debates and battles that follow Kant. Indeed, much of the history of nineteenth-century philosophy in Germany can be summarized as the attempt to continue,

I

improve on, defend, or demolish the philosophical rationalism established by Kant.

Kant's first appearance in philosophy was a professional but not particularly distinguished dissertation published in 1770, when the philosophy professor was already nearing 50. It caused some local controversy, but it is remembered and of interest today only in the reflected light of the great works that were to follow. Among these were three remarkable and remarkably difficult *Critiques*, the *Critique of Pure Reason* (1781), the *Critique of Practical Reason* (1788), and the *Critique of Judgment* (1790). The first *Critique* examined the capacities and limitations of reason and the necessary conditions for knowledge. The second explored and defended the concept of morality and autonomy in human action. The third, intended to be a synthesis of the first two and bring "the entire critical undertaking to a close," included wide-ranging discussions of aesthetic taste, and the concept of teleology in the biological sciences. Together, the three *Critiques* established philosophy as a new profession, and it is often said that Kant was its first true professor. The difficulty of the *Critiques* was more than compensated for by their brilliance and their importance. The *Critique of Pure Reason* in particular has often been called the most important philosophical text of modern times. Daniel Bonevac, in his essay on the first *Critique*, suggests that no one can call him- or herself a philosopher today without first mastering, or at least coming to terms with, that book.

Kant was an unabashed rationalist, a designation that will be explored in some depth in the chapters to follow. Although his first *Critique* announces itself as a "criticism" that is intended to show the limits of reason, he leaves no doubt that he is, first and foremost, a defender of reason, the essentially human faculty. But Kant's rationalism and the various conceptions of reason and rationality explored by the various German Idealists must be viewed against a background of religious piety and, in some instances, anti-rationalism. Kant himself was a pious Lutheran and sought to bring reason and faith together, defending faith itself as a rational attitude. But surrounding Kant were several philosophers who denied both the supremacy of reason and the rationality of faith, among them Jacobi and Hamann, who was one of Kant's best friends in Kønigsberg. So, too, that movement called "the Enlightenment," which took reason as its guide and found in Kant its most eloquent German defender, encountered stiff resistance and opposition in Germany. Herder attacked the Enlightenment in the name of what we would now call "multiculturalism," defending the distinctive features of German culture. Many of the German Idealists following Kant nevertheless turned a skeptical eye on the Enlightenment, which many of them considered overly utilitarian and insufficiently attentive to spiritual matters. Early in the nineteenth century, Fichte and Hegel would defend their concepts of reason against a growing school of romantic philosophers, incorporating many of their ideas and images in their philosophy. Their colleague Friedrich Schelling would actually join and lead the romantics in their critique of the Enlightenment, and by the end of the first decade or so of the new century the concepts of both reason and Enlightenment had been hopelessly muddied. By the middle of the century, Kant's celebrated faculty of reason had been attacked from all sides, by his self-proclaimed followers who altered it beyond recognition, by the young materialists Feuerbach and Marx who insisted that reason was secondary to the necessities of life even in the realm of thought, by the German Idealist Arthur Schopenhauer who demonstrated at great length the primacy and the irrationality of the Will, by the Danish philosopher Kierkegaard who rejected the very idea of a rational explanation of human life or a rational defense of Christianity. Indeed, if there is a single concern that ties together all of the figures and the chapters of this volume, it is the nature and place of reason in human affairs.

In the chapters to follow, we have allowed each author their own voice. As the themes, the philosophers, and their books vary, so do the approaches and styles that seem appropriate. Thus the chapter on German philosophy before Kant by Lewis White Beck is historically oriented, while Daniel Bonevac's chapter on Kant's first *Critique* is an unusually clear exposition and explanation of the strategy and difficulties of that text. Don Becker interprets Kant's well-known moral philosophy in the context of his less familiar political philosophy, while Patrick Gardiner explains how Kant attempts to bridge the "two jurisdictions" of the first two *Critiques* with his aesthetic conception of universal subjective judgments and teleological explanations in the *Critique of Judgment*. Daniel Breazeale introduces the complex philosophy of Fichte and Schelling, emphasizing the early works in Jena, the site of many of the new century's most dramatic philosophical innovations, and Robert Solomon traces a path through Hegel's notoriously labyrinthine *Phenomenology of Spirit*. Willem deVries describes Hegel's attempt to derive metaphysics from logic, traces the development of that logic, and evaluates its success. Leo Rauch explores Hegel's "philosophy of objective spirit" and the emergence of freedom and reason through history, especially in his *Philosophy of Right*. Robert Nola describes the philosophical turmoil following Hegel's death in 1831 and the emergence of "the young Hegelians," especially Marx and Feuerbach. Kathleen Higgins sympathetically discusses the pessimism of the crankiest Kantian, Arthur Schopenhauer, and, finally, Judith Butler discusses the despair of the Danish "existentialist" Søren Kierkegaard.

While the chapters were prepared separately, there are many points of contact and contrast – for instance, between the logical analysis of concepts in Kant, Fichte, and Hegel, the aesthetics of Kant, Schopenhauer, and Kierkegaard, and the political philosophies of Kant, Hegel, and Marx. We are deeply indebted to all of our contributors and grateful both for their good scholarship and for their respect for our deadlines. The volume is, we think, a feast of interpretation and commentary, and we hope that the reader enjoys reading it as much as we have enjoyed putting it together.

CHAPTER 1

From Leibniz to Kant

Lewis White Beck

❧ INTRODUCTION ❧

Had Kant not lived, German philosophy between the death of Leibniz in 1716 and the end of the eighteenth century would have little interest for us, and would remain largely unknown. In Germany between Leibniz and Kant there was no world-class philosopher of the stature of Berkeley, Hume, Reid, Rousseau, Vico, or Condillac. The life and philosophy of Kant, however, raised some not-quite-first-class philosophers to historical importance. The fame of these men is parasitic upon Kant's greater fame. There were philosophers who did not achieve even this derivative fame, for not all roads led from Leibniz to Kant. I think, nevertheless, that we can best orient ourselves in a brief account of eighteenth-century German philosophy by seeing it as a preparation for Kant.

Leibniz was the last great philosophical system-builder of the seventeenth century, and his bold speculations and systematic wholeness were more characteristic of the seventeenth- than of the eighteenth-century philosophers. His peers were Descartes, Malebranche, Arnauld, Hobbes, Locke, and Spinoza, and in comprehensiveness and variety of genius he surpassed each of them. His system had an answer to almost every question put to it; he was said to be "an academy of science all by himself," and the principal objection to his grand baroque philosophical system was that it was – simply unbelievable. To accept it all would have required a speculative faith and a blind confidence in the metaphysical powers of the human mind that few philosophers of the eighteenth century could muster.

Christian Wolff, his most important disciple, did not make a *summa* of Leibniz's philosophy, but both his followers and opponents saw Wolff as doing precisely that. They accordingly called his philosophy the "Leibniz–Wolffian philosophy," a name which has become fixed in spite of both Leibniz and Wolff's renunciation of it. Modern scholarship shows the degree to which this title is inappropriate,[1] yet the Leibniz–Wolffian philosophy was the dominant intellectual system and movement in Germany from about 1720 to about 1754, the death of Wolff, and it provided the main opposition to Kant's philosophy until near the end of the century. The rise and fall of the Leibniz–Wolffian philosophy in its controversies with its opponents is the subject matter of this chapter. I deal almost exclusively with topics now important chiefly for an understanding of Kant and German Idealism.

But before we turn to these topics, something must be said about the general climate of opinion in Germany at this time. In all Protestant countries of western Europe, there was an intellectual awakening called the Enlightenment. "Enlightenment," Kant wrote, "is man's release from his self-incurred tutelage." Tutelage is allowing or requiring someone else to do one's thinking, and it is self-incurred because most human beings do not develop the skill and the courage to use their own reason. They surrender their freedom to those who will think for them in matters political, religious, and moral. Kant did not believe he lived in "an enlightened age," but did say he lived in an "age of enlightenment" when progress was being made to independent thought. But the specific forms that Enlightenment took varied from country to country; it depended upon the particular form of tutelage in each country, from which thinkers strove to emancipate themselves.

The German Enlightenment took place in a feudal environment of scores of small absolute monarchies in which Lutheran passive obedience and the eye of the local monarch ensured that the established order of things was regarded with sacred awe by the *Bürger*.[2] While the *philosophes* of France were not merely anti-clerical but also antireligious (materialists, atheists, freethinkers, skeptics), what was unique to the German Enlightenment was that it originally had a profoundly religious motive.

Pietism was a religious awakening at the end of the seventeenth century which had much in common with the persecuted Jansenist sect in France and the Methodist movement still to come in England. Pietism meant a return to a simpler form of Lutheranism, emphasizing the emotional and moral rather than the ritual and dogmatic aspects of the established churches. Instead of churches, there were evening gatherings in the homes of individual Pietists for communal devotion; every man was a priest, drawing inspiration from his own reading of scripture and applying its lessons to everyday life. Though the movement was not free of irrational elements, it was enlightened in encouraging its members not to defer to someone else who would do their thinking for them. Naturally all this produced plurality of opinion and diversity of faith, but its emphasis upon good works (establishing

6

schools and orphanages, for instance) brought it in line with the Enlightenment movement in other countries where the motivation was perhaps more intellectual and political.

There were, in fact, two Enlightenments in Germany. Besides the intellectual Enlightenment pursued by the Leibniz–Wolffian philosophers, there was also a Pietistic Enlightenment. Surprisingly they both originated in the same place, the University of Halle, a Pietistic institution founded by the Elector of Brandenburg primarily for the training of the bureaucracy required by this largest and most important German state.

The father of the Pietistic Enlightenment was Christian Thomasius (1655–1728), who had been banished from Saxony on religious grounds. Thomasius was an active reformer but not a deep philosopher. His ideal of education was that it raise not the cloistered scholar but the *honnête homme*, imitating France in "polite learning, beauty of mind, good taste, and gallantry." In order to reach a larger audience, he lectured and wrote most of his books in German, not Latin. He claimed academic freedom, taught religious toleration, and attempted to reform legal practices by outlawing torture and removing heresy and witchcraft from the reach of the law. As a Pietist he did not doubt the authority and authenticity of revelation, but he established the basis of law in ethics, ultimately in reason and experience. Pietism is almost always associated with an occult and quasi-mystical philosophy of nature, and this kept the German Enlightenment Pietists from participating in the great scientific revolution at the end of the seventeenth century.

Unfortunately Wolff and Thomasius were on a collision course. Intellectually they were not in serious disagreement on most substantive questions (though their interests were widely divergent). Personally their relations were correct, though not close. Thomasius apparently took no part in the ignoble campaign which drove Wolff from Halle just as he had himself been driven from Leipzig. But their disciples carried on a running controversy for the next forty years, and it was marked by *odium theologicum* and general nastiness on both sides.

WOLFF

Life and works

Christian Wolff was born in Breslau in 1679. With support from Leibniz he was appointed lecturer in mathematics at the University of Leipzig in 1702 and, four years later, professor of mathematics at the University of Halle. Wolff was no creative mathematician, but he found in mathematics the model for rigorous thinking in other fields. In this he simply followed the lead of Descartes and Leibniz.

Soon Wolff was teaching and writing philosophy, philosophy then meaning both the natural sciences and the subject which is today called philosophy. He published copiously on the experimental sciences and also on logic, metaphysics, cosmology, psychology, political theory, and natural theology in a series of large German books, most of which were entitled *Vernünftige Gedanken* ("Rational Thoughts") on the different areas of knowledge.[3] The contents and expository skill of these books led to their widespread acceptance as textbooks. His successes in publishing extensively used books, and his victories in the annual competition for paying students, incited intense rivalry between Wolff and the less successful Thomasian Pietist professors. They seized the opportunity to charge Wolff with heresy when he held, in a public lecture as rector of the university, that the resemblances between Chinese and Western ethics showed that ethics was based on universal human reason and human nature, not on divine revelation vouchsafed only to Western civilization. They represented to the King of Prussia, Frederick William I, that Wolff's determinism and fatalism meant that he should not punish deserters from his army because, being determined, they could not have helped doing what they had in fact done.

Enraged by this *lèse-majesté*, the choleric King dismissed Wolff and threatened to hang him in forty-eight hours if he was still on Prussian soil. Wolff had already received a call from the Calvinist University of Marburg, which he now accepted. He taught in Marburg for seventeen years. Heard by an international student body, more of whom could understand Latin than German, he repeated and expanded his series of *Vernünftige Gedanken* into large volumes of scholastic Latin addressed to an international readership. So great was his fame, and so scandalous had been the behavior of Frederick William I and his "Tobacco Cabinet," that efforts were repeatedly made to recall him to Prussia. He returned only in 1740 when the new King, Frederick the Great, made him chancellor of the University of Halle and granted him a patent of nobility and a large stipend. At the time of his death in 1754 he was certainly the best-known thinker in Germany, fully deserving the honorific title of Praeceptor Germaniae.

The mathematical ideal in philosophy[4]

Hobbes, Descartes, Spinoza, and Leibniz all shared a common ideal for philosophy, that it should attain the clarity and certainty hitherto available only in mathematics. Wolff is quite explicit about the relation of mathematics to philosophy. "The rules of mathematical method," he says,[5]

> are the same as the rules of philosophical method. . . . The identity of philosophical and mathematical method will be a surprise only to one who does not know the common source from which the rules of both mathematics and philosophy are derived.

This common source is "true logic" or "natural logic" of the workings of the human mind, not a finished logic which is itself a science.

Lest the identity of philosophy and mathematics appear to be wholly quixotic, it is essential to remember that "philosophy" and "mathematics" did not then mean exactly what they mean now. Philosophy, well into the eighteenth century, included the sciences; and though work of the highest kind in pure mathematics was being performed by Leibniz and Lambert and others, the mathematics that was the cultural model for the Enlightenment was applied (or, as it was then called, "mixed") mathematics. Wolff's mathematical works contain far more information about astronomy, meteorology, geodesics, and even architecture than they do topics in pure mathematics. The root idea of the mathematical model is that computation and measurement are essential to any body of advanced scientific knowledge.

In the true method, formulated by Descartes and followed with little change by Wolff, everything certain in our thoughts depends upon the order of our thoughts, a step-wise procedure of moving from the simplest and most indubitable to the less certain and more problematical. Mathematics begins with definitions, proceeds to fundamental principles (axioms), and thence to theorems and problems (constructions). The product of a definition is a clear and distinct idea, evident to attention and communicable to others. Mathematical theorems are demonstrated by analysis of the contents of definitions and axioms, demonstration taking the form of showing that an alternative to a true theorem is self-contradictory or contradictory to another established truth.

In the syllabus for his mathematics lectures in 1731[6] Wolff tried to show both the importance and the inadequacy of mathematical knowledge. Mathematics deals only with the observable phenomena in space and time (which are subjective), and it operates with images; ontology, on the other hand, deals with being *qua* being and replaces images with exact concepts.

How well did the mathematical ideal stand? In 1762 the Royal Academy of Sciences in Berlin offered a prize for the best essay on the question: 'Whether metaphysical judgments generally, and in particular the fundamental principles of natural theology and morals, are capable of proofs as evident as those of geometry?" A disciple of Wolff,

Moses Mendelssohn, took the prize with an essay giving an affirmative answer, with which Wolff would have agreed. The runner-up, with a negative answer, was the unknown Immanuel Kant. In this respect history has followed Kant, not Wolff and Mendelssohn.

The marriage of reason and experience

One of the perennial problems of philosophy is to determine the roles of reason and experience in knowing. In the seventeenth and eighteenth centuries it was the subject of controversy between philosophers we now call rationalists and those we call empiricists. Among the empiricists we count Locke, Berkeley, Hume, Reid, and Condillac; among the rationalists, Descartes, Malebranche, Spinoza, and Leibniz.

Wolff is sometimes considered the arch-rationalist, but we must enquire into the *kind* of rationalist he was.[7] A rationalist like those just listed believes that *reason alone*, or rational intuition, is able to discover truths that are independent of experience and that could not be learned *from* experience, but that necessarily apply *to* experience. Such truths have been called, especially since Kant, *a priori*, in contrast to truths *a posteriori*, i.e. truths learned only from experience.

Wolff frequently insists that there are no *a priori* truths in *this* sense; he says that there is no human *pure* reason devoid of sense content; he agrees with the Scholastic teaching, "There is nothing in the intellect that was not first in sense." He rejects the theory of innate ideas, which has always been one of the principal tenets of the rationalist school. Hence Wolff may seem to be no rationalist at all; he is not a rationalist in the strictly defined sense of the preceding paragraph, but his style and vocabulary give a rationalistic veneer to his thoughts because he seems to generate *a priori* knowledge by improving upon empirical knowledge.

He attempted (successfully, in his own judgment) to derive the principle of sufficient reason from the law of contradiction.[8] Leibniz had attempted to keep these two principles separate and independent of each other, and had ascribed each to a very different metaphysical source (respectively the will and the intellect of God). Wolff, on the contrary, contends that it is a logical truth that every true judgment has a sufficient reason for being true. Though Wolff does not claim to derive empirical truths from the principle of sufficient reason (and, ultimately, from the law of contradiction), he does claim (and makes good his claim) to be able to give a rational account of what was originally perceived empirically.

He does so by drawing a distinction between two kinds of knowledge, which he calls historical and philosophical knowledge.[9] He does so in parallel with Aristotle's distinction (*Posterior Analytics*, Book I, ch. 13) between *knowledge of fact* and *knowledge of reasoned fact*. Historical knowledge is knowledge based on the perception of a raw fact, something existing or happening. But by memory, classification, measurement, hypothesis-formation, and perhaps simple experiments we clarify our knowledge of a fact by seeing it as a "certain kind" of fact. The ideas of sense become ideas of reason (the *vernünftige Gedanken* of Wolff's book titles), reason being the capacity for "seeing with the mind's eye" the connections of ideas and their sufficient conditions. All the knowledge that reason has or produces comes from experience – historical knowledge is the basis of philosophical knowledge – but it is so processed by reason into definitions, principles, axioms, probable hypotheses, and well-tested laws of nature that a subtle change is introduced into our historical knowledge of fact: knowledge of fact becomes knowledge of reasoned fact. Going beyond what has been actually observed, knowledge of reasoned fact extends to facts not yet experienced. Wolff likes to say that there is a marriage of reason and experience (*connubium rationis et experientiae*) which he does not wish to disturb.

There are two movements in knowledge. The ascent from knowledge of fact to principles and reasons is the analytical method of Descartes (Kant's regressive method); the descent from reason to experience is Descartes's synthetic (Kant's progressive) method. The knowledge of reasoned fact was commonly in Wolff's day called *a priori* knowledge[10] (knowledge from reason, not experience), even though for Wolff its ultimate and irreplaceable source is experience.

We can now summarize Wolff's kind of rationalism. He *is not a rationalist* in the sense of the belief that pure reason without need of experience can produce *a priori* knowledge (in mathematics and metaphysics, for example). He *is a rationalist* in a loose sense in that he emphasizes the function of reason in converting raw data of the senses into reasonable knowledge. With his armies of syllogisms in valiant array, Wolff demonstrated everything from the existence of God to theories in astronomy; he proves that German coffee houses should be modeled after those of England. No wonder Wolff is generally thought of as a rationalist!

Ontology and special metaphysics

The keystone of Wolff's stupendous edifice is his *First Philosophy, or Ontology*, published in Latin in 1729. In 1720 he had published a volume sometimes known as the *German Metaphysics* whose accurate and instructive title is *Rational Thoughts on God, the World, the Soul of Man, and All Things in General.*

The subject matter of ontology is being in general, demonstrative knowledge of what it is that makes something possible if it is possible and actual if it is actual. It is like Aristotle's "First Philosophy" which deals with being *qua* being (*Metaphysics*, Book IV, ch. 1). Ontology deals with questions and concepts common to all branches of knowledge.

Questions about the various kinds of being are reserved for the several volumes on special metaphysics, viz., the being of God, the existence of whom follows only from his possibility (the ontological argument), the being of the soul, and the being of the world. The actual world and the actual soul are made actual by "a complement of possibility"[11] which renders possible things actual. Kant destroyed this connection of possibility and actuality by asking the question: Is the complement possible? If it is not, it is impossible and cannot serve the purpose. If it is, it is just another possibility and contributes nothing toward actuality. There is no valid inference from possibility to actuality. The converse inference, from existence to possibility, is explored by Lambert, Crusius, and Kant.

Many of the 964 articles in the *Ontology* give definitions of metaphysical terms such as being, existence, possibility, essence, condition, thing, attribute, simplicity, substance, space, time, cause, quality, etc. These concepts are shuffled, combined and separated, contrasted, and compared in an almost mechanical procedure.

One of the most important concepts is that of substance, defined as follows: "What contains in itself a *principium* [roughly: a cause] of changes is a substance."[12] Each substance contains in itself a sufficient condition for a change in itself or in other substances. If the change is motion, the monad is a physical substance; if the change is mental, the monad is a spiritual substance. Only one substance contains the cause of its own being, and that substance is God. Thus arise the three divisions of special metaphysics: rational theology, rational psychology, and rational cosmology. It will be noticed that Wolff is closer to Descartes than to Leibniz, who had asserted that all substances are spiritual and had denied that one substance could cause a change in another. Wolff, very tentatively, holds the doctrine of pre-established harmony only for the case of relations between mind and body monads.

Wolff follows Leibniz in denying absolute Newtonian space, and agrees with Leibniz that space is a subjective order of appearances of substances. He holds a mechanical view of nature, which consists of simple unextended physical monads interacting by contact with each other, the whole showing intelligent design and especially purposiveness for human benefit.[13] The soul is a simple substance with a *vis repraesentativa* or a power of being conscious; the soul is immortal and the will free. Like Leibniz in his *Theodicy*, Wolff strove to reconcile freedom and necessity, but with equal ill-success.

Moral philosophy

Wolff wrote more on practical philosophy (ethics and law) than on any other subject. There is little new in Wolff's theory, but it is superbly organized and undoubtedly influenced Kant's articulation of ethical theory in his *Metaphysics of Morals*. Kant cites Wolff as the exemplary representative of the best of the four types of heteronomous ethics, the ethics of perfection.[14]

The intellect conceives of a perfection, which is the value aspect of truth as the perfect harmony and interconnection of the essential attributes of a thing following from its intrinsic essence. True being (as object of knowledge) and true good (as object of desire) are identified. The will necessarily strives for a perfection which the intellect has discerned. Rational willing is definitive of morality. The achievement of a perfection is attended with pleasure, but the test for an action is not its consequent pleasure, but its rational motivation and justification.

Natural law requires that each person strive to achieve their own perfection and also that of others. Revelation is not required to teach men their duties, nor is the promise of divine reward needful to move people to do the good.

The completion of Wolff's system in aesthetics

A great gap in Wolff's system was the lack of a theory of beauty and fine art. The last decade of Wolff's life was a time of extensive literary dispute concerning matters of taste. There were controversies between defenders of the classical forms and harbingers of the romanticism that was yet to come. There was great competition between those who would emulate French drama and those in favor of English models, and still others (e.g. Lessing) who wanted to develop a native drama with German themes.

It is easy to see why a comprehensive philosophical movement like Wolffianism should be concerned to develop a theory of art, in spite of the fact that there certainly are few philosophical theories less likely than Wolff's to be fruitful concerning beauty and art. Wolffian theories of art were produced by two disciples, Alexander Baumgarten of Halle (later Frankfurt on the Oder) and Moses Mendelssohn of Berlin.

Baumgarten[15]

In Leibniz–Wolffian philosophy the perfection of sense would be achieved when a sensuous idea was so clarified and rendered so distinct that it would become an abstract intellectual idea. Indeed the entire Wolffian program may be summed up in Wolff's efforts to replace facts given in sense with reasoned facts from which the unique, ineffable content of sense had been evaporated. The perfection of sense is reason, and there is only a difference of degree between the clarity of reason and obscurity of sense. To raise the perfection of sense means: to replace percepts with concepts.

This feature of Wolffian rationalism made it indifferent to the arts, for the artist is one whose skill makes it possible to achieve a perfection of sense which is the object of a perfect, direct intuition, not object of abstract thought got at by omitting the specificities of a singular perception. According to Baumgarten sensation can be perfected by so enhancing its vividness and clarity that there will be pleasure in its mere contemplation.

The irreducible sensory component in such a perception is called the aesthetic and the intuitive by Baumgarten. Sense, which is the lower cognitive faculty, is the higher faculty in the contemplation of beauty. A perfection (of form, color, sound) apprehended by sense instead of by reason is beauty. Aesthetics is the "science of the beautiful."

Mendelssohn

In 1755 Moses Mendelssohn published *On Feelings* (*Empfindungen*), a modification of Baumgarten's views which marks a sharp advance in the direction of Kant's mature aesthetic theory and the aesthetic theory of the later idealists and romantics.

The human mind, he holds, is too limited to be able to sensuously observe the variety-in-unity of ontological perfections, which is discernible only by reason. Thus far Mendelssohn stands with Wolff and Baumgarten, but he now adds: we can sensuously contemplate the variety in unity of the mind's own acts and passions, sensations, thoughts, and emotions. He calls this the "harmony of the powers of the soul." The directly felt perfection of perceiving, not the perception of an antecedent perfection in the perceived object, gives rise to disinterested aesthetic pleasure in the harmonious play of our faculties. Mendelssohn here makes an important and permanent contribution to the history of art and aesthetic theory. He teaches that beauty is not predicated upon an objective perfection (of color, design, morals, or whatever is found in the work of art); it is a perfection of perception, not a perception of perfection.

Pleasure usually accompanies the satisfaction of some previously existing desire, but art and beauty are not normally enjoyed because of the pleasure they afford by satisfying some antecedent desire. In addition to perception and will, each with its own attendant pleasure, there is another faculty of the mind which has its own peculiar pleasure. This faculty Mendelssohn calls *feeling* or approval (*Billigungsvermögen*) by which we experience "disinterested pleasure," a pleasure different from that of satisfied desire or curiosity.

Mendelssohn explains this pleasure by our satisfaction in the harmonious function of all the *Seelenkräfte*, when feeling and willing and perceiving go together to produce a delectable state of mind. Each person's taste will be affected by their physical and even physiological make-up, but with the advance of education and general culture more pervasive satisfactions will replace the doctrine of *à chacun son gout*. This harmony of the powers of the soul is involved in both the enjoyment of art and its creation by genius. Genius is an "imitator of divinity," a "second creator."

❧ CRUSIUS ❧

The Pietist campaign against Wolff was fought on two levels. Motivated by *odium theologicum*, envy, and nepotism as well as by genuine concern incited by Wolff's apparent affinity with Spinozistic pantheism and fatalism, the Halle Thomasians Budde, Lange, and Walch conducted a dirty campaign that continued even after Wolff had been banished. But these Thomasians, like Thomasius himself, were not systematic philosophers of Wolff's caliber; they found fault with Wolff, but offered no interesting alternative. The most important alternative was that of Crusius.

Christian August Crusius was born in Leuna near Merseburg (Saxony) in 1715 and died in Leipzig in 1775. Almost all the men in his family were Lutheran clergymen, and he held professorships in both philosophy and theology and was a pastor holding important posts in the Lutheran hierarchy. About 1750 he gave up philosophical work altogether and devoted himself to theological and biblical studies and the care of souls.

In place of mathematics,[16] Crusius thought of theology as the science whose relations to philosophy must be understood. Philosophy, according to him, is not a sufficient ground for religious faith and human virtue; it is not even essential to the conceptualization of theological truth, since the truths established in philosophy may be overturned by the greater authority of theology. "We cannot think something" was the mark for the impossible among most Enlightenment philosophers, but for Crusius there were conditions under which the inference from inconceivability to impossibility may be suspended: if the thing inconceivable by us may be conceivable by a more perfect mind, or if "We recognize an obligation to regard something inconceivable as possible or actual in order not to act contrary to the most important rules of human perfection" (which include, of course, revelations of the commands of God).[17]

From all this it is easily seen how opposed Crusius was to Wolff. Wolff as a leader of the intellectual Enlightenment was bent upon extending the scope and power of human reason and denying any constraints upon it; Crusius as a leader of Pietistic thought was more concerned to restrain the ambition to explain everything; he tried to determine and fix the boundaries of human intellect when dealing with the brute facticity of the contingent world and the mysteries of religion. That he did so without the obscurantism of the early Thomasians, by developing a sophisticated epistemology as an alternative to Wolff, is a mark of near greatness in this almost forgotten man.

Ontology and theory of knowledge

For Crusius existence, not possibility, is the fundamental concept. In this he differs markedly from Wolff, who asks what is the ground of the possibility of something prior to asking what it is that makes it actual if it is actual. Wolff's answer to this question concerns logical possibility, i.e. non-self-contradictoriness. Crusius's ontology is to challenge Wolff's account of the role of logical possibility in the explanation of existence. We reach the concept of possibility by first finding existent things and then, by "an abstraction from existence" (the reverse of the "complement of possibility"), we find that whatever exists is also possible, but not the converse. If nothing existed, nothing would be even possible. The concept of possibility requires the concept of existence, but not the converse.[18]

Crusius is here speaking, obviously, of what he calls real possibility, not ideal possibility (i.e. possibility of being thought, because noncontradictory). Real possibility is the possibility inhering in things that might exist outside and beyond our thought of something merely noncontradictory. There can be this real possibility only if there are in the world existing things with forces adequate to bring about the actualization of this possibility.

Understanding has the inexplicable faculty of being conscious of ideas. Reason is the perfection of understanding, consciously recognizing truth as truth. Two activities of reason are to be distinguished; reason *in concreto*, which is the capacity functioning in a single individual with their various quirks and dispositions; and reason *in abstracto*, which is the "complex" of the essential forces of human understanding in general. Only reason *in abstracto* is capable of objective knowledge.[19]

By a kind of denudation we find simplicity and clarity in sensations and other representations. We remove in thought all accidental properties of things, and we are left only with the essential relations that things necessarily bear to one another. Besides noncontradiction and identity there are relations that show the ultimate unanalyzable real forces of things. There is intuitive knowledge of simple, clear, and necessary relations of ideas stated by Crusius as basic laws of thought. Instead of Wolff's single supreme condition (law of contradiction) and its corollary (law of sufficient reason), Crusius states five laws:

(a) The law of inseparables: Whatever cannot be conceived without something else cannot exist without that other (*Metaphysics*, § 15); (b) The law of incompatibles: Whatever cannot be thought in connection with another thing cannot exist with that thing (§ 15); (c) The law of space: Everything that is is somewhere in space (§ 48); (d) The law of time: Everything that is is somewhen or at some time (§ 48); (e) The law of contingence: That whose nonbeing may be conceived may at some time have not existed (§ 33).[20]

These laws are based upon "the nature of human understanding" which is "the supreme criterion of possible and actual things."[21] Kant thinks that Crusius's epistemological principles can correspond to ontological truths only if there is a pre-established harmony between the knower and the known.[22] Crusius, of course, will not accept this Leibnizian theory, but he states repeatedly that God has "placed the marks of truth in the human understanding."[23]

Freedom and the principle of sufficient reason

The principle of sufficient reason is not listed among the basic laws of thought. Though a valid principle it is not an independent principle; it is, rather, a corollary deduced from the law of the inseparable. Crusius, who certainly had not read Hume, states that we cannot think of a happening or a coming-to-be without associating it, in intuition, with some other precedent event. (Hume, of course, about the same time flatly denied this impossibility.)[24] But Crusius says: "Anyone who observes himself clearly sees that nothing that comes to be may be thought except when one at the same time admits that there is another thing that has power sufficient to produce it."[25] He concludes, like Hume, that causation is neither analytically necessary nor an empirical generalization, but he does not draw Hume's skeptical conclusion.

For any coming-to-be we search for a substance or thing that has the force or power (otherwise inscrutable) to bring this about. Reason must accept the forces and powers it empirically discovers in nature without thinking that they are logically necessary.[26]

The law of efficient causation shown in the previous paragraphs to be a corollary of the law of the inseparable has several corollaries of its own, and they may be collectively called the law of sufficient reason. Crusius's Latin *Dissertation on the Use and Limits of the Principle of Determining Reason, Commonly Called Sufficient Reason* (1743) is based on his unwavering adherence to the freedom of the will, but uncompromising rejection of any theory of freedom of the will compatible with the Wolffian principle of sufficient reason. He distinguishes between *determining* reason and *sufficient* reason. The former is a reason which makes its consequence uniquely necessary, and that principle underlies determinism and fatalism. But that principle, he holds, is not demonstrable by the principle of contradiction, and therefore is not universally valid. A sufficient reason,[27] on the contrary, may have diverse consequences, and is compatible with freedom of the will.

Crusius's "solution" to the problem of free will is one of the standard ones: nature is the realm of strict determinism, but man is an exception to this rule of the law of determining reason. He believed that the will is free and therefore believed he had to relax the strict principle of determinant reason and accept the looser condition of sufficient reason. Then the same conditions may be "sufficient" for me to do A or to do B, and whichever I do I freely do because these reasons for A or B are supplemented by a free human decision. But it is patently wrong to call the conditions "sufficient" when they must be supplemented by a free act of will.

Here we have a fine example of Crusius's modifying epistemological conclusions when they conflict with faith and morals. This was not the first time, nor will it be the last, when moral conviction takes precedence over logical analysis.

Virtue is the agreement of human actions with the commands of God.[28] Hence Kant correctly lists Crusius as the exemplary representative of "theological moralists" who hold (correctly) that there is an objective standard of morality but also (incorrectly) that the standard lies in the will of God instead of in the rational will of man.[29]

Having established (to his satisfaction) the freedom of the will as the capacity for absolute spontaneity of action, Crusius believed that he had established the only possible foundation for imputing responsibility and for justifying reward and punishment. The duty of man is to obey God, not directly to seek perfection and pleasure.[30] The love of God is the pure moral motive, like respect for the moral law in Kant. For guidance in morality man has an inborn conscience and a will to virtue. Since mankind and its moral perfection are the final end of God, we human beings can believe that obedience to and love of God will in fact lead to blessedness, even if only in another world.

With these views and his Pietist *habitus* it is not hard to see why the young Crusius gave up his philosophical career after only twelve years. Theology's gain was philosophy's loss.

❧ LAMBERT ❧

Johann Heinrich Lambert was born in Mühlhausen, Alsace, in 1728. Unlike Wolff he was a creative mathematician; he was the first to demonstrate that e and π (*pi*) are irrational numbers, and he was a pioneer in non-Euclidian geometry. He is generally regarded as the father of the science of photometry, and his name is commemorated in the "Lambert–Beer law" of the absorption of light, and in the name of a fundamental unit of illumination, the "lambert."

Mathematics and simple ideas

Lambert speaks as an almost fanatical mathematician when he says: "What cannot be weighed and calculated doesn't concern me. I understand nothing of it." "One will not give the name of 'perfect scientific knowledge' to philosophy when it is not at the same time completely mathematical."[31] "Wolff brought about half of mathematics into philosophy; now it is a matter of bringing the other half."[32] The half Wolff had brought in was the method of definition and proof, but he did not bring to philosophy the part of mathematics which concerns intuition, postulation, hypothesis, and construction; by taking arbitrary definitions "as it were, gratis," "without noticing it he hid all the difficulties in them."[33]

When Lambert first read Euclid, long after he had studied Wolff's theory of geometry, he was astonished, he says,[34] to find that Euclid had begun with simple, clear, and distinct intuitions of lines, points, and angles, and not (as Wolff had done) with nominal definitions, the applicability of which to figures in space was at least questionable. He thought that Wolff had done nothing to establish the truth of his premises and correspondence between theorems and the actual structure of figures in space. Still, "The honor of bringing the right method into philosophy was reserved for Wolff," he says. "Whoever wants to profit most from Wolff's writings should begin with them, and then survey writings which more or less diverge from his. I do not hesitate to include here [the works of] Darjes[35] and Crusius." But the most Wolff

19

could establish was the possibility, not the necessity and objective reference, of mathematical knowledge. There was a gap between logical truth and experience, between possibility and existence.

How is a priori knowledge possible?

To fill this gap Lambert, like Wolff, distinguished between ordinary and scientific knowledge of things.[36] Scientific knowledge establishes clear and distinct ideas of experience and supplements them with hypothetical *Lehrbegriffe*. Lambert then asks: to what extent can scientific knowledge be *a priori*?, using the term *a priori* in a stricter sense than Wolff, and approximating Kant's usage to refer to concepts that could not have arisen out of experience.[37] Experience is only the occasion of our having *a priori* knowledge,[38] but it is experience that gives existential reference to *a priori* knowledge which, without experience, is limited to the possible and the necessary. Though we suppose that it applies to the actual, the specificities of the actual – i.e. which possibilities are actual in this world – are not known *a priori*. But we have *a priori* knowledge of the contents (objects) of simple ideas and not just of their formal relations to each other.

In giving the "mechanism," so to speak, of *a priori* knowledge, that is, in explaining *how* we know anything *a priori*, Lambert turns to the "anatomist of ideas," Locke, for the theory of simple ideas of which, and by means of which, Lambert believes we have *a priori* knowledge.

Simple ideas are said to have only one (atomic) predicate; they are equivalent to their *Merkmal* (sign or criterion) with no hidden predicates, and they have insufficient complexity to be liable to self-contradiction (and for that reason they are possible). Simple ideas are clear even in the mind of a solipsist, and so are not dependent on the real existence of their objects. What is most important about simple ideas is not their identities but their necessary and possible connections such as "what is solid is extended" and "cogito ergo sum." It is by virtue of these relations that we escape from an endless series of mere tautologies and, through combining them, formulate the sets of simple ideas which underlie, *a priori*, the various sciences. In true Leibnizian spirit of the *ars characteristica*, the more we can analyze empirical concepts into simple ones and empirical judgments into tautologies or possible combinations, the more our knowledge is *a priori*. The relations of simple ideas through comparison and combination are submitted to the criterion of thinkability (*Gedenkbarkeit*, like Crusius's inseparability – which Lambert calls combinability – and incompatibility), and each combination can be the *a priori* foundation of some science; each actual science can be submitted to the analytical discovery of what its simple, *a priori* ideas are. These simple ideas are called *Grundbegriffe*. Geometry is the science of simple ideas of extension in space; chronometry the science of simple ideas in duration; phoronomy the science of simple ideas in both space and duration; etc. The *Vernunftlehre* – science of the operations of the mind – depends on simple ideas of a thinking being and Locke's ideas of reflection. This gives rise to metaphysical knowledge which in point of certainty is on a par with geometry.[39]

Lambert and Crusius were the first among our philosophers to see the problematic aspect, yet also the extreme importance, of understanding necessary relations between simple ideas. No longer can the Wolffians equate impossibility with logical contradictoriness. Not all opposition is opposition of contradictories.[40] The necessity dependent upon the principle of contradiction is confined to the components of complex ideas, established by arbitrary definitions. It was the Wolffians' goal to show that all necessity was logical necessity, and all impossibility was logical incompatibility; but they failed to achieve it. To have seen the problem, which arises in trying to account for all necessities by means of identities, was the eminent contribution of Crusius and Lambert. Lambert confesses "that the *fons possibilitatis duos ideas combinandi* (the origin of the possibility of combining two [simple] ideas) has not been fully discovered."[41] It had hardly even been noticed, and it will not have been "fully discovered" until Kant will have generalized the problem into the question: How are synthetic judgments *a priori* possible?

Lambert himself attempted to find the *fons* of the necessary connections among simple ideas. There is in our minds, he held, an *actus reflexus*, a comparing of simple ideas which, in some unexplained way, gives rise to knowledge of their possible and/or necessary connections and combinations. Comparison is the fundamental *actus reflexus* of mind which is involved in analysis and synthesis of ideas.[42] In ways Lambert does not explain, out of the similarity and difference of simple ideas there issue necessary relational ideas, which indicate which simple ideas are validly synthesizable with others. This is not logical inference (where "synthesizable with" means "not contradictory to"); it involves an intuition, and in so concluding Lambert makes little or no progress beyond Crusius.

Nor were Lambert's efforts to avoid phenomenalism (and indeed solipsism) any more successful. Holding that possibility presupposes the actual existence of something, Lambert fallaciously thinks that it must be existence *extra mentem*.[43] He eventually follows Malebranche in calling upon God to give metaphysical status to some of our ideas.[44] In spite of the influence of Locke and his proximity to Kant, Lambert is a metaphysician in the grand style, and his epistemological acuteness does not restrain his speculative passions.

Lambert's correspondence with Kant

Lambert published his *Cosmological Letters* in 1761. It has a rather curious history. It was a product of a sudden *aperçu* which Lambert had into the structure of the heavens. He saw analogies between planetary systems and galaxies. Kant had presented somewhat the same plan in his *Universal Natural History and Theory of the Heavens* (1755) but had introduced a cyclical evolutionary dimension on the origin and dissolution of astronomical structures. This theory is now known as the Kant–LaPlace hypothesis on the origin of the solar system. This classic in the history of astronomy was almost unknown at the time because of the bankruptcy of Kant's publisher. When Lambert read Kant's *Only Possible Premise for a Demonstration of the Existence of God* (1764), which contained a brief account of Kant's astronomical views, he wrote to Kant exculpating himself for the apparent plagiary, expressed contempt for the belletrist philosophers in Berlin, and invited Kant to enter a philosophical correspondence with him. Lambert really does philosophy in his letters and is anxious to involve Kant in his plans; Kant, always a reluctant letter writer, fills his letters with *politesse* but does not engage with Lambert in any serious philosophical rumination.

In September 1770, Kant sent Lambert a copy of his Inaugural Dissertation, *On the Form and Principles of the Sensible and Intelligible World*. In his covering letter (2 September 1770) he spoke of having "arrived at a position that, I flatter myself, I shall never have to change." Little did he know!

Lambert replied on 13 October in a long, somewhat repetitious letter which shows that he had a good understanding of Kant's Inaugural Dissertation. In it he disagreed with Kant on the nature of time and on the method to be followed in metaphysics.

The Kantian position to which Lambert objected was very briefly this. We have sensible representations of things as they appear to us (phenomena) and intellectual representations of things as they are in themselves (noumena). It is an error in philosophy to apply predicates of sensible knowledge to objects of intellectual representation; there is (in Lambert's terminology) an absolute gap between ontology and phenomenology. Time and space are *a priori* forms of both pure and empirical sensible knowledge; therefore neither space nor time nor any predicates presupposing space or time may be applied to the reality of things as they are in themselves.

Lambert's most explicit objection was to the "unreal" state to which time was condemned in the Dissertation.[45] He tells Kant: "If time is unreal, then no change can be real. . . . Till now I have not been able to deny all reality to time and space, or to consider them mere images and *Schein*."[46]

To his regret, Kant did not answer Lambert's letter, but after Lambert's death in 1777[47] he replied, in § 7 of the *Critique of Pure Reason*, saying: "I grant the whole argument. Certainly time is something real, namely the real form of inner intuition." If, on the other hand, we take time and space to be transcendentally real, the status of bodies in time and space is "degraded to mere illusion (*Schein*)" and "the good Berkeley cannot be blamed" for so degrading them.[48] Kant's response to Lambert in the *Critique* is to show that the transcendental reality of time, which Lambert desiderated, leads to subjective idealism (illusionism) which Lambert rejected.

Lambert's second major objection to the Inaugural Dissertation anticipated a major shift of view between the Dissertation and the first *Critique*. Anticipated, yes; occasioned, perhaps not, though we do not know. Lambert's assertion of continuity between phenomenology and ontology conflicted with what Kant called "the all-important rule" in metaphysical thinking: "Carefully prevent the principles proper to sensitive cognition from passing their boundaries and affecting intellectual cognition."[49]

This rule was rescinded in the *Critique of Pure Reason* in the famous sentence: "Thoughts without content are empty, intuitions without concepts are blind."[50] Here "content" means sensible intuitions, and Kant is here saying that no exertion of thought can produce knowledge if there is no sensible intuition. The most decisive factor in this reversal was Kant's discovery (aided no doubt by his reading of Tetens) that without sensible intuition there can be no synthesis of concepts and hence no judgments. The Inaugural Dissertation had kept separated what the first *Critique* would tightly bind together. So much, then, for Kant's thinking that he would never have to change what he thought in 1770!

Whether Lambert's *obiter dicta* had anything to do with this turnabout in Kant's thinking is doubtful, yet the weighty remark of a man Kant so much admired *may* have had an influence on him. Lambert says:

> It is also useful in ontology to take up concepts borrowed from
> appearance (*Schein*), since the theory must finally be applied
> to phenomena again. For that is how the astronomer begins,
> with the phenomenon: deriving his theory of the construction
> of the world from phenomena, he applies it again to phenomena

and their predictions in his ephemerides. In metaphysics, where the problem of appearance (*Schein*) is so essential, the method of the astronomer will surely be the safest.[51]

Could there here lie the seed of Kant's Copernican analogy?

~~ TETENS ~~

Johann Nicolaus Tetens was born in Schleswig in 1736 or 1738. His teacher at the University of Kiel, Johann Christian Eschenbach, was the German translator of Berkeley, and from him must have come much of the extensive knowledge of, and sympathy for, British philosophy which Tetens so obviously shows. Tetens was professor at Kiel from 1776 to 1789, when he entered the service of the King of Denmark. He had a distinguished career as a minister of finance until his death in 1807.

Tetens's empiricistic orientation

Tetens was sometimes alluded to as "the German Locke." He repeatedly says that "We must go back to the path trodden by Locke" and build on his "physiology (*Physic*) of the human understanding."[52] He thought that Locke's "plain, historical method" must be practiced, deriving all our ideas from experience. But he also thought that the British (especially Bacon, Locke, and Hume) had interpreted empirical knowledge as a mere collection of observations, had minimized the role of theory and logical form in their theories of knowledge, and had never been able to develop a systematic speculative philosophy or ontology. Reid, Oswald, and Beattie likewise had failed to develop an ontology which would enable them to systematize their common-sense philosophy, and this had kept them from penetrating very deeply into explanations of the mental process underlying common-sense knowledge and everyday practice. Tetens does not oppose the common-sense philosophers as he does Hume, but sees his own task rather to be that of securing and clarifying the philosophy of common sense. He is so committed to Locke, however, that he never concerns himself with Reid's opposition to "the new way of ideas," which is Reid's preeminent claim to historical importance. Tetens writes contentedly of impressions and ideas just as if Reid had never thrown doubt on the entire movement from Descartes to its denouement in Berkeley, Hume, and unnamed "solipsists" in France.[53]

The possibility of metaphysics

In his *Universal Speculative Philosophy* Tetens asked the fundamental Kantian question: Is metaphysics possible? He asked: "Are the times right for systems of philosophy? Can one be more than an observing philosophical *raisonneur*?"[54]

Since Wolff, special metaphysics had been about either spiritual substances (God and the soul) or material substance. Rational theology, rational psychology, and rational cosmology each has its own fundamental concepts and principles, but they share some in common. Tetens calls the study of these common elements *transcendent philosophy* because it transcends the three divisions of special metaphysics.[55] It is first philosophy, ontology, *Grundwissenschaft*. Transcendent philosophy, however, is no longer to be the abstract, formal, almost lexicographical ontology of Wolff. It is, rather, epistemology (though the word did not exist in Tetens's lifetime). It is an empirical science, even though practiced in the armchair. What begins in the empirical sciences may end up in the *a priori* science of ontology.

When Tetens says, for instance, that "Nothing comes from nothing," he is formulating an *objectively necessary* principle of transcendent philosophy. But he sees the same judgment as an assertion of his reason, and he interprets it as an empirical proposition asserting only that his reason cannot think that something comes from nothing.[56]

How can this empirical, contingent judgment (even if true) serve (as it did for Crusius and Lambert as well as for Tetens) as a warrant for the objective principle expressed in the same words? For Tetens, the determination of the conditions of knowledge of the objective principle is itself an explicitly empirical task. Tetens believed that necessities of our mental operations, though discovered empirically, became necessities of transcendent philosophy. He asks us to consider whether "Nothing comes from nothing" is just a quirk of his individual mind; do others agree with him in asserting that nothing comes from nothing? These are all empirical questions that can be answered; but it is not obvious how a true and favorable answer to these questions has any standing when it is a question of ontology: *Can* something come from nothing?

Neither Crusius, Lambert, nor Tetens seems to have seen the problematical character of efforts to base the *a priori* claims of our cognitions upon contingent facts of psychology. Kant characterizes such efforts as "getting water from a pumice stone." Let us see how Tetens proceeds.

The cognitive faculties

Tetens draws a line between the active and the receptive powers of the soul. The active power is the will and the faculty of thought; the receptive faculty is feeling or sense. Cognition occurs only when the former works upon the latter. The first product of this working is the capacity to form representations and concepts; there are already impressions of sense and feeling, but these are brought to consciousness as representations only by the basic power of making representations and concepts; a representation is the first object of consciousness, but it is not an impression or a copy of an impression. Thought is necessary to form a representation as a *sign* of sensation; the sensations must be "run through" and "held together" in a certain way[57] by thought before they become representations of an object. The power of imagination (*Dichtkraft*) creates generic images of sensible *abstracta* such as space and time. When representations refer to things in space and time which presumably give rise to them, we are said to perceive objects, and we fail to notice that we have only representations of objects, not objects themselves. We identify and reidentify objects, associate them with one another, make abstractions from and classify them. In short, we obtain or form a concept of an object that can function in knowing in a way that a mere image cannot.

When representations become distinct concepts and their original felt association is replaced by a connection which is thought, there arises a concept of relation (*Verhältnissbegriff*) between concepts. Relational concepts are not confined to specific pairs of representations but may remain the same even when the specific content of the representations is different. Such concepts are the fundamental concepts of transcendent philosophy. Among them are sameness and difference, coexistence and succession (space and time), inherence of a property in a substance, and dependence of one thing on another (echoes of Hume's list of "philosophical relations," anticipations of Kant's categories). The relations among these concepts are *a priori*, because they are not restricted as to the empirical content of the representations related to each other. Since they are relations implicit in the formal structure of judgments and inferences, they are found in and apply to all knowledge.

We have seen repeatedly how Crusius and Lambert recognized a class of necessary judgments which are not based on logical necessity according to the laws of identity and contradiction. They tried to establish the objectivity of such judgments. Generally, they tried to do so by appealing to the fact (if it is a fact) that these judgments express a necessity of thought, not a logical necessity: one *just must* see that some things cannot be thought to coexist. That, however, is a fallible, contingent truth if it is true at all. What they needed was a proposition with the apodeictic certainty of the law of contradiction yet one that could not be proved by the law of contradiction. (In a word, they needed to recognize what Kant will later call synthetic *a priori* judgments.)

Tetens was keenly aware of the problem in 1776. The truths of geometry are necessarily true, but not because they depend on identity and contradiction; they are necessarily true of space as we constitute the *abstracta* of space by the functioning of our cognitive faculties. The laws of identity and contradiction are "mere ways of thinking without reference to what is peculiar to the ideas related,"[58] but the laws of mathematics deal with what is peculiar to space and time. Where the necessity of a judgment does not depend on the merely formal relationship between subject and predicate or the particular empirical content of the two concepts, it must depend upon "what is, in respect to certain general classes of representations (or objects), necessary and natural to the understanding."[59] What the features are that are necessary and natural to the understanding must be discovered, according to Tetens, empirically, though the relations themselves are *a priori* necessary.

The objective reference of perception

It is a quite different thing to show that a judgment is an expression of thought natural to our understanding, and to show that the judgment is objectively true. Tetens made an original and significant change in the mode of examining this question of subjectivity and objectivity.

Sensations and impressions are not normally objects of consciousness. They lack referentiality or intentionality. They get intentionality from being ingredient in representations, representations in our consciousness being representations *of something*. Tetens claims that this is a better account of the origin of our belief in external, independent objects than the different ones offered by Hume and Reid. But he also confesses,[60] however, that it does not touch the question: *Is objective reference veridical?*

Tetens does not have an answer to the demand for justification of objective knowledge-claims, regarded as a question of metaphysics. Epistemologically, however, he gives a criterion of objectivity which is independent of the ontological status of minds and objects.

Tetens examines the way some ideas are endowed with objective reference without presupposing an answer to the question of the ontology of subject and object. He empirically distinguishes the *unchangeable subjective* and the *changeable subjective*,[61] and sees that

the former captures the empirical and methodological, if not the ontological, meaning of "objective." Similarly there is the distinction
between the *intersubjective* and the *subjective*, where the former is
ordinarily called the objective.

This is as close as a writer of an empirical theory of knowledge
can come to the Kantian divisons between judgments of perception
and judgments of experience and between unattainable knowledge of
transcendent objects and attainable knowledge of objects immanent in
experience.

Kant's friend Hamann said that Kant had Tetens open upon his
desk while writing the *Critique of Pure Reason*. Kant regretted that
this powerful and original thinker did not review his *Critique of Pure
Reason* when it was published in 1781. We can be sure that the second
edition (1787) would have been improved if Kant had had the benefit
of Tetens's criticisms. There is a certain melancholy in some of Kant's
remarks about Tetens – how close he had come to what Kant saw as
truth, and yet how far short of it he had fallen. He wrote:

> Tetens investigated the concepts of reason subjectively, I
> objectively. His analysis is empirical, mine transcendental. No
> one considered the possibility of such *a priori* knowledge
> [ingredient in and presupposed by empirical knowledge]
> although Herr Tetens could have given rise to it.[62]

➤ THE MENDELSSOHN–JACOBI ➤ CONTROVERSY[63]

The philosophers we have been studying raised objections to Wolff's
philosophy, but with the possible exception of Crusius they did not
bring much against his *Weltanschauung*. They were all men of the
Enlightenment. They all were quite "safe" on the big issues of philosophy – God, freedom, and immortality – while they disputed technical
points such as the logical status of the principle of sufficient reason.

A little after 1780 the *pax philosophica* was shattered by a controversy that left its mark on Kant, Herder, Goethe, and the early German
Idealists such as Schelling. It was a turning point in German philosophy
and cultural life. If one decides that Jacobi was the "victor," one can
say that the Enlightenment in Germany was finished.

Moses Mendelssohn was a faithful disciple of Wolff and won the
prize essay contest of the Berlin Academy by defending the Wolffian
mathematical ideal, defeating Immanuel Kant. Kant praised the elegance
of his literary style, and in fact he is the best stylist among German
philosophers before Schopenhauer. He was an intimate friend of Les-

sing's and was the model of the wise man in Lessing's drama, *Nathan der Weise*.

Friedrich Heinrich Jacobi was born into a rich Pietistic family in Düsseldorf in 1743. He reacted against the naturalistic, empiricistic education he received in Switzerland and became a religious enthusiast (*Schwärmer*). Faith and feeling were the watchwords of his philosophy.

The conception of Spinoza as an atheist or pantheist, a blind fatalist, a destructive critic of Scripture who denied its authority, and a revolutionary political thinker was almost universally accepted in Germany. Wolff wrote extensively in criticism of Spinoza,[64] but nonetheless he was accused of Spinozism by his Pietist colleagues at Halle. Mendelssohn in his *Philosophical Conversations* (1763) pleaded for a better and more fair-minded appraisal of "the accursed atheist of Amsterdam," without, of course, taking any step that committed him to Spinozism and without effecting any change in the almost unanimous condemnation of Spinozism.

Imagine the shock, then, when it became known shortly after his death in 1781 that *Lessing had been a Spinozist*. Lessing – Germany's greatest man of letters, Germany's greatest thinker between Leibniz and Kant, a man whose character after more than two centuries still awakens feelings of affection and respect – a *Spinozist?* In conversations with Jacobi, Lessing had made this confession. Through mutual friends Jacobi imparted this information to Mendelssohn, ostensibly to contribute to a biography of Lessing that Mendelssohn was working on. Naturally the secret could not be kept; party lines were drawn.

There was a complicated exchange of letters through intermediaries, some of whom egged on one or the other of the protagonists. Finally there were publications in which spleen was hardly covered by civility: Jacobi's *On the Doctrine of Spinoza, in Letters to Moses Mendelssohn* (1785), Mendelssohn's *Morning Lessons or Lectures on the Existence of God* (1785), Mendelssohn's *To the Friends of Lessing* (posthumous, 1786), and Jacobi's *Against Mendelssohn's Accusations in his "To the Friends of Lessing"* (1786). To these should be added *David Hume on Belief* (1787) since it develops Jacobi's "philosophy of faith and feeling" which underlies the conversations with Lessing and the correspondence with Mendelssohn.

Nothing shows better the ill-nature of this controversy than the accusations that Jacobi was responsible for Mendelssohn's death in 1786 at the climax of the debate.

For three reasons what might have been a quiet *Auseinandersetzung* between two scholars was raised to the level of a public scandal. The first was the eminence of the recently deceased Lessing. Any surprising secrets about that good and famous man were bound to be objects of public curiosity. Second, there were many who hoped it was true that Lessing had been a Spinozist. These crypto-Spinozists were more numerous than anyone had reckoned, and with Lessing's Spinozism established they could come out of the closet.

Then there were the personal motives and traits of the principals. Fritz Jacobi was a name-dropper and a tuft-hunter. He prided himself on knowing everybody. (Goethe told Eckermann that Jacobi lacked something necessary for a poet or philosopher, but that he would have made a good ambassador.) Pride and snobbery were mixed in him with a genuine religious concern.

Mendelssohn was not shocked by Spinozism, as we have already seen. But it was a personal wound to him that Lessing, his intimate friend of thirty years, should have concealed his Spinozism from him and revealed it to some young man he hardly knew. At first he doubted the truth of what Jacobi said about Lessing; then he doubted the truth of what Lessing may have said about himself, citing as explanation Lessing's love of paradox, irony, and persiflage.

Much has been written about the strategy and tactics of the contestants, detailing how Jacobi laid traps for Mendelssohn, how these were dodged by Mendelssohn who was laying traps of his own, etc. Neither of the principals came out with clean hands. The stakes were too high for either man to be punctilious about the ethics of publication of personal documents. The stakes were the validity of the whole philosophical enterprise.

Jacobi saw the issue as a choice between the nihilistic Spinoza–Leibniz–Wolffian Enlightenment and the absolute but irrationalistic claims of faith and feeling. Jacobi's target was something even bigger and grander than Lessing and Spinoza: he aimed to overthrow the Enlightenment's rationalism and intellectualism and ideal of demonstrable metaphysical and theological truth. He tried to show that any system of demonstrations had to go in the direction of Spinozism; minor criticisms of Wolff had to give way to a frontal assault on the entire enterprise of philosophy as an intellectual discipline. Mendelssohn's strategy was to construct a form of Spinozism which Lessing *might* have held and which did not have the fatal consequences that Jacobi had found in his interpretation of Spinoza. In this way he could free the Leibniz–Wolffian philosophy of the atheism, pantheism, nihilism, and fatalism that Jacobi said it shared with Spinoza.

When Lessing remarked of Spinoza's substance "that we can think nothing about it doesn't imply its impossibility," Jacobi replied: "You go even farther than Spinoza. For him understanding is worth more than anything." Lessing replied: "For men only. Spinoza was far from thinking our miserable human acting for purposes was the best method, and far from making thought supreme."[65]

After an *excursus* in which Jacobi tries to show that Leibniz and hence the Leibniz–Wolffians were in essential agreement with Spinoza, Jacobi returns to his theme of the impotence and inferiority of abstract thought:

> In my judgment the greatest service of the enquirer is to uncover and reveal being (*Daseyn*). Explanation is only the means and the way to the goal; it is neither the next nor the ultimate goal. The final goal is what does not let itself be explained: the irresolvable, the immediate, the simple. . . . Since we only put together and hang together what is explainable in things, there is a certain illusion (*Schein*) in the soul which blinds more than it reveals. . . . [When we enquire] we close the eye of the soul with which the soul sees itself and God, so that by greater concentration it can see with the eye of the body.[66]

We do not, therefore, approach truth by rational thinking; rather, we embrace it in spite of rational thinking. A *mortal leap* (*salto mortale*) is needed. (An almost exactly parallel move can be found in Kierkegaard's distinction between approximation to the truth and appropriation of the truth.) But Jacobi was unable to persuade Lessing with his "tired head and old legs" to take the plunge; Lessing remained a Spinozist. Others who professed adherence to Spinozism, however, embraced a very different Spinozism from that of rationalism and geometrical rigor. For men like Herder,[67] Schelling, and Goethe, an organic, holistic, romantic conception of oneness replaced the quasi-mathematical perfection of Spinoza's substance. Spinoza came into his own, paradoxically, when rationalism was on the wain.

Having held Spinozistic nihilism (Jacobi's own word) to be the natural and inevitable last stage in the evolution of Enlightenment, it was to be expected that Kant's *Critique of Pure Reason*, published the year of Lessing's death, should come under criticism from Jacobi. But instead of appealing directly to religious "faith and feeling," he allied himself with David Hume. He appealed to Hume and to Hume's critic, Thomas Reid, to justify his doctrine of the impotence of reason even in the simplest actions of everyday life. Hume substituted belief for unattainable knowledge, and Reid found belief essential in establishing the existence of external objects when all that analytical reason could show was only impressions and ideas.

In his *Morning Lessons* (*Morgenstunden*) (1785) Mendelssohn does two things. First, he reasserts the correctness of Wolff's deism and its superiority over Spinoza's pantheism. He points out what seems to him to be a myriad of errors in Spinoza's philosophy. He shows, to his own satisfaction, that the demonstrative method does not necessarily produce the Spinozistic conclusions of pantheism and fatalism.[68]

Second, he formulates, in the name of his friend Lessing, a system of "purified pantheism" which Lessing might have held and which would not have the evil consequences that Jacobi thought were indigenous in Spinozism. Specifically, in the fourteenth Lesson he makes of substance a spiritual being endowed with intellect and will but not extension. Then the question whether God is the world (pantheism) or the world stands outside God (deism) does not have the portentous consequences which follow from identifying the human mind with a mode of substance whose essence is necessity, extension, and oneness.

In his *To the Friends of Lessing* (1786) Mendelssohn tries a new gambit. He commends "sound human understanding" (common sense in the Scottish philosophy) when high speculations like Spinozism or purified pantheism, formulated by fallible human reason, conflict or do not carry conviction. He says:

> When I speak of rational conviction . . . I am not speaking of metaphysical argumentation . . . or of scholastic demonstrations which have stood the test of the most subtle skepticism; rather, I speak of the expressions and judgments of simple and sound human understanding which directly grasps and contemplates things. I certainly respect demonstrations in metaphysics . . . but *my* conviction of religious truths does not depend so completely upon metaphysical argumentations that it would have to stand or fall with them. One can raise doubts about my arguments and show fallacies in them, and yet my conviction remains unshaken. . . . For the true and genuine conviction of natural religion . . . these artificial methods [of metaphysical speculation] are of no use. The man whose reason is not debauched by sophistry needs only to follow his own good sense.[69]

This was the state of things at the end of the Mendelssohn–Jacobi dispute: the proponent of faith and feeling sees his rationalist enemy take refuge in common sense. On both sides, reason has taken a beating. That is how it appeared to one man, Immanuel Kant, in an apostrophe to Jacobi and Mendelssohn:

> Men of intellectual power and broad minds! I honor your talents and love your feeling for humanity. But have you considered what you do, and where you will end, with your attacks on human reason? . . . Friends of the human race and of that which is holiest to it! . . . do not wrest from reason that which makes it the highest good on earth, the prerogative of being the ultimate touchstone of truth.[70]

German Idealism proper may be said to have begun when leading philosophers heeded Kant's words and made reason "the highest good on earth" and "the ultimate touchstone of truth."

❧ NOTES ❧

1 See, for instance, C.A. Corr, "Christian Wolff and Leibniz," *Journal of the History of Ideas*, 36 (1975): 241–62.

2 W.H. Bruford, *Germany in the Eighteenth Century* (Cambridge: Cambridge University Press, 1965), p. 222.

3 Wolff's *Gesammelte Werke*, ed. J. Ecole, J.E. Hofmann, *et al.* (Hildesheim: Olms, 1962–), are currently being published, but there is little Wolff in English. There is *Preliminary Discourse on Philosophy in General*, trans. R.G. Blackwell (Indianapolis: Bobbs-Merrill, 1963); selections from *Vernünftige Gedanken von Gott, der Welt, der Seele des Menschen, auch allen Dingen überhaupt* in *Eighteenth Century Philosophy*, trans. L.W. Beck (New York: Free Press, 1966); selections from *Vernünftige Gedanken von der Menschen Thun und Lassen* in *Moral Philosophy from Montaigne to Kant*, trans. J.B. Schneewind (Cambridge: Cambridge University Press, 1990).

4 See T. Frängsmyr, "Christian Wolff's Mathematical Method and its Impact on the Eighteenth Century," *Journal of the History of Ideas*, 36 (1975): 653–68.

5 Wolff, *Preliminary Discourse on Philosophy in General*, op. cit., § 139.

6 Wolff, *Von dem Unterschiede metaphysischer und mathematischer Begriffe* . . . , in *Gesammelte Werke*, op. cit., Series I, Vol. 22, pp. 286–343, esp. § 14.

7 J. Ecole, "En quel sens peut-on dire que Wolff est rationalist?" *Studia Leibnitiana*, XI (1979): 45–61.

8 Wolff, *Prima Philosophia sive Ontologia*, in *Gesammelte Werke*, op. cit., Series I, Vol. 2, §§ 70, 288–319; *Vernünftige Gedanken von Gott* . . . , op. cit., § 30. Wolff's "deductions" are so patently question-begging that it is not worthwhile repeating them.

9 Wolff, *Preliminary Discourse on Philosophy in General*, op. cit., §§ 7 ff.

10 Wolff defines *a priori* as follows: "Whatever is known *a priori* is elicited by the power of the intellect." "Whatever becomes known to us by ratiocination is said to be known *a priori*." *Psychologia Empirica*, in *Gesammelte Werke*, op. cit., §§ 438, 434.

11 Wolff, *Ontologia*, op. cit., § 174; *Vernünftige Gedanken von Gott* . . . , op. cit., § 14. Kant's rejection of the complement of possibility is in *Critique of Pure Reason*, A 231, B 284. On this difficult point, see C.A. van Peursen, "Wolff's Philosophy of Contingent Reality," *Journal of the History of Philosophy*, 25 (1987): esp. 75–6.

12 Wolff, *Ontologia*, op. cit., § 872.

13 Wolff tediously recites the benefits that earth-dwellers enjoy by virtue of the sun's existence, e.g. without the sun there could be no sundials and we could not detect compass deviations. What about suns (i.e. stars) that do not benefit earth-dwellers? There must be inhabitants of their planets, who do benefit from their suns. See also the exciting chapter on the benefits we have from the

existence of air. *Vernünftige Gedanken von der Absicht der natürlichen Dingen,* in *Gesammelte Werke,* op. cit., §§ 28, 44, 46, 60, 85, 91, *et passim.*

14 Kant, *Critique of Practical Reason,* trans. L.W. Beck (New York: Macmillan, 1993), p. 41.

15 Baumgarten's Latin Wolffian textbooks were used by Kant in his lectures. One book has been translated into English under the name *Reflections on Poetry,* trans. K. Aschenbrenner and W.B. Holtker (Berkeley: University of California Press, 1954).

16 Crusius, *Weg zur Gewissheit und Zuverlässigkeit der menschlichen Erkenntnis* (1747), §§ 5, 9, 10 (hereafter referred to as *Logic*); *Entwurf der notwendigen Vernunftwahrheiten* (1745), § 234 (hereafter referred to as *Metaphysics*). All citations are to *C.A. Crusius, Die philosophischen Hauptwerke,* ed. G. Tonelli, 4 vols (Hildesheim: Olms, 1987).

17 Crusius, *Metaphysics,* op. cit., § 14.

18 Ibid., §§ 56, 57. This startling thesis was accepted by Lambert and by the precritical Kant in his *Only Possible Premise for a Demonstration of the Existence of God,* trans. G. Treash, Part I, Observation 2 (New York: Abaris, 1979), p. 69; also *New Exposition of the First Principles of Metaphysical Knowledge,* in *Kant's Latin Writings,* 3rd edn (New York: P. Lang, 1993), p. 52.

19 Crusius, *Logic,* op. cit., § 62. Kant does not believe that the Crusian distinction permits an escape from psychological subjectivity.

20 All of these laws except the first two are rejected as "subreptitious axioms" in Kant's Inaugural Dissertation. They result from the application of sensible concepts to intelligible objects and are therefore invalid.

21 Crusius, *Metaphysics,* op. cit., § 15.

22 Kant's letter to Herz, 21 February 1772, in *Kant's Philosophical Correspondence,* ed. A. Zweig (Chicago: University of Chicago Press, 1967), pp. 72–3. Crusius may have been the target of Kant's attack on "preformationism" in *Critique of Pure Reason,* B 167–8; see G. Treash, "Kant and Crusius: epigenesis and preformation," *Proceedings of the Sixth International Kant Congress,* II (1989): 95–108.

23 Crusius, *Logic,* op. cit., § 185.

24 Crusius is closer to Hume when he speaks of "feeling a compulsion to grant another thing from which one thing comes" (*Metaphysics,* op. cit., § 63) but does not draw Hume's skeptical conclusion.

25 Crusius, *Metaphysics,* op. cit., § 31.

26 This is the principal theme of Kant's *Essay towards Introducing Negative Magnitudes into Philosophy* (1764), the work that shows more than any other the Crusian influence on Kant.

27 Crusius, *Dissertatio philosophica de usu et limitibus principii rationis determinantis, vulgo sufficientis,* §§ II, III.

28 Crusius, *Anweisung vernünftig zu Leben* (1744), § 175.

29 Kant, *Critique of Practical Reason,* op. cit., p. 41.

30 Crusius, *Anweisung vernünftig zu Leben,* § 176.

31 Lambert, *Anlage zur Architektonic,* § 683. This work, published with Kant's aid in 1765, aimed to be an ontology for all the sciences, but it lacks the architectonic, systematic order which might have come from the successful application of Lambert's adaptation of Leibniz's *ars characteristica.* It is to be

found in Lambert's *Philosophische Schriften*, ed. H. W. Arndt (Hildesheim: Olms, 1965), Vols 3 and 4.

32 Lambert, "On the Improvement of Method of Proof in Metaphysics, Theology, and Morals," p. 5. This was an uncompleted draft of a paper Lambert apparently intended to submit to the Berlin Academy in the prize competition of 1762. It was first published as the *Kant-Studien Ergänzungsheft* (1918). It shows some remarkable kinship with Kant's prize essay.

33 Lambert to Kant, 3 February 1766, in *Kant's Philosophical Correspondence*, op. cit., p. 51.

34 Lambert, *Abhandlung von Criterium veritatis* (1761), § 79, first published in *Kant-Studien Ergänzungsheft*, 36 (1915).

35 Joachim Georg Darjes (1714–63), professor in Jena and later in Frankfurt/Oder; originally a disciple of Wolff, he was influenced by Crusius. The quotation is from Lambert, *Anlage zur Architektonic*, op. cit., § 11.

36 Lambert, *Neues Organon*, Dianoiologie, §§ 601–5. This work was published in two volumes in 1764 and is reprinted as Lambert's *Philosophische Schriften*, op. cit., Vols 1 and 2.

37 Ibid., § 639.

38 Ibid., §§ 656–7.

39 Ibid., Dianoiologie, § 662.

40 This is the subject matter of Kant's *Essay towards the Introduction of Negative Magnitudes in Philosophy*, written under the Crusian influence before Kant had read Lambert.

41 Lambert, *On the Improvement of the Method . . .* , op. cit., § 19 μ; see Lambert, *Abhandlung von Criterium veritatis*, op. cit., § 92.

42 Ibid., *notanda* 4.

43 Lambert, *Anlage zur Architektonic*, op. cit., § 297.

44 Lambert, *Neues Organon*, op. cit., Alethiologie, § 234a.

45 See L. Falkenstein, "Kant, Mendelssohn, Lambert, and the Subjectivity of Time," *Journal of the History of Philosophy*, 29 (1991): 227–52.

46 *Kant's Philosophical Correspondence*, op. cit., pp. 63, 66.

47 Until Lambert's death it had been Kant's intention to dedicate the *Critique of Pure Reason* to him.

48 Quotations from Kant, *Critique of Pure Reason*, A 37, B 53, B 71.

49 Kant, *On the Form and Principles of the Sensible and the Intelligible World*, § 24, in *Kant's Latin Writings*, op. cit., p. 148.

50 Kant, *Critique of Pure Reason*, A 51 = B 75.

51 *Kant's Philosophical Correspondence*, op. cit., p. 65.

52 Tetens, *On Universal Speculative Philosophy* (1775), pp. 57, 66–7, in Tetens, *Philosophische Versuche über die menschliche Natur und ihre Entwickelung* (Berlin: Kant Gesellschaft, 1913). Both of Tetens's works cited are included in this volume.

53 The pervasive influence of the Scots on Tetens has been studied by M. Kuehn in his comprehensive *Scottish Common Sense in Germany, 1768–1800* (Montreal: McGill-Queen's University Press, 1987), ch. 7.

54 Tetens, *On Universal Speculative Philosophy*, op. cit., p. 66.

55 Ibid., p. 40. A like use of "transcendent" is found in Lambert (*Neues Organon*,

op. cit., Alethiologie, § 48; *Anlage zur Architektonic*, op. cit., § 301). "Transcendent" is not to be confused with Kant's "transcendental."

56 Tetens, *On Universal Speculative Philosophy*, op. cit., p. 27. There is a marked resemblance to Crusius here.

57 Kant, *Critique of Pure Reason*, A 99.

58 Tetens, *On Universal Speculative Philosophy*, op. cit., pp. 33–4.

59 Ibid., p. 28. Tetens accepts Kant's distinction between the necessity inherent in intuition and that belonging to "the transcendent principles of reason." Thus he is at one with Kant in asserting the discontinuity of mathematical and metaphysical reasoning, citing Kant's Inaugural Dissertation. See ibid., pp. 21–2 n.

60 Tetens, *Philosophical Essays* (1777), in *Philosophische Versuche . . .* , op. cit., p. 393.

61 Ibid., p. 527

62 *Kants gesammelte Schriften*, 29 vols, ed. Deutsche (formerly Königliche Preussische) Akademie der Wissenschaften (Berlin: de Gruyter [and predecessors], 1902—), Reflexion 4901, and Vol. 23, pp. 23, 57.

63 The best collection of documents is H. Scholz (ed.), *Die Hauptschriften zum Pantheismusstreit* (Berlin: Kant Gesellschaft, 1916). Selections from Scholz have been translated as *The Spinoza Conversations between Lessing and Jacobi*, trans. G. Vallée *et al.* (Canham, Md: University Press of America, 1988).

64 Wolff, *B. von S. Sittenlehre widerleget von . . . Christian Wolff* (Leipzig, 1744); *Theologia naturalis* (1749), Vol. II, §§ 671–716.

65 *The Teaching of Spinoza in Letters to Moses Mendelssohn*, in Scholz, op. cit., pp. 82–3.

66 Ibid., p. 91.

67 See, for example, Herder's *God, Some Conversations* (1787) (New York: Hafner, 1940).

68 Mendelssohn, *Morgenstunden*, Lesson XIV; Scholz, op. cit., p. 15.

69 Scholz, op. cit., p. 307.

70 Kant, "What is Orientation in Thinking?" in *Kant's Critique of Practical Reason and Other Writings in Moral Philosophy* (Chicago: University of Chicago Press, 1949), pp. 303, 305.

❧ BIBLIOGRAPHY ❧

1.1 Allison, H.E. *Lessing and the Enlightenment*, Ann Arbor: University of Michigan Press, 1968.

1.2 Anchor, R.E. *The Enlightenment Tradition*, New York: Harper & Row, 1967.

1.3 Baeumler, A. *Das Irrationalitätsproblem in der Aesthetik und Logik des achtzehnten Jahrhunderts.* Darmstadt: Wissenschaftliche Buchgesellschaft, 1967. (Originally published as *Kant's Kritik der Urtellskraft, Ihre Geschichte und Systematik*, Halle, 1923.)

1.4 Beck, L.W. *Early German Philosophy: Kant and His Predecessors*, Cambridge: Harvard University Press, 1969. Chs XI–XVI.

1.5 Beck, L.W. *Essays on Kant and Hume*, Yale University Press, 1978. Ch. 5: "Analytic and Synthetic Judgments before Kant."

1.6 Beiser, F.C. *The Fate of Reason. German Philosophy from Kant to Fichte*, Harvard University Press, 1987.

1.7 Bossenbrook, W.J. *The German Mind*, Detroit: Wayne State University Press, 1961.

1.8 Bruford, W.H. *Germany in the Eighteenth Century. The Social Background of the Literary Revival*, Cambridge: Cambridge University Press, 1935 (reprinted 1965).

1.9 Cassirer, E. *Das Erkenntnisproblem in der Philosophie und Wissenschaft der neueren Zeit*, Darmstadt: Wissenschaftliche Buchgesellschaft, 1971. Volume II.

1.10 Cassirer, E. *The Philosophy of the Enlightenment*, Princeton: Princeton University Press, 1951.

1.11 Copleston, F. *A History of Philosophy*, London: Burns & Oates, 1960. Volume 6: *Wolff to Kant*.

1.12 Edwards, P. (ed.) *The Encyclopedia of Philosophy*, New York: Macmillan and Free Press, 1967, 8 volumes. (Contains scholarly articles and bibliographies on all the philosophers mentioned in this chapter.)

1.13 Gawlik, G. and Kreimendahl, L. *Hume in der deutschen Aufklärung*, Stuttgart: Fromman Hoolzboog, 1987.

1.14 Hillebrand, K. *German Thought from the Seven Years' War to Goethe's Death*, New York: Holt, 1880.

1.15 Kantzenbach, F.W. *Protestantisches Christentum im Zeitalter der Aufklärung*, Gütersloh: Mohm, 1965.

1.16 Kuehn, M. *Scottish Common Sense in Germany, 1768–1800*, Kingston and Montreal: McGill-Queen's University Press, 1987.

1.17 Petersen, P. *Geschichte der aristotelischen Philosophie im protestantischen Deutschland*, Leipzig: Meiner, 1921.

1.18 Philipp, W. *Das Werden der Aufklärung in theologiegeschichtlicher Sicht*, Göttingen: Vanderhoek aund Ruprecht, 1957.

1.19 Philipp, W. (ed.) *Das Zeitalter der Aufklärung*, Bremen: Schünemann, 1963.

1.20 Sutton, C. *The German Tradition in Philosophy*, London: Weidenfeld & Nicolson, 1974.

1.21 Tonelli, G. "La Philosophie Allemande de Leibniz á Kant." In *Histoire de la Philosophie*, ed. Y. Beleval, vol. ii, pp. 728–85. Paris: Encylopédie de la Pléiade, 1973.

1.22 Wolff, H.M. *Die Weltanschauung der deutschen Aufklärung*, Bern: Francke, 1949.

1.23 Wundt, M. *Die deutsche Schulmetaphysik im Zeitalter der Aufklärung*, Tübingen: Mohr, 1945.

1.24 Zeller, E. *Geschichte der deutschen Philosophie seit Leibniz*, München, 1873.

CHAPTER 2

Kant's Copernican revolution

Daniel Bonevac

Immanuel Kant's *Critique of Pure Reason* was to transform the philosophical world, at once bringing the Enlightenment to its highest intellectual development and establishing a new set of problems that would dominate philosophy in the nineteenth century and beyond. As Richard Rorty has observed, Kant would turn philosophy into a profession, if for no other reason than that, after 1781, one could not be called a philosopher without having mastered Kant's first *Critique* – which, in the words of Kant's famous commentator, Norman Kemp Smith, "is more obscure and difficult than even a metaphysical treatise has any right to be."[1]

The *Critique*'s central character is "Human reason," which, Kant begins his first edition's preface by noting,

> has this peculiar fate that in one species of its knowledge it is
> burdened by questions which, as prescribed by the very nature
> of reason itself, it is not able to ignore, but which, as
> transcending all its powers, it is also not able to answer.

> (A vii)[2]

Reason develops principles to deal with experience; within the realm of experience, those principles are well justified. Reason finds itself driven, however, to ask questions extending beyond that realm. The very principles it has developed and upon which it properly continues to rely in dealing with experience there lead it "into darkness and contradictions" (A viii). Metaphysics, once Queen of the Sciences, now surveys the battlefield on which these principles clash and mourns. Kant's aim in the *Critique* is to rescue metaphysics, "to secure for human reason complete satisfaction" (A 856, B 884) by defining its proper sphere of application.

Kant's means for achieving this end is the critical method. The title of the work is ambiguous in both English and German: Pure reason may be the agent or the object of the critique.³ In fact, it is surely both. The critical method requires reason to critique itself, to determine its own limits, and then to devise rules for staying within them. This, Kant thinks, is the key to reason's "complete satisfaction": "there is not a single metaphysical problem which has not been solved, or for the solution of which the key at least has not been supplied" (A xiii).

Understood in this way, Kant's critical method hardly seems revolutionary. It had been exemplified already in Locke's *Essay concerning Human Understanding* and Hume's *Treatise of Human Nature*. Both were attempts to define the limits of human knowledge by employing reason in a reflective act of self-criticism. Kant's most important contribution is not the general idea of the critical method, but the specific form that method takes, for which he often uses the adjective *transcendental* rather than *critical*. Kant claims that he uses the transcendental method and establishes the truth of transcendental idealism.

What, then, is the transcendental method? To understand it, we need to focus on what, in the preface to the second edition of 1787, Kant considers the key to his advance: his Copernican revolution in philosophy. "[T]he procedure of metaphysics," Kant writes, "has hitherto been a merely random groping, and, what is worst of all, a groping among mere concepts" (B xv). Kant finds himself capable of setting metaphysics upon the secure path of a science by advancing a hypothesis analogous to that of Copernicus.

> Hitherto it has been assumed that all our knowledge must conform to objects. But all attempts to extend our knowledge of objects by establishing something in regard to them *a priori*, by means of concepts, have, on this assumption, ended in failure. We must therefore make trial whether we may not have more success in the tasks of metaphysics, if we suppose that objects must conform to our knowledge.
>
> (B xvi)

Copernicus explained the motions of the heavenly bodies as resulting, not just from their own motion, but also from the motion of the observers on earth. Just as he sought "the observed movements, not in the heavenly bodies, but in the spectator" (B xxii n.), so Kant seeks the laws governing the realm of experience not in the objects themselves but in us: "we can know *a priori* of things only what we ourselves put into them" (B xviii).

❧ THE PLATONIC HERITAGE ❧

Kant is a rationalist. We might define a *concept rationalist* as one who believes in innate concepts – that is, that we have first-order cognitive abilities that we do not derive from experience – and a *judgment rationalist* as one who believes that we can know some synthetic truths *a priori* – that is, that we can know independently of experience some truths that are not merely linguistic or verbal, that are not automatically true or false because of the meanings of the words that constitute them. Kant is plainly a rationalist in both senses. He argues that we can deduce pure concepts of the understanding *a priori*, independently of experience, from the mere possibility of experience, and moreover that there are synthetic *a priori* truths – that is, truths that we can know independently of experience but that are not merely verbal. Indeed, the establishment of rationalism in both senses seems to be a major goal of the *Critique*.

Like many rationalists, Kant understands himself as working within the Platonic tradition. The central problems he attacks and his solutions to them stem directly from that tradition. To understand Kant's Copernican revolution, therefore, we must consider the framework in which his thought is embedded.

Consider a judgment of perception, for example, (said pointing to a figure drawn on a blackboard) 'This is a triangle.' According to Plato, at one very influential stage of his thought, at least, the mind so judging is Janus-faced. It is turned toward a perceptual object, a triangle, if it judges correctly. It is also turned toward the abstract form of a triangle. Both the object and the form have real causal or explanatory power. The object is causally responsible for our perception of it. But we are able to perceive it as a triangle because we apprehend the general form of triangularity. The form of a triangle is exemplified in the triangle itself, which in turn is an instance of, or, in Plato's technical language, *participates* in, the form.

The forms constitute the most distinctive feature of Plato's philosophy of mind. They explain our ability to think general thoughts; they account for regularities as well as changes in experience; they explain how different people (or the same person at different times) can think the same thought; and they explain how thoughts can be veridical. We may think general thoughts, for example, by thinking about the forms and how they relate. Regularities in experience involve constant relations of forms; changes occur when an object of sense stops participating in one form and begins participating in another. Two different people can think the same thought by attending to the same forms. Finally, thoughts can depict reality accurately by involving the forms that are actually instantiated.

But the forms also generate a serious epistemological puzzle. By definition, the forms are not themselves objects of experience; we do not perceive triangularity as we perceive individual triangles. How, then, do we know anything about them? How is the realm of forms, which Philo of Alexandria later termed "the intelligible world," intelligible? In an Aristotelian philosophy of mind, we generate our own general concepts from experience through a process of abstraction. A Platonist may borrow this account for certain general concepts, but cannot use it for all, because it is central to Platonism that some forms are ultimately responsible for our abilities to think the corresponding thoughts. On Plato's view, we do not abstract the idea of a pure triangle from triangular objects we perceive; indeed, we never encounter a pure triangle in experience. Instead, we recognize objects as triangular because we apprehend the form of pure triangularity and recognize that the objects approximate that pure form. In this sense, the forms have causal power; we are able to think of things as triangular by virtue of our apprehension of the form.

Unfortunately, Plato has no theory that explains our interaction with the forms. He relies on two metaphors. In the *Meno*, he speaks of recollection; we apprehend the forms by recalling a time before birth when our souls were united with them. In the *Republic*, he speaks of the form of the Good as analogous to the sun, shedding light on the realm of forms and making possible our apprehension of them. Neither metaphor yields a satisfactory theory within the limits of Platonic metaphysics. Neither, moreover, seems to explain our apprehension of forms without begging the question. The *Meno* metaphor explains the causal efficacy of the forms now by appealing to their efficacy at some earlier time; the *Republic* metaphor, by appealing to the efficacy of the form of the Good. The Neoplatonic theory of emanation, according to which the entire realm of forms is ordered, with the causal efficacy of higher levels making lower levels possible and intelligible, does little to change the central epistemological difficulty.

Augustine, however, solves Platonism's epistemological problem by going beyond the resources of the original theory. To put it crudely, he adopts the *Republic*'s solution, but replaces the form of the Good with God. It is not clear why the form of the Good should be more causally efficacious than any other form. Causal efficacy, in contrast, is not a problem for God, who can do anything. Augustine thus follows Philo in identifying the forms with ideas in the mind of God, and describes the process by which we apprehend the forms as illumination, an act of revelation by which God allows us to make use of a portion of divine mental resources and by which, therefore, God makes our minds resemble the divine mind. We have innate cognitive capacities that reflect the principles according to which God created the world.

Platonism remained Augustinian throughout the medieval debates concerning realism and nominalism arising from the conflict between Platonic and Aristotelian theories of substance and knowledge. Descartes, however, advanced a new kind of skeptical argument that forced a change in Platonism and that brought the theory of knowledge to center stage in modern philosophy. He added to the traditional arguments of Sextus and Cicero the possibility of an evil deceiver, who systematically misaligns our minds to reality. This extends farther than traditional skeptical arguments, for it raises the possibility that not only sensible knowledge but even logic and mathematics might be mistaken. It thus challenges the Augustinian solution to Platonism's epistemological problem. Why should illumination produce veridical knowledge? Why should we believe that God reveals the portion of the divine mind relevant to the construction of the world, and not some counterfeit of it? Why should our innate ideas, and the *a priori* knowledge arising from them, have anything to do with the world?

Kant sees the force of this difficulty, and thinks that, within the Platonic framework, it is insoluble. He divides previous philosophers into dogmatists and skeptics (A ix; A 856, B 884). Dogmatists like Descartes and Leibniz assume that human reason can comprehend ultimate reality. Their dogmatism involves three factors:

1   *Realism.* Human thought can discover the nature of objective reality.
2   *Transcendence.* Real knowledge is capable of extending beyond experience to the supersensible. (See A 295–6, B 352.)
3   *Rationalism.*[4]

Descartes, for example, tries to demonstrate that God guarantees the veridicality of our *a priori* judgments by arguing that God exists and is entirely good. A good God, surely, would not be a deceiver. Granting Cartesian rationalism, we may see the problem generated by the possibility of the evil deceiver as precisely that of realism: Why should we believe that our thinking can discover the nature of objective reality? Descartes's solution relies on transcendence. We may take the form of thought implicit in the *cogito*, namely, the method of clear and distinct ideas, and apply it beyond the realm of our own thinking to reality – indeed, to reality that transcends all possible experience. But this, Kant sees, is just what is at issue. If realism is false – if our minds cannot discover the nature of objective reality – then why should we expect our modes of thinking, applied to the nature of that reality, to be reliable? It will not do to appeal to transcendence to justify realism, for the only argument for transcendence presupposes realism. For example, Descartes's third *Meditation*, arguing for the existence and moral excellence of God, appeals to the premise that there is at least as much reality in the cause as in the effect.[5] Why, given only the certain knowledge that I think and I exist, should I accept this principle as certain? Descartes derives it by applying the method of clear and distinct ideas beyond the mental realm of the *cogito*, which first justified it, to the realm of external, objective reality. Kant, for this reason, among others, rejects Descartes's proof. But his reasoning is broader. Any argument for realism within the dogmatist's framework will rely on transcendence and make a similarly illegitimate move.

Skepticism, as Kant conceives it, also involves three factors:

1   *Subjectivism*. Knowledge of objects reduces to knowledge of sense.
2   *Immanence*. Real knowledge is limited to the sphere of sense experience.
3   *Empiricism*. (The denial of rationalism in either of its forms.)

Skepticism, too, encounters difficulties. If dogmatism extends our knowledge too far and too uncritically, skepticism seems unable to account for the knowledge we do have. Hume's scandal of induction, for example, illustrates that we cannot justify any causal knowledge we claim to have. It would have to reduce to a knowledge of items directly presented in sensation, but, as Hume shows, it does not.

Kant's critical philosophy shares the immanence of skepticism, but also the rationalism of dogmatism. It transcends the distinction between realism and subjectivism, holding that in a sense each is correct. Kant's synthesis of dogmatism and skepticism comes at the cost of distinguishing between the world of appearance – the *phenomenal* world – and the world of things-in-themselves – the *noumenal* world. The former is essentially sensible, and human thought can discover its nature. Things-in-themselves, in contrast, lie beyond our cognitive capacities. The dogmatist is right about the possibility of knowledge of objects, even *a priori* knowledge of them; the skeptic is right about the limitation of knowledge to the realm of experience.

Both, however, misunderstand the status of objects of experience, thinking that they are in themselves as they appear to us. The phenomenal world is both sensible and knowable; the noumenal world is neither. With respect to phenomena, therefore, the skeptic is vanquished; we can have *a priori* knowledge of objects of experience. With respect to noumena, however, the skeptic triumphs, for we can have no knowledge of things-in-themselves.

Kant's solution to the epistemological problem of Platonism goes beyond the distinction between phenomena and noumena. It would be easy to build that distinction into Descartes's metaphysics, for example, without thereby making any headway on the skeptical problem. The key to Kant's solution resides in two additional changes to the traditional framework. First, Kant explains the causal efficacy of the forms by transforming them into *categories*, pure concepts of the understanding. They are innate cognitive capacities of a very general kind, but they are wholly mental; the question of their correspondence to abstract, mind-independent forms cannot arise. Without such forms there remains, of course, the possibility that the categories do not correspond to objective and concreté reality. So, second, Kant reverses the traditional conception of the relation between thought and its object, or, as he puts it, between object and concept. The Platonist traditionally sees the object as causally responsible for the veridical, perceptual thought of it. Kant's Copernican revolution is precisely to reverse this understanding, maintaining instead that thought is causally responsible for constituting the object. The result is not anarchy, a circumstance of "thinking making it so," for the constitution of objects proceeds according to the categories in a rule-governed way. The rule-governed character of the construction makes knowledge of objects possible. More, it makes *a priori* knowledge of them possible, for we can understand what we put into them – we can discover the rules according to which we constitute them. In this way Kant justifies his realism with respect to the phenomenal world without any appeal to transcendence – indeed, in the face of its outright denial.

❧ THE CATEGORIES ❧

Kant's first change to the traditional Platonistic framework is to substitute for the forms the categories, pure concepts of the understanding. These are innate ideas of the kind smiled upon by every concept rationalist. But there is no abstract realm of forms to which they must correspond. Their independence dissolves the epistemological difficulty arising for the aspect of the mind turned toward the forms in Platonic theories of mind.

All knowledge, Kant observes, involves concepts; all concepts, in turn, "rest on functions," "bringing various representations under one common representation" (A 68, B 93). The representations united in a concept may be sensible intuitions or other concepts. Kant here makes an important concession to empiricists such as Hume: the content of concepts traces ultimately to sensation. Kant makes much of this in the Transcendental Dialectic to refute the transcendence thesis. In deriving the categories, however, he focuses on the mediate character of concepts. Concepts of objects always relate to those objects indirectly:

> Since no representation, save when it is an intuition, is in
> immediate relation to an object, no concept is ever related to
> a concept immediately, but to some other representation of it,
> be that other representation an intuition, or itself a concept.
> Judgment is therefore the mediate knowledge of an object, that
> is, a representation of a representation of it.
>
> (A 68, B 93)

This has the consequence, critical to the Copernican revolution Kant means to effect, that both judgments and objects are products of synthesis.

Knowledge, Kant contends, always takes the form of judgments. (This is true at least for discursive knowledge, that is, knowing *that*, as opposed to knowing *how* or knowing *to*.) Judgments are combinations of concepts, which, in turn, are rules for synthesis, bringing together various sensations or concepts. Concepts relate to objects because they are such functions of synthesis. To discover the pure concepts of the understanding, therefore, we must find the functions of synthesis with *a priori* rather than empirical origins.

The content of judgments, we might say, always has an empirical source, for the content of the concepts that comprise them arises ultimately from sensation. A concept unites sensible intuitions or other concepts that themselves unite sensible intuitions or other concepts. The chain cannot proceed to infinity; at some point, it terminates in intuition. This may suggest that there are no pure concepts. But not all functions of synthesis operating in a judgment comprise part of its content. A judgment has both a content and a form. The content stems from experience, but the form does not. We can identify the pure concepts of the understanding, then, by examining the forms of judgment. Fortunately, there is already a science that abstracts from the content of judgments and examines only their forms – logic.[6]

Kant, using Aristotelian logic, derives the following table of judgments (A 70, B 95):

I
Quantity
Universal
Particular
Singular

II		**III**
Quality		*Relation*
Affirmative		Categorical
Negative		Hypothetical
Infinite		Disjunctive

IV
Modality
Problematic
Assertoric
Apodeictic

Every judgment, Kant contends, has a quantity, a quality, a relation, and a modality. In quantity, it is either universal ('every metal is a body,' for example), particular ('some metals are yellow'), or singular ('Socrates is a philosopher'). In quality, it is either affirmative ('Socrates is mortal'), negative ('Socrates is not mortal'), or infinite ('Socrates is immortal'). In relation, judgments may be categorical ('gold is a metal'), hypothetical ('if every metal is a body, gold is a body'), or disjunctive ('gold is a metal or a rare earth'). And, in modality, judgments are problematic ('gold may be a metal'), assertoric ('gold is a metal'), or apodeictic ('gold must be a metal'). The table of judgments thus gives what Kant takes to be an exhaustive account of the forms of judgment.

From the perspective of modern logic, the table seems incomplete. It does not include the quantity of 'most metals are heavy' or 'many metals oxidize'; it omits the modality of 'Socrates ought to avoid hemlock.' It has no place for judgments with complement clauses, such as 'Socrates knew that the hemlock would kill him,' and makes no provision for the abstraction relating 'kind' and 'kindness,' 'friend' and 'friendship.' It is silent about verb tense and aspect. (Kant considers time a form of sensibility, not of judgment, and so considers it beyond the province of logic.) It omits identity. Kant's table is not only incomplete from a modern point of view; it is redundant. Many entries can be derived from others with the help of forms recognized by contemporary logicians. There is no consensus on exactly what such a table would need to reflect all the forms of possible judgment. Kant is surely correct, however, that what we now call quantifiers, connectives, and modalities are required.

The functions of judgment are not themselves the pure concepts of the understanding, but they correspond to them one-to-one. Kant lists the pure concepts of the understanding in his table of categories (A 80, B 106):

I
Of quantity
Unity
Plurality
Totality

II
Of quality
Reality
Negation
Limitation

III
Of relation
Of inherence and subsistence
Of causality and dependence
Of community

IV
Of modality
Possibility–impossibility
Existence–nonexistence
Necessity–contingency

Some of these relate directly to a corresponding entry in the table of judgments – 'Negative' and 'Negation,' for example, or 'Problematic' and 'Possibility–Impossibility.' Other connections – 'Disjunctive' and 'Of community,' for instance – seem tenuous. How does Kant derive the table of categories? His detailed arguments are not terribly important, for, as we have seen, the entries on the table of judgments reflect an outdated logic. But it is important to understand what the categories are.

Roughly speaking, what the table of judgments is to judgments, the table of categories is to objects. Just as the table of judgments outlines the possible logical forms of judgment, so the table of categories outlines the possible logical forms of objects. This explains, for example, why, corresponding to the assertoric modality, we find 'Existence–nonexistence' rather than 'Truth–falsehood.' Synthesis of the manifold of intuition is essential to concepts. But synthesis alone does not suffice for knowledge. Knowledge of objects requires a unification of the pure synthesis of the sensible manifold. That is, the concept of an object is special: It is the concept of a unified thing. In different terminology, concepts of objects not only tell us when a certain predicable or general term applies, but also when it is being applied to one and the same thing.[7] The pure concepts of the understanding "apply *a priori* to objects of intuition in general" (A 79, B 105); they spell out the possible forms of such objects by indicating the possible kinds of unity.

Kant's key assumption in deriving the categories in this way is that "The same function which gives unity to the various representations *in a judgment* also gives unity to the mere synthesis of various representations *in an intuition*" (A 79, B 105). Each such unity is a pure concept of the understanding. Why are the unifying functions in judgments and objects the same? We have seen above that judgments and objects are both products of synthesis. Moreover, knowledge is always knowledge of objects through judgments. This suggests that judgments, at least of the sort appropriate to knowledge, are possible only by virtue of the unifying activity of the categories. Still, this does not suffice to establish the identity of function. It shows that the unifying activity in a judgment presupposes the unifying activity in an intuition, not that they have the same form.

Kant's argument turns on his notion of a concept. The unity of judgments and objects alike is a unity in a concept. This not only explains the link between the table of judgments and the table of categories; it also explains why the pure concepts of the understanding have *a priori* validity, avoiding the challenges of the skeptics.

> Concepts of objects in general thus underlie all empirical knowledge as its *a priori* conditions. The objective validity of the categories as *a priori* concepts rests, therefore, on the fact

49

that, so far as the form of thought is concerned, through them alone does experience become possible. They relate of necessity and *a priori* to objects of experience, for the reason that only by means of them can any object whatsoever of experience be thought.

(A 93, B 126)

To understand the role that concepts play in Kant's theory of mind, however, we must examine his account of the kinds of synthesis.

❧ THE SUBJECTIVE DEDUCTION ❧

Kant's argument for the first key to his solution to the problems arising from the Platonic framework – the pure concepts of the understanding – also defends and develops the second key, the Copernican revolution. The argument occupies the portion of the *Critique* he entitles "The transcendental deduction of the pure concepts of the understanding." There are, however, two very different versions of this argument in the first and second editions of the *Critique*. The first edition version presents a model of how the mind constructs objects from the data of sense, arguing that the pure concepts of the understanding are essential to the process. The second version presents no model, but analyzes the implications of the "I think." The general strategy, however, remains the same. The categories are "concepts of an object in general" (B 129); they are " *a priori* conditions of the possibility of experience" (A 94, B 126). We are able to experience objects, that is, only because we have the concept of an object. We do not derive this concept from experience, for we could not experience anything as an object without already having the general concept of an object.

The transcendental deduction of the first edition is notoriously difficult; Kant apparently pieced it together from four manuscripts composed at different times and reflecting four different stages of his thinking.[8] It moreover includes two arguments: an "objective" deduction seeking to establish "the objective validity of *a priori* concepts," and a "subjective" deduction investigating "the faculty of thought" (A x–xi).

The subjective deduction outlines a three-part model of mental activity – specifically, of the generation of a judgment of experience such as 'This is a triangle.' This model shows, in Kant's view, how judgments of experience require the categories. Kant defines a pure concept of the understanding as a concept without any empirical content, that is, as one that "universally and adequately expresses . . . a formal and objective condition of experience" (A 96). His strategy is to "prove that by their means alone an object can be thought" (A 97). This, he says, "will justify their objective validity," for, if the categories are necessary conditions of experience, nothing could be an object of experience without complying with the categories.

Sensation, Kant holds, is a manifold. It bombards us with a plethora of possible sources of information. Out of this multiplicity we synthesize representations, concepts, and judgments. The first act of synthesis is that of apprehension in intuition. All sensations occur in time.[9] We bind the multiplicity sensation offers into unified items of sense. A sensation of a triangle, for example, may consist of various visual and tactile impressions received over a short interval of time. We experience it as a single sensation, usually without being aware of its complex nature. In short, we organize the data of sense into discrete sensations. This organization is the synthesis of apprehension in intuition.

The second act is the synthesis of reproduction in imagination. Kant argues that "experience as such necessarily presupposes the reproducibility of appearances" (A 101–2). His premises concern pure intuitions of space and time – drawing a line in thought, for example, or thinking of a number – which, he maintains, are possible *a priori*. Kant's theory of pure intuitions is controversial and somewhat obscure. But we can argue the point on other grounds. Sensations, considered individually, are not full-blown objects of experience. We can have many sensations of the same object. We might view a triangle, for example, from many different perspectives. To make any judgment about such an object of experience, we must relate sensations to each other, being capable of recognizing them as sensations of the same object. How we do this is of course an empirical question. But do it we must if we are ever to form concepts of objects of experience.

That brings us to the third act, the synthesis of recognition in a concept. Throughout this discussion, Kant seems to operate with two ideas of what concepts are. The awareness of the unity of various sensations, Kant says, is a concept – etymologically, a "thinking together." Having related sensations in the synthesis of reproduction in imagination, we form a concept through our consciousness of their unity as an object. But Kant also speaks of a concept as a rule: "a concept is always, as regards its form, something universal which serves as a rule" (A 106). Specifically, a concept is a rule for the synthesis of the manifold of intuition. These two notions of concepts are intimately connected:

> the unity which the object makes necessary can be nothing else than the formal unity of consciousness in the synthesis of the manifold of representations. It is only when we have thus

produced synthetic unity in the manifold of intuition that we
are in a position to say that we know the object. But this unity
is impossible if the intuition cannot be generated in accordance
with a rule by means of such a function of synthesis as makes
the reproduction of the manifold *a priori* necessary, and renders
possible a concept in which it is united. Thus we think of a
triangle as an object, in that we are conscious of the
combination of three straight lines according to a rule by which
such an intuition can always be represented. This *unity of rule*
determines all the manifold, and limits it to conditions which
make unity of apperception possible.

(A 105)

Essential to recognizing something as an object, then, is a consciousness
of its unity. But this consciousness is possible only if the object is
constructed according to a rule. We can recognize a collection of
intuitions as constituting a single object only by having a rule for
uniting them into that object. We take a triangle as a single object
rather than three distinct line segments that happen to intersect because
we have a rule for uniting those segments. Without such a rule, we
would be left with a manifold. The two notions of concept are connected, then, in that we are aware of unity (concept in sense one) according
to a rule (concept in sense two).

The rule-governed character of object construction brings with it
a kind of necessity. To count as a triangle, for example, something
must be a plane figure with three sides and three angles. So, it is a
necessary truth that triangles have three sides and three angles. This,
it might seem, is not the sort of necessity that interests Kant; 'triangles
have three angles' is analytic. But when we ask what necessary truths
stem, not from the rule for constructing triangles or any other kind of
object, but from the rule-governed constructions of objects in general,
we obtain a more interesting answer. All objects must be unified, for
example; the concept of an object is the concept of a single thing.

Necessity, in turn, implies transcendental conclusions about our
contributions to objects.

All necessity, without exception, is grounded in a transcendental
condition. There must, therefore, be a transcendental ground
of the unity of consciousness in the synthesis of the manifold
of all our intuitions, and consequently also of the concepts of
objects in general, and so of all objects of experience, a ground
without which it would be impossible to think any objects for
our intuitions.

(A 106)

Kant's argument begins with the premise that necessity is grounded in a transcendental condition. He does not argue for it because he takes it as evident from Hume's writings. Necessary connections, Hume observes, cannot be found in experience. We are directly aware of a succession of things but not of the connections between items of the sequence. (In Frank O'Malley's words, "Life is just one damned thing after another.") Our concept of necessity, Hume concludes, must come from us, not from what we experience. So far, Kant agrees. But Hume goes on to attribute the source of our concept of necessity to the passionate side of our nature, to a feeling of expectation. Kant, in contrast, finds necessity's source in the unity of objects. We experience objects, not just a whirling mass of sensations. And, as we have seen, it is a necessary truth that all objects are unified. Kant concludes that there is a transcendental ground of that unity. The source of the unity of objects, moreover, is also the source of the concept of an object in general; it thus underlies our experience of any object.

The transcendental ground of the unity Kant terms *transcendental apperception*. When we reflect on the contents of our own consciousness, as Hume stresses, we are aware only of a succession of mental states; we do not confront a unified self. The contents of consciousness are always changing: "No fixed and abiding self can present itself in this flux of inner appearances" (A 107). Thus, we find no unity in what Kant calls empirical apperception or inner sense. But there must be a ground of unity in us. This brings us to Kant's key contention: The ground of the consciousness of unity is the unity of consciousness. The source of our consciousness of the unity of objects is the underlying unity of our consciousness itself. This unity of apperception is "the *a priori* ground of all concepts" (A 107), for all concepts unify the manifold of sensibility into objects. The most general concepts, relating to the form of an object in general, are the categories. The unity of apperception and with it the categories underlie the lawlike connections we find among objects of experience and the synthetic *a priori* knowledge we have of them.

The subjective deduction, then, means to spell out Kant's Copernican revolution in subjective detail. We can know certain truths about objects independently of experience, for we can uncover the pure concepts of the understanding relating to the form of an object in general. These concepts do not arise from experience; they underlie the possibility of experience. So, we can know *a priori* that any experience will conform to them. This establishes realism, the view that we can attain knowledge of objective reality, within the realm of objects of experience. It also establishes concept rationalism. Most importantly, it solves the traditional Platonic problem of the conformity of the world to our innate ideas without invoking God, *ex caelo* or *ex machina*.

❧ THE OBJECTIVE DEDUCTION ❧

Kant nevertheless views the subjective deduction as inessential to the success of the critical enterprise. He needs to establish the objective validity of the categories; he does not need to spell out the subjective details of the faculty of thought. Kant is trying to show that the categories underlie our judgments about objects. Judgments, however, are the products of the three-stage model of mental activity outlined in the subjective deduction, and the categories enter the model only in the third stage. The first two stages are thus inessential to the argument. The subjective deduction, moreover, treats the crucial third stage cursorily, leaving the role of the categories unclear. So, Kant begins another argument, the objective deduction, to treat only the relation between judgments and the categories. In the second edition, Kant omits the subjective deduction entirely and elaborates the objective deduction of the first edition.

Kant begins, not by considering the process of transforming the data of sense into judgments, but by reflecting on the form of sensibility itself. "We must begin with pure apperception," he says. "Intuitions are nothing to us, and do not in the least concern us if they cannot be taken up into consciousness" (A 116). That is, the model of mental activity presented in the subjective deduction presupposes, even at its earliest stage, the unity of consciousness. It relates the data of sense to a single consciousness or mind in which reside the faculties of sensibility, imagination, and understanding.

> For the manifold representations, which are given in an intuition, would not be one and all *my* representations, if they did not all belong to one self-consciousness. As *my* representations (even if I am not conscious of them as such) they must conform to the condition under which alone they *can* stand together in one universal self-consciousness, because otherwise they would not all without exception belong to me.
>
> (B 132–3)

The unity of consciousness thus underlies the possibility of sensation and thought. Kant obtains "the transcendental principle of the *unity* of all that is manifold in our representations, and consequently also in intuition" (A 116), which he terms "the highest principle in the whole sphere of human knowledge" (B 135). All representations are representations precisely because they can be represented in empirical consciousness. But an empirical consciousness requires a transcendental consciousness, for it is unified without containing its unity as an element. All representations therefore presuppose the transcendental unity of apperception.

To put Kant's argument differently: Empirical consciousness, as far as its contents are concerned, is a mixed bag. We cannot discover its unity from its contents. Nor can we determine that a given succession of mental states is unified into a single empirical consciousness by examining the contents of those states: "the combination (*conjunctio*) of a manifold in general can never come to us through the senses, and cannot, therefore, be already contained in the pure form of sensible intuition" (B 129). That a given representation is Jones's representation, therefore, we cannot analyze by appeal to monadic properties of that representation. We cannot analyze it by appeal to relations among representations. We must instead analyze it by appeal to a relation between the representation and something else. Whatever is responsible for the unity of consciousness is not to be found in empirical consciousness but in the relation between its contents and something else, outside and underlying empirical consciousness. That is the transcendental unity, "that which itself contains the ground of the unity of diverse concepts in judgment, and therefore of the possibility of the understanding, even as regards its logical employment" (B 131). At one point Kant even identifies the transcendental unity with the understanding (B 134 n.). The transcendental unity of apperception manifests itself in the 'I think' that we can append to all our judgments and representations:

> It must be possible for the 'I think' to accompany all my
> representations; for otherwise something would be represented
> in me which could not be thought at all, and that is equivalent
> to saying that the representation would be impossible, or at
> least would be nothing to me.
>
> (B 132)

This argument for the transcendental unity of consciousness allows Kant to speak of a transcendental *principle*: "a principle of the synthetic unity of the manifold in all possible intuition" (A 117). The principle of the unity of consciousness itself is analytic, roughly of the form 'I am I' (B 135). But the transcendental principle Kant obtains from it is nonetheless synthetic. We have seen that a sensation is part of Jones's empirical consciousness if and only if it stands in the appropriate relation to Jones's transcendental unity of apperception. This, Kant insists, is a necessary truth about our kind of consciousness, one which permits *a priori* knowledge of the unity of consciousness without manifesting that unity explicitly in its contents. It follows that Jones can receive a sensation only if it stands in relation to Jones's transcendental unity. We can know *a priori*, then, that any sensation must relate to the transcendental unity: "all the manifold of intuition should be subject to conditions of the original synthetic unity of apperception"

(B 136). This proposition, furthermore, is synthetic. We derive it, not by analyzing the concept of sensation or even the concept of the transcendental unity, but by connecting the two by way of the transcendental argument just reviewed. As we might expect concerning the argument for any synthetic truth, it rests on experience. But it permits *a priori* knowledge, knowledge that can be derived independently of experience and that holds necessarily, because it concerns the form of any possible experience.

Kant is driving toward the conclusion that "appearances have *a necessary relation to the understanding*" (A 119). Appearances, he says, are "data for a possible experience"; they therefore have to relate to the understanding. The transcendental unity of apperception is responsible for what Kant calls the *affinity* of our representations – that is, their being *our* representations, their constituting a single empirical consciousness – and also the rule-governed character of the synthesis of the manifold of intuition. If that synthesis were not rule-governed, the combination of the data of sense would not yield knowledge but random and "accidental collocations" (A 121) such as the products of imagination in the usual sense. We may freely combine concepts, to form the notion of a three-headed dragon or a golden mountain, but we gain no knowledge of what is actual from exercising that freedom. We attain knowledge of objects because the construction of objects actually presented in experience is rule-governed.

Sensibility presents us with the data of experience, giving it the form of space and time; the understanding formulates judgments. The rule-governed synthesis linking the two is a product of the imagination and is unified by pure apperception. Our perception of a triangle, for example, is rule-governed; we cannot connect any sensations we like, label them a triangle, and obtain knowledge. The rule, in this case, is quite specific about geometrical form. Underlying such specific rules, Kant points out, is a general set of rules for generating concepts of objects. We can call something a triangle only if it has three sides and three angles. More broadly, we can call something an object only if it meets certain conditions, that is, satisfies certain rules. Those rules are specified by the categories. Kant therefore characterizes the understanding as the faculty of rules.

The objective deduction, Kant maintains, shows that we can know objects because we construct them: "Thus the order and regularity in the appearances, which we entitle *nature*, we ourselves introduce. We could never find them in appearances, had not we ourselves, or the nature of our mind, originally set them there" (A 125). The understanding, consequently, is nothing less than "the lawgiver of nature" (A 126). This follows from Kant's argument, for it has shown that the transcendental unity is "an objective condition of all knowledge. It is not merely a condition that I myself require in knowing an object, but is a condition under which every intuition must stand in order *to become an object for me*" (B 138).

✦ THE DIALECTIC ✦

The Transcendental Analytic and related portions of the *Critique* attempt to justify Kant's rationalism. The Transcendental Dialectic, which comprises most of the second half of the book, tries to justify Kant's thesis of immanence. As Kant puts it, the topic of the Dialectic is illusion. Certainly, he means to show that the hope of extending knowledge beyond the realm of sense experience is illusory. But he uses the term 'illusion' in a more specific sense: "an *illusion* may be said to consist in treating the *subjective* condition of thinking as being knowledge of the *object*" (A 396; see A 297, B 353–4). The key to the Analytic is the Copernican revolution, the idea that the faculty of thinking constitutes objects. This should not tempt us to conclude, however, that subjectivity and objectivity – thinking and knowing – match effortlessly. Clearly we may think of things that are not objectively real through imagination. We may also make mistakes. Most seriously, our thinking extends easily beyond the realm of sense experience. We may engage in metaphysical contemplation, arguing about the freedom of the will, the existence of God, and the mortality or immortality of the soul. But Kant denies that we can attain any real knowledge of these matters.

Kant differentiates thinking and knowing, subjectivity and objectivity, by distinguishing the transcendental unity of apperception from the subjective unity of consciousness. To understand the distinction, we must return to the argument of the Transcendental Deduction, which uses the subjective unity to argue for the transcendental unity. The subjective unity of consciousness is a determination of inner sense. The manifold of intuition is given to us in experience, and our experience constitutes a single experience; this is the subjective unity. The manifold of intuition is united in the concept of an object through the transcendental unity. The subjective unity of consciousness is a condition of all thinking; the transcendental unity is a condition of all knowing.

This distinction is extremely important for Kant; transcendent metaphysics results from its confusion. We may think whatever we like in imagination. We may connect concepts and intuitions freely without concern for their presence in experience. The transcendental unity, however, directs our thought toward an object and toward reality. We can know a synthetic judgment only by some connection with experience. This is why we cannot have knowledge that transcends experience: "The *possibility of experience* is, then, what gives objective reality to all our *a priori* modes of knowledge" (A 156, B 195). Indeed, it explains Kant's first example of a synthetic *a priori* principle: "every object stands under the necessary conditions of synthetic unity of the manifold of intuition in a possible experience" (A 158, B 197).

Kant's distinction between the transcendental and subjective unities has two important consequences. First, a rational psychology – a discipline taking the 'I think' as its sole text (A 343, B 401) and amounting to a theory of the soul – is impossible. One might suppose, given the account of the transcendental unity, that the "I," or, to use Kant's term, the soul, is a simple, unified substance, and that we can discover this *a priori*. This, however, is a confusion. One can argue that the representation of the "I" is a representation of a substance, of something simple and unified. But to deduce that the "I" *is* a substance, simple and unified, is to commit a fallacy.[10] In fact, it is to invite the skeptic's objections all over again. Nothing here guarantees the veridicality of our representations. From the perspective of transcendental (rather than rational, that is, rationalist and transcendent) psychology, the "I" is "completely empty": "it is a bare consciousness which accompanies all concepts. Through this I or he or it (the thing) which thinks, nothing further is represented than a transcendental subject of the thoughts = X" (A 346, B 404).

As with the self, so with things-in-themselves. The second consequence of Kant's distinction is thus that knowledge of things-in-themselves is impossible; knowledge is limited to the sphere of experience. The limits of knowledge become clear in thinking about the role of the categories. The pure concepts of the understanding are conditions of the possibility of experience. They have *a priori* validity, against the claims of the skeptic, because "all empirical knowledge of objects would necessarily conform to such concepts, because only as thus presupposing them is anything possible as an *object of experience*" (A 93, B 126). Objects of experience must conform to the categories. Objects beyond the realm of experience, however, face no such constraint. In fact, we have no reason to believe that the categories apply to them at all. The categories conform to objects of possible experience because we synthesize those objects from the data of sensibility. What lies beyond sensibility lies beyond the categories, for we have no reason to believe that it results from such a process of synthesis.

This means that transcendent metaphysics is impossible. Metaphysical knowledge, to be interesting, must be knowledge of the world; it cannot be merely verbal. So, it must consist of synthetic propositions. Moreover, it cannot rely on experience; to be necessary and nonempirical, it must be *a priori*. Kant, as a rationalist, is committed to the possibility of synthetic *a priori* knowledge. But such knowledge is possible only transcendentally, that is, through the contemplation of what makes experience possible. We secure the possibility of synthetic *a priori* knowledge by arguing for the categories. They apply, however, only to objects of possible experience. Kant derives rationalism, therefore, only by undercutting transcendence.

> No other objects, besides those of the senses, can, as a matter of fact, be given to us, and nowhere save in the context of a possible experience; and consequently nothing is an object *for us*, unless it presupposes the sum of all empirical reality as the condition of its possibility.
>
> (A 582, B 610)

We can witness Kant's application of his principle of immanence in his refutation of the cosmological argument for the existence of God. That argument appears in Aquinas, for example, as follows:

> In the observable world causes are to be found ordered in series; we never observe, or even could observe, something causing itself, for this would mean that it preceded itself, and this is impossible. Such a series of causes, however, must stop somewhere. For in all series of causes, an earlier member causes an intermediate, and the intermediate a last (whether the intermediate be one or many). If you eliminate a cause, you also eliminate its effects. Therefore, there can be neither a last nor an intermediate cause unless there is a first. But if the series of causes goes on to infinity, and there is no first cause, there would be neither intermediate causes nor a final effect, which is patently false. It is therefore necessary to posit a first cause, which all call "God."[11]

Kant's transcendental critique of this argument alleges "a whole nest of dialectical assumptions," of which he points out several: (a) The argument assumes that each event in the observable world has a cause. Kant agrees; he regards it as a synthetic *a priori* truth. But, as such, "This principle is applicable only in the sensible world; outside that world it has no meaning whatsoever" (A 609, B 637). (b) Why can't a series of causes go on to infinity? Kant finds nothing to justify this assumption even in the sensible world. (c) Is it true that, if you eliminate a cause, you eliminate its effects? Even if this holds in experience, we have no justification for extending it beyond experience. (d) Finally, why should we identify the first cause as God? Philosophers have understood God as the perfect being, "that, the greater than which cannot be conceived," the being more real than any other, and the necessarily existent being. To conclude that the first cause is God, we must show at least that the first cause is perfect and necessary. Nothing in the proof accomplishes this. Consequently, Kant maintains that "the so-called cosmological proof really owes any cogency which it may have to the ontological proof from mere concepts" (A 607, B 635), for it assumes that perfection, necessity, and being the first cause all hold of the same thing.

The ontological proof appears in Anselm in the following form:

> Certainly, this being exists so truly that one cannot even think that it does not exist. For whatever must be thought to exist is greater than whatever can be thought not to exist. Hence, if that greatest conceivable being can be thought not to exist, then it is not the greatest conceivable being, which is absurd. Therefore, something so great that a greater cannot be conceived exists so truly that it cannot even be thought not to exist.[12]

The argument means to show that perfection entails necessity. That God is perfect Anselm takes as an analytic truth, as following from a definition of 'God.' He concludes that God exists necessarily.

Kant's assault on this argument is more complicated than his attack on the cosmological proof, but also more illuminating. This proof is a paradigm example of illusion, the mistaking of the subjective for the objective. It tries to establish the necessary existence of God from the mere concept of God. Kant is willing to grant that the argument shows that the concept of God, so defined, includes the concept of existence. But he denies that this implies anything at all about the existence of God in reality.

The key to Kant's attack on the ontological argument is his contention that 'being' is not a real predicate. Kant defines a determining predicate as "a predicate which is added to the concept of the subject and enlarges it" (A 598, B 626). It follows that a judgment with a determining predicate must be synthetic, for the predicate must enlarge the subject; it cannot already be contained in it. " 'Being'," Kant insists, "is obviously not a real predicate; that is, it is not a concept of something which could be added to the concept of a thing" (A 598, B 626). A real predicate is capable of serving as a determining predicate. 'Being,' evidently, is not.

We might be tempted to conclude that existential judgments such as 'God is' or 'God exists' are analytic, for 'being' cannot serve as a determining predicate. But Kant clearly maintains that all existential judgments are synthetic. He argues specifically that 'God exists' is not analytic, and concludes, "as every reasonable person must, that all existential propositions are synthetic" (A 598, B 626). It follows that 'being' cannot be contained in the concept of a thing. But how can existential judgments be synthetic if they lack determining predicates?[13]

A synthetic judgment is not merely verbal; its predicate, according to Kant, must add something not already included in its subject. 'Being,' then, must add something to every subject concept. Yet it is not determining; it does not add to and enlarge the subject concept. 'Being' adds something that does not enlarge the concept of the subject.

To understand how this is possible, we must return to Kant's theory of concepts. Concepts are functions of synthesis that organize and unify the material of sense. They mold the data of sense into perceptions of objects (A 68, B 93, B 95). Consequently, their content relates essentially to the manifold of sense. In language and in thought, we can manipulate items however we like. Only through links to intuition, actual or possible, can we move from thinking to knowledge, activating the transcendental unity and giving our thoughts objective validity. (See A 155, B 194–5, B 146, B 165–6.) In short, concepts have content by virtue of the patterns of possible intuitions falling under them. This entails that 'being' is not a real predicate, for it lacks this sort of content. It cannot enlarge a subject concept; any intuition falling under the concept of a dollar falls under the concept of an existing dollar, and vice versa (A 599–600, B 627–8). It follows, moreover, that existential judgments are synthetic, for existence cannot be part of the content of a subject concept (A 225, B 272).

If 'being' lacks content definable in terms of the manifold of sense, what does it contribute to a judgment? Existential judgments do not enlarge or alter a rule for the synthesis of the manifold of intuition, but express the relation of the rule to the understanding. For Kant, then, 'being' is relational. The same holds of possibility and necessity, which share the fourth, "Modality" portion of the table of categories.[14] Kant maintains that the modality of a judgment adds nothing to the judgment's content. Instead, it determines the judgment's relation to the understanding: "The principles of modality thus predicate of a concept nothing but the action of the faculty of knowledge through which it is generated" (A 234, B 286–7). Existence and the other modalities contribute "a relation to my understanding" (A 231, B 284), determining "only how the object, together with all its determinations, is related to understanding and its empirical employment, to empirical judgment, and to reason in its application to experience" (A 219, B 266).

Kant compares the 'being' at stake in existential judgments to the 'being' of the copula (A 74, B 100; A 598–9, B 626–7). Both "distinguish the objective unity of given representations from the subjective" (B 141–2). Only by relating the terms of a judgment to the transcendental unity of apperception

does there arise from this relation a *judgment*, that is, a relation
which is objectively valid, and so can be adequately
distinguished from a relation of the same representations that
would have only subjective validity – as when they are
connected according to the laws of association.

(B 142)

'Being' in both roles distinguishes the subjective from the objective.

This is why the ontological proof is Kant's paradigm case of
dialectical illusion. The advocate of the proof mistakes the subjective
for the objective, failing to recognize that God's existence or necessity
cannot be established analytically, from the definition of 'God' alone.
In saying that something exists, we assert a relation to the understanding; we assert that we may experience the object, or stand in relation
to it by way of empirical laws (A 219, B 266–7; A 234 n., B 287 n.;
A 616, B 644). And this cannot be derived from concepts alone. It
follows that nothing exists with analytic or logical necessity:

If I take the concept of anything, no matter what, I find the
existence of this thing can never be represented by me as
absolutely necessary, and that, whatever it may be that exists,
nothing prevents me from thinking its nonexistence.

(A 615, B 643)

We can now see how Kant can practice the transcendental method
while rejecting transcendent metaphysics. The latter confuses the subjective and the objective, failing to recognize that concepts have content
only in relation to experience. The transcendental method, however,
focuses directly on the relation to the understanding at stake in questions of modality. Kant deduces the categories by reflecting on the sort
of relation that must hold if experience of objects is to be possible.

∽ HUMANISM ∽

Kant carefully distinguishes his view from the idealism of Berkeley,
which assails the notion of a reality beyond the realm of ideas. Kant's
solution to Platonism's problems relies on distinguishing phenomena
from noumena. Kant thus insists on the need to recognize nonmental
objects, things-in-themselves, of which our appearances are appearances.

Kant nevertheless realizes that his theory is a form of idealism –
transcendental idealism, he calls it – for truth, objectivity, and existence,
within the theory, become fundamentally epistemic notions. The same
holds of all the modalities – possibility, truth or existence, and necessity

– for all have the same function of relating a judgment to the under-standing. Metaphysics is inseparable from epistemology; the root notions of metaphysics are all, in the end, epistemological notions.

Kant's epistemic conception of modality underlies his identifi-cation of *a priori* and necessary judgments. Saul Kripke has attacked this identification, pointing out that *a priori*city is a matter of epistem-ology – can something be known independently of experience? – while necessity is a matter of metaphysics. Kripke has alleged, against Kant, that there can be contingent *a priori* and necessary *a posteriori* truths.[15] This seems plausible on the metaphysical view of necessity that Leibniz and Kripke share, namely, that necessity is truth in all possible worlds. But Kant rejects that view. A judgment is *a priori* if it can be known independently of all experience; if, that is, it holds no matter what experience might yield, or, to put it differently, if it holds no matter what the world *looks* like. A judgment is necessary, on the Leibniz–Kripke view, if it holds no matter what the world *is* like. Kant does not confuse these notions; he rejects the latter precisely because it is metaphysical in a transcendent sense. The truth of skepticism is that we cannot know what the world is like. The only notion of modality we can use is epistemic, in which we consider possible experiences rather than possible worlds. On this conception, of course, the *a priori* and the necessary are not only equivalent, but obviously so.

Moreover, it becomes possible to attain knowledge of necessary truths about objects of experience. Reason gets itself into trouble when it tries to leave the realm of possible experience. Kant is able to defend our knowledge of necessary truths against skeptics such as Hume because, for him, the *a priori* and necessary extend to the immanent sphere only, not to the transcendent. They are limited to the realm of possible experience. If *a priori* judgments were necessary in a strong metaphysical sense, then Kant's immanence thesis would be hard to understand.

The epistemic character of the basic notions of metaphysics – when these notions and, correspondingly, metaphysics are properly construed – is the central consequence of Kant's Copernican revolution. It would become fundamental to virtually all nineteenth-century approaches to philosophy. Skepticism, perhaps the chief philosophical puzzle since Descartes, would give way to puzzles arising from Kant's uniquely humanistic idealism. For Kant, as for the ancient Sophist Protagoras, man is the measure of all things. Kant, of course, takes the definite article here seriously. There is one and only one measure: the categories underlie all possible experience. Not everyone would agree. The nature and especially the uniqueness of the measure would define the chief battleground for philosophers during the next two centuries.

❦ NOTES ❦

1 R. Rorty, *Philosophy and the Mirror of Nature* (Princeton: Princeton University Press, 1979), p. 149; N. Kemp Smith, *A Commentary to Kant's Critique of Pure Reason* (Atlantic Highlands, NJ: Humanities Press, 1962), p. vii.

2 This and other citations from the *Critique of Pure Reason* are from the translation of N. Kemp Smith (London: Macmillan, 1929; New York: St Martin's Press, 1965). Throughout, any emphasis in the quotations is Kant's; the pagination is that of the original first (A) and second (B) editions.

3 H. Vaihinger, *Commentar zu Kant's Kritik der Reinen Vernunft*, Vol. I (Stuttgart: Spemann, 1881), pp. 117–20.

4 The analysis is Vaihinger's. See ibid., p. 50; Kemp Smith, op. cit., pp. 13–14.

5 Descartes, *Meditations*, III.

6 Kant often speaks of the content and form of judgments in just this way. Introducing the table of judgments, he writes, "If we abstract from all content of a judgment, and consider only the mere form of understanding," we derive the table (A 70, B 95). At other times, however, he treats the form and content very differently. Modality, for example, differs from the other aspects of judgment in the table in that "it contributes nothing to the content of a judgment (for, besides quantity, quality, and relation, there is nothing that constitutes the content of a judgment)" (A 74, B 100). These are plainly inconsistent. In the former passage, Kant speaks of empirical content or, more precisely, the content of the impure concepts in a judgment; in the latter, he speaks of logical content. It is tempting to identify the form of a judgment with its logical content, but Kant's theory of the modalities makes that impossible. See my "Kant on Existence and Modality," *Archiv für Geschichte der Philosophie*, 64, 3 (1982): 289–300.

7 That is, concepts of objects are rules of individuation as well as application. For a sophisticated modern treatment of this distinction, see A. Gupta, *The Logic of Common Nouns* (New Haven: Yale University Press, 1984).

8 See H. Vaihinger, "Die transcendentale Deduktion der Kategorien," *Gedenkschrift für Rudolf Haym* (1902); Kemp Smith, op. cit., pp. 202ff.

9 Kant's theory of time occupies part of the Transcendental Aesthetic. In brief, time is the form of inner sense, the progression of sensations, thoughts, and, in general, representations that constitutes empirical consciousness. Space and time, Kant argues, are *a priori* forms of intuition, for they are necessary conditions of sensation. We cannot sense anything without sensing it in space and time, that is, as spatially and temporally located. Time is moreover the form of inner sense because we cannot think anything without thinking it in time, that is, without our thought being part of a temporal sequence.

10 See W. Sellars, "Some Remarks on Kant's Theory of Experience" and ". . . this I or he or it (the thing) which thinks . . .," in his *Essays on Philosophy and its History* (Dordrecht: Reidel, 1974), pp. 44–61, 62–92.

11 St Thomas Aquinas, *Summa Theologiae*, Ia. 2; my translation.

12 St Anselm of Canterbury, *Proslogion*, III; my translation.

13 For more on this apparent contradiction, see J. Shaffer, "Existence, Predication, and the Ontological Argument," *Mind*, 71 (1962): 307–25; W.H. Walsh, *Kant's*

Criticism of Metaphysics (Edinburgh: Edinburgh University Press, 1975), p. 7; G. Vick, "Existence was a Predicate for Kant," *Kant-Studien*, 61 (1970): 357–71, esp. 363–4; R. Coburn, "Animadversions on Plantinga's Kant," *Ratio*, 13 (1971): 19–29, esp. 21–2; R. Campbell, "Real Predicates and 'Exists'," *Mind*, 83 (1974): 96ff.; and my "Kant on Existence and Modality," op. cit., pp. 291–5.

14 One of the few commentators to observe this is H. Heimsoeth, *Transzendentale Dialektik* (Berlin: de Gruyter, 1969), Vol. III, p. 480.

15 See S. Kripke, *Naming and Necessity* (Cambridge, Mass.: Harvard University Press, 1972, 1980), pp. 34–9.

ᕦ SELECT BIBLIOGRAPHY ᕤ

Original language editions

2.1 Kant, I. *Critik der reinen Vernunft*, Riga: J.F. Hartknoch, 1781.

2.2 *Kants gesammelte Schriften*, 29 vols, ed. Deutschen (formerly Königlich Preussische) Akademie der Wissenschaften, Berlin: de Gruyter (and predecessors), 1902–.

2.3 Kant, I. *Werke, Academie Textausgabe: Anmerkungen der Bande I–IX*, Berlin: de Gruyter, 1977.

English translations

2.4 Kant, I. *Critik of Pure Reason*, trans. F. Haywood, London: W. Pickering, 1838.

2.5 Kant, I. *Critique of Pure Reason*, trans. J.M.D. Meiklejohn, New York: Colonial Press, 1899; London: J.M. Dent, 1934, 1940.

2.6 Kant, I. *Critique of Pure Reason*, trans. N. Kemp Smith, London: Macmillan, 1929; New York: St Martin's Press, 1965.

2.7 Kant, I. *Critique of Pure Reason*, trans. W. Schwarz, Aalen: Scientia, 1982.

Books on Kant (in English)

2.8 Beck, L.W. *Early German Philosophy: Kant and his Predecessors*, Cambridge, Mass.: Belknap Press of Harvard University Press, 1969.

2.9 Beck, L.W. *Essays on Kant and Hume*, New Haven: Yale University Press, 1978.

2.10 Beck, L.W. (ed.) *Kant Studies Today*, La Salle, Ill.: Open Court, 1969.

2.11 Beck, L.W. (ed.) *Kant's Theory of Knowledge*, Dordrecht: Reidel, 1974.

2.12 Broad, C.D. *Kant: An Introduction*, Cambridge: Cambridge University Press, 1978.

2.13 Cassirer, E. *Kant's Life and Thought*, trans. J. Haden, New Haven and London: Yale University Press, 1981.

2.14 den Ouden B.D., and Moen, M. (eds) *New Essays on Kant*, New York: Peter Lang, 1987.

2.15 Guyer, P. (ed.) *The Cambridge Companion to Kant*, Cambridge: Cambridge University Press, 1992.

2.16 Korner, S. *Kant*, Harmondsworth: Penguin, 1955.

2.17 Scruton, R. *Kant*, Oxford: Oxford University Press, 1982.

2.18 Walker, R.C.S. *Kant*, London: Routledge & Kegan Paul, 1978.

2.19 Werkmeister, W.H. *Kant, the Archetectonic and Development of his Philosophy*, La Salle, Ill.: Open Court, 1980.

2.20 Wolff, R.P. (ed.) *Kant: A Collection of Critical Essays*, Notre Dame: University of Notre Dame Press, 1968.

2.21 Wood, A.W. (ed.) *Self and Nature in Kant's Philosophy*, Ithaca: Cornell University Press, 1984.

Books on the Critique of Pure Reason (in English)

2.22 Allison, H.E. *Kant's Transcendental Idealism: An Interpretation and Defense*, New Haven: Yale University Press, 1983.

2.23 Ameriks, K. *Kant's Theory of Mind*, Oxford: Clarendon Press, 1982.

2.24 Aquila, R.E. *Representational Mind: A Study of Kant's Theory of Knowledge*, Bloomington: Indiana University Press, 1983.

2.25 Bennett, J. *Kant's Analytic*, Cambridge: Cambridge University Press, 1966.

2.26 Bennett, J. *Kant's Dialectic*, Cambridge: Cambridge University Press, 1974.

2.27 Brittan, G.G. *Kant's Theory of Science*, Princeton: Princeton University Press, 1978.

2.28 Ewing, A.C. *A Short Commentary to Kant's Critique of Pure Reason*, Chicago: University of Chicago Press, 1938.

2.29 Forster, E. (ed.) *Kant's Transcendental Deductions: The Three Critiques and the Opus Postumum*, Stanford: Stanford University Press, 1989.

2.30 Kemp Smith, N. *A Commentary to Kant's Critique of Pure Reason*, Atlantic Highlands, NJ: Humanities Press, 1962.

2.31 Paton, W.E. *Kant's Metaphysic of Experience*, London: Allen & Unwin, 1970.

2.32 Prichard, H.A. *Kant's Theory of Knowledge*, Oxford: Oxford University Press, 1909.

2.33 Rescher, N. *Kant's Theory of Knowledge and Reality: A Group of Essays*, Washington: University Press of America, 1983.

2.34 Schaper, E., and Vossenkuhl, W. (eds) *Reading Kant: New Perspectives on Transcendental Arguments and Critical Philosophy*, Oxford: Blackwell, 1989.

2.35 Sellars, W. *Science and Metaphysics: Variations on Kantian Themes*, London: Routledge & Kegan Paul, 1968.

2.36 Seung, T.K. *Kant's Transcendental Logic*, New Haven: Yale University Press, 1969.

2.37 Strawson, P.F. *The Bounds of Sense: An Essay on Kant's Critique of Pure Reason*, London: Methuen, 1966.

2.38 Walsh, W.H. *Kant's Criticism of Metaphysics*, Edinburgh: Edinburgh University Press, 1975.

2.39 Wilkerson, T.E. *Kant's Critique of Pure Reason*, Oxford: Oxford University Press, 1976.

2.40 Winterbourne, A. *The Ideal and the Real: An Outline of Kant's Theory of Space, Time, and Mathematical Construction*, Dordrecht: Kluwer, 1988.

2.41 Wolff, R.P. *Kant's Theory of Mental Activity*, Cambridge, Mass.: Harvard University Press, 1963.

CHAPTER 3

Kant's moral and political philosophy

Don Becker

Practical philosophy, for Kant, is concerned with how one ought to act. His first important work in practical philosophy, *Foundations of the Metaphysics of Morals*, provides Kant's argument for the fundamental principle of how one ought to act, called the "categorical imperative," which basically requires one to act only according to principles that are themselves fit to be universal law. In Part I of this chapter we will focus on Kant's argument for the categorical imperative, and see how it functions as the fundamental principle of his moral philosophy. In Part II we will look at Kant's political philosophy, seeing both that it is grounded in this fundamental principle of how one ought to act, and that it gains support from other aspects of Kant's philosophical thinking.

❧ PART I: KANT'S MORAL PHILOSOPHY ❧

Inasmuch as Kant thinks that the fundamental principle of how one ought to act must be capable of grounding a definitive answer in all circumstances, he recognizes that no empirical study, which is dependent on the contingent nature of the world as we experience it, can provide the sort of principle that he seeks. Instead, Kant will proceed with an *a priori* study of how one ought to act, which, insofar as it is independent of the contingent nature of the world as we experience it, can provide a definitive principle. Two forms of *a priori* study that Kant employs are the analysis of concepts and transcendental arguments. According to the former, insofar as some concept applies, whatever is entailed in that concept is true. According to the latter, insofar as some concept applies, whatever is a necessary condition of its application is true. Thus, Kant begins with the two concepts that are fundamental to his intended study, "morality" and "rational being," and determines that they reveal the truth of the categorical imperative. (Although the concept "rational being" is really the fundamental concept employed by Kant, the concept "morality," which he could have derived from the concept "rational being," plays a central role in his presentation.) Kant's presentation includes two basic steps. First, he asks what is meant by the concept "morality," and argues that it entails rational beings acting in accord with the categorical imperative. This, however, only answers the question of what morality is on the assumption that morality exists. Kant then considers the concept "rational being," and argues that a necessary condition of a being thinking that this concept applies to itself is that it think of itself as free. Furthermore, since Kant equates freedom in this sense (i.e. "positive freedom") with what he calls autonomy, and autonomy with subjection to the categorical imperative, it follows that beings who think of themselves as rational must consider themselves to be subject to the categorical imperative that he has described.[1]

"Morality" and "rational beings"

Kant engages in the *a priori* study of ethics, or metaphysics of morals, because this is the only way to gain definitive knowledge of how one ought to act. He proceeds by first considering what is meant by "morality," and determining that it means neither more nor less than acting according to the categorical imperative (*FMM*, 58).[2] Although more must be said before it is possible to explain the categorical imperative fully, and the exact nature of the moral principle that it designates, nevertheless, if one merely considers the two words that make up the term, an important aspect of its nature is revealed. "Categorical" means absolute, without qualification or exception, and "imperative" refers to a type of command. Thus, a categorical imperative is an absolute command.

According to Kant, "Everyone must admit that a law, if it is to hold morally (i.e. as a ground of obligation), must imply absolute necessity" (*FMM*, 5). Thus, Kant treats it as obvious to everyone that morality ultimately entails an absolute command or categorical imperative. Furthermore, since nothing absolute can be derived from something contingent, he argues that the only way to determine the exact nature of this absolute command is to engage in the *a priori* study of practical reason (i.e. reason related to acting):

unless we wish to deny all truth to the concept of morality and renounce its application to any possible object, we cannot refuse to admit that the law is of such broad significance that it holds not merely for men but for all rational beings as such; we must grant that it must be valid with absolute necessity and not merely under contingent conditions and with exceptions. For with what right could we bring into unlimited respect something that might be valid only under contingent human conditions? And how could laws of the determination of our will be held to be laws of the determination of the will of any rational being whatever and of ourselves in so far as we are rational beings, if they were merely empirical and did not have their origin completely *a priori* in pure, but practical reason?

(FMM, 24)

Kant holds that morality entails absolute laws; that, insofar as they are absolute, these laws must hold not only for human beings but for all similar, i.e. rational, beings; and that to have such general applicability these laws cannot be learned through experience or any empirical study, but must be derived through a purely *a priori* study.

Kant thinks that people, insofar as they are rational, are subject to an absolute moral law. Kant thinks that the fact that rational beings are subject to an absolute moral law is what fundamentally distinguishes them from all of the other material things in the world, which he recognizes to be subject to the laws of nature. Thus, Kant distinguishes physics, which is concerned with those objects that are subject to the "laws of nature," from ethics, which is concerned with those objects that are subject to the "laws of freedom" (*FMM*, 3). As will become clear, these laws of freedom constitute the absolute moral law.

This distinction between physics and ethics can be somewhat confusing; after all, isn't everything subject to the laws of nature? Maybe not. Think for a moment of a world in which *everything* were subject to the laws of nature. This would be a world of strict causal determinism; everything that happened would have followed inexorably from what preceded it. Among other things, all human behavior would be completely determined by these laws. But if all human behavior is causally determined according to laws of nature, then in what sense could people be considered morally responsible for their acts? Thus, if the concept "morality" is to make sense, then it must be possible to think of people not only as common physical entities subject to the laws of nature, but also, in another sense, as rational beings, subject to the laws of freedom (see *FMM*, 68–73).

Kant thinks of people in just this dual way, as sensible or physical beings, causally determined according to the laws of nature, and as intelligible or purely rational beings, independent of causal determinism and capable of acting in accord with the laws of freedom. Accordingly, Kant suggests that the human will is subjected to two influences (see e.g. *FMM*, 16, 42). As sensible or physical beings, human beings have desires that arise from their physical nature and corresponding physical needs, which Kant broadly characterizes as the desire to be happy. This universal desire, as well as other indiosyncratic particular desires, is the source of inclinations, which exert a potentially controlling influence on the will. However, insofar as human beings are intelligible or purely rational beings, they recognize the laws of freedom, resist the force of inclination, and determine their will for themselves, independently of external influences and inclinations. Furthermore, and recognition of this is crucial for a correct understanding of Kant's moral philosophy, Kant thinks that *all* rational beings, insofar as they determine their will for themselves independently of their inclinations, will recognize the very same principle, the categorical imperative, as expressing the law of freedom in accord with which they ought to act (*FMM*, 71).

Thus far we have seen that the concept of "morality" entails the notion of an absolute law or "categorical imperative," and that it can only apply to (rational) beings who can resist their inclinations and choose to follow such a law of freedom. Let us now look more closely at exactly what Kant means by a "categorical imperative."

Kant's concept of a categorical imperative

Imagine that the human will were influenced only by pure reason. Whatever pure reason recognized as right would necessarily be willed, and whoever was possessed of pure reason would never do wrong. But Kant has said that the human will is influenced by both reason and inclination. Therefore, human beings don't necessarily will (and consequently act) as pure reason reveals is right, because they can be led astray by their inclinations. Thus, if a human will is to be determined in accordance with the objective moral law, it must be constrained. Kant calls the formula that expresses the command that constrains this will an imperative. Kant holds that there are two types of imperatives:

> All imperatives command either *hypothetically* or *categorically*. The former present the practical necessity of a possible action as a means to achieving something else which one desires (or which one may possibly desire). The categorical imperative would be one which presented an action as of itself objectively necessarily, without regard to any other end.
>
> (*FMM*, 30)

Two points that are rather important to Kant are expressed in this passage.

First, Kant reveals the basic difference between hypothetical and categorical imperatives. All imperatives determine the will to some good, but hypothetical imperatives say only that some action is good given that one has a particular purpose. Hypothetical imperatives reveal the means to given ends. Since these ends are contingent, however, as are all the ends that one commonly imagines (including the desire for happiness) inasmuch as there is no necessity for human beings to be so constituted that they have any of the particular desires that they experience, these ends cannot give rise to a categorical imperative. A categorical imperative, as Kant says, cannot depend on any contingent end, but "would be one which presented an action as of itself objectively necessary."

Second, by saying of a categorical imperative that it "*would* be one . . . ,' Kant is making it clear that there may be no categorical imperative. Kant is only talking about what a categorical imperative *would* be like if one existed. This is very important, and is consistent with a point made earlier. Human beings can only be subject to a moral law if they are capable of resisting the influences of their inclinations, and determining their wills through reason in accord with a principle or law that is known *a priori*. There can be no moral responsibility for beings whose actions are all causally determined. Thus, before Kant can actually assert that there is a categorical imperative, he must first show that human beings have reason to believe themselves capable of determining their wills through reason. Nevertheless, Kant's argumentative strategy is to hold off on the question of whether human beings are actually subject to the categorical imperative, and to first pursue the question of what a categorical imperative would be, assuming that one exists.

The first formulation of the categorical imperative

Kant argues that there can be only one categorical imperative, and that, from the very idea of *a* categorical imperative, one can deduce a formula of *the* categorical imperative. Kant's argument can be expressed as follows (see *FMM*, 37–8). A categorical imperative is an absolute law. Although it is obvious that a categorical imperative entails an absolute law, it is not at all clear what this law will command. Imagine any possible content of this law, say, to maximize human happiness. Insofar as what constitutes human happiness is contingent (human beings could be constituted differently), all that one can construct is a hypothetical imperative directed to a particular contingent end. Thus, a categorical imperative cannot be directed to any particular contingent end.

But if the imperative cannot be directed toward any particular contingent ends, then what is left? Although later a formulation of the categorical imperative that is based on an end that is not contingent will be considered, for now it seems that the imperative can require nothing more than conformity to absolute law. But since there is nothing in particular to which this absolute law can be directed, it can command only that one act in a way that is at least consistent with the possibility of absolute law. Kant expresses this categorical imperative as follows: "Act only according to that maxim by which you can at the same time will that it should become a universal law" (*FMM*, 38). This imperative does not rely on any specific content, but states the formal requirement that one always act in a way that one could will to be required to act by an absolute law.

The application of the categorical imperative and the distinction between perfect and imperfect duties

What does it mean to act only according to that maxim by which you can at the same time will that it should become a universal law? First, what is a maxim? A maxim is a general principle according to which an individual acts. Thus, one might hold the maxim "I will watch television when bored," or "I will steal things when I desire more goods." Kant is saying that it is morally permissible to act according to one's maxim only if it is possible at the same time to will that it should become a universal law.

One of the most famous examples that Kant uses to help make his point clear is that of the maxim to make a false promise to honor one's debt when seeking a loan that one does not intend to pay back (see e.g. *FMM*, 18–19, 39). Can one hold this maxim and, at the same time, will that it should be a universal law? Well, imagine that there were a universal law to make false promises. In such circumstances, inasmuch as no one could be trusted, the institution of promising itself could not exist. Now, since it is logically impossible for one at the same time to will both to make a false promise and that the institution of promising not exist, it is immoral to act on the maxim to make a false promise when desirous of another's money. Thus, the categorical imperative, as well as stating a restriction on permissible behavior, also provides a test of whether the restriction applies. If one cannot conceive of acting on the maxim while, at the same time, the maxim holds as a universal law, as is the case in the example of the false promise, then the maxim fails the test and may not be acted upon.

Immediately after introducing the categorical imperative, Kant provides four examples of its application, which are designed to represent a common division of duties into four basic categories. Kant provides examples of perfect duties and imperfect duties both to oneself and to others, which can be classified as shown below.

	Duty to oneself	Duty to others
Perfect duty	Do not commit suicide	Do not falsely promise
Imperfect duty	Develop talents	Be beneficent

While the distinction between duties to oneself and duties to others requires no explanation, this is not the case with the distinction between perfect and imperfect duties. Kant was not the first to distinguish between perfect and imperfect duties, but his distinction does not correspond exactly with that of his predecessors (*FMM*, 38 n.). As Kant employs the concepts, perfect duties are those with which one's every action must conform. Thus, in all but one special case (i.e. the duty to join the state), perfect duties actually entail prohibitions against actions that should never be performed under any circumstances, e.g. stealing and murder. Imperfect duties, for Kant, entail principles that one must adopt, but that one need not (and, in fact, cannot) act upon in every instance. One would not think of another as moral who did not hold, and in some appropriate circumstances act upon, the principle "Be beneficent." However, it is also clear that it is not possible for one's every act to be the fulfillment of an imperfect duty. For one thing, one's every act cannot be, say, beneficent, since one also must tend to one's own physical needs. Even more obviously, one's every act cannot be one of beneficence, and also one of developing talents, and also one that furthers every other imperfect duty. Thus, Kant distinguishes between those duties with which one's every act must accord, and those duties that require one to adopt a principle, but leave one leeway in deciding when to act upon it.

With this distinction between perfect and imperfect duties in mind, it is important to look back to the categorical imperative, and to the test of the permissibility of actions. There are two ways that a maxim can fail the test of the categorical imperative. There are maxims for which it is logically impossible, and thus inconceivable, for one to will the maxim and its universalization at the same time, as in the false promise example discussed above, and there are maxims for which there is merely a contradiction in the will of an individual who wills both the maxim and its universalization at the same time, as in the example discussed below. Kant recognizes that there is an exact correspondence both between the duties generated by maxims failing the test of the categorical imperative in the former manner and perfect duties, and between the duties generated by maxims failing the test of the categorical imperative in the latter manner and imperfect duties (*FMM*, 40–1).[3] Both Kant's test of duties entailed in the categorical imperative and his reformulation of the distinction between perfect and imperfect duties gain support from this correspondence.

Having already seen in the example of a false promise how perfect duties are related to maxims for which it is inconceivable to will both the maxim and its universalization at the same time, let us turn to an example of an imperfect duty. Consider the maxim "I will not develop my talents when I seem to be doing fine without bothering." There is no logical contradiction that results from holding this maxim and, at the same time, willing that it should become a universal law. After all, one can very well imagine a rather easy life on a tropical island where one need do nothing more than pick fruit when hungry. Thus, adopting this maxim does not violate a perfect duty.

Remember, however, that the categorical imperative says to "act only according to that maxim by which you can at the same time will that it should become a universal law." While the test of perfect duties focuses on whether one *can* will that the maxim should become a universal law, thereby focusing on the logical possibility of holding the maxim and its universalization at the same time, the test of imperfect duties focuses on the question of whether one can *will* that the maxim should become a universal law. It may be logically possible to live a human life without developing one's talents, and yet it may be impossible, without contradiction, to *will* to live such a life. Although Kant's treatment of the examples of imperfect duties is very unclear, I think that one can make the best sense of his discussion if one reads him as saying that the human will is essentially unlimited in that it can hold anything imaginable as its object, and that a contradiction therefore results if one wills to place a limitation on one's own will. Thus, it is not logically impossible for people to will not to develop their talents (it doesn't violate a perfect duty) but it entails a contradiction in their will, since, on the one hand, their wills are essentially unlimited, but, on the other hand, willing the nondevelopment of one's talents yields a limitation on what one can effectively will. According to this analysis, it follows that there is an imperfect duty to develop one's talents.

The second formulation of the categorical imperative

Although Kant thinks that there is only one categorical imperative, he thinks that it can be formulated in more than one way. Of course, any other formulation of the categorical imperative, if it is to be a formulation of the *same* imperative, must require and prohibit exactly the same actions as the first formulation. Although Kant maintains that the first formulation discussed above is the most fundamental and precise, he develops alternative formulations of the categorical imperative because they make the demands of morality more intuitively plausible (*FMM*, 53).

The derivation of the first formulation of the categorical imperative can be thought of as based on a consideration of the necessary form of a categorical imperative. The idea is that the imperative must express an absolute law, but, since the law cannot command any contingent particular and still be absolute, all that can be commanded is that any particular maxim to be acted upon must be of such a *form* that it could be universal law. The second formulation of the categorical imperative, in contrast, focuses on the proper *content* of one's maxims (*FMM*, 48, 53). Kant bases the second formulation of the categorical imperative on his view that rational beings have absolute value as ends in themselves (*FMM*, 45–6).

Although Kant's argument in support of this view of rational beings is not very clear, it appears to rely on two fundamental claims. Kant has elsewhere said that the only thing that is good without qualification is a good will (since anything else can be put to a bad end, but not good willing itself) (*FMM*, 9–10), and seems to allude to this position during the argument. He also begins the discussion of which this argument is a part by reminding his readers that only rational beings have a will (*FMM*, 44). From these two claims it is reasonable to conclude that rational beings are of absolute value because they are the only possible source of that which is good without qualification. An imperative with content can therefore be a categorical imperative, provided that the end of that imperative is for rational beings to be treated as ends. Thus, the second formulation of the categorical imperative is: "Act so that you treat humanity, whether in your own person or in that of another, always as an end and never as a means only"[4] (*FMM*, 46). This imperative includes an absolute prohibition against treating others as means only, and to do so would violate a perfect duty. It also requires one actively to treat others as ends, and this requirement is an imperfect duty. A reconsideration of the examples introduced earlier will help make this clear.

Consider what happens when Mary makes a false promise to John, say to pay back a loan when, in fact, she intends to flee to Brazil. Mary has used John as a means for gaining the money she needs to go to Brazil. It is true that virtually any time two people make an agreement they are treating one another as means, but the important thing is that when the agreement is honest they are not treating one another as a means *only*. When making an honest agreement, people know more or less how they are furthering the interests of another, and this furthering of the other's interests is an explicit part of their own act. Thus, in honest agreements people treat one another as means, but they also respect one another as ends, insofar as the other has been able to make a free and informed decision as to whether to participate in the agreement. However, when Mary exploited John's trust by making a false promise, she treated him as a means only, in that he was not given the relevant information with which to decide whether he wanted to provide the benefit to Mary that she actually received. He was not treated as an end at all, in that he was not provided the opportunity to embrace the results of their interaction as an end of his own. Thus, Mary violated a perfect duty by treating another rational being, not as an end, but as a means only.

Now imagine that Mary is a botanist fascinated by, and extremely talented at, studying tropical deforestation, and she asks John, who won $50 million in the lottery, to help fund a research trip to Brazil. Here there is no question of perfect duties. Neither Mary's request for support, nor John's either providing it or refusing to do so, entails treating a rational being as a means only. But should John provide the support? Were John to provide the funding, he would be treating Mary as an end, insofar as he would be acting to facilitate her realization of her own ends. Of course, as was pointed out in the previous discussion of imperfect duties, it is not humanly possible for one's every action to be one of actively treating (in the sense of furthering) others as ends. Nevertheless, there is an imperfect duty to hold the principle of actively treating or furthering others as ends, and to act on this principle in appropriate circumstances. John may not be specifically required to provide funding for Mary, but he does have an imperfect duty, in a range of circumstances that seem appropriate to him, to use his personal resources to actively treat or further other rational beings as ends. Thus, it is a perfect duty never to treat oneself or another rational being as a means only, and an imperfect duty to actively treat or further all rational beings as ends in themselves.

The third formulation of the categorical imperative, the principle of autonomy, and duty

Although Kant expresses his third formulation of the categorical imperative in a number of ways, its clearest statement may be in the "principle of autonomy." According to this principle one is only subject to the moral law that one has legislated for oneself: "Never choose except in such a way that the maxims of the choice are comprehended as universal law in the same volition" (FMM, 57). Although this principle seems quite similar to the first formulation of the categorical imperative, the important difference is that this principle requires one to think of the universal laws as issuing from one's own volitions, and thus that the constraints to which one is subject come from one's own will. Kant's point is that rational beings are not merely subject to the moral law, but subject to the law because they created it themselves, i.e. because the law comes from their own will.

To understand the importance of autonomy for morality one must consider Kant's views on "good will" and "duty." While other things might be good toward one end or another, or when employed in one way or another, Kant says that the only thing that is good without qualification is the good will (see *FMM*, 9–10). Kant then reveals the nature of the good will in a discussion of duty (see *FMM*, 12–15). Kant argues that acts do not have moral worth merely because they accord with duty, but only if they are done from (the motive of) duty. For example, if a shopkeeper gives a young child the correct change because they know that it is good for business, or even if someone helps another in need because they like to be helpful, although the acts accord with duty, they have no true moral worth. Kant is not saying that it is bad for people to behave in these ways, but only that they do not warrant *moral* esteem. In all the cases in which people behave in accord with duty, but for reasons other than just the requirements of duty, the person is moved by some particular interest, even if it is only the good feeling that they get inside. In all of these cases the person is acting out of some particular interest, and not merely manifesting a good will. The good will is only manifest when one does one's duty, not from any particular interest, but precisely because it is one's duty.

Now the importance of the principle of autonomy can be clear. Imagine that rational beings were subject to a moral law that they had not created for themselves. If the moral law did not come from the rational being's own will, then there would have to be some influence external to this being that moved it to act in conformity to the law. Obedience to the moral law would then be conditional on rational beings responding in a certain way to this external influence. For Kant, however, this would be antithetical to morality. Obedience might accord with duty, but it would not be from duty, it would not manifest a good will, and it would have no true moral worth.

Kant concludes that the principle of autonomy expresses the fundamental claim of his moral theory:

> That the principle of autonomy, which is now in question, is the sole principle of morals can be readily shown by mere analysis of concepts of morality; for by this analysis we find that its principle must be a categorical imperative and that the imperative commands neither more nor less than this very autonomy.

(FMM, 58)

The concept of morality entails the idea of an absolute law, and, therefore, the fundamental moral principle must be a categorical imperative. But when one thinks about this imperative one recognizes that, since the imperative must be absolute, it cannot be based on anything of contingent interest. This requirement eliminates all principles that have their source outside of the individual, and leaves only the principle of autonomy.

Why people are subject to the categorical imperative

So far it has been shown that if there is such a thing as morality, then its rule is expressed by the categorical imperative (in all of its alternative formulations) that Kant has provided. What has not been shown is that beings like ourselves are subject to this morality. Kant has shown that it is essential to the concept of the categorical imperative, through the principle of autonomy to which it leads, that, if there is to truly be a categorical imperative, then it must be adopted by rational beings for themselves. But why would rational beings adopt the categorical imperative? Kant's answer is that, insofar as rational beings take themselves to be rational, they necessarily recognize the categorical imperative as a constraint upon themselves. Kant is saying that a necessary component of the self-image of rational beings is their recognition of the fact that they must constrain themselves in accord with the categorical imperative. Here again one can see that Kant is using an *a priori* argument based on the concept "rational being" to support his moral theory.

Kant's transcendental argument for his moral theory takes the following form. First he argues that there is a relationship between freedom and autonomy such that all beings who consider themselves free must accept the principle of autonomy, which, as was previously discussed, entails the categorical imperative (*FMM*, 64). Then he shows that rational beings, because of how they experience the world, and, specifically, their own activity in the world, must consider themselves free (*FMM*, 65). Thus, it follows that rational beings must think of themselves as constrained by the categorical imperative. An explanation of this transcendental argument for the categorical imperative best begins with an account of his view of freedom.

Rational beings have wills, and they cause things to happen in the world through their wills. Kant says of the will of rational beings that

> freedom would be that property of this causality by which it can be effective independently of foreign causes determining it,

79

just as natural necessity is the property of the causality of all irrational beings by which they are determined to activity by the influence of foreign causes.

(FMM, 63)

This is Kant's view of negative freedom, i.e. freedom from determination by something external to the will. The idea is that if one's will is free in this negative sense, then, as opposed to existing merely as a sensible or physical being, subject to strict causal determinism, one must also exist as an intelligible or purely rational being that can have effects on the world independently of any foreign influences one experiences.

Kant claims that this negative conception of freedom opens the door to a positive one. Kant has said that the will is a kind of causality that, free in the negative sense, is not determined by foreign influences. One must recognize, however, that "the concept of a causality entails that of laws according to which something (i.e. the effect) must be established through something else which we call cause" *(FMM, 63)*.

So how is a will that is free in the negative sense determined? It is clear from the concept of "causality" that a free will must be determined in accord with some law. This is also confirmed by common sense. To imagine a will that is not determined in accord with some law, is to imagine a will that is random. But a being whose will appears to be random is not thought of as free, but is ushered away by people in white coats. Such a will does not accord with the concept of "freedom."

To be free, therefore, a will must be determined in accord with some law. It cannot be determined by the laws of nature, for determination by the laws of nature is exactly what accounts for the lack of negative freedom in sensible or physical beings. Thus, a will that is free in the positive sense must determine itself, it must act in accord with a law that it adopts for itself, a law of freedom. This, however, is exactly what it is to be autonomous, and therefore to recognize oneself as subject to the categorical imperative. After all, the categorical imperative is the only principle of the will that beings can adopt for themselves, since all other imperatives are based on ends that are of contingent value, and, thus, entail rational beings' determination by things external to themselves. Kant concludes this discussion by stating that "a free will and a will under moral laws are identical" *(FMM, 64)*.

Kant still hasn't shown either that rational beings have free wills, or that there are any beings in the world that are subject to the morality that he has described. What has been shown is that only free beings can be subject to morality, and, more importantly, that all beings that think of themselves as free must think of themselves as subject to morality. Thus, if Kant demonstrates that rational beings necessarily think of themselves as free, then he will have shown that rational beings must think of themselves as subject to the categorical imperative. And if this demonstration is based on the way that rational beings necessarily experience themselves in the world, then Kant will have provided a transcendental argument that rational beings are subject to the categorical imperative. So the question is: Do rational beings experience themselves in the world in a way that requires them to think of themselves as having a free will?[5]

What is it to think of oneself as a rational being? To think of oneself as rational is to think that one applies reason (competently) when making judgments. The following is an example of applying reason when making a judgment: If a rational being knows that if statement P is true then statement Q is true, and also knows that P is, in fact, true, then, if it actually manifests its rationality, it will conclude that Q is true, through the application of a certain, in this case obvious, principle of logic. A being that came to hold that Q is true without having applied the principle of logic, say because Q just popped into its mind, would not be thought of as having made a rational judgment (regardless of the truth of its belief). Furthermore, even a being who applied the principle of logic, if it did so out of instinct, or because it was forced to by some external power, would not be thought of as having (itself) made a rational judgment. Calling a judgment rational, and, by extension, a being rational insofar as it makes rational judgments, is only appropriate when the being has itself adopted and correctly applied the relevant principle of logic. If the being does not do this for itself then it is like a simple computer (one for which there is no question of artificial intelligence). It never deserves credit for the conclusions that it draws because its application of logical principles is solely the result of forces external to itself, e.g. the skill of its programmer.

Thus, with respect to logical judgments, a being can only think of itself as rational if it thinks that it has adopted and applied the principles of logic for itself. Of course, one can adopt and apply these principles for oneself only if one is free in Kant's positive sense. Thus, to think of oneself as rational, at least in one's logical judgments, one must think of oneself as free, and as having freely adopted the laws of logic. Nevertheless, although one must *freely* adopt these laws if one is to think of oneself as rational, that does not necessarily mean that one could adopt some other laws of logic and still think of oneself as rational. It is quite possible (though there are some who would question this claim) that there is only one set of fundamental logical laws that one can adopt without belying one's rationality. One's freedom is still manifest, however, by the fact that one has adopted the laws of logic for oneself, even though there is only one set of logical laws that one can adopt as a rational being.

The situation with regard to morality is analogous. To consider oneself possessed of practical reason, i.e. to think that one applies reason in determining one's will and consequently one's actions, one must think of oneself as freely adopting one's principles of action. In other words, one must think of oneself as having a free will. However, the fact that one must be free in adopting one's principles of action does not mean that there must be some range of options for one to select from among. As appears to be the case with logic, in the case of morality, there is exactly one fundamental principle of action that can be freely adopted, and that is the categorical imperative.

These considerations lead to a common confusion with respect to Kant's views on freedom, which can be expressed in the following question: How is it possible for one both to be free and to *have* to adopt the categorical imperative? This question manifests a misunderstanding of what Kant means by freedom. By freedom Kant does not mean the option of choosing one thing or another (which one might also call liberty), but rather, the power of self-determination (which can also be called autonomy).

Kant's point is that if the moral law is truly to be freely adopted, then it cannot get its force from any contingent conditions external to the individual. However, the only principle of action that is independent of determination by any contingent external influences is the categorical imperative. Therefore, insofar as one thinks of oneself as a rational being, possessed of practical reason, one must think of oneself as subject to the categorical imperative.

A second common confusion with respect to Kant's views on freedom is that he thinks that people are free only when they act in accord with the categorical imperative. The concern is that Kant is claiming that people are not acting freely on those occasions when they succumb to the influence of their inclinations and act contrary to the categorical imperative. If this were true it would raise quite a problem, because it entails the claim that people who act immorally are not free, and therefore cannot be held responsible for their actions. Kant, however, thinks of all rational beings as free insofar as they recognize the categorical imperative as a constraint upon their actions. Those who violate this constraint, insofar as they are rational, recognize that they have done wrong exactly because they recognize the categorical imperative as a proper constraint upon their wills (*FMM*, 41). A being who violates the categorical imperative, and does not recognize that it has done wrong, must not have adopted the categorical imperative as a constraint upon its will. Such a being cannot think of itself as rational. Thus, the categorical imperative expresses the definitive principle of how rational beings ought to act.

❧ PART II: KANT'S POLITICAL PHILOSOPHY ❧

In his political writings Kant builds upon the foundations he established principally in his moral philosophy to provide a rather strong argument supporting the necessity and the legitimacy of the state. In particular, he argues that there must be a single institution among a people, which he calls the state, that has the authority to use coercion to force people to leave others free to formulate and pursue the ends of their choice, provided that they are not violating the similar freedom of another. Kant argues both that morality requires people to exist within a state that secures their freedom to formulate and pursue the ends of their choice, provided that they do not violate the similar freedom of others, and that morality permits people to use coercion to force others to be members of such a state.

Kant suggests that his argument for the state grows out of the consideration of how human beings are actually to apply the categorical imperative (*MM*, 16).[6] Nevertheless, this approach does not reveal all of Kant's concerns in his argument for the state. Accordingly, I will also discuss Kant's argument that people necessarily view themselves as having a certain role to fulfill in the world, and that they can only perform this role successfully if their freedom to formulate and pursue the ends of their choice is secured within a state.

The domain of jurisprudence, the ends of nature, and the value of external freedom

Kant's *Metaphysics of Morals* addresses the issue of how the categorical imperative is to be applied by human beings. This work is divided into two parts: the "Doctrine of Right," in which Kant expresses much of his political philosophy, and the "Doctrine of Virtue," which is concerned exclusively with other aspects of his moral philosophy. Ostensively, the basis for Kant's division of the work is the difference between duties of justice, juridical (legal) duties, and duties of virtue, ethical duties (*MM*, 18–21). Kant says that all legislation (juridical and ethical) consists of two elements: the law, and the incentive to obey the law.

Although two different types of legislation may agree about the law, e.g. both juridical and ethical legislation may prohibit murder, they can at the same time differ with respect to their incentives:

> If legislation makes an action a duty and at the same time makes this duty the incentive, it is *ethical*. If it does not include the latter condition in the law and therefore admits an incentive other than the Idea of duty itself, it is *juridical*.
>
> (*MM*, 19)

Kant is distinguishing ethics, according to which one must always do one's duty exactly because it is one's duty, and never for any other reason, from jurisprudence, according to which one can have some other incentive for one's actions that fulfill one's duties. In fact, Kant begins the "Doctrine of Right" by defining jurisprudence as "the body of those laws that are susceptible of being made into external laws, that is, externally legislated" (*MM*, 33).[7] Thus, one must determine exactly what laws can be externally legislated.

First we should consider the difference between perfect and imperfect duties, and whether the laws that correspond with each of these can be externally legislated. Perfect duties require the performance or nonperformance of specific actions. It is easy to imagine how laws corresponding to these duties could be externally legislated, as it is easy to imagine how external incentives could be employed to coerce people either to perform or to refrain from performing specific actions.

It seems impossible, however, for external incentives to be employed to coerce people to perform imperfect duties (*MM*, 45). After all, imperfect duties require people to adopt certain principles (e.g. beneficence), and to act on those principles in circumstances that they deem appropriate. But people cannot be coerced either to adopt principles or to act on them. Since people's wills are always free, and adopting a principle is an act of will, people cannot be forced to adopt principles. Furthermore, although people can be coerced to perform acts that follow from specified principles, since the act is merely a response to the coercion, it cannot be construed as an attempt to act in accord with the specified principle. Thus, people cannot be forced to act on a principle. Therefore, only imperfect duties can be the subject matter of jurisprudence, imperfect duties cannot.

It might appear, then, that all perfect duties can be addressed by jurisprudence. Actually, however, there is good reason to believe that Kant means to exclude perfect duties to oneself from the domain of jurisprudence.[8] One clear statement to this effect follows: "The concept of justice . . . applies only to the external and – what is more – practical relationship of one person to another" (*MM*, 34). One can best understand Kant's political philosophy, and specifically his exclusion of perfect duties to oneself from the domain of jurisprudence, by considering the broadest concerns that motivate him to write about the state.

In a number of his writings, including some essays on history and, more importantly, the *Critique of Judgment*, Kant reveals a great concern for the development of humanity. In the *Critique of Judgment*, Kant's interest in the development of humanity is revealed in the context of an extended discussion of teleology or purpose. He argues that people can only make sense of a thing insofar as they understand it in terms of its purpose (*CJ*, 280).[9] The notion of a thing having a purpose, however, is ambiguous, raising two issues, each of which is relevant (CJ, 312–13). Something can be organized in a way that manifests a purpose internal to the entity, as a tree is organized to grow and reproduce, or the manifest purpose can be external to the entity, as a tree is organized to help maintain the proper oxygen level in the atmosphere for animals to survive.

When the question of purpose is asked of nature itself, the answer is quite revealing about humanity. Kant thinks that the ultimate internal purpose of nature is human culture, by which he means the ability of human beings, as sensible or physical beings constrained by the laws of nature, to formulate and pursue whatever ends they may set for themselves (CJ, 317–21). But human culture in this sense can only develop if people are secure from others interfering with their ability to formulate and pursue the ends of their choice. Thus, the greatest development of human culture, the ultimate end of nature, can only be realized if people do not violate their perfect duties to others ("UH," 45–6).[10] However, since the violation of perfect duties to oneself would also inhibit the development of human culture, it is not yet clear why Kant restricts the role of the state to include the enforcement of only perfect duties to others.

Kant's reason for excluding perfect duties to oneself from the domain of jurisprudence is revealed through the consideration of his views on the final external purpose of nature (CJ, 322–3). The final external purpose of nature can only be manifest in something that makes use of nature, but is not itself a part of nature, i.e. is not subject to the laws of nature, otherwise it would merely be one more internal purpose of nature. It is human beings, insofar as they are intelligible, or purely rational, beings subject to the moral law, who provide the final purpose for all that exists within nature. However, to the extent that people are not acting on the moral law, but are responding to their inclinations, nature is not being used toward any ends that themselves come from outside of nature. Thus, the final end of nature is only realized to the extent that humanity has developed toward moral perfection.

Kant, however, thinks that the final end of nature cannot be realized so long as people remain in the state of nature because morality is necessarily inefficacious when people remain in this condition. Among people who choose to remain in the natural condition, without a state that enforces the fulfillment of perfect duties to others, it is as if they have agreed with one another that anything goes:

> If men deliberately and intentionally resolve to be in and to remain in this state of external lawless freedom, then they cannot wrong each other by fighting among themselves; for

whatever goes for one of them goes reciprocally for the other as though they had made an agreement to that effect.

$$(MM, 72)$$

In such circumstances, there is reason to believe that none of the duties that people have to one another will be fulfilled. Thus, only if there is a state that enforces the fulfillment of perfect duties to others is it possible that morality will develop to the point that all duties to others can regularly be fulfilled. Therefore, the existence of the state is viewed by Kant as a necessary condition for the development of morality.

It is now clear that Kant requires a state that enforces at least the fulfillment of perfect duties to others, but why should it not also enforce the fulfillment of perfect duties to oneself? The problem is that the enforcement of perfect duties to oneself would undermine the development of the moral character necessary among people who are to fulfill all of their ethical duties. Although the argument is too involved to pursue fully here, the basic point is that one's perfect duties to oneself are fundamental, and only one who truly fulfills these duties, i.e. fulfills them precisely because they are duties, can develop the character necessary for the fulfillment of all of their duties. But if one is coerced to fulfill these duties to oneself, instead of fulfilling them solely because they are one's duties, this will undermine the development of one's character as one who fulfills all one's duties.[11] Thus, although the external legislation of perfect duties to oneself may facilitate the realization of the ultimate end of nature, it would actually undermine the development of humanity toward moral perfection, the final end of nature. Kant's greatest interest, the development of humanity toward both the ultimate and final ends of nature, can be realized only within a state that enforces the fulfillment of perfect duties to others, thereby securing people's external freedom and permitting them to formulate and pursue the ends of their choice, provided that they leave a similar freedom for others.

External freedom and the concept of justice

Having, at least briefly, explained Kant's non-political reasons for being concerned with securing people's external freedom, the foundation has been laid for showing how Kant argues within his political philosophy from the presumed value of external freedom to the necessity and legitimacy of a state that uses coercion to force people to fulfill their perfect duties to others. The outline of Kant's argument is as follows:

1   People have an innate right to external freedom.

2   The only legitimate limitation on this right to external freedom is the right of others to a similar freedom.

3   The condition of the universal realization of this right to external freedom is the condition of justice.

4   Justice entails the authorization to use coercion, as necessary, to support the condition of justice.

5   The innate right to external freedom entails both
   a   the right to security in oneself, and
   b   the right to possess things external to oneself.

6   Someone who remains in proximity, and in the natural condition relative to others, i.e. not in a state, interferes with their external freedom by not providing them a guarantee of security with respect to both
   a   their right in themselves, and
   b   their rightful possession of objects external to themselves.

7   Existing within a state, subject to juridical law, is the only way to guarantee this security to others.

8   It is just to use coercion to force anyone in proximity into a state, subject to juridical law.

Kant claims that there are two types of rights: innate rights and acquired rights (*MM*, 43). Innate rights belong to people by nature, independently of any act of law. Acquired rights, on the other hand, only come to exist through an act of law. Since acquired rights are dependent on acts of law, they cannot themselves provide the basis for considering people obligated to accept the lawful authority of a state. Any right that is to provide a legitimate basis for considering people obligated to accept the authority of a state must be an innate right. The innate right of external freedom plays this crucial role in Kant's argument for the necessity and the legitimacy of the state. Kant begins the section entitled "There is only one innate right" as follows:

> Freedom (independence from the constraint of another's will),
> insofar as it is compatible with the freedom of everyone else
> in accordance with a universal law, is the one sole and original
> right that belongs to every human being by virtue of his
> humanity.

> (*MM*, 43–4)

The innate right to external freedom, therefore, is the only right that can provide the justification for imposing a system of juridical law on others.

This innate right to external freedom provides the basis for Kant's conception of "justice," which he defines as "the aggregate of those conditions under which the will of one person can be conjoined with the will of another in accordance with a universal law of freedom" (*MM*, 34). What are the conditions under which people's wills can be conjoined in accordance with a universal law of freedom? Kant thinks that two wills can be conjoined if they include no incompatibility. But what does this mean? Following Kant's description of willing as "the summoning of all the means in our power" (*FMM*, 10), two wills can be conjoined if each will, while summoning all of the means in its power applicable toward its end, does nothing incompatible with the activity of the other.

Suppose that two people will to hold the same political office. They will both summon all of the means that are in their power to gain this office, which, taken to its literal extreme, will undoubtedly include the violent elimination of their rival. In this case their wills cannot be united since each of them, by seeking to eliminate the other, is acting in a manner that is incompatible with the other's pursuit of the goal. It is not possible for them jointly to will that they act in the manner described, since it entails both of them willing their own death, and also willing to survive after the death of the other.

The question of justice, however, is not merely whether their wills can be conjoined, but whether they can be conjoined in accordance with a universal law of freedom. This restricts the range of maxims upon which they can will to act to those that are in accord with the universal law of freedom, which, for human beings, is expressed in the categorical imperative. If the rivals restrict their wills to maxims that meet this requirement, then they each will act on no maxim (employ no means) the universalization of which would be incompatible or inconsistent with the freedom of the other to act on similarly acceptable maxims. If the politicians so restrict themselves, then all of their acts, e.g. distributing buttons, or advertising their virtues on television, will be compatible with the like freedom of others. Their wills can be conjoined since there is no incompatibility or inconsistency between their willing to act in this restricted manner, and others willing to act similarly.

Although it was made to seem above, during the discussion of the universal law of freedom and its relationship to the categorical imperative, that justice requires one to act fully in accord with the categorical imperative, it is clear from Kant's definition of justice that it is limited to perfect duties to others. The exclusion of duties to oneself is clear from the reference to conjoining the will of one person with the "will of another." The exclusion of imperfect duties is entailed by the reference to the conditions in which one person's will *"can be conjoined"* with that of another. When asking if the wills *can* be conjoined, one is asking only whether it is logically possible for the maxims to hold at the same time, the test for perfect duties, not whether one could will them to hold at the same time, the test for imperfect duties.

With this understanding of Kant's conception of justice, it is easy to see that it amounts to nothing more than the condition of the universal realization of the innate right to external freedom. For all people to be independent of the constraint of others' wills, to the extent that this is compatible with the freedom of everyone else in accordance with a universal law, i.e. for the innate right to external freedom to be universally realized, requires neither more nor less than that people be in a condition in which their wills can be conjoined in accordance with a universal law of freedom, i.e. that people be in a just condition. Thus, if Kant can argue that the concept of justice logically entails the right to use coercion in support of the condition of justice, then he will have shown that there is no inconsistency in using coercion to support and maintain external freedom.

Kant wants to show that such coercion as is truly employed in opposition to injustice is itself consistent with justice (*MM*, 35-6). It follows from Kant's definition of justice that injustice would be *any condition* in which one person's will could not be conjoined with the will of another in accordance with a universal law of freedom. This condition cannot be eliminated, but can only be furthered, by an act that is itself unjust. Since every unjust act entails a will that cannot be conjoined with at least one other will in accordance with a universal law of freedom, every unjust act itself necessarily furthers the existence of the condition in which one person's will cannot be conjoined with the will of another in accordance with a universal law of freedom, i.e. the condition of injustice. Thus, any coercion that actually opposes the condition of injustice must, by definition, itself be just.

Kant goes on to argue that it is not merely just, but required by justice, to use coercion against anyone who acts unjustly (*MM*, 36-7). Of course, there are conditions on how that coercion is to be justly applied, but, assuming that these conditions are met, the application of coercion in support of the innate right to external freedom is itself a requirement of justice. It is particularly important to Kant, in light of the broadest concerns of his political philosophy, that external freedom can be supported by coercion. He is concerned with external freedom because it is a necessary condition for the development of humanity toward the final end of nature, moral perfection. But if people have to be moral to respect one another's external freedom, then Kant would have a circular argument in which the conditions for the development of morality were themselves dependent on morality. Kant needs the condition in which people respect one another's external freedom to be established entirely independently of the morality of the people. Thus, it is essential for Kant's argument that external freedom can be supported entirely by external legislation (independent of people's internal moral motivations).

The components of external freedom

Having shown that coercion can and ought to be used in support of the innate right to external freedom, the question of exactly what is entailed in this right must now be addressed. Based on his definition of the innate right to external freedom it is clear that Kant wants people to be independent of constraints that come from the will of others, when they are formulating and pursuing the ends of their choice in a manner consistent with others having a like freedom. It would seem then that Kant thinks that the innate right to external freedom entails independence from others *willfully acting* in a way that interferes with one's right to formulate and pursue the ends of one's choice. A right to this sort of freedom may be commonly recognized, and may provide an adequate basis for a derivation of the necessity and legitimacy of the state. However, it is clear from Kant's argument for the state that he has a significantly stronger sense of "freedom" in mind. This freedom includes independence from others willfully acting in a way that interferes with one's right to formulate and pursue the ends of one's choice in a manner consistent with the similar freedom of others, but it also includes independence from others even *willfully maintaining a condition* that interferes with this right (see *MM*, 35).

If he is to provide an *a priori* argument for the necessity of the state, Kant has to be concerned with the possibility of one's external freedom being interfered with by the conditions that others maintain, and not only by their actions. Kant's argument is dependent on the fact that someone who is in proximity, and in the natural condition relative to others, necessarily interferes with their external freedom. If Kant based his argument for the state on the fact that people will commit acts that interfere with the external freedom of others, then his argument for the state would be contingent on people actually committing such acts. Thus, Kant says:

> I am injured by the condition of other people who are in the natural state. For [when others remain in the natural condition] I have no security and my property is always in danger. I am not obligated to remain in this fear.[12]

Kant's point is that people who remain in proximity, and in the state of nature relative to others, interfere with others' freedom by interfering with both their security in themselves and their right to things external to themselves. Furthermore, one need not tolerate this situation of insecurity that undermines freedom, because people can be forced to join the state, the only condition in which freedom is guaranteed, without violating their freedom.

The last two sentences constitute, in effect, a restatement of steps 5–8 of Kant's argument as outlined above. According to the innate right to external freedom, people have the right to formulate and pursue the ends of their choice, provided that they leave a similar freedom for others. Kant thinks that this right entails both the right to security in oneself and the right to possess things external to oneself.

Any violation of one's right in oneself, which would seem necessarily to involve some sort of assault, clearly entails the victim's being constrained by the will of another (the perpetrator). Furthermore, Kant thinks that even the threat of a violation of one's right in oneself interferes with one's external freedom, as Hobbesian reasoning reveals. If people are in fear for their personal security, they will have to focus a great portion of their efforts on securing themselves, and will not be able to formulate and pursue those ends that truly interest them. Thus, the innate right to external freedom entails the right to security in oneself.

The explanation of why the innate right to external freedom entails the right to possess things external to oneself is much more complicated. One simple explanation that Kant alludes to at times is that human culture is advanced through people engaging in complex projects, but people will only engage in such projects if they have a fixed expectation of their efforts being undisturbed, and of being able to work from the results of earlier efforts in subsequent, more involved projects. Thus, the right to possess things external to oneself is necessary for the development of human culture, the ultimate end of nature. Kant's more complicated explanation of the right to property is basically that freedom can only be restricted to preserve the like freedom of others, owning property does not restrict the like freedom of others, and, therefore, freedom includes the right to own property. Thus, to restrict the possibility of the rightful possession of things external to oneself is to restrict freedom for something other than freedom, which is necessarily inconsistent with the final end of nature (*MM*, 52–3).

The necessary conditions of external freedom

What remains to be shown is that anyone who remains in proximity, and in the natural condition relative to others, interferes with both of the rights that are entailed in the innate right to external freedom. First we shall look at Kant's argument that such an individual interferes with others' right to possess things external to themselves. Kant maintains that the right to possess anything, although land is the most important example, depends on a relationship of the wills of all those who are in proximity (*MM*, 65). There are no material conditions, which could be verified empirically, that constitute having a right to a thing. Although Locke argued that one can make something one's property by mixing one's labor with it, Kant would respond that this begs the question, since it can now be asked: By what right does one mix one's labor with something?

Kant thinks that a person can rightfully possess something only if everyone in proximity relinquishes their right to will the use of that thing. Thus, one cannot take rightful possession of something through one's own will alone; there must be a union of wills manifesting the agreement of all to respect the property of each:

> Now, with respect to an external and contingent possession, a unilateral Will cannot serve as a coercive law for everyone, since that would be a violation of freedom in accordance with universal laws. Therefore, only a Will binding everyone else – that is, a collective, universal (common), and powerful Will – is the kind of Will that can provide the guarantee required. The condition of being subject to general external (that is, public) legislation that is backed by power is the civil society. Accordingly, a thing can be externally yours or mine only in a civil society.
>
> (*MM*, 65)

For Kant, existing within a state is the form in which the people express their mutual respect for one another's rightful possession of things external to themselves. What happens, however, if there are people in proximity, and in the state of nature relative to the others? These people are not parties to the union of wills by which each person's rightful possessions are guaranteed. These people are in a position to will the use of things that would otherwise be rightfully possessed by others. But since rightful possession depends on the agreement of the wills of all those in proximity, the presence of these people who are outside the union of wills makes rightful possession impossible, thereby interfering with the freedom of those within the union. Thus, Kant concludes this discussion by saying that if rightful possession must be possible (and it is entailed in the innate right to external freedom), "then the subject must also be allowed to compel everyone else with whom he comes into conflict over the question of whether such an object is his to enter, together with him, a society under a civil constitution" (*MM*, 65). In summary, Kant argues that the innate right to external freedom includes the right to possess things external to oneself; that this right can only be realized within a state; that anyone in proximity and outside of the state interferes with this right; and, therefore, that it is just to use coercion to force such people to enter the state.

Kant also argues for the necessity and the legitimacy of the state from the fact that the innate right to external freedom entails a right to security in oneself that can only be realized within a state. While it is true that everyone has an ethical duty to respect everyone else's rights in themselves, nevertheless, since people have no way of knowing the intentions of others, they are not secure in their rights in themselves until such time as they guarantee to one another that they will respect these rights:

> The necessity of public lawful coercion does not rest on a fact, but on an a priori Idea of reason, for, even if we imagine men to be ever so good natured and righteous before a public lawful state of society is established, individual men, nations, and states can never be certain that they are secure against violence from one another.
>
> (*MM*, 76)

Kant's point is that, despite the requirements of morality, people's rights in themselves are insecure outside of a state. Paralleling his argument for the state from the right to possess things external to oneself, Kant argues here that the only way that the rights entailed in the innate right to external freedom can be realized is if people make their will not to violate these rights publicly known, and that the form of this mutual guarantee is the state.

Kant's argument that the necessity and the legitimacy of the state can be derived from the fact that people have the right to security in themselves is well summarized in the following:

> It is usually assumed that one cannot take hostile action against anyone unless one has already been actively *injured* by them. This is perfectly correct if both parties are living in a *legal civil state*. For the fact that one has entered such a state gives the required guarantee to the other, since both are subject to the same authority. But man (or an individual people) in a mere state of nature robs me of any such security and injures me by virtue of this very state in which he coexists with me. He may not have injured me actively (*facto*), but he does injure me by the very lawlessness of his state (*statu iniusto*), for he is a permanent threat to me, and I can require him either to enter into a common lawful state along with me or to move away from my vicinity.
>
> ("PP," 98 n.)[13]

The innate right to external freedom can be universally realized only within a state, in which each person guarantees this right of everyone else by participating in a union of wills resolved to use coercion in support of this right. Furthermore, since it is just to use coercion in support of the innate right to external freedom, it is just to use coercion to force into the state those people who would otherwise maintain a condition that interferes with the external freedom of others (e.g. by remaining in proximity and outside of civil society).

Kant on international relations

Before discussing Kant's views on how one is forced to join a state, and the version of hypothetical social contract theory toward which these concerns lead Kant, it is interesting to consider the relationship between Kant's argument for the necessity of the state and his views on international relations. Kant has argued that people who remain in proximity, and in the natural condition relative to others, because they necessarily interfere with the freedom of those others, may therefore justly be forced to join together with them in a state that secures their freedom. However, what if these people are already members of a state, but a different neighboring state? Two related problems arise: First, the members of each state interfere with the freedom of the members of the other state just as they would if they were not members of a state at all: if there is no formal relationship between the states, there is no guarantee that the members of each state will respect the rights of the members of the other state. Second, the two states, which can each be thought of as a "moral person," are in the state of nature relative to one another, and suffer all the difficulties that led Kant to argue for the need for civil society.

Kant recognizes that these are serious difficulties which, unchecked, would very much undermine the possibility of the sort of human development that he thinks should be facilitated. His solution to the problem is to suggest that the same forces that lead individuals into a state should lead states into a federation of states ("PP," 102–5; "UH," 47; "TP," 90).[14] This federation of states would then fulfill the same role among states that a state fulfills for its citizens, and would also provide the necessary guarantee of external freedom among the citizens of different states.

Although it is clear what Kant provides through his suggestion of a federation of states, there is also a significant problem raised by this suggestion: Who is ultimately sovereign? Since Kant argues that for a state effectively to fulfill its role it must be ruled by an absolute sovereign, it would seem to follow that the federation of states can effectively fulfill its role only if it is ruled by an absolute sovereign. Thus, it appears to be a clear implication of Kant's argument that there should be a single world nation, without lesser sovereign states. However, Kant never supports the notion of a single world state, and at one point discusses the concern that such a world state "may lead to the most fearful despotism" ("TP," 90). Thus, while Kant was right to recognize that his argument for the necessity and the legitimacy of the state has important implications for international relations, he was never able to give a clear and satisfactory account of how those international relations should be organized.

Kant's hypothetical social contract theory

Kant has shown that people who remain in proximity, and in the natural condition relative to others, can be forced to join together with others in a state. Before one can understand what Kant thinks is entailed in forcing someone to join a state, one must understand what Kant thinks is entailed in being a member of a state, and how this membership is manifest. These issues are all addressed by what might best be described as a hypothetical social contract theorist.

Kant's hypothetical social contract theory follows from his *a priori* reasoning about human beings, and his recognition of both the rights of human beings, and the impossibility of realizing those rights outside of a state:

> A state (*civitas*) is a union of a multitude of men under laws of justice. Insofar as these laws are necessary a priori and follow from the concepts of external justice in general (that is, are not established by statute), the form of the state is that of the state in general, that is the Idea of the state as it ought to be according to pure principles of justice. This Idea provides an internal guide and standard (*norma*) for every actual union of men in a commonwealth.
>
> (*MM*, 77)

Kant is concerned with the Idea of the state, which is based on *a priori* necessary laws of justice, and thus ought to serve as the blueprint for all actual states. It is the possibility of deriving the state *a priori* that grounds the possibility of a hypothetical social contract theory.

Kant is a social contract theorist, maintaining that one's political obligations can only result from one's having consented, along with others, to be subject to the authority of the state. Kant, however, departs from the more traditional social contract theorists in that he does not think that this consent is actual, either explicit or tacit. Thus, Kant's social contract theory is best described as hypothetical, to distinguish it from those theories according to which people must actually manifest their consent through their behavior. Under Kant's hypothetical social contract, human beings can be treated *as if* they have consented to the social contract, because their consent is a necessary manifestation of their humanity, i.e. it is known *a priori* that, inasmuch as a being is rational, and one to whom the concept "human" applies, this being necessarily consents to the social contract. Thus, Kant says that being a member of a state is a "requirement of pure reason, which legislates *a priori*" ("TP," 73).

It is in accord with this pure reason that people are parties to the social contract, and organize themselves into a state. Being organized into a state, however, does not require that individuals actually apply their own reason and recognize the necessity and the legitimacy of the state; rather, the state is legitimate because *a priori* reason reveals it to be so: "The act by means of which the people constitute themselves a state is the original contract. More precisely, it is the Idea of that act that alone enables us to conceive of the legitimacy of the state" (*MM*, 80).

Kant places himself in the contract tradition through his reference to the "original contract." However, he then avoids any reliance on the actuality of this contract, and introduces what I have called a hypothetical social contract theory. It is not any actual social contract, to which people have actually consented either explicitly or tacitly, that lies at the foundation of the state and accounts for its legitimacy. Rather, it is the "Idea" of the original contract, a necessary idea of *a priori* pure practical reason that must, therefore, necessarily be assented to by all human beings inasmuch as they manifest their rationality, that provides the foundation of the state, and accounts for its legitimacy.

All that is required for one to be a member of a state, remembering that it requires no actual consent, is to exist in a condition in which each individual has the rights and obligations that are necessary for the maintenance of a just condition, and which are enforced by the state through coercion. In fact, Kant argues that even if the state does not enforce exactly those rights and obligations that are necessary for the maintenance of a just condition, people must still accept its authority (for reasons that will be revealed shortly). In any case, membership in the state amounts to nothing more than the fact that citizens have an obligation to obey the law, and will be punished if they do not. There is nothing that manifests citizens' membership in the state save the fact that *a priori* pure practical reason requires people, as intelligible beings, to subject themselves to this system of laws, and that people, as sensible or physical beings, are actually subjected to the authority of the state.

What about those people existing either within the borders of the state, or otherwise in proximity, who, as intelligible beings, do not recognize the *a priori* practical necessity of subjecting themselves to the authority of the state, and, therefore, as sensible or physical beings, do not necessarily obey the authority of the state? Kant has said that such people can be forced to join the state. But, since there is no particular behavior by which people actually manifest their consent to the social contract, there is no act that people can be forced to perfom that will manifest their joining the state.

In the end, what it is to force such people to join the state can be seen by considering why it is necessary to do so. The fact that such people, as intelligible beings, do not recognize the *a priori* practical necessity of the state is irrelevant, since justice is concerned with only the external relations among persons. The fact that such people, as sensible or physical beings, do not obey the authority of the state, however, means that, were they members of the state they would have been subjected to coercion, as necessary, to maintain the condition of justice. Membership in the state amounts to nothing more than being subject to the threat of coercion in response to violations of the law. Kant's claim, that people who do not accept the authority of the state should be forced to join the state, really amounts to the claim that, in accord with the hypothetical social contract that they necessarily accept insofar as they are rational beings, they should be treated as members of the state.

Kant on rebellion and resistance

Kant has argued from the fact that people have an innate right to external freedom, and the fact that this freedom is not violated by the use of coercion against someone who is violating the freedom of another, to the fact that people can be treated as if they were parties to an original contract by which they agreed to accept the authority of the state. The idea of an original contract, however, not only explains the political obligations of the members of a state, but also accounts for the limitations that exist on the authority of the state:

> [The original contract] is in fact only an *idea* of reason, which
> nonetheless has undoubted practical reality; for it can oblige
> every legislator to frame his laws in such a way that they could
> have been produced by the united will of a whole nation. . . .
> This is the test of the rightfulness of every public law. For if a
> law is such that a whole people could not *possibly* agree to
> it . . . it is unjust; but if it is at least *possible* that a people could

agree to it, it is our duty to consider the law as just, even if the people is at present in such a position or attitude of mind that it would probably refuse its consent if it were consulted.

("TP," 79)

The idea of the original contract, to which all human beings, insofar as they are rational, necessarily consent, includes restrictions on the possible legislation of a legitimate state. Basically, legislation is legitimate if it would be possible for the people to consent to it. The fact that the people would be likely to choose not to consent to a given piece of legislation is not relevant to its legitimacy, provided that it does not require the violation of a perfect duty, and, thus, could at least possibly receive the people's consent.

Accordingly, it would not be surprising if Kant went on to argue that rebellion and resistance against a state whose laws are legitimate is absolutely prohibited, but that it is permissible to rebel against a state that passes unjust legislation, or at least to resist the specific unjust laws. Such a position would be consistent with the fact that Kant, on certain grounds, applauded the French Revolution. This line of reasoning is also supported by a passage in which Kant implies that resistance to illegitimate legislation, which requires the violation of a perfect duty, is permissible, or even required: "When men command anything which is itself evil (directly opposed to the law of morality) we dare not, and ought not, obey them."[15] Despite this apparent endorsement of resistance to unjust legislation, however, Kant repeatedly states that rebellion against states that enact unjust legislation, and resistance to illegitimate legislation, are both absolutely prohibited. At first blush this is rather surprising. After all, Kant's interest in the state is grounded in his concern for the development of morality, which fundamentally entails the autonomy of the individual, and, yet, submission to an unjust state seems undeniably to entail the violation of morality and the denial of individual autonomy. Nevertheless, Kant's arguments for the absolute prohibition against rebellion and resistance are well grounded in his most fundamental concerns.

Kant's absolute prohibition against rebellion and resistance, while holding a theory of illegitimate legislation, is evident. He says that "the people too have inalienable rights against the head of state, even if these cannot be rights of coercion" ("TP," 84). Kant both recognizes that there are things beyond the legitimate authority of the state, and asserts that the people cannot use coercion in response to such transgressions. The absolute nature of this prohibition is stated unequivocally: "it is the people's duty to endure even the most intolerable abuse of supreme authority" (MM, 86). Another passage both expresses this absolute prohibition, and begins to reveal Kant's justification for it:

It thus follows that all resistance against the supreme legislative power, all incitements of the subjects to violent expressions of discontent, all defiance which breaks out into rebellion, is the greatest and most punishable crime in a commonwealth, for it destroys its very foundations. This prohibition is *absolute*.

("TP," 81)

Kant not only thinks that the prohibition against rebellion and resistance is absolute, but that it must be absolute, because rebellion and resistance destroy the very foundations of a state. Even a state that is unjust must be supported because the state is necessary for the realization of the innate right to external freedom, and to rebel or resist any state is to act on a maxim that makes all states insecure:

For such resistance would be dictated by a maxim which, if it became general, would destroy the whole civil constitution and put an end to the only state in which men can possess rights.

("TP," 81)

For such procedures, if made into a maxim, make all lawful constitutions insecure and produce a state of complete lawlessness (*status naturalis*) where all rights cease at least to be effectual.

("TP," 82)

In his political philosophy, Kant argues for the necessity and the legitimacy of the state because, without a state, the rights that people have under the innate right to external freedom cannot be secured, and humanity will not progress toward the ultimate and final ends of nature. Rebellion and resistance, however, entail the adoption of maxims that make the state impossible, rights ineffectual, and the hope for human progress vain. Thus, it is only if people live within secure states, that are themselves members of a healthy federation of states, that humanity can possibly progress toward the ultimate and final ends of nature, the complete development of human culture and the attainment of moral perfection.

❧ NOTES ❧

1 For Kant these identities are necessary, thus obviating the claim that he is substituting into an intentional context.
2 *FMM* stands for Kant, *Foundations of the Metaphysics of Morals*, 2nd edn, revised, trans. L.W. Beck (New York: Macmillan, 1959).
3 Kant wouldn't consider this correspondence mere coincidence, but space does not permit a discussion of its grounds.

4 It is clear that by "humanity" here Kant is referring to rational beings generally.

5 Kant argues only that insofar as we think of rational beings as actors in the world, i.e. from the point of view of practical philosophy, can we argue that these beings are free. This argument does not constitute a theoretical proof of the freedom of rational beings.

6 *MM* stands for Kant, *The Metaphysics of Morals*, the Preface, Introduction, and most of Part I ("Doctrine of Right") of which constitute *The Metaphysical Elements of Justice*, trans. J. Ladd (New York: Macmillan, 1965).

7 The word that is here translated as "jurisprudence" is the same word as is translated "doctrine of right," but the former corresponds to colloquial English. Furthermore, the root of this word, "*Recht*," can be translated as either "right" or "justice" depending on the context. Thus, the "Doctrine of Right," Kant's theory of jurisprudence, is concerned with those duties that are duties of justice.

8 There is rather good evidence both for and against this claim; however, I think that much better sense can be made of Kant's political philosophy on the assumption that it is correct.

9 *CJ* stands for Kant, *Critique of Judgment*, trans. W.S. Pluhar (Indianapolis: Hackett, 1987).

10 "UH" stands for Kant, "Idea for a Universal History with a Cosmopolitan Purpose," in *Kant's Political Writings*, 2nd edn, ed. H. Reiss, trans. H.B. Nisbet (Cambridge: Cambridge University Press, 1991).

11 Kant, *Lectures on Ethics*, trans. L. Infield (Indianapolis: Hackett, 1963), pp. 117–18.

12 Kant, Reflection 7647 (my translation), in *Kant's gesammelte Schriften*, 29 vols, ed. Deutschen (formerly Königlich Preussische) Akademie der Wissenschaften (Berlin: de Gruyter [and predecessors], 1902-), Vol. 19, pp. 476–7.

13 "PP" stands for Kant, "Perpetual Peace: A Philosophical Sketch," in *Kant's Political Writings*, op. cit.

14 "TP" stands for Kant, "On the Common Saying: 'This May be True in Theory, but it does not Apply in Practice'," in *Kant's Political Writings*, op. cit.

15 Kant, *Religion within the Limits of Reason Alone*, trans. T.M. Greene and H. H. Hudson (New York: Harper & Row, 1960), p. 90 n.

❧ SELECT BIBLIOGRAPHY ❧

Original language editions

3.1 *Kants gesammelte Schriften*, 29 vols, ed. Deutschen (formerly Königliche Preussische) Akademie der Wissenschaften, Berlin: de Gruyter (and predecessors), 1902–; the complete collection of Kant's work.

English translations of Kant's work

3.2 *Anthropology from a Pragmatic Point of View*, trans. M.J. Gregor, The Hague: Nijhoff, 1974.

3.3 *Critique of Judgment*, trans. W.S. Pluhar, Indianapolis: Hackett, 1987.

3.4 *Critique of Practical Reason*, trans. L.W. Beck, New York: Bobbs-Merrill, 1956.

3.5 *Critique of Pure Reason*, trans. N. Kemp Smith, New York: St Martin's Press, 1965.

3.6 *Foundations of the Metaphysics of Morals*, 2nd edn, trans. L.W. Beck, New York: Macmillan, 1990.

3.7 *Lectures on Ethics*, trans. L. Infield, Indianapolis: Hackett, 1963.

3.8 *The Metaphysics of Morals*, trans. M. Gregor, Cambridge: Cambridge University, 1991.
  Preface, Introduction, and Part I ("Doctrine of Right"), trans. J. Ladd, in *The Metaphysical Elements of Justice*, New York: Macmillan, 1965.
  Preface, Introduction, and Part II ("Doctrine of Virtue"), trans. J.W. Ellington, in *Ethical Philosophy*, Indianapolis: Hackett, 1983.

3.9 *Religion within the Limits of Reason Alone*, trans. T.M. Greene and H.H. Hudson, New York: Harper & Row, 1960.

3.10 "Idea for a Universal History with a Cosmopolitan Purpose";

3.11 "On the Common Saying: 'This May be True in Theory, but it does not Apply in Practice' ";

3.12 "Perpetual Peace: A Philosophical Sketch":
  All appear in:
  Reiss, H. (ed.) *Kant's Political Writings*, 2nd enlarged edn, trans. H.B. Nisbet, Cambridge: Cambridge University Press, 1991.
  Humphrey T. (ed.) *Perpetual Peace and Other Essays*, Indianapolis, Hackett, 1983.

Commentaries on Kant's moral and political philosophy

3.13 Allison, H.E. *Kant's Theory of Freedom*, Cambridge: Cambridge University Press, 1990.

3.14 Arendt, H. *Lectures on Kant's Political Philosophy*, ed. R. Beiner, Chicago: University of Chicago Press, 1982.

3.15 Aune, B. *Kant's Theory of Morals*, Princeton: Princeton University Press, 1979.

3.16 Beck, L.W. *A Commentary on Kant's "Critique of Practical Reason"*, Chicago: University of Chicago Press, 1960.

3.17 Carnois, B. *The Coherence of Kant's Doctrine of Freedom*, trans. D. Booth, Chicago: University of Chicago Press, 1987.

3.18 Gregor, M.J. *Laws of Freedom: A Study of Kant's Method of Applying the Categorical Imperative in the "Metaphysik der Sitten" ["Metaphysics of Morals"]*, New York: Barnes & Noble, 1963.

3.19 Mulholland, L.A. *Kant's System of Rights*, New York: Columbia University Press, 1990.

3.20 Murphy, J.G. *Kant: The Philosophy of Right*, London: Macmillan, 1970.

3.21 Nell, O. *Acting on Principle: An Essay on Kantian Ethics*, New York: Columbia University Press, 1975.

3.22 Paton, H.J. *The Categorical Imperative: A Study in Kant's Moral Philosophy*, London: Hutchinson, 1947.

3.23 Riley, P. *Kant's Political Philosophy*, Totowa, NJ: Rowman & Littlefield, 1983.

3.24 Shell, S.M. *The Rights of Reason: A Study of Kant's Philosophy and Politics*, Toronto: University of Toronto Press, 1980.

3.25 Sullivan, R.J. *Immanuel Kant's Moral Theory*, Cambridge: Cambridge University Press, 1989.

3.26 Williams, H. *Kant's Political Philosophy*, Oxford: Blackwell, 1983.

3.27 Wolff, R.P. *The Autonomy of Reason: A Commentary on Kant's "Groundwork of the Metaphysics of Morals"*, New York: Harper & Row, 1973.

3.28 Yovel, Y. *Kant and the Philosophy of History*, Princeton: Princeton University Press, 1980.

CHAPTER 4
Kant: *Critique of Judgement*
Patrick Gardiner

Kant's third *Critique*, the *Critique of Judgement*, was published in 1790 and was intended – as he himself put it – to bring his "entire critical undertaking to a close." So conceived, it was certainly in part designed to build upon and develop ideas that had already been introduced in its two predecessors but which he had come to regard as requiring further elaboration and supplementation. Thus Kant included in its ambitious scope wide-ranging discussions impinging upon the spheres of scientific enquiry, ethics, and religion, his aim being to approach these apparently diverse realms within a perspective distinguishable in significant ways from any he had hitherto adopted. At the same time, however, it should be recognized that the book was composed not only in the light of theses he had advanced in his own previous writings. For it may also be seen as involving responses or allusions to positions that had been put forward by other thinkers and which had attracted considerable attention among his contemporaries. This was especially true in the case of aesthetics, an area he had not so far subjected to systematic critical scrutiny; but they arose as well both from developments in the emergent biological sciences and from theoretical studies relating to history and to the nature of social change. Further, and at a more general level, Kant was sharply aware of recent contributions to the existing climate of opinion that had been made by philosophers who wished to challenge many of the rationalistic assumptions associated with the eighteenth-century *Aufklärung*, particularly those felt to threaten or undermine cherished dogmas of religious orthodoxy. All in all, German thought in the 1780s can be said to have been the focus of a variety of competing intellectual preoccupations and trends. Hence it is hardly surprising that his own treatise, appearing at the end of an ideologically turbulent decade, bore the imprint of current controversies, some of which had indeed been sparked off by the publication nine years earlier of the *Critique of Pure Reason* itself.

The outcome of these disparate concerns and influences was a complex and seminal work. It was also, at least in certain respects, an elusive one. The sections into which the *Critique of Judgement* is divided fall into four main groups, each centering round a dominant topic or theme. But although the individual subjects treated are of great intrinsic interest, they are apt to strike the reader as belonging to markedly different categories; moreover, the actual manner in which some of the constituent sections are suppose to fit together is not always easy to discern. It may therefore be tempting to regard the book from one point of view as amounting to a series of somewhat loosely related essays rather than as representing a unified enquiry controlled by a single overarching objective. Nonetheless, Kant makes it pretty clear at the outset that this was not how he himself envisaged the project on which he was engaged. Instead, he presents it as following a course determined by, and closely integrated with, the overall plan informing his earlier investigations, the assumed connection deriving from the theory of mental powers or faculties in terms of which he tended to articulate the basic principles governing human thought and conduct. The functions of two of those faculties – namely, understanding and reason – had already been examined and their respective provinces charted. Thus in the Preface he writes that his first *Critique* was largely devoted to analyzing the role of the understanding in supplying the *a priori* principles essential to our cognitive experience; while in the second he demonstrated how reason – here identified in its practical employment as the source of moral prescriptions – performed a comparable *a priori* role in legislating at the level of human action and desire. He now maintains that a third faculty remains for consideration which forms "a middle term" between the other two and whose claims as a possible source of independent *a priori* principles have still to be assessed. The faculty in question is the power of judgment (*Urteilskraft*), the important issues its mediating position raises indicating that a further *Critique* is called for. Accordingly, and with the completion of his system in mind, it is this that Kant sets out to provide. Let us see how he proceeds, beginning with the contents of the formidable Introduction which in effect constitutes the first major division of his new work.

REFLECTIVE JUDGMENT AND THE CONCEPT OF PURPOSE

Kant wrote two Introductions to the *Critique of Judgement*, discarding the first as being "disproportionately extensive" and replacing it with the shorter version he decided to publish in its stead. Even in its abbreviated form, however, it amounts to an involved and demanding piece of work, containing retrospective references to conclusions so far reached in his philosophy as well as anticipations of matters he intends to cover in the main body of the text that is to follow. Since it is in terms of the former conclusions that he offers a preliminary clue to what he conceives to be a guiding concern of the present *Critique*, it will be best to start with his somewhat condensed remarks in that connection. For they indicate that his conception of judgment as playing a mediating role between understanding and reason was intimately linked to a distinction which was fundamental to the doctrine of transcendental idealism propounded in his previous writings.

This was the radical contrast he had drawn between the realm of empirical phenomena, comprising reality as it appears to us as cognitive subjects endowed with a certain sensory and intellectual apparatus, and a postulated non-empirical realm of noumena or "things in themselves." So far as the phenomenal sphere was concerned, Kant had argued that our familiar awareness of a spatio-temporal and causally governed world of perceivable entities and events presupposed a framework of universal forms and categories which was imposed upon the data or raw material of sensation by the human mind. Such an *a priori* framework determined the basic structure of the empirical consciousness, constituting the conditions upon which all everyday and scientific knowledge depended for its possibility. At the same time, it must clearly be understood that any knowledge we might legitimately claim to possess of reality was confined to the sphere of observable nature, i.e. to what fell within the scope of sensory experience: it did not extend to the noumenal realm, the latter being a supersensible field that was necessarily inaccessible to theoretical cognition or investigation. However, it did not follow that the notion of the supersensible had no substantive part to play in our thought. On the contrary, Kant regarded it as being crucial to the conception we were obliged to have of ourselves when considered from a practical and, more specifically, a moral point of view. For here it was essential that we should think of ourselves as possessing free will and as being thereby able to act in compliance with practical imperatives prescribed by reason as opposed to following the natural promptings of sensuous impulse or inclination. Such a capacity for rational self-determination appeared to be excluded on the supposition that we belonged solely to the phenomenal domain, since on Kant's own principles everything occurring within that sphere was subject without exception to the laws of natural causality. On the other hand, the requirements of morality could be preserved if it were accepted that there were two aspects under which people might be viewed, the first of which involved treating them as items in "the world of sense" and the second of which involved regarding them as belonging to the "intelligible" or supersensible sphere which necessarily lay outside the range of the causal categories that were universally applicable within the empirical realm. Thus, while from a theoretical standpoint we were indeed bound to consider ourselves as governed by natural laws, from the standpoint of practical motivation and choice we could at the same time consistently conceive of ourselves as exercising freedom and rational autonomy of the kind presupposed by the moral consciousness. Kant was careful to point out that the latter conception, depending as it did for its possibility upon our membership of the supersensible as well as the natural world, was not capable of being cognitively established; for nothing whatsoever could be *known* by us at the level of noumenal reality. Nonetheless, the "two-world" doctrine invoked might be said to leave room for the idea of human free will in a way that rendered it compatible with the acceptance of a fully deterministic account of nature, thereby resolving an antinomy commonly believed to arise between the claims of scientific enquiry and the presuppositions of ethical thought.

Problematic though it has often been felt to be, the above solution to this apparent conflict was certainly the one that Kant had adopted in his two preceding *Critiques*. And it recurs in the Introduction to his third inasmuch as he speaks there of theoretical understanding and practical reason as having "two distinct jurisdictions," neither of which need be thought of as interfering with the other – "it is possible for us at least to think without contradiction of both these jurisdictions, and their appropriate faculties, as coexisting in the same Subject" (Introduction, p. 13). However, although in the present context he briefly refers to this thesis as having been established in the *Critique of Pure Reason*, at the same time he indicates here that it leaves in its wake a further issue whose significance has still to be faced. For it raises the question of what connection, if any, may be presumed to exist between the spheres of natural necessity and practical freedom, given their supposed independence. Kant certainly writes of there being "a great gulf fixed" between the provinces to which the concepts of nature "as the sensible" and of freedom "as the supersensible" respectively apply, the first of these being "powerless" to exercise an influence upon the second. The fact remains nonetheless that the two realms cannot be thought of as totally insulated from each other, for it is a condition of moral agency that the principles and objectives which reason prescribes should be understood to be realizable in the phenomenal world, achieving expression within the empirical course of events. As he himself goes on to say: "the concept of freedom is meant to actualize in the sensible world the end proposed by its laws," and he holds it to follow that nature must be "capable of being regarded in such a way that in the conformity to law of its form it at least harmonizes with the possibility of the ends to be effectuated in it according to the laws of freedom" (ibid., p. 14). In other words, we should be able, though without violating the principle of natural causality, to consider the phenomenal domain under an aspect that would allow us to view it as amenable to the behests and aims of morality; at the very minimum, it would not present itself as being wholly alien to the fulfillment of the latter. Such an aspect is specifically connected by Kant with the notion of a purposiveness or "finality" in nature which is supplied by the faculty of judgment; and it is in these terms that he envisages the possibility of judgment's providing a "mediating concept" or requisite link between the two modes of thinking – theoretical and practical – whose spheres of application he has found it essential to distinguish.

The implications of this suggestion, which Kant relates somewhat obscurely to his conception of phenomenal nature as itself having a "supersensible substrate" or noumenal ground, only appear at a later stage of the *Critique* where it is evaluated in the light of certain qualifications to which it is held to be inevitably subject. Within the context of the Introduction, however, its chief importance lies in its being the cue for him to initiate a general account of judgment and its functions. It is necessary to speak in the plural of its role, since Kant certainly regards the power of judgment as operating at more than one level of our thought and as being relevant to discriminable philosophical concerns. That, indeed, quickly becomes apparent from the discussion which directly follows and which actually forms the centerpiece of this section of his book. For there it is issues pertinent to scientific procedure, rather than questions arising from reflection on our moral experience, that immediately occupy him. Moreover, it is with reference to such methodological considerations that he first broaches the problem of what kind of *a priori* employment may legitimately be assigned to the mental faculty he has in mind.

Kant opens his account by making a preliminary distinction between what he respectively calls the "determinant" and the "reflective" dimensions of judgment. In both it is said to involve relating universals and particulars, but the manner in which it does so is radically different in the two cases. Thus judgment is asserted to be determinant when it involves applying a "given" universal – that is, a concept or general law known or presupposed in advance – to particulars recognized as falling under it: it was in this sense that Kant referred to judgment in his first *Critique*, where the relevant universals were the formative categories and principles of the understanding and where it was simply characterized as "the faculty of subsuming under rules." He now wishes to compare that capacity with another one in which the above process is, so to speak, reversed; here it is the particular, or particulars, that is or are given, the task of judgment being taken instead to consist in seeking a universal beneath which the latter can appropriately be brought. Engaging in such a task is the business of reflective judgment, and it is with the operations of judgment so understood that Kant is presently concerned.

What does this amount to in less abstract terms? As we have seen, it was central to the standpoint Kant adopted in his critical philosophy that everything falling within the sphere of empirical reality conformed to an overall framework whose universal applicability to phenomena was transcendentally guaranteed. And, since the forms of order embodied therein were constitutive of all objective experience, it followed that they must be taken to hold of whatever occurred within the areas explored by the empirical or natural sciences. However, it was one thing to recognize the *a priori* validity for any experience of such a categorical principle as that every event must have a determining cause. It was quite another to discover *from* experience what particular causal laws or regularities actually obtain within a given domain and to try to identify their possible connections and interrelations. Neither enquiry can be undertaken without recourse to the findings of empirical observation and scrutiny, but Kant lays especial stress on the second as expressing something that he considers to be intrinsic to the very notion of scientific thinking. That is the idea of system.

The claim that "systematic unity is what . . . raises ordinary knowledge to the rank of science" had already been emphasized in the first *Critique* in connection with what was there called "the logical employment of reason." Here Kant takes it up, though with the difference that the exercise of judgment is implicitly substituted for that of theoretical reason. At the level of everyday life there are innumerable generalizations which reflect the "manifold forms of nature" and which may be said to contribute to the stock of our ordinary or common-sense knowledge of the world. Even so, a mere aggregate of such perceived regularities, however comprehensive, is never by itself sufficient to qualify as a science. To satisfy that description, and to meet theoretical requirements of the kind deemed essential to scientific understanding, it is necessary that the relevant empirical laws should be seen to constitute an interdependent and hierarchically related system; as Kant puts it, from this point of view it is essential to establish "the unity of all empirical principles under higher, though likewise empirical, principles, and thence the possibility of the systematic subordination of higher and lower" (Introduction, p. 19). And that leads him to formulate what he conceives to be a fundamental presupposition of scientific enquiry. For he goes on to maintain that to embark upon such a project is to proceed on the assumption that the multiplicity of nature's laws will be found to exhibit a unitary order which is intelligible to the human mind, so that it is as if "an understanding (though it be not ours) had supplied them for the benefit of our cognitive faculties." Nature, in other words, must be approached as though its workings were purposively adapted to our intellectual capacities and powers of comprehension, this being a conception which he specifically ascribes to reflective judgment. And in so ascribing it he at the same time contends that it amounts to an *a priori* principle possessed of an independent validity in its own right.

Kant is insistent that the distinctive status of the principle in question, together with that of subsidiary "maxims of judgement" like those which attribute economy and continuity to nature's operations, should be fully appreciated. In his own terminology, it is not "constitutive": unlike the transcendental rules imposed by the understanding, it does not represent a necessary condition of phenomenal reality as such, being prescriptively related to our modes of empirically investigating nature rather than being objectively determinative of the natural realm considered in itself. Nor, Kant holds, does it justify us in affirming the existence of an actual designer in the form of a divine or superhuman intelligence responsible for harmonizing the natural world with the needs and capacities of our finite intellects. Instead it functions purely as a principle of enquiry which, while *a priori* in the sense of being something brought to rather than derived from experience, is only "regulative" or heuristic in character. Nevertheless, although we can never justifiably claim to know that nature objectively conforms to a purposively conceived order of the sort postulated, we are subjectively obliged even so to pursue our investigations *as if* it did. For otherwise scientific thought and research, conceived as a quest after system within the *prima facie* untidy conglomeration of facts and regularities that empirically confronts us, could not be meaningfully undertaken: "were it not for this presupposition we should have no order of nature in accordance with empirical laws, and, consequently, no guiding-thread ... for an investigation of them" (Introduction, p. 25). It appears, therefore, that a view of nature invoking purposive conceptions – which, as was intimated earlier, might ultimately be found to serve judgment as a means of mediating between the spheres of freedom and natural causality – can at least be said to have received positive, if limited, endorsement within the context of scientific methodology. For here it is taken by Kant to underlie, as an indispensable regulative idea, the general project of comprehending phenomena within a unitary scheme of interconnected laws. It has, moreover, a further implication to which he briefly alludes. For it follows from the account he has given that, although as scientists we must always conduct our enquiries on the supposition that nature is adapted to meet our systematizing ambitions, we cannot in this case – as we can in the case of its conformity to the categories of the understanding – have any guarantee that it will necessarily do so; if on a particular occasion it turns out to accord with our theoretical concerns, that can only be for us a contingent result. But the attainment of every objective where failure is possible is accompanied by a feeling of pleasure. Hence whenever the scientific quest after systematic unity is crowned with success, such an achievement is bound to be pleasing: the discovery, Kant notes, "that two or more empirical heterogeneous laws of nature are allied under one principle that embraces them both is the ground of a very appreciable pleasure" (ibid., p. 27). Thus it emerges that the exercise of judgment can be viewed as being intimately connected with the experience of a certain kind of pleasurable feeling, one that has its source in the satisfaction afforded to our faculties of cognition rather than in the fulfillment of any practical aims or desires we may happen to entertain.

The above concludes what Kant has to say in the Introduction about the part played by reflective judgment in rendering the scientific enterprise possible. In effect, it constitutes a prelude that leads – admittedly somewhat obliquely – to the two central sections of his *Critique*, the first comprising a comprehensive analysis of judgment in relation to the aesthetic consciousness and the second a discussion of its role that focuses chiefly on the interpretation of organic phenomena of the sort studied in biology. At first sight these might seem to represent very dissimilar fields of interest. Nevertheless, they are both ones in which Kant again treats the idea of purposiveness as occupying a pivotal position. Furthermore, the intellectually oriented conception of pleasure he associated with the use of reflective judgment in scientific contexts may be regarded as anticipating, if only in some respects, a notion that lies at the heart of his aesthetic theory.

❧ AESTHETIC JUDGMENT AND EXPERIENCE ❧

Kant's concern with aesthetics – the subject to which Part I of the *Critique of Judgement* is exclusively devoted – was by no means new. It is true that his appreciation of art itself was limited in both scope and depth. That was especially so in the case of music, to whose appeal he appears to have been largely insensitive; yet even with regard to literature he seems to have confined himself to a somewhat narrow diet, while his lifelong residence in the city of Königsberg meant that he had practically no direct awareness of what had been achieved in the spheres of painting, sculpture, or architecture. All the same, these constraints did not prevent him from taking a considerable interest in the nature and sources of aesthetic experience. He had long been familiar with eighteenth-century writing on aesthetic matters, an essay he published in 1764 on the feeling of the beautiful and sublime suggesting that by that time he was already broadly acquainted with the contributions made by such British thinkers as Hutcheson, Addison, and Burke. He referred, however, to the piece in question as having been undertaken "more with the eye of an observer than a philosopher," and it was in fact only when he returned to the topic more than two decades later that he felt able to accord it the type of theoretical treatment it merited.

This was due to the circumstance that during the years immediately preceding the composition of the third *Critique* Kant underwent a fundamental change of mind concerning the character of aesthetic claims. Generally speaking, he regarded earlier theorists, who included men like Baumgarten, Lessing, and Hume, as having tended to favor one or other of two radically opposed approaches to what these involved. Either they viewed them as being essentially related to psychological reactions or sentiments which were subject to a purely empirical investigation, or else they interpreted them instead as answerable to conceptual criteria or rules in a way that implicitly assimilated them to the status of cognitive assertions about objective reality. While he had previously been inclined to sympathize with the first position, Kant was now of the opinion that neither of them was finally acceptable. Both distorted what was basically at issue, each – though in contrasting ways – failing to do justice to distinctive peculiarities of judgments of taste that rendered them problematic. He therefore concluded that it was necessary to provide a fresh analysis of their implications, one that was designed moreover to show that the possibility of such claims ultimately depended upon the satisfaction of certain *a priori* conditions. Given that he had at the same time come to regard aesthetic appreciation and the pleasure it afforded as representing a specific form in which reflective judgment manifested itself, this was not an unexpected aspiration.

Beauty and the problem of taste

Many of the elements central to Kant's revised account are set out in the section that opens this part of the *Critique* and is called "Analytic of the Beautiful." As its title indicates, he considers the judgments with which he is dealing to be propositions ascribing beauty to things, subdividing his discussion of them into four "moments" – quality, quantity, relation, and modality – which purport to elucidate their essential nature under distinguishable aspects. Although schematically separated, however, the different features thereby identified tend (somewhat questionably) to be spoken of as logically interdependent, and Kant also introduces additional points about their import that await clarification or elaboration further on in the book. Thus close attention to the order and detail of his exposition at this stage is liable to encounter obscurities or uncertainties that raise difficulties of interpretation. Nonetheless, and despite such complications, it is possible to view what he writes as contributing to a developing pattern of argument whose general tenor and purpose become evident as he proceeds.

Right at the beginning of the "Analytic" Kant makes it apparent that he wishes to draw a sharp distinction between aesthetic judgments and ones that are objectively cognitive; to that extent at least he is in agreement with previous theorists who adopted a basically subjectivist position. Judgments of taste are not concerned with, nor can their truth be determined by reference to, observable properties of phenomena in the sense in which those may be said to underlie claims to knowledge about how matters stand in the world. Rather, they crucially have to do with the manner in which particular representations affect us so as to produce a "feeling of pleasure or displeasure," the latter being something that "denotes nothing in the object." It follows, Kant thinks, that aesthetic judgments are ones whose "determining ground *cannot be other than subjective*," and he goes on to stress the contrast between, on the one hand, apprehending a building from a strictly cognitive standpoint and, on the other, being "conscious of this representation with an accompanying sensation of delight" (Part I, pp. 41–2). *Qua* subjective feeling, such a pleasurable reaction can contribute or add nothing to our knowledge of the building considered as an independent object of perception; it is, however, indispensable as forming the basis of a favorable judgment of taste.

It appears, then, that pronouncing something to be beautiful necessarily implies finding it to occasion an experience of satisfaction. But satisfaction of what kind? Unlike some of his predecessors, who had also assigned pleasure a central place in their accounts, Kant was not content merely to regard the notion as referring to an isolable mental state, identifiable apart from the varying conditions of its occurrence. We have seen that traces of a different approach were already discernible in the Introduction to the *Critique*; but it is only here, where Kant emphasizes the need to discriminate the type of enjoyment intrinsic to the appreciation of beauty from the kinds of satisfaction experienced in other contexts, that it is explicitly formulated and developed. Thus he insists that the delight relevant to such appreciation must be carefully distinguished from pleasures which are, as he puts it, "allied to an interest" and which presuppose the presence of determinate appetites or wants on the part of the subject. Pleasures of the latter sort fall into two main groups, respectively categorized as ones that relate to the agreeable and ones that relate to the good. So far as the agreeable is concerned, Kant singles out immediate pleasures of sense, speaking at the same time as if these involved the gratification of particular desires or inclinations. By contrast, pleasure in the good is not a matter of sensuous enjoyment, the satisfactions in question being determined instead by rational considerations of a characteristically practical nature – we may, for instance, be pleased by something's serving a certain purpose or again by its meeting certain standards or requirements we have in mind, including those prescribed by morality. Delight in the beautiful, however, stands on a completely different footing from either of the above. It derives from no specific interest, whether sensuous or practical, that we may take in the existence of a given object or state of affairs. On the contrary, our attention in this case is directed solely to what strikes us as worthy of contemplation in its own right, the pleasure afforded being dependent neither upon sensory gratification nor upon a recognized conformity to the demands of practical rationality or volition. Hence it can be said that, of the triad of delights mentioned, taste in the beautiful constitutes "the one and only disinterested and *free* delight; for with it, no interest, whether of sense or reason, extorts approval" (Part I, p. 49). It is related to "favour," as opposed to "inclination" or "respect," and "favour is the only free liking."

The view that an attitude of disinterested contemplation is essential to aesthetic appreciation is one that has acquired widespread currency since Kant's time. He may not have been alone among eighteenth-century philosophers in subscribing to it, but he was certainly the most explicit and influential of its original proponents. He saw it, moreover, as having a significant bearing upon a feature of judgments of taste that was vital to a proper interpretation of their meaning. For he thought that, if the delight we take in a particular object is believed to owe nothing to conditions or preoccupations peculiar to ourselves, we feel we have reason for claiming that it should elicit a similar delight from everyone. And it was just such a claim to general agreement that he held to be necessarily embodied in aesthetic appraisals, a claim which he initially encapsulated in the contention that "the beautiful is that which, apart from concepts, is represented as the object of a *universal* delight" (Part I, p. 50). The grounds and implications of this contention are examined and explored in the second and fourth "moments" of the "Analytic."

The fact that we are typically prone to speak as if beauty were a quality of things in the world is pertinent to what Kant has in mind. As one might expect, he implies that such a form of words is misleading insofar as it suggests that aesthetic judgments can legitimately be assimilated to objective judgments of a cognitive kind. Nevertheless, it is also revealing in pointing to a genuine analogy between the two; for the former, despite being subjectively founded on feeling, resemble the latter in that they "may be presupposed to be valid for all men." This becomes apparent, Kant thinks, if one compares the ways in which we refer to the merely pleasant or agreeable, where what we say is restricted in scope to our own private sensations, with the pronouncements we make about the beautiful, these being understood to have universal import in that they lay claim to the assent of others. Appealing to ordinary usage, Kant argues that when someone says that a particular wine is agreeable he will readily admit that he is asserting no more than that it is agreeable *to him*. There is therefore no contradiction between his judgment and a divergent judgment about its agreeableness expressed by somebody else, with the consequence that neither can properly criticize or condemn the taste of the other as "incorrect": here, as in all cases of what is found personally pleasing to our various senses, the familiar dictum "Everyone has his own taste" holds good. When, on the other hand, we turn to ascriptions of beauty, the situation markedly changes. A person cannot in the same fashion confine him- or herself to saying of, for example, a building or a poem, "It is beautiful *for me*," as if that again were just a matter of the pleasure it happened to give them. For, according to Kant,

> if it merely pleases *him*, he must not call it *beautiful*. Many things may for him possess charm or agreeableness – no one cares about that; but when he puts a thing on a pedestal and calls it beautiful, he demands the same delight from others. He judges not merely for himself, but for all men, and then speaks of beauty as if it were a property of things.
>
> (Part I, p. 52)

Such an implicit call upon the agreement of others, which Kant sharply distinguishes from a mere empirical conjecture as to how they are likely to react, explains how it is that divergent judgments of beauty, as distinct from ones concerning the agreeable, represent genuine instances of conflict. For here we express ourselves as if we were entitled to their assent; in his own words, we "formulate judgements demanding this agreement in its universality," and if it is not forthcoming we are apt to regard those who dissent as being mistaken or wrong – we do not shrug off its absence as simply a difference in individual response. To that extent, then, aesthetic appraisals may justifiably be likened to cognitive judgments about matters of fact, where a similar claim to universal acceptance is implied and where divergences of opinion give rise to imputations of error.

There, however, the apparent resemblance ends. For the validity to which aesthetic appraisals lay claim is subjective only; as such it in no way depends upon the use of concepts, whereas these play an essential role in ascribing validity to cognitive judgments about items in the world. Judgments of the latter type, in addition to presupposing the formal conditions imposed by the categories, necessarily involve subsuming what is perceptually presented under determinate empirical concepts whose applicability to the given is governed by publicly recognized rules. The validity of a particular cognitive claim is thus objectively decidable according to whether what it purports to denote and describe has been correctly characterized in a manner that conforms to the relevant rules or criteria. But it is Kant's emphatic contention that judgments of taste cannot be understood or assessed in these terms: "in forming an estimate of objects merely from concepts, all representation of beauty goes by the board," appeals to specific rules or principles as a means of compelling agreement or resolving disputes in aesthetic contexts being out of place (Part I, p. 56). If that were not so, aesthetic judgments would – as certain theorists have earnestly hoped – be "capable of being enforced by proofs." Yet their hopes are vain, disregarding as they do something that is intrinsic to the very notion of aesthetic appraisal and failing which nothing can rightfully qualify as a judgment of the kind in question. For, as Kant has already insisted, what is crucial in grounding such a judgment about a given object is the pleasure we subjectively experience when we contemplate it; we must "get a look at the object with our own eyes, just as if our delight depended on sensation." If the requisite delight is lacking we cannot properly or sincerely pronounce the thing to be beautiful, nor *a fortiori* can agreement that it is be wrung from us by others, however numerous they may be and whatever supposed "rules of beauty" laid down by distinguished critics they may invoke in their support. As he puts it elsewhere, in such circumstances I can only "take my stand on the ground that my judgement is to be one of taste, and not one of understanding or reason" (ibid., p. 140). The contrast with the claims to validity implicit in cognitive assertions could not, it would appear, be more trenchantly affirmed.

Nevertheless, and as Kant himself was well aware, the position he had reached raised a considerable problem from a philosophical point of view. If aesthetic appraisals differed from expressions of personal liking in claiming universal and – as he further maintained – necessary agreement, and if they differed from cognitive judgments in virtue of their essentially subjective orientation, the question inevitably arose as to whether, and if so in what manner, they could be said to be justifiable. It was one thing to offer an analysis that aimed to exhibit their logical and epistemological peculiarities. It was another to contend that, given such features, we were actually entitled to make them. In our ordinary practice we might speak as if we were, but with what right? When I say of an object that it is of a certain shape or dimensions, there are determinate criteria to which reference can be made;

granted that its empirically identifiable properties satisfy them, I may legitimately require general assent. When, on the other hand, I call it beautiful, it is intersubjective agreement in response, not agreement in objective description, that is centrally at issue. And here, it seems, I have ultimately to consult and rely upon my own felt reactions to the thing, "to the exclusion of rules and precepts" and without the availability of empirical or conceptual proofs. But if so, what valid grounds can I or anyone else possess for purporting to speak with a "universal voice" that lays claim to the concurrence of all? In Kant's own summary formulation of the problem, "how are judgements of taste possible?" (Part I, pp. 144–5).

An early intimation of his approach to the question he posed had already appeared when he was discussing the disinterestedness of aesthetic pleasure and when he there implied that the absence of personal idiosyncrasies in determining our delight might naturally lead us to regard it as resting on what we "may also presuppose in every other person." As originally introduced, however, this seems to be presented as a mere conjecture which is uninformative as to the content of the presupposition referred to and which in any case stands in need of independent substantiation. And much of what Kant wrote in subsequent sections may be interpreted as being designed to provide such substantiation. Thus he went on to argue that a careful examination of the inner nature and sources of our pleasure in the beautiful showed it to be due to the satisfaction of subjective conditions of judgment which must indeed be assumed to be universally present in every human being. Hence if we could be sure that the pleasure we experienced was produced in accordance with these conditions, we should in fact be entitled to call upon the agreement of others in the manner distinctive of judgments of taste. Although his reasoning in support of this conclusion takes an intricate and on occasions bewilderingly circuitous course, the salient points covered are not hard to discern.

What, then, are the "subjective conditions" to which allusion has been made? Kant's answer derives from his faculty psychology and turns on something he calls "the free play of the cognitive powers." In the account of perceptual knowledge originally given in the *Critique of Pure Reason* and briefly recalled in the present work, such cognition was portrayed as involving the operations of both imagination and understanding. The imagination, as "the faculty of intuitions or representations," holds together and synthesizes items of the sensory manifold so as to allow them to be subsumed by the understanding under appropriate concepts; in this connection, therefore, it can be said to be at the service of the understanding, "in harness" to the latter in its task of categorizing and conceptualizing the presentations of sense. Now it is Kant's contention that the same two faculties are also operative at the level of aesthetic experience. Here, however, there can be no question of there being a specific cognitive purpose which requires the subordination of the imagination to the ends of the understanding; in consequence, the roles they respectively perform do not conform to this pattern. Instead they should be regarded as engaging or meshing together in a fashion that enlivens or "quickens" both while setting "irksome" constraints upon neither: in the ideal case, that takes the form of a harmonious accord, a mutually satisfying interaction whereby each faculty is proportionately attuned to the other in an unconstrained "entertainment of the mental powers." The resultant "feeling of free play" is one of pleasure, and it is of such pleasure that we are conscious when our experience is of an authentically aesthetic kind.

Kant believed that the above account provided the basis for a "deduction," or justification, of the intersubjective validity to which judgments of taste laid claim. For with those the delight involved was not dependent upon merely contingent capacities for sensuous enjoyment which notoriously varied from individual to individual. On the contrary, it had been shown to presuppose the operation of intellectual faculties that must be presumed to be identical in all human beings as *a priori* conditions if communicable knowledge was to be possible; hence it was pleasure of a type which everybody, in appropriate circumstances and undistracted by irrelevant considerations, could rightfully be expected to share. Kant indicated, moreover, that the position he had advanced had an additional consequence to which he attached great importance, a consequence that concerned the aspects under which an object must strike us if it was to produce the requisite response. In explaining what this consisted in, he introduced the notion of "formal finality" or "purposiveness without a purpose" (*Zweckmässigkeit ohne Zweck*).

How are these curious expressions to be understood? At first sight Kant might be taken to mean that, in ascribing beauty to products of nature, we are subjectively disposed to think of them as somehow purposively adapted to our faculties but without being thereby justified in asserting this to be actually the case. And that is suggestive of a partial analogy with what he wrote in the Introduction about the conception of nature presupposed by reflective judgment in relation to scientific enquiry. But while in contexts involving natural beauty he is apt to speak in this vein, he also makes it clear that he has something further in mind. For he also argues that for pleasure of the relevant kind to be possible our response must be occasioned by the perceptual *form* an object displays, this form being experienced as manifesting a self-subsistent coherence or order which is apprehended neither as serving an assignable objective end or utilitarian purpose nor as conforming to some prior notion of what the thing is supposed or intended to be. The point is elaborated in a celebrated distinction drawn between what he respectively calls "pure" or "free" beauty and "dependent" or "adherent" beauty: the first, he writes, "presupposes no concept of what the object should be; the second does presuppose such a concept and, with it, an answering perfection of the object" (Part I, p. 72). Thus if we appreciate a natural product in terms of its suitability to its biological function or a human product in terms of its meeting requirements specific to objects of that type, we are assessing it from the standpoint of dependent beauty and any pleasure we derive therefrom partakes of what Kant earlier referred to as being pleasure in the good. In judging something as an instance of free beauty, on the other hand, we are concerned solely with what "pleases by its form," the form in question presenting an appearance of design or purposive organization that is satisfying on its own account and without any reference to identifiable objective ends or preassigned specifications. The latter would introduce considerations of a conceptual or cognitive character, whereas it is essential to formal relationships of the sort proper to a "pure" judgment of taste that they should not be reducible to some "universally applicable formula" and that they should be grasped and enjoyed in a way that is altogether free from the constraint of determinate rules.

In giving examples of objects that impress us with the requisite pleasingness of form, Kant selects as "beauties of nature" certain birds, flowers, and crustaceans; in general, indeed, it is to natural products that he tends to accord precedence throughout this part of his text. But he also illustrates what he has in view by mentioning various human artifacts. Thus abstract "designs à la grecque" and wallpaper patterns are said to be "free beauties" inasmuch as they have "no intrinsic meaning" or representative function – "they represent nothing – no object under a definite concept"; and he further asserts that art forms such as painting and sculpture, where "the *design* is what is essential," and musical works, where "composition" has an analogous status, are likewise capable of disposing the mind to the harmonious interplay of the faculties that is productive of aesthetic satisfaction. Whether his emphasis on exclusively formal features followed from, or was even wholly consistent with, his overall account of the character and grounds of judgments of taste may be questioned. It cannot, however, be denied that his asseverations on that particular score have frequently been seen as anticipating certain substantive critical doctrines which were to achieve considerable prominence more than a hundred years after he wrote. The conception of visual art as pre-eminently a matter of "significant form," popularized early in the twentieth century by British writers like Roger Fry and Clive Bell, has often been cited in this connection. It is noteworthy, too, that the American critic and advocate of formalism, Clement Greenberg, later explicitly referred to him as a precursor of modernist theory. Such comparisons and parallels are understandable enough if viewed in the context of some of the claims Kant put forward in the "Analytic of the Beautiful." Nevertheless, they accord less comfortably with what he had to say when, in the second of the two main sections into which Part I of the *Critique of Judgement* is divided, he effectively widened the scope of his investigation of aesthetic experience.

The sublime and fine art

Both the title of this lengthy second section and the manner of its organization have – not surprisingly – troubled commentators. Kant called it "Analytic of the Sublime," thereby giving the impression that he would be centrally concerned with sublimity considered as a distinguishable dimension of the aesthetic consciousness. But the heading chosen turns out to be misleadingly restrictive. Not only does the implied contrast with beauty lead him back into picking up and elaborating on matters regarding the status and justification of judgments of taste that had already been alluded to in the preceding section. He also goes on to undertake an extended examination of the nature and value of artistic achievement which reaches far beyond anything suggested by his previous, rather cursory remarks on that topic. And while it is possible to descry some connection between the treatment of art he is now concerned to provide and his treatment of the sublime, the links discernible remain at best tenuous. Following the order of Kant's own account, we shall begin with the latter.

Kant's interest in sublimity as a distinctive aesthetic category dates back to his 1764 essay on its relation to beauty which was mentioned earlier on. As in the case of the beautiful, however, his approach to the sublime underwent a profound transformation, the setting in which his observations were originally framed being replaced by one that eschewed "merely empirical" considerations of the kind adduced by Edmund Burke in his famous study of the subject in favor of a "transcendental exposition" that involved conceptions deriving from Kant's mature critical system. In giving such an exposition, he makes it clear that he does not wish to deny the presence of significant similarities in our appreciation of the two. Thus he claims at the outset that both are "pleasing on their own account" and without reference to any further end. Moreover, judgments of the sublime are like pure judgments of beauty in not presupposing the application of any determinate concept and in the fact that, while being singular and noncognitive, they nonetheless lay claim to universal validity. Yet, despite these affinities, there are important differences which Kant is at pains to point out. In his eyes, they are sufficiently impressive to make an independent explanation of how sublimity can figure as a recognizable aspect of our aesthetic experience seem an imperative requirement.

The need for such an explanation becomes plain when we compare the satisfaction we take in the beautiful with that aroused by the sublime. As has been seen, the former is held to involve the apprehension of a formal or self-subsistent purposiveness in objects which engages our faculties of imagination and understanding in harmonious free play. Furthermore, so far as natural beauty is concerned we are elevated by the thought of nature as being in some sense teleologically ordered to elicit this pleasurable response, "a finality in its form making the object appear, as it were, preadapted to our power of judgement" (Part I, p. 91). In the case of the sublime, however, nature confronts us in quite another light. For what is striking here is the circumstance that we assign sublimity to natural effects which present themselves to us as limitlessly vast or chaotic in a way that may be totally devoid of form. And this is connected by Kant with additional points of difference. Whereas what we find beautiful in nature is experienced as being happily attuned to our mental faculties, natural products of the kind typically referred to as sublime are said to "contravene the ends of our power of judgement"; they overwhelm our capacity for sensuously taking them in, thereby constituting what he calls an "outrage on the imagination" rather than anything conducive to its unconstrained accord with the understanding. It follows (Kant thinks) that sublimity, unlike beauty, is incorrectly ascribed to the phenomena themselves; for how can what is apprehended as "inherently contra-final" be noted with an expression of approval? Instead, we should properly attribute it to the sentiments and attitudes of mind they evoke in us, these being essentially associated with the presence of rational ideas that exceed the bounds of sensory presentation. As he himself puts it: "the sublime, in the strict sense of the word, cannot be contained in any sensuous form, but rather concerns ideas of reason" (ibid., p. 92).

Kant's stipulations concerning the use of the term, and the accompanying contrast drawn with beauty, consort somewhat oddly with what he says elsewhere about the grounds and subjective orientation of aesthetic judgments in general. Given that – as he here allows – objects can properly be called beautiful in virtue of their aptitude for affecting our faculties in certain ways, why should not the same considerations apply to the phenomena we call sublime, even if these are said to affect them in a radically dissimilar manner? In fact, it is his reference to reason and its ideas that is crucial in the present context and that chiefly underlies the distinction he wishes to make. For, insofar as particular natural phenomena cause us to entertain conceptions that outrun our powers of imaginative representation, they arouse us to a consciousness of reason as an independent faculty which leads us "to esteem as small in comparison with [its] ideas . . . everything which for us is great in nature as an object of sense." And that, Kant claims, helps to explain the pleasurable exaltation induced by the sublime, springing as it does from a presentiment of "our superiority over nature" that awakens us to our rational vocation and makes the mind "sensible of the sublimity of the sphere of its own being." Accurately construed, therefore, sublimity "does not reside in any of the things of nature, but only in our own mind" (Part I, p. 114).

The invocation of reason as a separate "supersensible" faculty, which according to his previous *Critiques* is capable of both a theoretical and a practical exercise, underpins the account Kant goes on to give of two different modes wherein the above presentiment is held to manifest itself and which he refers to respectively as the "mathematically" and the "dynamically" sublime. In the case of the first, it is the sheer magnitude and formlessness of what appears before us that is paramount, conveying a perceptually intractable impression of unlimited extent and absence of boundary. But the failure of the imagination to encompass within a comprehensive intuition what is thus intimated to it, and the consequent dissatisfaction we feel in the face of its inadequacy, is counterbalanced by the fact that we are able to grasp in *thought* the notion of the infinite as a totality or "absolute whole," the latter being an indeterminate idea ascribable to reason in its theoretical capacity. Hence the very limitations displayed by the imagination in its fruitless endeavors to measure up to this idea at the level of sensuous representation serve to highlight by contrast the supremacy of our rational powers, indicating that we are endowed with "a faculty of mind transcending every standard of sense" (Part I, p. 102). A broadly analogous conclusion is reached in Kant's discussion of the dynamically sublime, although here the focus is on reason in its practical employment and what he writes assumes a distinctively ethical character. Whereas in the preceding case it was the vast dimensions of certain phenomena that impressed us, it is now the apparently "irresistible might" exhibited by such natural occurrences as violent storms and volcanic eruptions. Like Burke before him, Kant insists that the aesthetic appreciation of nature under this threatening aspect, which brings home "a recognition of our physical helplessness," is only possible when we view it from a position of safety; on the other hand, he fundamentally diverges from his predecessor in the interpretation he offers of the satisfaction involved. That is not (as Burke had implied) due to the moderation of our sentiments which the absence of personal danger produces and which thereby allows us to find pleasantly invigorating and stimulating what would otherwise be experienced as disagreeably frightening. On the contrary, Kant holds its actual source to lie once again in a sense of the superiority of our rational powers to those of sensibility. This time, however, it is not a theoretical capacity to surpass in thought the limits of the sensuously oriented imagination that he has in mind. Rather, it is a supposed ability at the level of our practical life to respond to hostile or menacing circumstances in such a manner as to withstand the pressures of sensuous inclination. The dynamically sublime, in other words, awakens us to the conception of ourselves as self-determining moral agents who can rise above the solicitations of sensuous impulse and make our conduct conform instead to the principles and ends laid down by practical reason. Thus in experiencing it we are conscious of being more than mere creatures of sensibility – here conceived as a susceptibility to natural desires or fears – and are raised to a presentiment of the pre-eminence of our rational stature. This, moreover, is something we may properly expect of all human beings in virtue of their assumed capacity for moral feeling. It follows, therefore, that judgments of the sublime, like judgments of the beautiful, may rightfully command general assent, although they do so on different grounds.

The emphasis on pride in the supremacy of reason in Kant's theory of the sublime, together with the prominent place he assigned to moral considerations, may not be felt to conform very happily to our intuitive understanding of the concept as applied in aesthetic contexts. In tackling the problems it poses, however, he at least showed a novel insight into their complexity, as well as demonstrating a salutary readiness to extend the range of his enquiry beyond the somewhat narrow limits suggested by his initial analysis of taste. And a similar sensitivity to the variety of forms that aesthetic experience can take emerges in the passages he specifically devoted to the importance and value of art. In his earlier treatment of beauty he had tended to accord paradigmatic status to natural objects, with the accompanying implication that the aesthetic quality of works of art was estimable in comparable terms. Here, by contrast, it is the distinguishing features of the latter that he goes out of his way to stress.

One such feature concerns intentionality. Kant does not retract his original claim that to be beautiful natural objects must convey an impression of formal design, even appearing to us as if they had been "chosen as it were with an eye to our taste" (Part I, p. 217). But that is very different from appreciating something in the knowledge that it is the product of *actual* deliberation, consciously made with a view to affecting us in a manner that will be found satisfying in its own right. Artistic works are intentional in this full-blooded sense and realizing them to be so is vital to their appraisal – "a product of fine art must be recognized to be art and not nature." That is not to suggest that they should look artificially contrived or "laboured"; rather, they must be "clothed *with the aspect* of nature" in not seeming to owe their creation to an obtrusive observance of constrictive or "mechanical" rules. Thus an unstudied "pleasingness of form," consonant with the conditions of taste, remains a necessary component of artistic worth. But it is not – Kant now insists – sufficient. Acknowledgment of the intentional dimension of art requires us to take account of a further factor, one that relates to the content of a work or to what it is meant to represent.

Reference to the relevance of representational considerations in evaluating artistic achievement certainly constitutes a significant departure from the restrictively formalist preoccupations evident in some of Kant's previous pronouncements on the subject. Yet it would be wrong to conclude from what he writes about artistic representation that he simply had in mind the mimetic reproduction of natural phenomena in another medium, however elegantly or harmoniously that might be accomplished. For his discussion of it is integrally connected with the role he ascribed to "genius" in art, this being described as completely opposed to the "spirit of imitation" and as involving capacities additional to merely technical skills that can be picked up and learned through academic training. Genius, according to Kant, is an esentially original and creative power, exhibiting itself among other things in the portrayal and expression of what he termed "aesthetic ideas": taste may impart a universally pleasing appearance to art, but it is genius, as the source of and ability to communicate such ideas, that animates genuine examples of fine art with "soul" or "spirit." Thus questions concerning the nature of aesthetic ideas and the manner in which they can be presented by artists in a publicly accessible form assume a critical importance in his account. How should what he says about them be interpreted?

In looking for an answer, it is worth noting some remarks Kant makes about their relation to ones of the kind that figured in his theory of the sublime. Ideas like those of absolute totality or transcendental freedom were "indemonstrable concepts of reason" to which nothing could objectively correspond at the level of possible experience and for which a "commensurate intuition" could therefore never be given. Aesthetic ideas, it is now suggested, may be appropriately viewed as constituting the counterpart of such purely rational conceptions. They resemble the latter in not belonging to the sphere of objective cognition, but they do so for a diametrically opposite reason. For what are here under consideration are representations or intuitions of the imagination "for which an adequate concept can never be found." Kant elaborates on the point as follows:

By an aesthetic idea I mean that representation of the imagination which induces much thought, yet without the possibility of any definite thought whatever, i.e. *concept*, being adequate to it, and which language, consequently, can never get quite on level terms with or render completely intelligible.

(Part I, pp. 175–6)

It appears, then, that insofar as works of art are understood to embody aesthetic ideas, their inner content can never be finally or exhaustively articulated in alternative terms. The multiplicity of thoughts and associations conveyed by such works overflows the boundaries of determinate formulation and definition, outrunning the resources of conceptual or linguistic expression.

Kant develops and illustrates this theme in subsequent passages. He does not dispute that, in seeking to give sensuous shape to the ideas that inspire them, artists are obliged to draw upon material which is furnished by perception and which is itself susceptible to objective description. He stresses, however, that they do not do this in a merely imitative spirit, but rather in a fashion that imbues familiar phenomena with an unfamiliar meaning or symbolic resonance, thereby "animating the mind by opening out for it a prospect of kindred representations stretching beyond its ken." Far from simply copying nature, art "surpasses" it, seizing upon the elusive intimations and fragmentary aspects of ordinary life and experience and "bodying them forth to sense with a completeness of which nature affords no parallel." Thus imagination, regarded in the context of artistic activity as a productive rather than a reproductive capacity, can be affirmed to be "a powerful agent for creating, as it were, a second nature out of the material supplied to it by actual nature" (Part I, p. 176): it does not so much mirror the everyday world as transform it. It must be admitted that Kant's allusions to the imaginative faculty are at times confusing, and not least in the apparently very different status accorded to it here from the one he typically assigned to it in his treatment of the sublime – he is even prepared to speak of it in its artistic employment as "emulating the display of reason in its attainment of a maximum." But notwithstanding such difficulties and obscurities, his suggestive account of the imaginative potential of aesthetic ideas may be seen in retrospect to have been at once arresting and seminal. In emphasizing the revelatory though conceptually "inexponible" nature of specifically artistic representation, he anticipated in outline approaches followed by both Schiller and Hegel, particularly the latter's detailed portrayal of the various arts as modes of expression in which thought and sensuousness are to be found indissolubly united or fused.

The aesthetic and the ethical

It was indeed Hegel who, referring to Kant's aesthetic theory as a whole, described him as having spoken "the first rational word" on the subject. Whatever Hegel himself may have meant by this, there can be no question that Kant's overall contribution proved to be of cardinal importance for the future development of aesthetics as a separate branch of philosophy. Rich in content and comprehensive in scope, it stands out as a historical landmark in the field, bringing into view considerations whose deeper significance had eluded the notice of earlier writers and whose ramifications have continued to haunt later ones. Furthermore, by underlining though not finally resolving problems unique to judgments of taste, it did much to encourage the notion that the aesthetic consciousness forms an autonomous or self-contained sphere, irreducible to other areas of human experience and demanding independent investigation in its own right.

Yet while Kant's influence in promoting such an outlook seems incontrovertible, a certain qualification regarding his own position is in order. It may be true that he never diverged from his fundamental claim that aesthetic judgments can no more be assimilated to practical or moral judgments than they can be to those of cognition or mere sensory liking. However, that did not prevent him from suggesting in a variety of places and contexts that connections exist between our capacities for aesthetic appreciation and broader concerns relating to our lives and conduct. This was clearly evident in his analysis of the dynamically sublime, with its pronounced ethical overtones. But discernible variations on the same general theme occur elsewhere. At one point, for example, he contends that the cultivation of taste and the communication of the delights it affords play a noteworthy role in social development, exerting a civilizing impact upon human behavior and intercourse. And at others he draws attention to analogies between the aesthetic and the moral points of view: in both cases we can be said to prescind from a preoccupation with personal gratification or advantage, regarding things instead from a universally shareable perspective; insofar as taste is conducive to such a mental state, it makes "the transition from the charm of sense to habitual moral interest possible without too violent a leap" (Part I, p. 225). Finally, Kant indicates that a concern with the beauty of nature – though not, it transpires, with that of art – is linked in a special way to our aspirations as moral beings. His point seems to turn on the often reiterated idea that natural beauties strike us as if they were designed to accord with and satisfy our mental powers in the enjoyment of aesthetic experience, intimations of such an apparent harmony between mind and nature being said to awaken an "interest . . . akin to the moral" (ibid., p. 160).

What he writes on this score is admittedly condensed and somewhat elusive, but he can partly be taken to mean that the interest in question derives from the notion of nature's being capable of displaying a comparable accordance with our ethical ideals and ends. If so, the moral significance he wishes to attach to the appreciation of natural beauty differs markedly from – though without necessarily conflicting with – the moral import he attributed to our experience of the dynamically sublime. For the latter was essentially related to our assumed ability as self-determining rational agents to rise above the promptings of natural inclination at the level of inward choice and intention. Here, on the other hand, it is the conception of nature's ultimately harmonizing with the fulfillment of ethical ideas and projects at the level of external reality that is relevant. And that may recall what Kant wrote about the faculty of judgment in general when, at the start of the third *Critique*, he contemplated its playing a mediating role in relating our moral aspirations to the world. Nor need this seeming echo of his wider preoccupations surprise us. Although at times only faintly in evidence, they were seldom – if ever – altogether absent from his mind.

TELEOLOGICAL JUDGMENT AND EXPLANATION

In Part II of the *Critique of Judgement* Kant takes leave of aesthetics and returns to topics in the philosophy of science, the notion of purposiveness as "the characteristic concept of the reflective judgement" once again being prominent in what he has to say. Even so, he is at pains to point out that the issues that now occupy him must be distinguished from those he was dealing with when considering the fundamental presuppositions of scientific enquiry in the Introduction. Thus it was one thing to ascribe purposiveness to nature in the sense of conceiving the natural sphere to conform to a "logical system" of empirical laws which was adapted to our cognitive capacities and powers of comprehension. It was another to postulate or assume the applicability of purposive conceptions to particular types of *objects* falling within the natural realm. And it is to the specific question of whether, and if so in what manner, it may be justifiable to interpret from a scientific standpoint certain phenomena in purposive or teleological terms that the present part of the *Critique* is to a large extent directed. As quickly emerges, the particular phenomena Kant has in view are living or organic beings of the sort studied in biology.

Internal purposiveness and the concept of an organism

Generally speaking, and given the preconceptions of the age in which Kant was writing, the belief that organic phenomena presented special problems for the development of science is not hard to understand. The adoption of mechanical principles of explanation, founded upon the notion of "matter in motion" and according to which natural objects and events were universally subject to quantitatively determinable causal regularities, appeared acceptable enough when applied to the inanimate domain; by the close of the eighteenth century, indeed, the Newtonian framework of material particles and forces seemed already to have been triumphantly vindicated through the formulation of experimentally confirmed hypotheses whose explanatory power extended over a very wide range. When, however, it was proposed that the same approach should be transferred to the sphere of the organic the position looked a good deal less straightforward. For living things possessed features that apparently distinguished them sharply from inanimate entities and substances. In particular, they exhibited a degree of internal organization and complexity which made it difficult to regard them as the merely contingent products of "blind" causal forces or mechanisms and which suggested instead that it would be more apposite to invoke notions like design and purposive function in accounting for their structure. Thus a division tended to open up between those who steadfastly maintained that in the final analysis all phenomena, animate and inanimate alike, were explicable in mechanistic terms and those who claimed that the phenomena of organic life required for their proper interpretation a quite different set of ideas.

The broad outlines of this emerging controversy were already clearly visible in Kant's time. Teleological conceptions might have been effectively extruded from the sphere of physics, but the belief that they were nonetheless requisite in some form for the understanding of living things found adherents in contemporary biology. Moreover, quasi-Aristotelian ways of thinking about nature had been revived at a more general level by the philosopher J.G. Herder whose principal work, *Ideas toward a Philosophy of the History of Mankind*, was severely criticized by Kant himself on its publication in 1784. That such views impinged crucially upon his own position will be evident from what has already been said about the epistemological theses he had advanced in his first *Critique*. For according to these the very possibility of objective experience and knowledge was dependent upon the application of *a priori* concepts and rules in unifying the data of sense, the latter being held to correspond in essentials to the basic principles of Newtonian science. It appeared to follow, therefore, that nature was universally subject to regularities that conformed to the accepted paradigm of scientific explanation: in Kant's words, "appearances must . . . be capable of complete causal explanation in terms of other appearances in accordance with natural laws" (*Critique of Pure Reason*, B 574). Claims of this sort, suggestive of an unqualified commitment to the tenets of the Newtonian scheme, might thus lead one to suppose that he would have ranged himself firmly with those who argued that organisms, no less than the rest of the natural world, were susceptible to mechanistic modes of explanation, and that he would have set his face against any attempt to reintroduce – even within a limited field of enquiry – conceptions that apparently harked back to an earlier epoch of scientific thinking. In fact, however, he followed another route; the opinions on the subject he eventually arrived at were altogether more complex, with reflective judgment being invoked to resolve the matters in dispute.

At a preliminary stage of his approach to what he calls "objective finality in nature," Kant distinguishes between the notions of "external" and "internal" purposiveness. With reference to the first of these, he points out that various natural products may be regarded as being designed either for our own benefit or else for the use and advantage of other living creatures. For example, grass may be said to exist in order to support herbivores like sheep or cattle, and the existence of the latter may in turn be viewed as answering to the needs of human beings. But although we may be led to look at things in this light if we make certain further assumptions, we are in no sense bound to do so. Taken simply by themselves, we can causally account for and sufficiently explain such externally adaptive relationships without recourse to any teleological ideas.

By contrast, understanding the internal structure and development of organic phenomena seems positively to demand their employment. Thus we find it not merely natural but necessary to treat a living object like a plant or an animal as being something of which "every part is thought as *owing* its presence to the *agency* of all the remaining parts, and also as existing *for the sake of the others* and of the whole, that is as an instrument" (Part II, p. 21). So conceived, an organism can be termed a "natural end" (*Naturzweck*), an entity whose inner constitution appears to be governed by an idea of what it is meant to be or become and whose component elements variously contribute to this purpose in a fashion suggestive of the operations of a constructive intelligence; indeed, the very notion of living things as "organized beings" may be felt to carry this implication. Moreover, in the case of internal as opposed to external purposiveness, Kant insists that objects which exemplify it are such that we are unable to imagine how their nature and production could be accounted for in terms of "mechanical principles" alone. It is impossible for human reason to hope to understand the generation of even "a blade of grass" from merely mechanical causes: "such insight," he roundly declares, "we must absolutely deny to mankind" (ibid., p. 54).

Pronouncements of the above kind strongly suggest that it is primarily to teleological modes of thought rather than to ones presupposing the operations of physical causality that we should look when investigating organic phenomena – a proposal encapsulated in Kant's dictum that an organism is a natural product in which "nothing is in vain, without an end, or to be ascribed to a blind mechanism of nature" (Part II, p. 25). Hence we may gain the impression that he was prepared after all, and despite expectations to the contrary, to side with the anti-mechanist camp in biology. And on the face of it this would seem to entail his accepting a dualism regarding our understanding of the empirical world which was hard, if not impossible, to reconcile with his own stated epistemological commitments. It turns out, however, that he only subscribed to it in a form that imposed important restrictions upon both the significance and the actual implications of the teleological principles involved.

Teleology and empirical science

In the first place, Kant was concerned to emphasize that similarities discernible between natural organisms and purposively constructed human artifacts must not be allowed to obscure no less striking differences. An artificial contrivance such as a watch fulfills its function because the parts of which it is composed interact by moving one another in ways that have been independently determined by its maker. Living phenomena, by contrast, are apprehended as "self-organizing" entities, endowed with a "formative power" (*bildende Kraft*) which remains for us basically mysterious in its workings and for which no close analogue exists among the products of human art or technique. The various components of an organism are interrelated in a distinctively intimate and reciprocal manner, both "producing" and "sustaining" one another: for example, if an essential part of a tree is damaged or destroyed, the deficiency is apt to be repaired or made good "by the aid of the rest" so as to preserve the life of the whole to which they severally belong. Thus in considering the role of the concepts of design and purpose in biology it is necessary to recognize the constraints that govern their meaningful use in that context.

Second, Kant indicates that in any event teleological principles of the sort employed in the interpretation of biological processes ultimately possess no more than a regulative status. In this view, to be sure, they are indispensable to our thought about these, affording modes of understanding and suggesting fruitful lines of enquiry at a point where the resources of explanation in terms of efficient causality seem to fail us. And that, indeed, may also encourage us to enlarge the field of their application to nature as a whole, adopting a perspective on reality wherein it is assumed that "everything in the world is good for something or other; nothing in it is in vain" (Part II, p. 28). In conformity with the reservations he has already expressed about attributions of "external" purposiveness, however, Kant is careful not to ascribe to such an extended employment of teleological conceptions the indispensability he thinks these have for us within the more limited sphere of organic phenomena; we are not obliged to contemplate nature in general in this way. Nevertheless he holds that, even in the case of the organic sphere, to say that we find it subjectively necessary to bring purposive notions to its interpretation is not to say that these can be accredited with objective validity. It is one thing to assert that we are intellectually so constituted that we cannot render organic phenomena intelligible to ourselves other than by treating them *as if* they were – in some admittedly mysterious sense – designed or organized to accord with a preconceived idea or intention regarding their final form. It is another to assert this to be so as a matter of objective fact, their possibility being dependent upon the agency of a nonhuman intelligence or creative mind. The latter, according to Kant, is something we could never justify or prove: strictly speaking, "we do not *observe* the ends in nature as designed" but "only read this conception into the facts as a guide to judgement in its reflection upon the products of nature" (ibid., p. 53). Here as elsewhere, in other words, we occupy the standpoint of reflective judgment, operating with heuristic concepts and principles that play a vital role in directing our thought about nature but without being in a position to affirm the actual existence of a supernatural designer or "author of the world."

In effect, and whatever concessions he may have made to the opponents of mechanism in biology, Kant did not abandon the conviction that explanation of a cognitively acceptable kind must conform to the mechanical paradigm. It is noteworthy, for instance, that he consistently speaks of our "estimating" (*beurteilen*) organic processes through teleological conceptions, not of our explaining them thereby. Moreover, he reiterates the point that we should always press the search for mechanical causes as far as we can, since if we do not follow this procedure there can be "no knowledge of nature in the true sense at all." And while he undoubtedly asserts, quite categorically, that we can never hope to arrive at purely physical explanations of organic phenomena, he stresses that it would even so be "presumptuous" dogmatically to conclude that some "mechanism of nature," sufficient to account for them, does not in fact exist. That is something which we have simply no means of knowing; the most that can reasonably be affirmed is that such a possibility lies beyond the limits of human comprehension.

Despite its considerable ingenuity, Kant's attempt to do justice to the rival claims of mechanism and teleology is not free from difficulty. It is true that at one point he writes as if the "antinomy" to which these approaches may be said to give rise can be surmounted by understanding each of them to be endorsing a particular methodological "maxim" for the investigation of nature rather than a principle purportively constitutive of its objective character. Thus a rule enjoining us invariably to seek causal explanations as far as we are able is not inconsistent with a rule legitimizing a resort to purposive interpretations when "a proper occasion" presents itself: to that extent the two standpoints can be reconciled. One trouble with this proposal, however, is that the causal principle was originally portrayed by Kant *as* being constitutive; to treat it now as having no more than the regulative status he has ascribed to its teleological counterpart would represent an apparent departure from that position. Furthermore, it is one thing to assert of certain phenomena, which at a given stage of enquiry seem to resist physical or mechanical explanation, that they may be accounted for instead along teleological lines. It is a different and more questionable matter to say of them that a complete causal explanation must forever be beyond our reach; indeed, the subsequent history of the biological sciences makes such a contention look somewhat bizarre. Even so, Kant certainly implied that, insofar as we found ourselves obliged to understand the functional structure of organisms in purposive terms, it was impossible for us to regard them as the mere products of what he himself called "blind efficient causes"; nor was he alone among his contemporaries in feeling that the two conceptions *prima facie* excluded one another in their application. Consequently, and notwithstanding the qualifications he introduced, he appears to have been committed to holding that we were precluded from fully assimilating organic phenomena to the framework within which all objective knowledge and genuinely scientific explanation are set. And it was perhaps partly a recognition of the problems this ostensibly presents that led him to entertain the notion of a possible understanding, "higher than the human," which would comprehend the mechanical and teleological principles as cohering within a single uniting principle that transcended them: "if this were not so," he writes, "they could not both enter consistently into the same survey of nature" (Part II, p. 70). He argues, however, that such a principle can only be referred to what, as the supersensible or noumenal ground of the phenomenal realm, lies outside the range of empirical representation. Thus so far as we ourselves are concerned it must be one of which, from a theoretical point of view, we are unable to form "the slightest positive determinate conception."

⤙ TELEOLOGY, MORALITY, AND GOD ⤚

Kant's contention that the supersensible constitutes a realm necessarily inaccessible to human knowledge and understanding of a theoretical kind is one that recurs in the Appendix which forms the long concluding section of the *Critique of Judgement*. This comprises a careful and wide-ranging discussion of the conceivable relevance of teleological interpretations of the natural world to the claims of theology. It is true that the question of whether the apparent evidence of purposiveness in nature could be invoked in support of such claims had already been broached in the *Critique of Pure Reason*, where it was examined along with other attempts that had classically been made to establish the existence and character of God from a speculative standpoint. Kant clearly felt, however, that the comprehensive investigation he had now undertaken of the general status and limitations of teleological judgment in relation to natural science warranted his embarking upon a more extended analysis than hitherto of the issues which the so-called "argument from design" involved. Furthermore, such an analysis seemed especially called for in the light of what he had written in his second *Critique* concerning the possibility of justifying belief in God from a moral or practical point of view as opposed to a theoretical one.

As has been seen, Kant specifically denied the legitimacy of deriving theological conclusions from the fact that we find ourselves subjectively obliged to interpret certain natural products in teleological terms. It may be that the best sense we can make of such apparently purposive phenomena as organisms is by thinking of them as the creations of "a supreme intelligence"; he implies, indeed, that this is the case. But at the same time he reiterates the point that such an hypothesis is devoid of objective authority and that its import must instead be comprehended heuristically; it can never do more than

> point to this cause in the interests of the reflective judgement
> engaged in surveying nature, its purpose being to guide our
> estimate of the things in the world by means of the idea of such
> a ground, as a regulative principle, in a manner adapted to our
> human understanding.

(Part II, pp. 75–6)

The latter claim certainly accords with his critical objections to any theoretical attempt to transcend the limits of possible experience. Yet he thinks that, even if his strictures on that score were disregarded, other important difficulties would remain. By no means all natural phenomena impress us as bearing the marks of design; nor is it true that everything that occurs in the empirical world is *prima facie* easy to reconcile with the thought that nature in general has issued from the hand of a wise and beneficent creator. It would seem, in fact, that the most we could reasonably hope to establish by following this path would be the formative operations of a suprahuman "artistic understanding" (*Kunstverstand*) sufficient to account for "miscellaneous ends" of the sort natural organisms exemplify. But that is a far cry from being entitled to infer that the world as a whole is the product of a presiding moral divinity with an overarching end or purpose in view. And if we confine ourselves to the theoretical contemplation of nature alone it is unclear how such an inference could conceivably be justified. There is nothing in the natural order when considered solely by itself which can properly be held to qualify as an unconditioned or final end of creation capable of endowing it with meaning and value in our eyes.

The various weaknesses of the argument from design, referred to by Kant himself as "physico-theology," do not however require us to suppose that no such ultimate end can be identified. This becomes apparent if we turn aside from theoretical considerations and approach the matter from the standpoint of practical reason as exhibited in our moral experience. When looked at in that perspective it is evident that man emerges as the only possible candidate – "without man . . . the whole of creation would be a mere wilderness, a thing in vain, and have no final end" (Part II, p. 108). In our capacity as moral agents we are aware of having a status which sets us apart from the rest of the natural order and which uniquely assigns to our existence intrinsic worth. For it is a presupposition of the moral consciousness that, regarded as rational beings possessing freedom of choice and volition, we are able to act under laws and pursue objectives that originate, not in nature, but in ourselves. In Kant's words:

> Only in man, and only in him as the individual being to whom the moral law applies, do we find unconditional legislation in respect of ends. This legislation, therefore, is what alone qualifies him to be a final end to which entire nature is teleologically subordinated.
>
> (Ibid., p. 100)

How is this supposed to be relevant to the issue that physico-theology tries but fails to resolve – the existence of God as "the supreme cause of nature and its attributes"? It is Kant's contention that, while a theoretical appeal to our experience of nature cannot legitimize theological claims, there is a sense in which a recognition of what is essentially involved in our vocation as moral agents may be said to do so. Following the line of thought articulated in his second *Critique*, he argues that practical reason sets before us as an *a priori* obligation the project of promoting what he calls the *summum bonum*, "the highest good *in the world* possible through freedom" (Part II, p. 118). Such a goal is held to constitute an ideal state of affairs wherein human happiness would be appropriately proportioned to moral desert, a condition that manifestly does not obtain in life as we know it but which we are nonetheless called upon to help to realize. Granted, however, that this is something morality obliges us to pursue as a duty, it follows that we must believe it to be ultimately attainable; and that consideration, when taken in conjunction with the limitations to which we are inescapably subject as finite and imperfect members of the world, requires us to assume the existence of a "moral author" of nature capable of ensuring that our efforts will not turn out to be finally vain. Kant thinks that someone who, though in general right-eously disposed, does not assume this will inevitably be "circumscribed in his endeavour," eventually abandoning any attempt to further the project in question on the ground of its impracticability. If, on the other hand, such a person resolves to be faithful to the call of their "inner moral vocation" and acts accordingly, they thereby show them-selves to be committed to "the existence of a *moral* author of the world, that is, of a God" (ibid., p. 121). Such an assumption, in other words, is essential if we are to "think in a manner consistent with morality"; to employ the terminology of the second *Critique*, it repre-sents a "postulate" of pure practical reason. Admittedly, and as Kant points out in an important footnote, this argument still does not amount to an "*objectively* valid proof" of God; on critical principles that remains forever impossible. But it is nonetheless "sufficient *subjec-tively* and for moral persons" (ibid., p. 119). And given the necessary primacy for us of the moral law, he implies that it is all that we can properly ask for or need.

The priority that Kant assigns to what he calls "the moral proof" in the last part of the *Critique of Judgement* raises the question of what significance, if any, he is prepared to attribute to teleological conceptions of nature from a theological point of view. He certainly concedes that the traditional argument from design is worthy of respect; unlike other speculative arguments, it has appeared as persuasive to the understanding of the ordinary "man in the street" as it has to that of the "subtlest thinker." He implies, though, that this tends to be due to an unnoticed confusion between an ostensible reliance upon purely empirical factors and the underlying influence of "moral considerations to which everyone in the depth of his heart assents." When these two strands are carefully distinguished, it becomes clear that it is the second that actually produces conviction, any presumed dependence of the conclusion reached upon the "physico-teleological evidence" being in fact illusory. And he drives the point home by claiming that, even if as rational beings we inhabited a universe in which nature showed no trace of features suggestive of physical teleology, the asseverations of practical reason regarding the existence of God would still retain their force. Yet all the same, and notwithstanding his insistence that "physico-theology is physical teleology misunderstood" (Part II, p. 108), he does not go so far as to declare that such a teleology is wholly irrelevant or otiose in the present context. Considered as affording the premises for a theoretical demonstration it is certainly useless to the theologian. But it does not follow that it has no subsidiary role to play.

Kant indicates, for instance, that it may at least function "as a preparation or propaedeutic," disposing the mind to entertain the idea of there being an "intelligent" source of nature and thereby rendering it "more susceptible to the influence of the moral proof." Furthermore, he also goes on to suggest that the abundance of material for teleological judgment which the actual world supplies can be said to serve us "as a desirable confirmation of the moral argument, so far as nature can adduce anything analogous to the ideas of reason (moral ideas in this case)" (Part II, p. 155). In trying to interpret this rather cryptic remark, it will be worth recalling again the notion – initially advanced in the Introduction to the *Critique* – of judgment's affording a mediating link between practical reason as the supersensible source of moral requirements and nature as constituting the sensible sphere wherein they are to be given effect and realized. Now according to Kant's moral proof we must believe that the pre-eminent objective reason sets before us is an attainable one, this belief involving as an indispensable condition our acceptance of the existence of God. But it is not easy from a human standpoint to give content to that idea without envisaging nature to be designed in a manner that makes the attainment of such an end possible. Thus the fact that innumerable natural phenomena seem to demand for their intelligibility the employment of teleological concepts may be welcomed as lending some reinforcement to the thought of nature's being purposively adapted to the practicable fulfillment of what the moral consciousness enjoins; for as Kant puts it: "the conception of a supreme cause that possesses intelligence ... acquires by that means such reality as is sufficient for reflective judgement" (ibid.).

Even so, the problem of ultimately reconciling teleological and mechanistic interpretations of the natural world remains; and while Kant has allowed that a transcendent principle capable of subsuming or accommodating both might conceivably obtain at the level of a higher understanding, he at the same time reiterates the point that, so far as human knowledge is concerned, the conception of nature as a product of intelligent design can never be theoretically established or proved. Reflective judgment may perform a salutary service in supplementing assumptions to which, as a matter of moral necessity, we find ourselves committed by practical reason. As, however, he has consistently maintained throughout the third *Critique*, in none of its forms can judgment itself be accredited with cognitive insight into what lies beyond the bounds of the phenomenal sphere. Such assurance as we have on the latter score can never be other than a moral assurance, one that holds good for us "from a purely practical point of view" (Part II, pp. 143–4).

SELECT BIBLIOGRAPHY

Original language editions

4.1 Kant, I. *Kritik der Urteilskraft*, Berlin, 1790.
4.2 *Kants gesammelte Schriften*, 29 vols, ed. Deutschen (formerly Königlich Preussische) Akademie der Wissenschaften, Berlin: de Gruyter (and predecessors), 1902–, Vol. V.

English translations

4.3 *Kant's Critique of Judgement*, trans. J.C. Meredith, Oxford: Oxford University Press, 1952: all references in the text are to this translation.
4.4 *Kant's First Introduction to the Critique of Judgement*, trans. J. Haden, New York: Bobbs-Merrill, 1965.

Bibliographies

4.5 Cohen, T., and Guyer, P. (eds) *Essays in Kant's Aesthetics*, Chicago: University of Chicago Press, 1982, pp. 308–23.
4.6 Guyer, P. (ed.) *Cambridge Companion to Kant*, Cambridge: Cambridge University Press, 1992, pp. 467–9.

Influences

4.7 Addison, J. "On the Pleasures of the Imagination," *The Spectator* (1712); trans. into German 1745; in Addison, J. *The Spectator*, 5 vols, ed. with introduction and notes by D.F. Bond, Oxford: Clarendon Press, 1965, pp. 535–82.
4.8 Burke, E. *A Philosophical Enquiry into the Origin of Our Ideas of the Sublime*

and Beautiful (1757), ed. with introduction and notes by J.T. Boulton, London: Routledge & Kegan Paul, 1958.

4.9   Hume, D. *Essays Moral, Political and Literary* (1693), Oxford: Oxford University Press, 1963.

General surveys

4.10 Cassirer, E. *Kant's Life and Thought* (1918), trans. J. Haden, New Haven and London: Yale University Press, 1981.

Specific topics

4.11 Cassirer, H.W. *A Commentary on Kant's Critique of Judgement*, London: Methuen, 1938.

4.12 Caygill, H. *Art of Judgement*, Oxford: Blackwell, 1989.

4.13 Cohen, T., and Guyer, P. (eds) *Essays in Kant's Aesthetics*, Chicago: University of Chicago Press, 1982.

4.14 Crawford, D. *Kant's Aesthetic Theory*, Madison: University of Wisconsin Press, 1974.

4.15 Crowther, P. *The Kantian Sublime*, Oxford: Clarendon Press, 1989.

4.16 Guyer, P. *Kant and the Claims of Taste*, London and Cambridge, Mass.: Harvard University Press, 1979.

4.17 Kemel, S. *Kant and Fine Art*, Oxford: Clarendon Press, 1986.

4.18 McCloskey, M. *Kant's Aesthetics*, London: Macmillan, 1986.

4.19 McFarland, J.D. *Kant's Concept of Teleology*, Edinburgh: Edinburgh University Press, 1970.

4.20 McLaughlin, P. *Kant's Critique of Teleology in Biological Explanation*, Lewiston, NY: Edwin Mellen Press, 1990.

4.21 Mothersill, M. *Beauty Restored*, Oxford: Clarendon Press, 1984.

4.22 Podro, M. *The Manifold of Perception: Theories of Art from Kant to Hildebrand*, Oxford: Clarendon Press, 1972.

4.23 Savile, A. *Aesthetic Reconstructions: The Seminal Writings of Lessing, Kant and Schiller*, Oxford: Blackwell, 1987.

4.24 Schaper, E. *Studies in Kant's Aesthetics*, Edinburgh: Edinburgh University Press, 1979.

4.25 Walsh, W.H. "Kant's Moral Theology," *Proceedings of the British Academy*, 49 (1963): 263–89.

4.26 Wood, A. *Kant's Rational Theology*, Ithaca and London: Cornell University Press, 1978.

4.27 Yovel, Y. *Kant and the Philosophy of History*, Princeton: Princeton University Press, 1980.

CHAPTER 5

Fichte and Schelling: the Jena period

Daniel Breazeale

❧ FROM KANT TO FICHTE ❧

An observer of the German philosophical landscape of the 1790s would have surveyed a complex and confusing scene, in which individuals tended to align themselves with particular factions or "schools," frequently associated with specific universities or, in some cases, periodicals, and engaged in often bitter public controversies with their opponents. Within this context, Kantianism (or "the Critical philosophy," as it was styled by both its opponents and its exponents) was simply one party among others. Self-appointed representatives of "Enlightenment," inspired by English and French examples and pledging their allegiance to the legacy of Lessing, dominated more urbane intellectual circles, such as that of Moses Mendelssohn and his associates in Berlin. A more academic variety of rationalism was defended by the many proponents of the Leibnizian–Wolffian philosophy, which still dominated the philosophy departments of most German universities. At the same time, there was a widespread vogue for what was then called "popular philosophy," the adherents of which, though they usually shared the liberal assumptions and conclusions of the *Aufklärer* and Wolffians, based their philosophy not upon *a priori* reasoning, but upon an appeal to the testimony of "healthy common sense." In opposition to the dominant spirit of the age, these "popular philosophers" distrusted the systematic impulse and were suspicious of all attempts to turn philosophy into a well-grounded "science."

An even more extreme rejection of philosophy as a systematic science was associated with Friedrich Jacobi and J.G. Hamann, two idiosyncratic but influential thinkers who employed skeptical arguments in order to reveal the fragility of human reason and hence the necessity and superiority of "faith." Another eccentric but influential figure was J.G. Herder, a philosophical naturalist who challenged the prevailing mechanistic models of the mind and of society and sought to replace them with more organic or vitalistic ones. Herder's groundbreaking work on the origin of languages and the role of history in the formation of human consciousness eventually led him to call for a "meta-critique" of philosophy's alleged neglect of the influence of language, culture, and history upon thought itself. Finally, there were also a few straightforward representatives of philosophical skepticism, such as G.E. Schulze and Ernst Plattner.

All of these contending parties were united, however, in their opposition to the new Kantian philosophy, which was steadily gaining in prominence. Not only were several new journals dedicated to the promulgation of Kantianism, but a university chair was established for this purpose as well (at Jena in 1787). It is noteworthy, however, that the single work which played the greatest role in calling public attention to the Critical philosophy was not a book by Kant himself, but rather a series of popular "Letters on the Kantian Philosophy" published in 1786–7 in the widely circulated *Allgemeine Literatur-Zeitung*. These "Letters" were the work of K.L. Reinhold (1756–1823), an ex-Jesuit and enthusiastic convert to the new Critical philosophy. The most striking feature of Reinhold's "Letters" is their strong emphasis upon the *practical* or *moral* consequences of Kant's thought. Consequently, it was not as a new theory of knowledge or even as a critique of metaphysics that Kant's philosophy first attracted widespread attention, but instead, as an ingenious defense of freedom, morality, and religion: a doctrine of "practical belief" which was simultaneously able to acknowledge the (limited) legitimacy of the modern scientific worldview. On the strength of his fame as author of the "Letters," Reinhold was named as the first occupant of the new chair in Critical philosophy established at Jena in 1787.

To the consternation of many of Kant's more literal-minded followers, Reinhold proved to be a rather unorthodox adherent of the new transcendental philosophy and immediately embarked upon an ambitious project of reformulating and revising Kant's philosophy. Though Reinhold was quite prepared to endorse all of Kant's conclusions, he found Kant's specific arguments and "derivations" to be somewhat lacking in inner coherence and systematic rigor. According to Reinhold, transcendental philosophy could become genuinely "scientific" only by being recast in the form of a deductive system based upon a single, self-evidently certain, "absolutely first principle," from which, in turn, everything else (e.g. the famous distinction between "thought" and "intuition," with which Kant's theoretical philosophy begins) could be "derived."

Reinhold gave the name "Elementary Philosophy" (or "Philosophy of the Elements") to his revised version of Kantianism, and argued that the latter alone was able to provide Kant's writings with the systematic form and scientific foundation which they themselves lacked. By analyzing the bare concept of "representation," Reinhold obtained the first principle of his system, the "principle of consciousness," and from this first principle he then proposed to derive the distinction between intuition and thought, along with all of familiar Kantian faculties and categories.

Reinhold's Elementary Philosophy is historically significant for two reasons: First of all, Reinhold's explicit criticism of the "letter" of Kant's own presentation of his philosophy, and especially his criticism of the duality of Kant's starting point and the *ad hoc* character of some of his arguments, promoted a general demand for a more coherent and systematic exposition of Kant's philosophy. Second, Reinhold's specific program for accomplishing this task – viz., by deriving the entire Critical philosophy from a single first principle – stimulated others (above all, Fichte) to seek an even more "fundamental" first principle upon which philosophy in its entirety could be "grounded."

Another prominent feature of Kant's philosophy which was subjected to early criticism (though in this case not by Reinhold) concerned the problematic status of "things in themselves" within the Critical philosophy. The most influential early critic of Kant on this point was F.H. Jacobi (1743–1819), who was a well-known author of sentimental novels, as well as of several influential philosophical (or rather, anti-philosophical) works. In 1787 Jacobi devoted the Appendix to his *David Hume on Belief, or Idealism and Realism* to an examination of transcendental philosophy, and he focused his criticism upon Kant's apparently conflicting remarks concerning the status of "things in themselves." Jacobi concluded that the entire doctrine was incoherent, since, as he put it, one had to assume the existence of things in themselves in order to obtain entry in Kant's philosophy, only to discover upon entry into the same that such a doctrine is incompatible with the transcendental account of "objectivity" made possible by that same philosophy. For followers of Kant, therefore, the challenge was clear: to defend transcendental idealism from Jacobi's criticism without following Jacobi himself into a wholesale rejection of philosophical speculation and embrace of a fideistic celebration of "not-knowing."

Similar objections to treating the thing in itself as the transcendent ground of sensations were advanced by Salomon Maimon (c. 1752–1800), a largely self-educated Polish-Russian Jew and the author of the extraordinarily original *Examination of Transcendental Philosophy* (1790). For Maimon, however, the lesson to be drawn from the untenability of Kant's doctrine of things in themselves was not the need to abandon reason for immediate feeling and faith, but rather, the desirability of constructing a more "skeptical" variety of Kantianism, one shorn of all transcendent remnants and aware of its own limitations. To this end, Maimon attempted to rehabilitate the Leibnizian notion of an "infinite understanding," from the perspective of which the distinction between sensibility and thought, content and form, would disappear.

Another influential critic of the new transcendental philosophy was G.E. Schulze, self-styled "Humean skeptic" and author of the anonymously published *Aenesidemus, or concerning the Foundations of the Elementary Philosophy Propounded at Jena by Prof. Reinhold, Including a Defense of Skepticism against the Pretensions of the Critique of Reason* (1792). In attacking the Critical philosophy, Schulze not only repeated many of Jacobi's and Maimon's specific criticisms but added some new ones of his own, including an objection to the very idea of "the primacy of practical reason."

In addition to the various internal difficulties within Kant's writings, Kant's first generation of readers also had to grapple with what might be thought of as the external problem of the relationship between the various *Critiques*, a problem which, of course, ultimately concerns nothing less than the systematic *unity* of the Critical philosophy. How is the worldview of the first *Critique* to be squared with that of the second? Despite Kant's own attempt to address this problem, first in the Transcendental Dialectic of the *Critique of Pure Reason*, and then in the Introduction to the *Critique of Judgment*, many readers remained uncertain about how the deterministic worldview of Kant's theoretical philosophy could be reconciled with the account of freedom and self-determination presented in his practical philosophy. There was also widespread confusion regarding the relationship between the various "subjects" (or "I's") encountered in the various *Critiques*. Is the pure subjective spontaneity that accounts for the transcendental unity of apperception (i.e. "the transcendental I") identical with the freely acting and self-legislating practical agent ("the practical I")? And how are these "I's" related, in turn, to empirical self-consciousness and to embodied persons? Finally, many sympathetic readers expressed serious reservations concerning the overall "architectonic" of the Critical philosophy. How, precisely, are the claims of theoretical philosophy related to those of practical philosophy? Indeed, what is the epistemic status of philosophical claims themselves? What kind of "knowledge" does philosophy convey, and how is such knowledge established?

Such was the philosophical context within which the achievements of Fichte and Schelling must be understood and evaluated. Everyone agreed that, for better or for worse, philosophy was in a period of extraordinary crisis and ferment. Even as the magnitude of Kant's accomplishment was becoming increasingly apparent, it was also becoming obvious – to Kant's more perspicacious defenders as well as to his critics – that any successful defense of the Critical philosophy would have to be more than a mere restatement of the same. Instead, what would be required would be a further advance down the road first opened by Reinhold's Elementary Philosophy; only by abandoning the "letter" of Kantianism, or so it seemed, could its "spirit" be preserved.

❧ J.G. FICHTE'S JENA ❧
WISSENSCHAFTSLEHRE

Johann Gottlieb Fichte (1762–1814), son of a Saxon ribbon weaver, university dropout, and itinerant tutor, first encountered Kant's writings in 1790, and the effect was immediately galvanizing. "I have been living in a new world ever since reading the *Critique of Practical Reason*," he reported to a friend.

> Propositions I thought could never be overturned have been overturned for me. Things have been proven to me which I thought could never be proven – e.g. the concept of absolute freedom, the concept of duty, etc. – I feel all the happier for it. . . . Please forgive me for saying so, but I cannot convince myself that prior to the Kantian critique anyone able to think for himself thought any differently than I did, and I do not recall ever having met anyone who had any fundamental objections to make against my [previous, deterministic] system. I encountered plenty of sincere persons who had different – not *thoughts* (for they were not at all capable of thinking) but different – *feelings*.
>
> (III, 1: 167)[1]

As this passage poignantly testifies, what attracted Fichte to transcendental idealism was his conviction that it alone was able to reconcile human freedom and natural necessity, moral sentiments and rational judgments, "feelings" and "thoughts." It is no exaggeration to say that Fichte devoted the rest of his life to the task of explaining and expounding the philosophy which, he believed, makes such a reconciliation possible. Though he soon confessed to nagging doubts concerning certain details of Kant's own presentations of his philosophy, Fichte never entertained any doubts concerning the fundamental truth of the latter, at least insofar as its "spirit" was concerned – a spirit which Fichte was convinced was even better expressed in his own philosophy, which he succinctly characterized in 1795 as "the first system of human freedom" (III, 2: 298).

Barely two years after his first encounter with Kant's writings, Fichte was unexpectedly propelled to fame with the publication of his first book, *Attempt at a Critique of All Revelation* (1792). Through circumstances which have never been adequately explained, the book in question, issued by Kant's own publisher and dealing with an important topic (viz., revelation, considered as the "appearance" of noumenal reality within the phenomenal world) raised by the Critical philosophy but not yet explicitly dealt with by Kant himself, was originally published anonymously. Not surprisingly, it was immediately and widely hailed as the latest publication by Kant himself. Thus, as soon as the author's true identity became known, Fichte's fame as a philosophical author was assured, since it was now too late to retract all of the extravagant praise the book had already received.

The young author's notoriety was only increased by his next two publications, *A Discourse on the Reclamation of the Freedom of Thought from the Princes of Europe, who have hitherto Suppressed it* and the first installment of *A Contribution toward Correcting the Public's Judgment of the French Revolution*. Though both works were published anonymously in 1793 in Danzig (where Fichte was once again employed as a private tutor), the author's identity was widely known. Thus, in addition to his growing renown as the "third sun in the philosophical heaven," Fichte also acquired an early reputation as a fiery Jacobin, a reputation which guaranteed him political as well as philosophical enemies during his career at Jena.

When Reinhold unexpectedly resigned his chair at Jena in the spring of 1794 it was immediately offered to Fichte, who at this point was living in Zurich in the home of his new father-in-law and was completely engrossed in a vast project of constructing his *own* version of transcendental idealism, one which would heed Reinhold's call for a system based upon "a single first principle," but would do so in a manner which would avoid the published criticisms of Jacobi, Maimon, and Schulze. It was during this period that Fichte decided that his new philosophy deserved a new name. Accordingly, since he wished to emphasize that his new, "rigorously scientific," philosophy would represent something more than mere "love of wisdom" (or "philosophy"), he baptized it *"Wissenschaftslehre"* (that is, "theory of science" or "doctrine of scientific knowledge" – *not* "science of knowledge").

Fichte, who more than anything else wished for his own philosophical efforts to make a positive contribution to the improvement of human life, could hardly afford to decline the offer from Jena, which would guarantee the maximum amount of exposure for his new system.

Accordingly, he began lecturing on his new philosophy in the summer of 1794, though not before publishing a brief and "hypothetical" introduction to the same in the form of a meta-philosophical treatise entitled *Concerning the Concept of the Wissenschaftslehre, or of so-called "Philosophy"* (1794).

Even though Fichte had not yet completed the task of thinking through even the rudiments of his new system at the time of his arrival at Jena, he nevertheless immediately began lecturing on the "Foundations of the Entire *Wissenschaftslehre*." These lectures, which continued through the winter semester of 1794–5, represent Fichte's first attempt at a full-scale public presentation of his philosophy. For the convenience of his students, he had the text of his lectures printed and distributed (in fascicles) over the course of the two semesters. However, he soon agreed to have these printed fascicles bound together and issued as a book, or rather, as several books: *Foundations of the Entire Wissenschaftslehre*, Parts I and II (1794) and Part III (1795), and *Outline of the Distinctive Character of the Wissenschaftslehre with respect to the Theoretical Power* (1795) – though the title page of each of these volumes still included the words "published as a manuscript for the use of his students."

There is considerable historical irony in the fact that this "book," the first parts of which appeared in print well before the later portions had even been drafted, became (and to this day remains) Fichte's best-known and most influential philosophical work. It is intriguing to wonder what the "history of German Idealism" would have been like if the call to Jena had not come in 1794 and if, instead, Fichte had been allowed the leisure to develop and to publish his philosophy at a somewhat less frantic pace. But, of course, such speculation is as idle as it is intriguing, for the fact is that the full text of the *Foundations*, along with that of the *Outlines*, was fatefully set before the reading public in the summer of 1795.

Fichte himself was, from the first, deeply dissatisfied with the *Foundations*, which he wished his auditors and readers to treat as no more than a provisional presentation of the basic principles of his system. Accordingly, when he next returned to this topic, that is, in the lectures on the "Foundations of Transcendental Philosophy (*Wissenschaftslehre*) *nova methodo*" which he first delivered in 1796–7, he offered his students a completely revised and very different presentation of the basic principles and outlines of his philosophy. Apparently, he was relatively satisfied with this new presentation (the so-called "*Wissenschaftslehre nova methodo*"), for he repeated these lectures twice more during his career at Jena. Indeed, he fully intended to revise them for publication and, in 1797–8, succeeded in publishing two "introductions" to, as well as the first chapter of, this new version, under the title *An Attempt at a New Presentation of the Wissenschafts-lehre* in the *Philosophisches Journal einer Gesellschaft Teutscher Gelehrten*, of which he was then co-editor.

However, Fichte did not confine himself to refining his presentation of the foundations of his philosophy; he also devoted a great deal of effort to fleshing out the systematic scheme merely alluded to in his programmatic writings. He did this in his lectures on *Naturrecht* (or "natural right") and ethics, subsequently published as *Foundations of Natural Right according to the Principles of the Wissenschaftslehre* (1796–7) and *The System of Ethical Theory according to the Principles of the Wissenschaftslehre* (1798). Though he announced that he would lecture on a third systematic subdivision of the *Wissenschaftslehre*, viz., philosophy of religion, during the summer semester of 1799, the lectures in question were never delivered.

Fichte was embroiled in one controversy or another (often involving his political views) from the moment of his arrival in Jena, but the final one, the so-called "atheism controversy," proved to be his undoing. In 1798 he had published a brief article entitled "Concerning the Basis of our Belief in a Divine Governance of the Universe," in which he bluntly criticized all attempts by philosophers to infer the existence of God from the fact of the moral law – or from anything else. His many local enemies seized upon this article to incite broader opposition. He was officially charged by the Saxon authorities with atheism, which provoked a very public controversy between Fichte's opponents and defenders. Eventually, and largely as a result of his own tactical miscalculations, he was dismissed from his academic post. In the summer of 1799 he moved to Berlin.

For Fichte, 1799 was a year filled with disappointment. Not only did he lose his job, but he also began to lose many of his most prominent philosophical allies, including Reinhold, who had briefly become an enthusiastic exponent of the *Wissenschaftslehre*. Schelling, the most conspicuous and prolific of the young "Fichteans," continued, despite Fichte's disapproval, to pursue his interest in "the philosophy of nature," while Jacobi, whom, for all their philosophical differences, Fichte greatly admired, published a long *Open Letter to Fichte*, in which he devastatingly characterized the *Wissenschaftslehre* as "nihilism." Finally, in August 1799, Kant himself issued a public "declaration" in which he repudiated Fichte's system and disavowed any relationship between his own philosophy and the *Wissenschaftslehre*. "One star sets, another one rises," shrugged Goethe, when informed of Fichte's departure from Jena.

When Fichte arrived in Berlin (where there was, as yet, no university) he was forced to earn his living from his writings and from occasional, privately subscribed lessons and lectures. His first project was a "popular" presentation of his philosophy, one specifically designed to rebut the charge of atheism and to reply to Jacobi's more general criticisms of transcendental philosophy. The resulting book, *The Vocation of Man*, was published in 1800, closely followed by a rather bold foray into political economy (*The Self-Contained Commercial State*). Still attempting to defend himself against what he viewed as widespread misperceptions of his position, Fichte then published the pathetically titled *Crystal-Clear Report to the General Public concerning the Actual Essence of the Newest Philosophy: an Attempt to Force the Reader to Understand* (1801), in which he emphasized the philosophical differences between the *Wissenschaftslehre* and rival systems of thought.

At the same time, he continued to revise and recast his "scientific" presentation of the first principles of his system; indeed, he himself accurately characterized the period 1800–4 as one of "ceaseless work on the *Wissenschaftslehre*." Finally abandoning his efforts to revise for publication his 1796–9 lectures on *Wissenschaftslehre nova methodo*, he once again drafted an entirely new version of the foundations of his philosophy, which he presented in a course of private lectures delivered in Berlin in 1801–2. Once again, however, dissatisfaction with the results prevented him from publishing this new version and impelled him to embark upon yet another, even more thoroughgoing systematic overhaul of his presentation. These efforts culminated in the year 1804, in the course of which Fichte delivered three separate sets of lectures on the *Wissenschaftslehre*. Though he expressed complete satisfaction with this latest version and readied it for publication, he appears finally to have concluded that he himself was simply incapable of producing a written exposition of his own philosophy which could stand on its own and avert the sorts of misunderstanding to which his Jena writings had been subjected. For the rest of his life he vowed "to confine himself to oral communication, so that misunderstanding can thereby be detected and eliminated on the spot" (III, 5: 223). In 1804 he also delivered a well-received series of more popular lectures *On the Characteristics of the Present Age* (subsequently published in 1806), in which he dealt, for the first time, with the philosophy of history.

Fichte spent the summer semester of 1805 at the Prussian University at Erlangen, where he prepared and lectured upon yet another presentation of the first principles of his philosophy. Upon his return to Berlin in 1806 he delivered yet another set of "popular" lectures, *Directions for a Blessed Life*, which were published later that same year. These lectures reveal the strong influence of the Gospel of St John on Fichte's thinking at this point and contain what is perhaps the most accessible presentation of the new, more religiously oriented, and "mystical" tendency of his thought during his final years.

With the defeat of Prussia by Napoleon's armies in 1806 and the occupation of Berlin, Fichte took refuge in Königsberg, where he served briefly as a professor, producing for his lectures yet another version of the *Wissenschaftslehre*. After the Peace of Tilsit, however, he returned to Berlin, where he delivered his celebrated *Addresses to the German Nation* under the noses of the occupying forces. These lectures, in which Fichte attempted to kindle a sense of distinctively "German" patriotism and outlined a program of national education for this purpose, were published in 1808 and subsequently exercised a wide influence upon the development of German nationalist sentiment.

Fichte was also instrumental during this period in establishing the new University of Berlin. When the university was finally opened in 1810, he served as head of the philosophical faculty and, briefly, as rector of the university. He remained a professor at the new university until his death in 1814. During these years he lectured on a variety of subjects, including the first principles of his *Wissenschaftslehre* (of which he produced at least four more versions after 1810), political philosophy (or "doctrine of the state"), philosophy of right, and a popular introduction to philosophy under the title "the facts of consciousness." None of these new lectures were published by Fichte, though in 1810 he did publish a cryptic overview of the latest version of his system, *The Wissenschaftslehre in its General Outline*. Fichte died unexpectedly at the age of 51, of typhus, which he contracted from his wife, who had been infected by wounded soldiers she was nursing.

Let us now turn to a consideration of Fichte's *Wissenschaftslehre*, limiting ourselves to the version which exercised the greatest influence upon his contemporaries, that is, the "Jena *Wissenschaftslehre*" of 1794–9. In doing so, it is vital to recall that the term "*Wissenschaftslehre*" does not refer to any particular book or even any specific presentation of Fichte's system. In its broadest sense, "*Wissenschaftslehre*" is simply Fichte's proposed new name for "philosophy" itself, understood not as a form of "practical wisdom," but rather as a rigorous, systematic "science." Thus, in *Concerning the Concept of Wissenschaftslehre*, Fichte identifies *Wissenschaftslehre* with "the science of science itself," with knowledge about the very conditions, foundations, and limits of knowledge. (To be sure, this means that philosophy, *qua* "science of science" or "knowledge of knowledge," involves a certain, unavoidable degree of circularity. But, as Fichte argues persuasively in *Concerning the Concept*, such circularity – once it has been clearly grasped – is not an objection to philosophy, but is, instead, one of its most distinctive and unavoidable features.)

Somewhat more narrowly construed, "*Wissenschaftslehre*" is Fichte's new name for "transcendental idealism" or "Critical philosophy"

– in contrast to the previously prevailing systems, which Fichte lumped together under the name "dogmatism" and believed was best represented by Spinoza. The essential features of a *Wissenschaftslehre* in this narrower sense are, first of all, that it follows Kant in insisting that genuinely philosophical questions are those of justification or warrant (*quid juris*) rather than questions of "fact" (*quid facti*). Consequently, the actual arguments and deductions which constitute philosophy as *Wissenschaftslehre* cannot be based upon an appeal to the so-called "facts of consciousness," since the task of such a science is to "explain" or account for these very "facts." More specifically, the particular set of facts which a *Wissenschaftslehre* has to account for in the first instance are those associated with our experience of an external world of objects. Or rather, limiting ourselves to the standpoint of consciousness, what philosophy has to explain is the presence within human consciousness of "representations accompanied by a feeling of necessity." Hence the question posed by the *Wissenschaftslehre* is as follows: "What is the connection between our representations and their objects? To what extent can we say that something independent of our representations, something altogether independent of and external to us, corresponds to our representations?" (I, 3: 247). What has to be explained, in short, is "how representing becomes knowing."

Second, the "explanation" of cognition provided by the *Wissenschaftslehre* must be rigorously "transcendental" in character, in the sense that it must begin with something it regards as certain or beyond controversy (e.g. in Kant's case, the continuous self-identity of the knowing subject over time) and then enquire into the necessary conditions for the possibility thereof.

Third, a *Wissenschaftslehre* takes very much to heart the Kantian insistence upon "the primacy of practical reason." This does not mean simply that it recognizes the integrity and autonomy of the moral or "practical" sphere and resolutely refuses to countenance any standpoint that treats our consciousness of our own freedom as illusory. Instead, the *Wissenschaftslehre* insists that "the practical power is the innermost root of the I" (I, 3: 332); and, basing itself upon this insight, it attempts to demonstrate that "our freedom itself [is] a theoretical determining principle of our world" (I, 5: 77). What a transcendental idealism of this sort has to demonstrate is that only a free and practically striving I can have any experience of a world of spatio-temporal, material objects, and the overall deductive strategy of the *Wissenschaftslehre* is to demonstrate this by showing that the latter is a condition for the former. This is the sense in which "theoretical reason" is based upon "practical reason." (Of course, there is also an important sense in which the converse is true: since, according to Fichte anyway, practical striving presupposes theoretical awareness of a goal.)

Finally, there is a third, even narrower sense of "*Wissenschafts-lehre*," in which the term is synonymous neither with philosophy in general nor with transcendental idealism as such, but refers instead to Fichte's own, distinctive version of the latter. Although Fichte himself never relinquished his long-standing claim that "the *Wissenschaftslehre* is nothing other than the Kantian philosophy properly understood" and consequently always sought to minimize the differences between his own system and Kant's, it must nevertheless be conceded that there are many striking differences between the "letter" of his philosophy and that of Kant's.

For example, Fichte's version of transcendental idealism follows Reinhold in claiming to base everything upon a single, absolutely certain "first principle." By proceeding in this rigorously "deductive" manner, Fichte believed, the *Wissenschaftslehre* would be able to produce a more elegant and successful derivation of the *a priori* categories of possible experience – including space and time. (The deductive strategy of the *Wissenschaftslehre* makes it possible to dispense with the Kantian distinction between "transcendental aesthetics" and "transcendental logic," and thus tends to identify "forms of intuition" and "categories of thought.") By deriving everything from a single starting point the *Wissenschaftslehre* could also hope to avoid the problems of systematic unity which plagued Kant's writings. Not only would it be able to exhibit the "common root" of intuition and thinking, but, even more significantly, it would be able to demonstrate, in a systematic manner, the intimate link between theoretical and practical reason, the realm of nature and that of freedom. (This last point marks a major advance beyond Reinhold's Elementary Philosophy, which confined itself almost entirely to an account of theoretical reason.)

Or, to cite another example of the manner in which Fichte's philosophy advanced beyond the letter of Kant's, there is no room within the *Wissenschaftslehre* for any reference, however minimal or tangential, to "things in themselves." Having absorbed the arguments of Kant's critics, Fichte firmly rejected any appeal – within the context of a philosophical account of experience, though not, of course, within the context of everyday life, where such appeals are not only appropriate but unavoidable – to what he characterized as the "non-thought of things in themselves." In contrast to philosophical "dogmatism," which vainly attempts to explain representations as "produced" within the mind by external objects, and which thus pretends to derive consciousness from things, a genuine transcendental idealism or *Wissenschaftslehre* adopts the opposite strategy; that is, it tries to show how our experience of "things" is a consequence of the character of consciousness itself. If philosophy is to remain transcendental and is not to become transcendent, then the undeniable "objectivity" of the world of ordinary experience will have to be accounted for purely in terms of consciousness and its acts. This means that transcendental philosophy must demonstrate that "the representation and the object that is supposed to correspond to it are one and the same thing – merely regarded from two different points of view" (I, 3: 252). It accomplishes this by showing that consciousness must operate in certain ways if self-consciousness (which, for Fichte as for Kant, is the starting point of the entire deduction) is to be possible at all. It is the "necessity" of these modes of acting which accounts for the "feeling of necessity" which accompanies certain representations, and thereby accounts for the experienced "objectivity" of the world. (The sort of idealism which merely asserts that mind "constructs" reality but does not offer a rigorous deduction of the *necessity* with which it acts in doing so is dismissed by Fichte as "transcendent idealism.")

Turning now to the Jena *Wissenschaftslehre*, let us begin with an examination of its first principle or starting point. Obviously, it is not sufficient that the "first principle" of all philosophy be a proposition from which all of the other propositions of the system can be derived; in addition, the principle in question must also be *true*. But how can the truth of this highest principle be established? Its truth cannot be derived from some higher principle or set of principles, for then the principle in question would not be "first." Hence the first principle, if it is to be true at all, must be immediately true; it must express something that is self-evidently certain. (To be sure, *that* this self-evident certainty is *also* the "first principle" of all philosophy is by no means self-evident; instead, this can be established only by actually erecting a system upon the certainty in question.)

What then is the first principle of the Jena *Wissenschaftslehre*? Though casual readers of the *Foundations of the Entire Wissenschaftslehre* sometimes assume that Fichte begins with the logical principle "A = A," a closer reading of the famous § 1 of this text reveals that the first principle in question is not the abstract logical principle of identity, which is employed purely as a preliminary "clue" for the discovery of the actual first principle of the system: viz., the material proposition which states that "the I simply posits itself." This principle expresses what Fichte believes to be the supreme act of the mind, an act in which the I is simultaneously subject and object. (Such an act is "supreme" in precisely the same, transcendental sense in which Kant considered the transcendental unity of apperception to be "supreme.")

Though there is certainly a sense in which the *Wissenschaftslehre* may be construed as a continuation of the Cartesian project of basing philosophy as a whole upon the alleged self-evidence of the *cogito*, there is also a crucial difference concerning the status of "self-consciousness." For Fichte, self-consciousness (and hence all consciousness, since the underlying strategy of the entire enterprise is to show that the latter is but a special instance of the former) cannot be understood as a "fact," no matter how privileged; nor can it be comprehended as an accident of some substance or a modification of some "being." Instead, it must be understood as an *activity*, albeit of a most extraordinary, self-productive type. To employ Fichte's own terminology, the self-positing of the I, which alone makes possible every act of empirical self-consciousness, and indeed, object-consciousness, is a "fact/act" or *Tathandlung*. It presupposes no prior "subject" which acts; it constitutes itself, *qua* self-consciousness, in the very act of becoming conscious of itself.

From this it follows that the "being" of the I is, so to speak, a consequence of its self-positing. Indeed, this, according to Fichte, is precisely what it means to be a "free being." A similar thought has been expressed in our own century in the formula that, where human beings are concerned, "existence precedes essence."

Thus, in order to "explain representations" Fichte invokes an original act of consciousness which is not an act of mere "representing" at all, but is equally and at the same time an act of production, indeed autoproduction. Thus the starting point of the Jena *Wissenschaftslehre* is equally "practical" and "theoretical," for the act described in its first principle ("the I simply posits itself") is a "doing" as well as a "knowing." Indeed, it is precisely because Fichte's system commences with and proceeds from "that supreme point from which the practical and the speculative appear as one" (III, 2: 395) that it can hope to succeed in its overall goal of reconciling freedom and necessity, morality and nature.

This choice of a starting point has equally dramatic implications for the narrower field of theoretical philosophy proper (that is, for that portion of philosophy which accounts for our experience of an external world of spatio-temporal objects), for it establishes, from the very start, the essential identity of *ideality* (being for consciousness) and *reality* (being in itself). An I is an I only insofar as it posits itself – i.e. is aware of itself as an I. Since the unity of being and thinking is explicitly present in our original starting point, it follows that it will be (implicitly) present in everything derived therefrom. Everything that "is" is only insofar as it is "for the I"; i.e. "being" is not an original category within the *Wissenschaftslehre*, but is only a subsidiary or "derived" one.

The nature of this starting point is further clarified in Fichte's second attempt at a presentation of the outlines and first principles of his system (viz., in the *Wissenschaftslehre nova methodo* and the fragmentary *Attempt at a New Presentation*). It is here, in the presentation of 1796–9, that the initial act of self-positing with which the

Wissenschaftslehre begins is described as an "intellectual intuition." Though Fichte's use of this term has produced a great deal of confusion (and though his remarks on the topic are not always as clear or as consistent as one might wish), the term "intellectual intuition" simply designates the previously described "act" (*Tathandlung*) of pure self-consciousness, within which the I is supposed to be immediately present to itself, thereby constituting itself as an I, at the same time that it distinguishes itself as an object of consciousness from itself as the subject thereof. Such an act deserves to be called an "intuition" (in the Kantian sense) because the object of consciousness is in this case *immediately* present. But since the object in question (the I itself) is not "given" to consciousness in this case, but is *produced* thereby, the intuition is "intellectual" rather than sensory.

One should note that it is not Fichte's claim that such an original intellectual intuition can *ever* occur within empirical self-consciousness. On the contrary, he frequently reminds his readers that "this absolute identity of subject and object within the I can only be inferred and cannot be immediately evinced as a 'fact of consciousness' " (I, 5: 21). However, philosophical reflection upon our own, necessarily divided self-consciousness can lead us to *the inference* that such an original unity must necessarily underlie and condition every empirical act of consciousness (within which the reflecting subject is in fact never discovered to be identical with the object of reflection). Only if there is an original unity of self-consciousness can we account for our abiding sense of our own identity, despite the fact that within every moment of empirical consciousness we find our identity divided between that of the subject and that of the object.

Thus, whereas the formal presentation of the "foundations" of the system begins with a description of the ungrounded *Tathandlung* or self-positing of the I, actual philosophizing, i.e. recapitulating for oneself the series of deductions which constitute the *Wissenschaftslehre*, begins instead with a free act of reflective abstraction on the part of the would-be philosopher. This act of turning one's attentions away from all objects and toward the operations of one's own consciousness is not an act of "intellectual intuition" of the sort attributed to the pure I which the philosopher is trying to study. (If Fichte sometimes uses the term "intellectual intuition" to designate the act of introspection or self-observation engaged in by the philosopher, then one must carefully distinguish *this* use of the term from its other, more fundamental employment to designate the I's original act of self-positing.)

The philosopher, meanwhile, after having abstracted from the "facts of consciousness," then seeks (within the artificial context of their philosophical account) to re-establish that same realm of facts, and they accomplish this by showing *why* and *how* the I must posit such a realm if it is to posit itself at all. This is how transcendental philosophy answers the *quid juris*.

But why should a philosopher begin with precisely *this* abstraction? Why should we commence with the bare thought of what Fichte calls variously "the absolute I," "I-hood," "the intellect," or simply "reason" (rather than beginning, for example, with the abstraction of a "thing in itself")? What is it that makes this mere idea of an original self-positing subject *certain*? Fichte's reply is instructive: The initial certainty of his proposed starting point is not theoretical at all, but is, instead, *practical*. The autonomy of the I, which is, after all, what is asserted in the formula that "the I simply posits itself," is something one must confirm for oneself within one's own moral experience. To the extent that one is aware of oneself as a free agent, to this extent one is *actually* aware of oneself as a self-positing I.

To be sure, theoretical/philosophical doubts concerning such an awareness always remain possible. This is why skepticism cannot be avoided by purely theoretical means. Instead, what keeps us from doubting the proposed starting point is our sense of moral obligation to determine our own actions, that is to say, our indefeasible awareness of our own freedom. The reason, therefore, why the transcendental idealist comes to a stop with the proposition "the I freely posits itself" is not because they are unable to entertain theoretical doubts on this point or because they cannot continue the process of reflective abstraction. Instead, as Fichte puts it:

> I *cannot* go beyond this standpoint because I am not *permitted* to do so . . . I ought to begin my thinking with the thought of the pure I, and I ought to think of this pure I as acting with absolute spontaneity – not as determined by things, but rather, as determining them.
>
> (I, 4: 220–1)

Thus the "categorical imperative" is invoked to secure the first principles of the entire *Wissenschaftslehre* (not merely of ethics), which illuminates Fichte's striking claim that the "*Wissenschaftslehre* is the only kind of philosophical thinking that accords with duty" (I, 4: 219).

This also may help explain the notoriously *ad hominem* character of Fichte's polemic against those (the "dogmatists") who are unable or unwilling to accept the *Wissenschaftslehre*. What ultimately prevents them from doing so, according to Fichte, is not any deficiency of their intellect or any lack of philosophical acumen. Instead, the reason some people persist in attempting to understand consciousness in terms of things (rather than vice versa) is because they lack a lively sense of their own freedom. The defect in question is thus one which concerns their moral character. As Fichte put it in a sardonic footnote: "most men could more easily be convinced to consider themselves a piece of lava on the moon than an I" (I, 2: 326 n.). The *Wissenschaftslehre*, however, is a philosophy for those who can and do conceive of themselves as free agents, and it is in precisely this sense that Fichte could describe it as "from first to last, nothing more than an analysis of the concept of freedom" (III, 4: 182).

After one has established for oneself via abstract reflection the first principle of the *Wissenschaftslehre* and has confirmed the truth of this starting point by appealing directly to one's own practical experience, one is then in a position to discover – again, by reflection and self-observation – all of the other acts which must *necessarily occur as well* if the postulated original act is to occur. Of course, just as we are never directly aware of the original act of self-positing which constitutes subjectivity as such, so we are not usually aware of these other, "necessary but unconscious" acts which are derived as conditions necessary for the possibility of this first act (though, of course, the transcendental philosopher becomes aware of them in the course of their enquiry). The *Wissenschaftslehre* is therefore described by Fichte as both (a) a process of raising to consciousness those unconscious acts by means of which the I "constitutes" the world of its experience and (b) nothing more than a complete (and often exceedingly complex) analysis of its own first principle.

The results of such an analysis, however, are sometimes surprising. For example, one of the more striking conclusions of the "analysis" of freedom carried out in the "foundational" portion of the Jena *Wissenschaftslehre* is that, although "the I simply posits itself," freedom is never "absolute" or "unlimited"; instead, Fichte unequivocally demonstrates that freedom is conceivable only as limited. Only finite freedom is actual, just as the only sort of consciousness which is actual is finite, empirical, and embodied. Only "limited" subjects exist as subject.

The conclusion of the *Foundations* and the *nova methodo* is the same: an I must posit itself in order to be an I at all; but it can posit itself only insofar as it posits itself as limited (and hence divided against itself). The limitation in question is first posited as a "feeling," then as a "sensation," then as an "intuition" of a thing, and finally as a "concept." All that we can say, from a transcendental perspective, concerning the original character of the "limitation" in question is to describe it in terms of the I's practical striving. This limitation is first described (in the 1794–5 presentation) as a "check" or *Anstoß* to the I's striving, a "check" which manifests itself within consciousness as "feeling." Though Fichte certainly demonstrates that such an *Anstoß* must in fact occur if self-consciousness is to be actual, he never claims that such a limitation is *produced* by the self-positing I, though he does, of course, observe that a limitation cannot exist (as a limitation of the I) unless it is "posited" as such (i.e. taken up into consciousness) by the I. On the other hand, Fichte steadfastly opposes all attempts to "explain" the *Anstoß* as an "effect" produced by the Not-I. The point is simply this: like the I itself, even the most rigorously "scientific" and *a priori* philosophy finally must admit that there are *limits* to what can be explained. Philosophy can explain, for example, why the world has a spatio-temporal character and a causal structure, but it cannot explain why objects have the particular sensible properties they happen to have. This is simply what the I discovers – albeit "within itself" and not "out there" – when it reflects upon its own original limitations.

To be sure, philosophy can show that the I cannot posit its own freedom, i.e. cannot posit itself, *unless* it finds itself to be limited (and then, in turn, posits a world of objects as the ground of its own limited state – thereby, as it were, "explaining" to itself its own limitation). However, *that* the I, in fact, finds itself to be limited – and limited in a specific manner (= "feeling") – is something that cannot be demonstrated *a priori*; instead, this is something "that everyone can prove to oneself only through one's own experience" (I, 2: 390).

This first account of the original limitation of the I is supplemented (in the *Wissenschaftslehre nova methodo*) by an account of how the practically striving I is originally called upon to *limit itself* freely in response to a "summons" (*Aufforderung*) received from what it takes to be another free being similar to itself. To this degree, the 1796–9 presentation goes well beyond the 1794–5 version in demonstrating that self-consciousness also presupposes a recognition of and by others; for one can be conscious of oneself only as an individual, which in turn requires consciousness of a realm of rational beings of which one is but a single member. This important argument, which demonstrates that recognition of and by others is a condition for self-recognition, was first elaborated by Fichte in his *Foundations of Natural Right* and was subsequently incorporated into his presentation of the very "foundations" of the *Wissenschaftslehre* – though it must be admitted that the precise, relative roles of *Anstoß* and *Aufforderung* in the constitution of self-consciousness remain somewhat unclear.

Let us now turn from a consideration of the starting point and deductive strategy of the Jena *Wissenschaftslehre* to an examination of the overall, systematic structure of the same (as explained in the concluding section of the *Wissenschaftslehre nova methodo*). The presentation of a complete, transcendental system of philosophy should begin with a discussion and demonstration of the "basic principles" or "foundations" of such a system, and this is precisely what Fichte himself attempted to do, first in the *Foundations of the Entire Wissenschaftslehre* and *Concerning the Distinctive Character of the Wissenschafts-*

lehre with Respect to the Theoretical Power, and then, in a revised form, in his lectures on the *Wissenschaftslehre nova methodo*.

The "foundational" portion of the system begins by calling upon the reader to isolate for him- or herself the concept of the freely self-positing I ("think the I!"). Once this initial starting point has been established, it is followed by an elaborate, transcendental account of subjectivity as such, an account which includes step-by-step analysis (which Fichte calls "genetic explanation") of the various unconscious acts of the mind which are required for the possibility of self-positing and which are involved in the constitution of everyday experience. This analysis includes an extended account of the creative activity of the "productive imagination," understood by Fichte as that power of the I which mediates between free self-positing (*Tathandlung*) and limited self-feeling (*Anstoß*). This first, "foundational" portion of the *Wissenschaftslehre* demonstrates how the "entire mechanism of consciousness is based upon various ways of viewing the separation of the subjective and the objective within consciousness, and, in turn, the union of both" (I, 5: 21): hence the explicitly "dialectical" structure of the argument, which constantly oscillates between moments of relative identity and moments of relative difference.

Next come what Fichte terms the various "real" philosophical sciences which make up the further subdivisions of the entire *Wissenschaftslehre*. There are three such systematic subdivisions: "theoretical philosophy," "practical philosophy," and "philosophy of the postulates," within each of which the mind's general principles, laws, and modes of acting (all of which have previously been derived within the "Foundations") are applied and extended within a specific and limited field.

A "specifically theoretical *Wissenschaftslehre*" or "*Wissenschaftslehre* of cognition" (not to be confused with the "theoretical" portion of the *Foundations*) concerns itself with the general features of what consciousness "discovers" in the course of its experience. Accordingly, this portion of transcendental philosophy presents us with a complete "theory of the world." It deals with what is *given* to consciousness, and it explains – to the severely limited extent that this can be explained philosophically – the necessary features of such a world. Hence, theoretical philosophy is limited to a consideration of *cognition*, that is, to an analysis of the specific type of consciousness within which the conscious subject considers itself to be "determined" by its objects. Theoretical philosophy shows what objects must be like for such consciousness to be possible, and in this sense it constitutes an *a priori* account of empirical reality as a whole, or of "nature." It thus determines the content of experience, but only to the extent that this content reflects the form of consciousness. This sort of theoretical philosophy of nature can indeed circumscribe experience, but it is in no way intended to supplant or to rival the empirical, natural sciences.

Though clearly Fichte envisioned such a "distinctively theoretical *Wissenschaftslehre*" (modeled, no doubt, upon Kant's *Metaphysical Foundations of Natural Science*), he himself never completed such a science. The closest he came was in his *Concerning the Distinctive Character of the Wissenschaftslehre with Respect to the Theoretical Power*, which barely proceeds beyond the transcendental deduction of space, time, and causality.

In contrast with the purely "theoretical" portion of the system, the specifically "practical" *Wissenschaftslehre* views the object of consciousness as freely determined by the subject. Thus it treats objects (or "being") not as *given* to consciousness, but rather, as *produced*, and produced by a freely acting and conscious subject attempting to accomplish its own goals: hence Fichte's assertion that the practical *Wissenschaftslehre* views "being as a product of concepts." The usual name for such a science is "ethics" or "ethical theory" (*Sittenlehre*). Ethics, or the distinctively practical portion of the overall system of the *Wissenschaftslehre*, examines not what is, but what ought to be. The "world" with which it is concerned is the world as it ought to be constructed by rational beings. Thus, in this portion of his system (though not elsewhere) Fichte really does interpret the world purely as an arena for moral striving – for this is how the world is actually viewed by the practically striving I (just as the theoretical or "knowing" I views it as something given to consciousness).

Fichte's *System of Ethical Theory* begins with a recapitulation of certain conclusions established in the "Foundations": e.g. (a) an awareness of one's own efficacy (i.e. of one's capacity to realize one's goal concepts) is a condition for the very possibility of self-consciousness, and (b) the I finds itself called upon (or "summoned") to limit itself freely in relation to other free beings. The specific task of *The System of Ethical Theory* is to indicate the particular duties and practical corollaries which follow from the general obligation to limit oneself freely. Accordingly, this portion of the system can be described as a detailed analysis of conscience as such, or as an expanded enquiry into the form and content of the "categorical imperative." The result is a systematic account of duty as such, that is, of those duties which apply to all rational beings, without taking into account any of the individual differences between persons. Here again, the argument by means of which Fichte purports to establish this system of duties is strictly transcendental in character: the various "oughts" it establishes are presented as so many conditions for the possibility of the original "ought," i.e. as conditions for the possibility of autonomous self-determination.

The third and in many respects most original systematic subdivision of the *Wissenschaftslehre* is called by Fichte "philosophy of the postulates." This portion of the system is concerned with the relationship between the theoretical and the practical realms and examines the specific demands (or "postulates") which each realm addresses to the other. Those postulates that theory addresses to the practical realm are the subject of the portion of the system entitled "theory of right" (*Rechtslehre*) or "natural right" (*Naturrecht*), whereas those postulates that practical philosophy addresses to the theoretical realm are the subject of the philosophy of religion.

Unlike ethics, which deals with rational (i.e. free) beings as such, the "theory of right" considers these same practical agents in their *individuality*, that is, as individual members of a community of free individuals. Such a philosophical science poses the question: How must the freedom of each individual be externally *limited* in order to permit every individual to pursue their individual goals to the fullest extent possible?

The *Foundations of Natural Right* begins with a general deduction of "intersubjectivity," that is, with a transcendental demonstration that a free individual can recognize itself as such only insofar as it recognizes the freedom of others, while simultaneously distinguishing itself from all of these other freely acting individuals. The next step is to stipulate the conditions for the possibility of such "mutual recognition" among free beings, the chief one of which is free acknowledgment of the legitimacy of the general rule of "right" or "justice," namely: "limit your own freedom in accordance with the concept of the freedom of all other persons with whom you come into contact" (I, 3: 320).

Since the mutual recognition in question, that is, the sway of the "rule of right," can be shown to be possible only within a free society, Fichte's examination of "natural right" quickly turns into a consideration, deeply indebted to Rousseau, of the nature of a just social order, the sources of political legitimacy, and some of the specific features of a "just state." Indeed, the *Foundations of Natural Right* could be described as a systematic effort to re-establish the *Social Contract* on purely transcendental foundations. It is the most important early presentation of Fichte's political philosophy.

From a purely systematic perspective, the most distinctive feature of Fichte's *Rechtslehre* is his clear awareness of the distinctively "mixed" character of such a discipline. It is "theoretical," because it speaks of a "world" (viz., the juridical or political order which is designed to constrain the activities of freely self-positing individuals in such a way that each can pursue their own goals); yet it is also "practical," because such a world is never simply "given" to us, but must be produced by free action. The just state is a human product, not something "natural"; but at the same time it is something *external*, something which, unlike purely ethical ends, cannot be achieved merely by internal self-limitation – though, to be sure, the "external limitations" required by the concept of "right" must be freely self-imposed (i.e. must be expressions of the "general will").

This is precisely what distinguishes the "science of right" from the "theory of ethics" (and distinguishes Fichte's treatment of the former from that of Kant, for whom the "theory of right" constitutes a subdivision of ethics): whereas ethics deals with the sphere of our duties, and thus with what is *demanded* of us as free individuals, the theory of natural right deals with those limitations of freedom which are required by the concept of a community of free individuals; i.e. it deals with what is *permitted*. Whereas ethics is concerned with the inner world of conscience, the theory of right is concerned only with the external, public realm – though only insofar as the latter can be viewed as an embodiment of freedom. Hence the concept of right obtains its binding force, not from the ethical law, but rather from the general laws of thinking and from enlightened self-interest. Such a force is hypothetical rather than categorical. If one is to posit one's own freedom, then one must posit the freedom of others and limit one's own freedom accordingly. It follows that a just political order is a demand of reason itself, since "the concept of justice or right is a condition of self-consciousness" (I, 3: 358).

The other subdivision of the theory of the postulates, that is, the philosophy of religion, is described as that philosophical science which concerns itself with the postulates which morality addresses to nature. As such, the philosophy of religion considers the manner in which the sensible realm of nature is supposed somehow to accommodate itself to the goal of morality, and thus it deals primarily with what is sometimes called the problem of "divine providence." Fichte himself, as we have noted, was prevented from fully developing this portion of his system while at Jena by, ironically enough, the outbreak of the atheism controversy. Nevertheless, one can gain some idea of his thoughts on this subject from the short essay, "On the Foundation of Our Belief in a Divine Government of the Universe," which precipitated the controversy in question. What one finds in this essay is, first of all, an attempt to draw a sharp distinction between religion and philosophy (corresponding to the all-important distinction between the "ordinary" and "transcendental" standpoints), and second, a defense of our right to postulate something like a "moral world order." But whereas Fichte argues that we are justified in believing that our conscientious actions will in fact "make a difference" in the real world, he resolutely insists (against the Kantians) that such a postulate does not require the postulate of a personal deity, a.k.a., "moral lawgiver." Thus the argument of the essay in question is primarily negative. It does not deny the existence of God, but it does deny that such a postulate is morally required or justified.

Finally, a word is perhaps in order concerning the general tenor or "spirit" of Fichte's Jena *Wissenschaftslehre*. Before finally settling upon a distinctive name for his new philosophy, Fichte considered various possibilities, one of which was *Strebungsphilosophie*, or "philosophy of striving" (II, 3: 265). As a description of "the first system of human freedom" this discarded appellation is particularly apt, for the general conclusion of the Jena *Wissenschaftslehre* is as follows: Freedom is possible and actual only within the context of natural necessity, where it is never "absolute," but always limited and finite. Though it must posit its freedom "absolutely" – that is to say, "purely and simply" (*schlechthin*) or "for no reason" – a genuinely free agent can actually exist only as a finite individual striving to overcome its own limitations and to transform the natural world in accordance with its own goal concepts. To be an "I" is thus to be involved in an endless process of self-overcoming, a process which necessarily takes place in reciprocal interaction with other self-overcoming agents and in the context of a spatio-temporal, material world. Without such limits, there can be neither freedom nor self-consciousness.

Such is the philosophical "vision" which presides over and gives direction to the often bewildering complexities of Fichte's Jena writings. The *Wissenschaftslehre* is a philosophy of projects, a "philosophy of the future." The famous "absolute I" with which the system begins is a mere abstraction, just as the final unity of the I with itself toward which it aspires is a sheer ideal. Between the abstraction and the ideal lies the entire realm of actual consciousness and experience, which, as we have seen, is necessarily a realm of finite, constrained freedom and of real, empirical nature, which exists only "for consciousness" – even though the specific determinacy of this natural world remains philosophically inexplicable. What we *can* grasp is that the world is not now as it ought to be and that it is up to us to change it. Hence Fichte's parting injunction to the students who flocked to his lectures during his first semester at Jena: "Act! Act! That is what we are here for" (I, 3: 67).

❧ SCHELLING'S *NATURPHILOSOPHIE* AND ❧ SYSTEM OF IDENTITY

Even in a period when observers were in the habit of keeping a weather eye on the philosophical horizon for the emergence of the newest star, Friedrich Wilhelm Joseph Schelling was a phenomenon: a philosophical

Wunderkind who lived a long life, marked by what at least appeared to be dramatic and frequent shifts of philosophical orientation. Accordingly, it is customary to divide Schelling's philosophical career into a number of more or less distinct phases or periods, though scholars disagree among themselves over the precise number of periods and the degree of underlying continuity in Schelling's development. Here, in any case, we will confine our attention to the period prior to his departure from Jena in 1803.

Born near Stuttgart in 1775, Schelling was the son of a Schwabian pastor and duly attended the seminary at Tübingen, where he became close friends with Hölderlin and Hegel. His first philosophical publication, an essay on "the philosophy of mythology," appeared in 1793, when its author was barely 18 years old. With the publication of Fichte's first systematic writings, Schelling immediately became an enthusiastic exponent of the same and devoted his next two publications, *On the Possibility of a Form for All Philosophy* (1794) and *On the I as the Principle of Philosophy* (1795), to expounding and defending this latest version of transcendental idealism.

After leaving Tübingen in 1795, Schelling spent three years as a tutor to the children of a wealthy nobleman, a post which provided him ample opportunity for travel and independent study (including an extended period during which he studied physics, medicine, and mathematics at the University of Leipzig). During these years he became a regular contributor to the *Philosophical Journal*, where he published his *Philosophical Letters on Dogmatism and Criticism* (1795), as well as his *New Deduction of Natural Right* (1796)

A growing enthusiasm for Spinoza began to become increasingly evident in Schelling's writings of this period, along with mounting reservations concerning the *Wissenschaftslehre*. Above all, Schelling was dissatisfied with the status assigned to "nature" by Fichte's system. Indeed, one could characterize Schelling's philosophical project at this point as an attempt to replace Fichte's "lifeless" conception of nature with a more adequate one modeled on Spinoza's notion of *natura naturans*, but to do so without overstepping the bounds of transcendental idealism (e.g. by assimilating Spinoza's "infinite substance" or God to the idealists' "transcendental I").

Stimulated both by his enthusiasm for Spinoza and by his own scientific studies, Schelling gradually became preoccupied by efforts to construct a systematic *Naturphilosophie* or "philosophy of nature." To be sure, he was not alone. Others, for example Goethe, were also vocal in their dissatisfaction with what they regarded as the unnecessarily mechanistic and reductive character of the Newtonian worldview. Nevertheless, Schelling gave a distinctive twist to this project, inasmuch as he attempted to develop a more holistic view of nature which would at the same time be at least compatible with (if not actually a systematic subdivision of) the new transcendental philosophy of Kant and Fichte. Of his many publications on this topic, the more important include *Ideas for a Philosophy of Nature* (1797) and *On the World-Soul* (1798), as well as the *Journal of Speculative Physics* (1800–3).

In 1798 Schelling received an academic appointment at Jena, where he remained until 1803. Though he had frequent contact with Fichte during his first year in Jena, he was even more intimately associated with a younger and more artistically inclined circle, which included the Schlegel brothers, Tieck, and Novalis. Indeed, his philosophy of this period exercised a seminal influence upon the birth of "German romanticism," just as the latter, in turn, deeply influenced the subsequent development of Schelling's own thinking.

Even as he was exploring "speculative physics" and attempting to supplement transcendental idealism with *Naturphilosophie*, Schelling was also engaged in an attempt to construct a revised and improved presentation of transcendental idealism itself. His lectures on this subject resulted, in 1800, in the publication of what is perhaps, from both a literary and a philosophical point of view, his most successful single publication, *The System of Transcendental Idealism*.

Because of the quite privileged status assigned to art at the conclusion of the latter work, this phase of Schelling's thought is sometimes characterized as "aesthetic idealism." But Schelling's interest in art was not a merely passing phase, nor was it purely theoretical in character. Just as he had previously supplemented his efforts to construct a *Naturphilosophie* by studying the empirical sciences, so too, under the tutelage of Friedrich Schlegel, he attempted to cultivate himself aesthetically by making a systematic, empirical study of the history of art. The fruits of this intensive effort are apparent in the richly detailed lectures on the philosophy of art he delivered first at Jena (1801–3) and then at Würzburg (1803–4).

Schelling's Jena philosophy culminates in his efforts, in the years immediately following the publication of his *System of Transcendental Idealism*, to make explicit the implicit harmony between the philosophy of nature and transcendental idealism. In order to accomplish this goal, he incorporated both of these "sciences" within a larger, more encompassing system, which he dubbed the "System of Identity" or "Absolute Idealism" and expounded in a series of publications, including the *Presentation of my System of Philosophy* (1801), *Bruno, or On the Natural and the Divine Principle of Things* (1802), and what is unquestionably the most accessible and "popular" presentation of this phase of his thought, *On University Studies*.

This was also the period of close and regular collaboration between Schelling and Hegel, who arrived in Jena in 1801. For the next two years the two were allied in a collaborative effort to explicate and to defend the new System of Identity. In pursuit of this goal, they founded and co-wrote the entire contents of a short-lived new *Critical Journal of Philosophy*. During this same period the rift between Schelling and Fichte – a rift which originally arose over Fichte's misgivings at Schelling's efforts to "supplement" transcendental philosophy with *Naturphilosophie* and then turned into a more general disagreement concerning the nature and limits of philosophy itself – became permanent and public.

In 1803 Schelling, accompanied by his new wife Caroline (ex-wife of A.W. Schlegel), left Jena for a chair at the University of Würzburg, which had only recently come under the protection of the Bavarian Crown. In 1806 Schelling moved to Munich, where he served as general secretary of the Academy of Fine Art and delivered occasional public lectures as a member of the Bavarian Academy of Science. Later, following the establishment of the University of Munich, Schelling was appointed to a professorship. As a Protestant in a Catholic state increasingly dominated by ultramontane forces, Schelling found himself under growing pressure, but he nevertheless remained in Munich until his move to Berlin in 1841 (except for the period from 1820 to 1827, which he spent as a professor at the Protestant University of Erlangen).

For the next several years Schelling continued to develop and to defend his System of Identity (see e.g. his *System of Philosophy as a Whole and of the Philosophy of Nature in Particular*, 1804), while continuing to cultivate his interests in the philosophy of art (see e.g. *Concerning the Relationship of the Plastic Arts to Nature*, 1807) and *Naturphilosophie* (establishing yet another new journal, the *Yearbook for Medicine as Science*, 1805–8). However, the most distinctive feature of Schelling's thought during this period was a growing concern with religious issues and a particular fascination with the Gnostic tradition, as embodied, for example, in the theosophical writing of Jakob Boehme. This new interest is reflected in all of Schelling's post-Jena writings, and is especially prominent in his well-known *Philosophical Inquiries into the Nature of Human Freedom* (1809).

Eventually, Schelling's public forays into religious issues embroiled him in a bitter public controversy with Jacobi. At roughly the same time he also broke with his erstwhile ally Hegel, who, without mentioning Schelling by name, had mercilessly lampooned the System of Identity in the Preface to his *Phenomenology of Spirit*. Following the death of Caroline in 1809, Schelling's activity as a philosophical author virtually ceased. He began to associate more and more with conservative social and religious elements, defended the reactionary alliance of "throne and altar" represented by the Karlsbad decrees, and proudly identified himself as an opponent of "old-Jacobin views and of shallow Enlightenment."

From 1811 to 1813 Schelling worked on an ambitious speculative interpretation of human history, *The Ages of the World*. He went so far as to have text set in type, but withdrew it from publication at the last moment. He also began to lecture on the history of philosophy, and his lectures on this subject reveal an extraordinary animus against his erstwhile philosophical allies and a special resentment toward the growing success of Hegel's dialectical idealism. More and more, however, his lectures and writings focused upon the same three subjects: art, mythology, and religion.

In 1841 Schelling relocated to Berlin, where he was appointed Privy Councilor to the court as well as Professor of Philosophy, charged with the task of stamping out the "dragon's seed of Hegelianism." To the disappointment of the civil authorities, as well as that of his auditors (whose ranks included Kierkegaard, Bakunin, and Engels), Schelling barely touched upon political and social philosophy in his lectures at Berlin. Instead, he devoted them almost entirely to the development of his new philosophy of revelation and methodology. By this point he had begun to characterize his new standpoint as "positive philosophy," in contradistinction to the purely "negative" philosophy of Kant, Fichte, and Hegel – as well as of his own Jena period. Increasingly isolated from his students and contemporaries, Schelling finally died in 1854 in Bad Ragaz in Switzerland, where he had gone to recover from a cold.

It is difficult to comment briefly upon the thought of a philosopher whose intellectual development went through as many apparent "shifts" and phases as Schelling's. Nevertheless, some brief description of Schelling's philosophical itinerary prior to 1804 is called for, beginning with his first, self-consciously "Fichtean" phase. First of all, there is some question concerning the extent to which Schelling was ever an orthodox follower of Fichte, since important differences between his views and Fichte's are apparent even in his earlier writings. In hindsight, anyway, most scholars would agree with Schelling's own judgment of 1807, that "there was certainly a time when I sought to find something higher and deeper in [Fichte's] philosophy than I could in fact find there" (7: 23).[2] Still, the differences are hardly overwhelming, and it is hard to blame the young Schelling's contemporaries for initially classifying him as little more than "the town-crier of the I."

In retrospect, of course, one can detect the seeds of future development in Schelling's reluctance to endorse Fichte's view of the I as a pure activity and in his insistence, already apparent in *On the I*, on talking about the "being" of the I, and the various "spiritual properties" of the same. As has already been mentioned, however, the most striking difference between Schelling and Fichte at this point concerned the status of "nature" – both within transcendental philosophy itself and as an object of a special philosophical science.

The growing differences between Schelling and Fichte are even more apparent in the former's *Philosophical Letters on Dogmatism and Criticism*, in which the system of Spinoza ("dogmatism") is compared to that of Fichte ("criticism"), ostensibly to the advantage of the latter. Even here, however, it is apparent that Schelling's deeper interest is not so much to demonstrate the incommensurability of these rival systems as it is to find some way of combining Spinoza's superior grasp of objective reality with Fichte's transcendental analysis of subjective freedom.

Another significant difference between Schelling and Fichte, even at this early date, is hinted at in the former's casual reference to an "intellectual intuition of the world" (I: 285). Whereas for Fichte, "intellectual intuition" designated the abstractly conceived "self-positing" of the I, Schelling was prepared to employ this same term in a much broader sense to designate an allegedly "higher," non-sensible type of "direct perception" of objective reality, so that one could speak of an intellectual intuition of the Not-I as well as of the I. Understood in this manner, "intellectual intuition" was transformed into a special "faculty of truth" possessed by at least some individual human beings. It is this sense of "intellectual intuition" which attracted the attention of Novalis and Friedrich Schlegel and finally led Schelling himself to assert that "art is the organ of philosophy."

Schelling's dissatisfaction with the purely formal or "negative" concept of nature defended by Fichte, together with his admiration for Spinoza's interpretation of nature as a self-developing whole (*natura naturans*) soon led Schelling to make his first truly independent contributions to philosophy. Initially, this took the form of an effort to *supplement* transcendental idealism, which attempts to derive our knowledge of objects from an initial act of self-positing, with a "philosophy of nature" or *Naturphilosophie* that attempts just the opposite: i.e. the derivation of consciousness from objects. *Naturphilosophie* begins with nature as "pure objectivity" and then shows how nature undergoes a process of unconscious self-development, culminating in the production of the conditions for its own self-representation, that is, in the emergence of mind of spirit. *Naturphilosophie* thus shows how subjectivity emerges from pure objectivity. As precedents for this way of viewing nature, Schelling could refer, not only to Spinoza and Goethe, but also to Kant. Not only are features of Schelling's view of nature anticipated in Kant's discussion (in the *Critique of Judgment*) of natural teleology, but Kant had also attempted (in his *Metaphysical Foundations of Natural Science*) to develop a "metaphysico-dynamical" theory of matter as an equilibrium of opposed forces. Indeed, Schelling called explicit attention to the parallels between Kant's theory of matter and his own, though he noted that the "positive elements" in Kant's theory "remained too subordinate" (5: 332).

Rather than viewing nature merely as the "other" of consciousness, Schelling's *Naturphilosophie* seeks to interpret it as an analogon of the same: to treat nature as "visible spirit" and spirit as "invisible nature" (2: 56). So viewed, nature no longer appears to be the mechanically ordered, lifeless realm of the Not-I; instead, it becomes a living, self-organizing system in its own right, one not of mechanical relations between material "things," but of dynamic relations between forces, a self-developing, organic whole, containing within itself its own end or purpose: viz., the production of ever higher natural forms, culminating in mind itself.

In contrast with the approach of the experimental sciences, the method of *Naturphilosophie* is fundamentally *a priori*. It begins with the concept of the *unity* of nature (*natura naturans*) and then deals with the *diversity* of the same (*natura naturata*) by interpreting nature as a *system* of opposed forces or "polarities." The task of *Naturphilosophie* or "speculative physics" is to describe this system, from its highest, self-organizing principle ("the world soul") to the various specific oppositions or "polarities" (e.g. attraction and repulsion, positive and negative forces, light and darkness), which manifest themselves in ever more complex levels of organization, referred to by Schelling as "powers" or "potencies" (*Potenzen*). At the first level or "power," nature appears as a system of independent physical bodies; at the second, it is a realm of dynamic processes; whereas at the third and highest level it appears as a completely organic realm, indeed, as a single "organism." This hierarchical scheme reflects the teleological character of nature itself, inasmuch as the lower levels of organization can be adequately "explained" only in terms of the higher.

Whereas Schelling, in the first edition of his *Ideas for a Philosophy of Nature*, still sought to provide something resembling a 'transcendental deduction" of the "idea of nature," he dispensed entirely with such a derivation in the second edition (1803). In the new System of Identity the duality between nature and spirit proceeds directly from the point of "absolute indifference" with which the system begins; and thus the requisite concept of nature is immediately available for philosophical analysis.

In fact, the very idea of a *Naturphilosophie* was based from the start upon the idea of the "Absolute" (not to be confused with the "absolute I" of transcendental philosophy), an idea which can be warranted neither on empirical nor on transcendental grounds. Instead, as in Spinoza and in Schelling's own System of Identity, the idea of the

Absolute must simply be asserted as the philosophical starting point. Hence, by 1801 at the latest, Schelling had come to the clear recognition that the philosophy of nature is not an autonomous, self-grounded science, but "can proceed from nothing but a system of identity" (5: 116).

As has been emphasized, Schelling never considered his interest in the philosophy of nature to be in any way incompatible with his commitment to transcendental idealism. Instead, he viewed the two as complementary, as two sides of the same coin and two branches of a single, more comprehensive system, which he eventually names the "System of Identity." Before commenting upon the latter, however, let us consider a few of the more distinctive features of Schelling's own essay into transcendental philosophy in his *System of Transcendental Idealism*.

Whereas *Naturphilosophie* traverses the path from sheer objectivity to subjectivity, transcendental idealism proceeds in the diametrically opposed direction: pure subjectivity (self-consciousness) to objectivity (the necessary positing of the Not-I, or nature). This latter path, of course, was already blazed by the *Wissenschaftslehre*, and Schelling's description of it resembles Fichte's in many of its details. Adapting Fichte's characterization of transcendental philosophy as a "pragmatic history" of the human mind, Schelling's presentation of transcendental idealism takes the form of an analysis of successive "epochs" of consciousness; hence it moves from "sensation" to "sensible intuition," from "intuition" to "reflection," and from "reflection" to "willing." At the same time, Schelling also attempts to indicate how each of these stages in the transcendental "history" of self-consciousness is correlated with a specific *Potenz* of nature itself.

After having derived "willing," Schelling turns to what is (at least in comparison with Fichte's treatments of these topics) a rather perfunctory account of the "practical" portion of transcendental idealism, that is, to a deduction of intersubjectivity, the categorical imperative, the system of moral duties, and finally, the system of rights or laws. An innovation in Schelling's account of "natural right" and the just state is his explicit attention to the temporal, that is to say, historical, evolution of a just social order. Thus the *System of Transcendental Idealism* presents us, almost in passing, with an interpretation of human history as a process of *endless progress* toward the full realization of freedom, and thus as a "continual and gradual self-revelation of the absolute" (3: 603). Schelling's remarkable suggestion that history bears the same relation to practical philosophy that nature bears to theoretical philosophy implies that Fichte overlooked one of the "real sciences" which should constitute a separate subdivision of any complete transcendental system, viz., philosophy of history.

By far the most innovative and influential portion of Schelling's *System of Transcendental Idealism*, however, is its concluding section, "Deduction of the Universal Organ of Philosophy, or, Essentials of the Philosophy of Art according to Transcendental Idealism." Here Schelling treats art, not merely as capable of providing us with an "as if" glimpse of noumenal reality (Kant), nor as capable of assisting in the transition from the ordinary to the transcendental standpoint (Fichte), but rather as accomplishing – albeit in a concrete rather than in an abstract form – the very task of transcendental idealism. It is precisely within aesthetic experience, according to Schelling, that the identity between the subjective and the objective, what is conscious (freedom) and what is unconscious (nature), becomes an *object* to the experiencing I itself. This unity is present in the *art product*, the "beauty" of which is explicable only as a finite display of the infinite. The art product, in turn, can achieve this synthesis only because of the distinctive character of the activity which produces it. Artistic production, unlike all other human activities, is simultaneously free and unfree, conscious and unconscious.

Rather than attempting to explicate further the distinctive character of artistic production, Schelling simply invokes at this point "the obscure concept of 'genius'," (3: 616). Thus he was led by the force of his own argument to the conclusion that it is here and only here – in the productive activity of the artistic genius, in the "art product" which results from this activity, and finally, in the secondary type of "genius" required for genuine aesthetic appreciation – that the fundamental insight of transcendental idealism (viz., the identity of the ideal and the real) becomes apparent *within empirical consciousness*. This, therefore, is the meaning of the oft-quoted claim that art is "the only true and eternal organ and document of philosophy" (3: 627), for it is within aesthetic experience – and there alone – that the philosopher encounters in an objective form that intuition which allegedly grounds their entire transcendental system. By appealing to (objective) aesthetic intuition, the transcendental philosopher can defend him- or herself from the charge that the "intellectual intuition" with which they begin is nothing but a subjective illusion.

With this typically bold move, Schelling elevated the philosophy of art or aesthetics into a central position within his overall system. In fact, it could be argued that the "philosophy of art" outlined by Schelling during this period (1800–4) should really be viewed as constituting a third, co-equal branch of his overall System of Identity, one which should take its rightful place alongside *Naturphilosophie* and transcendental idealism. If, as Schelling maintains, art is "a necessary appearance which flows directly from the Absolute" (5: 345), then art, nature, and spirit are merely three different expressions or manifestations of the underlying reality.

In the years following the publication of the *System of Transcendental Idealism* the philosophy of art sketched at the conclusion of that work was elaborated by Schelling along Platonic (or Neo-platonic) lines. Thus, in his *Bruno*, as in his lectures on *The Philosophy of Art*, he interprets individual works of art as participating in or reflecting the various divine "Ideas." No aspect of Schelling's philosophy exercised a greater influence upon his contemporaries than his remarks on art, which fell on fertile ground and were further developed into what amounted to a religion of art by the early German romantics. Schelling himself, however, was never guilty of trying to supplant philosophy with art (even though he may have come perilously close to this at the conclusion of his *System of Transcendental Idealism*, where he calls for a "new mythology" which will represent the triumphant return of science to poetry and the synthesis of both). Instead, he insisted that art and philosophy should be viewed as correlative: art as the *real* and philosophy as the *ideal* reflection of one and the same absolute reality. What is present to the philosopher as a "subjective reflection" is present to the artist as an "objective reality"; but for this very reason the artist, who is inspired by a "genius" he himself does not clearly comprehend, remains unconscious of the true and "absolute" nature of his or her object, whereas the philosopher can acquire genuine "knowledge" of the identity in question. "This is why philosophy, despite its inner identity with art, remains always and necessarily science – i.e. ideal – and art remains always and necessarily art – i.e. real" (5: 349).

If transcendental idealism traces the path from "the ideal" to "the real" and *Naturphilosophie* the path from "the real" to "the ideal," and if it is also true that the basic presupposition underlying all true science is "the essential unity of the unconditionally real and the unconditionally ideal," a unity which is identical to "the idea of the Absolute" (5: 216), then surely it behooves the systematic philosopher to make this underlying unity as explicit as possible. This is precisely the task of Schelling's "System of Identity": to give philosophical substance to his frequently repeated assurance that transcendental idealism and *Naturphilosophie* are mutually complementary. Since this new system recognizes the total interpenetration of the real and the ideal at every level, Schelling called it "objective" or "absolute idealism" (5: 112). Since it asserts the underlying identity of mind and nature, as well as of all other experienced differences (including the philosophical differences between the systems of Spinoza and Fichte), he also called it the "System of Identity."

The most distinctive feature of this new system is that it *begins* with a bald assertion of the unity of thought and being, that is, with the idea of the "Absolute" or "reason." As Schelling explains, "this is the idea of the Absolute: viz., that in relation to the absolute, the idea is also being, and thus the absolute is also the first presupposition of knowing and is itself the first knowledge" (5: 216). Consequently, it is futile to demand any sort of philosophical deduction of or justification for the idea of Absolute Identity. Instead, the unity expressed by this idea must simply be presupposed.

The System of Identity commences not with the transcendental idealist's principle of self-identity, but with the still broader principle of identity as such, an identity which transcends and comprises every conceivable difference (hence Schelling's description of his own starting point as the "point of indifference"). To express this bare logical idea of an identity underlying every difference, Schelling utilized the abstract formula "A=A," which he consequently characterized as expressing "the supreme law of reason." From this undifferentiated or "indifferent" starting point, he then proceeded to a description (albeit a remarkably abstract one) of reality as a whole, considered as a differentiated system within which unity is maintained by various synthetic relationships, such as substance and attribute, cause and effect, attraction and repulsion, etc. As in his philosophy of nature, Schelling's System of Identity utilizes the notion of various hierarchically related *Potenzen* as its basic organizing principle. For since, as Schelling notes, there is only *one* absolute and identical reality, it follows that "diversity among things is possible only to the extent that the undivided whole is posited under various determinations [or 'powers']" (5: 366).

It must be confessed that, for all of Schelling's dialectical ingenuity, the details of his exposition of this system remain extraordinarily obscure. Though this is especially true of his attempts at a systematic presentation modeled on Spinoza's *Ethics* (e.g. in the *Presentation of my System of Philosophy*), it is also true of the "conversational" presentation contained in the dialogue *Bruno*, as well as of the informal exposition contained in the first of his lectures *On University Studies*. However, few critics of Schelling's System of Identity even bother to examine the details of his exposition and most limit themselves to pointing out the alleged emptiness or incoherence of the first principle of the same. Generations of students and scholars have been content to echo Hegel's famous characterization of Schelling's Absolute as "the night in which all cows are black."

However, even if one overlooks the difficulty of grasping its abstract starting point, the System of Identity still suffers from an even more serious problem, viz., its inability to give an adequate explanation of the *why* and the *how* of the initial movement from the point of indifference or identity to a (real) system of differentiated elements. The difficulty in question concerns the relationship between the "indifferent absolute" and everything else (and indeed, the very intelligibility of positing anything "else" beyond or outside of the "Absolute"). How, precisely, is one to understand the transition, demanded by this philosophy, from unity to difference, from the one to the many, from the eternal to the temporal, from the infinite to the finite, from the abstract to the concrete, from form to content, etc.? Schelling himself was clearly dissatisfied with his own solution to these questions, though not with the questions themselves; indeed, they may be said to have set the agenda for his entire subsequent philosophical development.

The more one reflects upon the problem of the transition from the Absolute to its finite manifestations, the easier it is to see why, in the period immediately after his departure from Jena, Schelling was increasingly attracted to various forms of Platonism and Neo-platonism and was particularly fascinated by the works of Bruno and Boehme; for all of these preceding philosophies explicitly address the question of how the finite can be said to "proceed from" the infinite. Furthermore, all of them tend to interpret the former merely as an "appearance of" or "way of looking at" the latter – albeit a necessary one.

Ultimately, Schelling seems to have acknowledged the intractability of this problem, at least within the framework of his earlier philosophy. Indeed, beginning with his *Philosophical Inquiries into the Nature of Human Freedom*, all of his later works may be seen as attempts to resolve this very problem, and to do so by moving from a purely abstract or formal philosophy of logical relations – a "negative" philosophy incapable of addressing questions of "existence" – to a "positive" philosophy, better able to open itself to the mystery of existence.

If Fichte's philosophy may be called a "philosophy of striving," Schelling's may be characterized as a philosophy of speculative salvation, inspired, above all, by a deep longing to restore a presumably lost unity or harmony. This longing is expressed in the profoundly "metaphysical" character of all of Schelling's writings, including his earliest ones. As early as 1795, he characterized philosophy's task as "solving the problem of the existence of the world" (1: 314), a formulation which certainly betrays a radically different spirit from that expressed in Fichte's description of philosophy's task as "explaining the origin of representations accompanied by a feeling of necessity," though not inconsistent with it.

It is quite in keeping with this difference that Schelling should have soon discarded the strictly transcendental approach to philosophy and should have transformed his system into a doctrine of the Absolute, for only such a doctrine is capable of addressing the "riddle of existence." A genuinely Critical or transcendental philosophy, in contrast, while not denying the presence of such a "riddle" within human life, also acknowledges philosophy's utter inability to solve it.

But the differences between Schelling and Fichte extend beyond their disagreement concerning the limits of philosophy, and include – if indeed they are not based upon – a disagreement concerning the very aim of human life. In Fichte's view, consciousness is necessarily divided against itself and the world; freedom is expressed through practical striving; and harmonious self-identity remains an unobtainable ideal. For Schelling, on the other hand, unity is always present, however obscured by appearances; all that prevents us from acknowledging this, and thereby obtaining a kind of salvation, is our lack of knowledge.

Moreover, according to Schelling, philosophy itself – that is, a misguided philosophy of "mere reflection" – is largely responsible for our present, torn condition, our separation from nature and from our own true selves. We suffer from a "spiritual sickness"; we long for restoration of a "lost unity." But the way to recover our health and restore this unity is not to reject philosophy, but to replace a shallow and false philosophy with a profound and true one: "to abolish the split at a higher power by means of speculation" (5: 121).

In the end, there is no better way to characterize the "presiding spirit" of Schelling's thought than to contrast it with that of Fichte's, and this contrast is nowhere better expressed than by Schelling himself, in his first lecture *On University Studies*, where he wrote, in a transparent allusion to Fichte: " 'Action! Action!' is the call that resounds from many quarters, most loudly however from those who do not wish to proceed with knowledge" (5: 452) Though Schelling undoubtedly included himself among the ranks of the latter, he never considered knowledge to be an end in itself, but only a means: a means for overcoming our divided selves, a means toward salvation. It is no accident that, whereas Fichte's most original philosophical contributions were to ethics and social philosophy, Schelling's were to the philosophy of art and philosophy of religion.

∽ THE LATER PHILOSOPHIES OF FICHTE ∽ AND SCHELLING

Even the most casual reader must be struck by the obvious superficial differences between the many versions of the *Wissenschaftslehre* Fichte wrote after 1800 and the two presentations of the "foundations" of the same he produced while in Jena. Experts continue to differ among themselves, however, concerning the depth and significance of the differences in question, with some arguing for a radical break in Fichte's intellectual development after the move to Berlin and others emphasizing the continuity of his writings and the similarities between the systems of his Jena and Berlin periods. (Fichte himself never renounced his earlier writings nor did he emphasize the differences between the various versions of the *Wissenschaftslehre*; on the contrary, he tended to describe them simply as so many different expressions or presentations of one and the same "spirit.")

So too in the case of Schelling, though here the differences are, if anything, even more striking (and of course Schelling himself called explicit attention to the differences between his earlier, "negative" philosophy and the "positive" philosophy of his Berlin years). Nevertheless, there are distinguished scholars who attempt to emphasize the continuity of Schelling's intellectual development and scorn the traditional division of his works into a series of separate "periods." Still, no reader of the *Philosophical Inquiries into the Nature of Human Freedom* or the posthumously published Berlin lectures on *Philosophy of Mythology* and *Philosophy of Revelations* can fail to note the tremendous difference between these works and the writings of Schelling's Jena period.

Moreover, even those scholars who acknowledge the fundamental differences between Fichte's earlier and later works, or between Schelling's earlier and later writings, disagree concerning the causes or reasons for these differences. Whereas some emphasize the role of "external" factors (such as, in the case of Fichte, the atheism controversy, the dispute with Jacobi, and the French occupation of Prussia, or, in the case of Schelling, the influence of figures such as Franz von Baader, Schelling's resentment at the successes of his contemporaries, and the general reactionary mood which engulfed Europe in the wake of the Congress of Vienna), others point to internal, philosophical reasons for the specific changes they purport to find in Fichte's and Schelling's post-Jena writings.

It has been said of Fichte that whereas his earlier thought and writings belong to the history of philosophy, his later work – with the exception of such "popular" efforts as *The Way toward the Blessed Life* and the *Addresses to the German Nation* – are of purely biographical interest, and the same could be said of the works of Schelling's final period. The point of such observations, presumably, is to call attention to the greater influence the early writings of each man had upon the subsequent history of "German Idealism." This, of course, is hardly surprising, given the fact that the most important theoretical writings of both Fichte's and Schelling's later years were not published until years after their deaths. However, this fact alone should not be allowed to suggest that the later writings of either are somehow lacking in intrinsic, philosophical merit. On the contrary, it is precisely the later, posthumously published writings of both Fichte and Schelling which have received the most concentrated attention from recent and contemporary scholars.

Large claims have been made on behalf of the later versions of Fichte's philosophy, and especially concerning the 1804 *Wissenschaftslehre* (which replaces the first principle of the Jena versions – viz., "the I simply posits itself" – with the lapidary proposition, "there is truth"). So too, far more attention has been paid in recent decades to Schelling's post-1803 writings than to his earlier works. In particular, his 1809 *Philosophical Inquiries into the Nature of Human Freedom* has been the subject of studies by such eminent thinkers as Karl Jaspers, Paul Tillich, and Martin Heidegger, all of whom agree in interpreting this text as a harbinger of twentieth-century existentialism. Other scholars have pointed to the lectures Schelling delivered during his final Berlin years as representing, not merely the logical conclusion of his own protracted philosophical development, but the culmination of German Idealism as a whole. Consequently, no well-informed contemporary student of either Fichte or Schelling would be likely to dismiss the later writings of either as lacking in interest or value.

Nevertheless, from the standpoint of a "history of German Idealism" it remains true that the Jena writings of Fichte and Schelling are the ones that matter most. They are the ones upon which their contemporary reputations were largely based, just as they are the writings which most influenced the immediately subsequent history of philosophy (unlike the later works, which exercised a negligible influence upon the "history of German Idealism"). To take a particular case in point, Hegel's philosophy, at least in the form in which we are familiar with it, is quite inconceivable apart from Fichte's Jena *Wissenschaftslehre* and Schelling's *Naturphilosophie* and System of Identity.

Hence there is some justification in the present context for ignoring the later published and unpublished writings of Fichte and Schelling. This, however, should not be taken as an implicit judgment upon the relative philosophical worth of the earlier and later writings of either Fichte or Schelling, nor is it meant as an endorsement of Hegel's self-serving interpretation of the philosophical merits of Fichte and Schelling, whom he tended to treat as little more than stepping stones toward his own version of speculative idealism. On the contrary, one must strenuously guard against such an interpretation, even if limited to the Jena writings of Fichte and Schelling. To interpret these solely in the light of their reception and critique by Hegel and others is to distort and to misunderstand them, a misunderstanding not unlike the one which would be involved if one were to read Plato merely as forerunner of Aristotle, or Descartes simply as a step along the path to Spinoza.

Quite apart from its historical influence, Fichte's Jena *Wissensch-*

aftslehre stands on its own as a unique and enduring, albeit widely misunderstood, contribution to philosophy, and the same can be said of Schelling's *System of Transcendental Idealism*, as well as of his various attempts to construct a "philosophy of nature" and to articulate his "System of Identity." Nobody today interprets Kant's *Critiques* merely as an "influence" upon the development of Hegelianism, even though they manifestly were such. So too, it is high time that the early writings of Fichte and Schelling be accorded the same intellectual courtesy – that is, the courtesy of being allowed to stand or to fall on their own merits.

❧ NOTES ❧

1 Fichte's writings and letters are cited, by series, volume, and page number, according to the text of the (still incomplete) new critical edition: *J.G. Fichte: Gesamtausgabe der Bayerischen Akademie der Wissenschaften*, 24 vols (to date) ed. R. Lauth *et al.* (Stuggart and Bad Cannstatt: Frommann, 1964–. All English translations are by the author (though Fichte's italics have not always been retained).

2 Schelling's writings are cited, by volume and page number, according to the first collected edition, edited by his son, F.K.A. Schelling: *Friedrich Wilhelm Joseph von Schellings sämmtliche Werke*, 14 vols (Stuttgart: Cotta, 1856–61). Translations are by the author.

❧ SELECT BIBLIOGRAPHY ❧

Fichte

Original language editions

5.1 *J.G. Fichte: Gesamtausgabe der Bayerischen Akademie der Wissenschaften*, 24 vols (to date), ed. R. Lauth, H. Jacobs, and H. Gliwitzky, Stuttgart and Bad Cannstatt: Frommann, 1964–.

5.2 *Johann Gottlieb Fichtes nachgelassene Werke*, 3 vols, ed. I.H. Fichte, Bonn: Adolph-Marcus, 1834–5.

5.3 *Johann Gottlieb Fichtes sämmtliche Werke*, 8 vols, ed. I.H. Fichte, Berlin: Veit, 1845–6.

English translations

5.4 *Attempt at a Critique of All Revelation* (1792, 1793), trans. G. Green, New York: Cambridge University Press, 1978.

5.5 *Fichte: Early Philosophical Writings*, trans. and ed. D. Breazeale, Ithaca: Cornell University Press, 1988.

5.6 *Fichte: Science of Knowledge (Wissenschaftslehre)*, trans. P. Heath and J. Lachs, New York, Appleton-Century-Crofts, 1970; 2nd edn, Cambridge: Cambridge University Press, 1982.

5.7 *Foundations of Transcendental Philosophy (Wissenschaftslehre) nova methodo* (1796–9), trans. and ed. D. Breazeale, Ithaca: Cornell University Press, 1992.

5.8 "On the Foundation of our Belief in a Divine Government of the Universe" (1798), trans. P. Edwards, in P.L. Gardiner (ed.) *Nineteenth Century Philosophy*, New York: Free Press, 1969.

5.9 *The Vocation of Man* (1800), trans. P. Preuss, Indianapolis: Hackett, 1987.

5.10 "A Crystal Clear Report to the General Public Concerning the Actual Essence of the Newest Philosophy: An Attempt to Force the Reader to Understand" (1801), trans. J. Botterman and W. Rash, in E. Behler (ed.) *Philosophy of German Idealism*, New York: Continuum, 1987.

5.11 *The Popular Works of Johann Gottlieb Fichte*, trans. W. Smith, 2 vols, London: Chapman, 1848–9; 4th edn, 1889.

5.12 *Addresses to the German Nation* (1808), trans. R.F. Jones and G.H. Turnbull, ed. G.A. Kelly, New York: Harper & Row, 1968.

5.13 "The Science of Knowledge in its General Outline" (1810), trans. W.E. Wright, *Idealistic Studies*, 6 (1976): 106–17.

Bibliography

5.14 Baumgartner, H.M. and Jacobs, W.G. *J.G. Fichte: Bibliographie*, Stuttgart and Bad Cannstatt: Frommann, 1968.

5.15 Breazeale, D. "Fichte in English: A Complete Bibliography," in D. Breazeale and T. Rockmore (eds) *Fichte: Historical Context and Contemporary Controversies*, Atlantic City: Humanities Press, 1993.

5.16 Doré, S. *et al.* "J.G. Fichte – Bibliographie (1968–1991)," *Fichte-Studien*, 4 (1992).

Influences and development

5.17 Baumanns, P. *Fichtes ursprüngliches System. Sein Standort zwischen Kant und Hegel*, Stuttgart and Bad Cannstatt: Frommann, 1972.

5.18 Gueroult, M. *L'Evolution et la structure de la doctrine de la science chez Fichte*, 2 vols, Paris: Société de l'édition, 1930.

5.19 Wundt, M. *Fichte-Forschungen*, Stuttgart: Frommann, 1929.

General surveys

5.20 Adamson, R. *Fichte*, Edinburgh: Blackwood, 1881.

5.21 Baumanns, P. *Fichte*, Freiburg: Alber, 1990.

5.22 Jacobs, W.G. *Johann Gottlieb Fichte*, Reinbeck bei Hamburg: Rowohlt, 1984.
5.23 Léon, X. *Fichte et son temps*, 3 vols, Paris: Armand Colin, 1922–7.
5.24 Philonenko, A. *L'Oeuvre de Fichte*, Paris: Vrin, 1984.
5.25 Rohs, P. *Johann Gottlieb Fichte*, Munich: Beck, 1991.
5.26 Widmann, J. *Johann Gottlieb Fichte*, Berlin: de Gruyter, 1982.

Interpretations of the Jena Wissenschaftslehre

5.27 Everett, C.C. *Fichte's Science of Knowledge: A Critical Exposition*, Chicago: Griggs, 1884.
5.28 Hohler, T.P. *Imagination and Reflection: Intersubjectivity. Fichte's Grundlage of 1794*, The Hague: Nijhoff, 1982.
5.29 Pareyson, L. *Fichte: Il sistema della libertà*, 2nd edn, Milan: Mursia, 1976.
5.30 Philonenko, A. *La Liberté humaine dans la philosophie de Fichte*, 2nd edn, Paris: Vrin, 1980.
5.31 Talbot, E.B. *The Fundamental Principle of Fichte's Philosophy*, New York: Macmillan, 1906.

Studies of the post-Jena Wissenschaftslehre

5.32 Brüggen, M. *Fichtes Wissenschaftslehre. Das System in den seit 1801/02 enstandenen Fassungen*, Hamburg: Meiner, 1979.
5.33 Widmann, J. *Der Grundstrukture des transzendentalen Wissens nach J.G. Fichtes Wissenschaftslehre 1804²*, Hamburg: Meiner, 1977.

Specific topics

5.34 Engelbrecht, H.C. *Johann Gottlieb Fichte: A Study of his Political Writings, with Special Reference to his Nationalism*, New York: Columbia University Press, 1933.
5.35 Henrich, D. *Fichtes ursprüngliche Einsicht*, Frankfurt/Main: Klostermann, 1967; trans. D. Lachterman, "Fichte's Original Insight," *Contemporary German Philosophy*, 1 (1982): 15–52.
5.36 Lauth, R. *Die transzendentale Naturlehre Fichtes nach den Prinzipien der Wissenschaftslehre*, Hamburg: Meiner, 1984.
5.37 Neuhouser, F. *Fichte's Theory of Subjectivity*, Cambridge: Cambridge University Press, 1990.
5.38 Renaut, A. *Le Système du droit: Philosophie et droit dans la pensée de Fichte*, Paris: Presses Universitaires de France, 1986.
5.39 Rockmore, T. *Fichte, Marx, and the German Philosophical Tradition*, Carbondale: Southern Illinois University Press, 1980.
5.40 Stolzenberg, J. *Fichtes Begriff der intellektuellen Anschauung*, Stuttgart: Klett-Cotta, 1986.
5.41 Williams, R.R. *Recognition: Fichte and Hegel on the Other*, Albany: State University of New York Press, 1992.

Recent collections and special issues of journals

5.42 Breazeale, D., and Rockmore, T. (eds) *Fichte: Historical Context and Contemporary Controversies*, Atlantic City: Humanities Press, 1993.
5.43 Hammacher, K. (ed.) *Der transcendentale Gedanke. Die gegenwärtige Darstellung der Philosophie Fichtes*: Hamburg, Meiner, 1981.
5.44 *Idealistic Studies*, 6, 2 (1979).
5.45 *Philosophical Forum*, 19, 2 and 3 (1988).

Schelling

Original language editions

5.46 *Schellings Werke*, 12 vols, ed. M. Schröter, Munich: Beck/Oldenbourg, 1927–54.
5.47 *Friedrich Wilhelm Joseph von Schellings sämmtliche Werke*, 14 vols, ed. F.K.A. Schelling, Stuttgart: Cotta, 1856–61.

English translations

5.48 *The Unconditional in Human Knowledge: Four Early Essays (1794–1796)*, trans. F. Marti, Lewisburg, Pa: Bucknell University Press, 1980.
5.49 *Ideas for a Philosophy of Nature* (1797), trans. E.E. Harris and P. Heath, Cambridge: Cambridge University Press, 1988.
5.50 *System of Transcendental Idealism* (1800), trans. P. Heath, Charlottesville: University Press of Virginia, 1978.
5.51 *Bruno, or On the Natural and the Divine Principle of Things* (1802), trans. and ed. M.G. Vater, Albany: State University of New York Press, 1984.
5.52 *On University Studies* (1803), trans. E.S. Morgan and N. Guterman, Athens: Ohio University Press, 1966.
5.53 "Of the Relationship of the Philosophy of Nature to Philosophy in General" (1802), trans. and ed. G. di Giovanni and H.S. Harris, in *Between Kant and Hegel: Texts in the Development of Post-Kantian Idealism*, Albany: State University of New York Press, 1985.
5.54 *The Philosophy of Art* (1801, 1804), trans. and ed. D.W. Stott, Minneapolis: University of Minnesota Press, 1989.
5.55 "Concerning the Relation of the Plastic Arts to Nature" (1807), trans. M. Bullock, in H. Read *The True Voice of Feeling: Studies in English Romantic Poetry*, New York: Pantheon, 1953.
5.56 *Philosophical Inquiries into the Nature of Human Freedom* (1809), trans. J. Gutmann, Chicago: Open Court, 1936.
5.57 *Ages of the World* (1813), trans. F.D. Bolmon, New York: AMS Press, 1942.
5.58 *Schelling's Treatise on the Deities of Samothrace* (1815), trans. R.F. Brown, Missoula, Mont.: Scholars' Press, 1976.
5.59 "On the Source of Eternal Truths" (1850), trans. E.A. Beach, *Owl of Minerva*, 22 (1990): 55–67.

Bibliographies

5.60 Sandkühler, H.J. *Friedrich Joseph Schelling*, Stuttgart: Metzler, 1970.
5.61 Schneeberger, G. *Friedrich Wilhelm Joseph von Schelling. Eine Bibliographie*, Bern: Francke, 1954.

Influences and development

5.62 Benz, E. *Schelling: Werden und Wirken seines Denken*, Zurich: Rein, 1955.
5.63 Frank, M., and Kurz, G. (eds) *Materialen zu Schellings philosophischen Anfangen*, Frankfurt: Suhrkamp, 1975.
5.64 Görland, I. *Die Entwicklung der Frühphilosophie Schellings in der Auseinandersetzung mit Fichte*, Frankfurt: Klostermann, 1973.
5.65 Lauth, R. *Die Entstehung von Schellings Identitätsphilosophie in der Auseinandersetzung mit Fichtes Wissenschaftslehre, 1795–1801*, Freiburg: Alber, 1975.

General surveys

5.66 Jaspers, K. *Schelling: Grösse und Verängnis*, Munich: Piper, 1955.
5.67 Marquet, J.-F. *Liberté et existence: étude sur la formation de la philosophie de Schelling*, Paris: Gallimard, 1973.
5.68 Tielette, X. *Schelling: Une philosophie en deviner*, 2 vols, Paris: Vrin, 1970.
5.69 White, A. *Schelling: An Introduction to the System of Human Freedom*, New Haven: Yale University Press, 1983.
5.70 Zeltner, H. *Schelling*, Stuttgart: Frommann, 1954.

Schelling's earlier philosophy (1794–1808)

5.71 Esposito, J.L. *Schelling's Idealism and Philosophy of Nature*, Lewisburg, Pa: Bucknell University Press, 1977.
5.72 Meier, F. *Die Idee der Transzendentalphilosophie beim jungen Schelling*, Winterthur: Keller, 1961.
5.73 Watson, J. *Schelling's Transcendental Idealism: A Critical Exposition*, Chicago: Griggs, 1882.

Schelling's later philosophy (1809–54)

5.74 Brown, R.F. *The Later Philosophy of Schelling: The Influence of Boehme on the Works of 1809–1815*, Lewisburg, Pa: Bucknell University Press, 1977.
5.75 Fuhrmans, H. *Schellings letzte Philosophie: Die negative und positive Philosophie im Einsatz des Spätidealismus*, Berlin: Junker und Dünnhaupt, 1940.
5.76 Heidegger, M. *Schelling's Treatise on the Essence of Human Freedom*, trans. J. Stambaugh, Athens: Ohio University Press, 1985.

5.77 Holz, H. *Spekulation und Faktizität. Zum Freiheitsbegriff des mittleren und späten Schelling*, Bonn: Bouvier, 1970.
5.78 Schulz, W. *Die Vollendung des deutschen Idealismus in der Spätphilosophie Schellings*, 2nd edn, Pfullingen: Neske, 1975.

Specific topics

5.79 Gibelin, J. *L'Esthetique de Schelling*, Paris: Vrin, 1934.
5.80 Haynes, P.C. *Reason and Existence: Schelling's Philosophy of History*, Leiden: Brill, 1967.
5.81 Knittermeyer, H. *Schelling und die romantische Schule*, Munich: Reinhardt, 1929.
5.82 Tillich, P. *The Construction of the History of Religion in Schelling's Positive Philosophy: Its Presuppositions and Principles*, trans. V. Nuovo, Lewisburg, Pa: Bucknell University Press, 1974.

Recent collections and special issues of journals

5.83 *Archives de philosophie*, 38, 3 (1975).
5.84 Baumgartner, H.M. (ed.) *Schelling: Einführung in seine Philosophie*, Freiburg: Alber, 1975.
5.85 *Les Etudes philosophiques*, 2 (1974).
5.86 *Idealistic Studies*, 19, 3 (1989).
5.87 Koktanek, A.M. (ed.) *Schelling-Studien*, Munich: Oldenbourg, 1965.
5.88 *Studia Philosophica*, 14 (1954).

CHAPTER 6

Hegel's *Phenomenology of Spirit*

Robert C. Solomon

G.W.F. Hegel (1770–1831) was the greatest systematic philosopher of
the nineteenth century. As a young man he followed and was (at least
at first) enthusiastic about the French Revolution. Then came the Reign
of Terror of 1793, and Hegel, like many early followers of the revolution, had second thoughts. With the new century came Napoleon.
Hegel and all of Germany watched with mixed fascination, anticipation,
and anxiety as Napoleon began his political and military campaign
eastward, forming alliances with many of the tiny principalities and
city-states of Germany, threatening and swallowing others. By 1806,
Napoleon was at the height of his powers, and in the battle of Jena in
October of that year, he put an end to the 800-year-old Holy Roman
Empire. The international success of French revolutionary liberalism
impressed Hegel, who was then teaching at the University of Jena. The
battle also put him out of a job. But in the wake of Napoleon Hegel
envisioned the birth of a new world, and he announced in the Preface
of the book he was completing, albeit in rather ponderous philosophical
terms, the ultimate liberation and final unification of the human spirit.
The book was called *The Phenomenology of Spirit*. Its influence in
philosophy would be as profound and as enduring as Napoleon's bold
ventures in European history, in terms of both its positive impact and
the reactions it engendered. It is Kant, perhaps, whose "Copernican
revolution" is usually compared to the upheaval in France, but it is
Hegel who deserves credit for consolidating and spreading that revolution. If Heine could compare Kant to Robespierre, then Hegel, with
comparable philosophical hyperbole, deserves comparison to Napoleon.[1]

 Hegel began studying and writing philosophy soon after Kant
had redefined the philosophical world, and just as Europe was entering

the turbulent new century. As a young man, Hegel was educated in the Tübingen seminary but seemed to have little religious ambition or theological talent. In fact, his first philosophical essays were somewhat blasphemous attacks on Christianity, including a piece on "The Life of Jesus" which went out of its way to make Jesus into an ordinary moralist, who in his Sermon on the Mount espoused Kant's categorical imperative.[2] As a student, however, Hegel entertained the idea of inventing a new religion that stressed our unity with nature, a "synthesis of nature and spirit" drawn from the ancient Greeks and crudely formulated with great poetic flair by Hegel's college friend and room-mate Friedrich Hølderlin. Hølderlin was without doubt one of the poetic geniuses of his generation and a powerful influence on young Hegel. Drawing from not only the ancient Greeks but the romantic culture that surrounded them, Hølderlin promulgated a grand metaphor of **effusion**, cosmic spirit making itself known to us and to itself throughout all of nature, in human history, and, most clearly of all, in poetry and the "spiritual sciences." Their younger friend Friedrich Schelling had already converted that metaphor into philosophical cur-rency by 1795, and when Hegel finally decided to turn to serious philosophy in 1801, it was with the encouragement and sponsorship of Schelling. He sought and obtained a teaching position, and, in opposition to the clear polemical tone of his earlier, "anti-theological" essays, he began to write philosophy in a terse, academic style.[3] Hegel joined Schelling in his bold attempt to forge a new form of philosophy, following Kant and the radical neo-Kantian Johann Gottlieb Fichte, and together they published a journal, the *Critical Journal of Philo-sophy*. His first professional essay was a comparison of the philosophies of Fichte and Schelling, making clear the superiority of the latter.[4] For several years, Hegel was known in the German philosophical world only as a disciple of Schelling. But then he published his *Phenomenology*.[5]

Hegel's original intentions and initial approach to the *Phenomen-ology* were rather modest and for the most part derivative of earlier efforts by Fichte and Schelling to "complete Kant's system." The idea of a "system" of philosophy comes from Kant, who aspired to provide a unified and all-encompassing "science" of philosophy. But according to Fichte and Schelling and several other philosophers who greatly admired and emulated Kant, he had not succeeded. He left us instead with a fragmentary philosophy which, however stunning in its indi-vidual parts, failed to show the unity of human experience. In particu-lar, Kant left a gaping abyss between his theory of knowledge – in the first *Critique*, the *Critique of Pure Reason* – and his conception of morals in the *Critique of Practical Reason*, and so left the human mind as if cleft in two. The third *Critique* was supposed to be a synthesis of the two, but in the opinion of many of Kant's closest followers, some of whom preferred the third *Critique* above all, that book failed to provide the synthesis required for a genuine system.[6] Moreover, Kant's conception of the "thing in itself," while central to his philosophy and the key to his division between the phenomenal world of knowledge and the noumenal world of free will, morality, and religion, was greeted by these post-Kantians as a mistake, a serious flaw that threatened to undermine the whole critical enterprise. The idea that there could be any intelligible conception of things as they are in themselves and not as phenomena – that is, as experienced by us – left room for the skeptic to dig in their wedge with the challenge: How can we know that we really know anything at all? How can we have true or "absolute" knowledge – that is, self-reflective knowledge that does not permit the possibility of skepticism? How does the world of practical reason tie in with what we know, and vice versa? In his philosophy, therefore, Hegel would argue against the intelligibility of skepticism, against the intelligibility of any conception of the "thing in itself" as distinct from things as we know them, and against the bifurcation of human experience into incommensurable theoretical and practical realms. The fact that Hegel expresses this reasonably modest and academically well-established set of problems and their solution in the language of "absolute knowing" has understandably led to much misunderstanding and considerably exaggerated claims on behalf of Hegel's efforts. What Hegel was after, however, was a continuation, a correction, and the "completion" of some of Kant's key themes, the unity of knowledge, the unintelligibility of skepticism, the importance of the first-person, "subjective," Cartesian, or "phenomenological" standpoint as the origin of all knowledge, and the *a priori* necessity of certain forms of consciousness. It was not a particularly ambitious program, and Kant, Fichte, and Schelling, among others, had clearly shown the way.[7]

What emerged in 1807, however, was a book very different from anything that had been seen in philosophy before. True, the Kantian themes and the post-Kantian ambitions were still in evidence, and the book did conclude with a modest chapter entitled "Absolute knowing." But in between the introduction and opening chapters, on the one hand, in which these themes were quickly dispatched, and the brief conclusion, on the other, in which the post-Kantian ambitions were summarily concluded, the book grew into something of a beautiful monster. There are chapters on various Greek philosophies and on various eccentric movements in ethics, as well as an open attack on Kant's categorical imperative, commentaries on contemporary history including the Enlightenment and the French Revolution, bits of literary criticism, philosophy of science, and an oddly shaped survey of the world's religions, all put forward in a barely intelligible abstract neo-Kantian jargon that makes even the Kantian *Critiques* read like vacation novels by comparison. The *Phenomenology* is not, as originally intended, merely a demonstration of "the Absolute." It is a magnificent conceptual odyssey which carries us through the most elementary conceptions of human awareness to some of the most all-encompassing and complex forms of consciousness. Its stated purpose is still to comprehend the truth – the absolute truth – but this should not be understood as a merely epistemological enterprise. What Hegel comes to mean by philosophical truth is an all-encompassing vision, and this will include not only a variety of philosophical theories but much material from religion, ethics, and history as well.[8]

❧ THE SPIRIT OF THE *PHENOMENOLOGY* ❧

The fact that Hegel so obviously followed in Kant's great footsteps too easily misleads us into thinking that Hegel, supposedly like Kant, was just another academic philosophy professor, worried about abstruse and abstract problems that an ordinary person would neither comprehend nor care about.[9] The truth is, of course, that this picture is unfair to Kant, and it is mistaken about Hegel as well. Kant was moved in philosophy not only by David Hume, who famously awakened him from his dogmatic Leibnizian slumbers, but by his religious piety, his firm moral convictions, and his enthusiasm for Newtonian science. He was troubled by the conflict between science and religion, and he was deeply interested in such speculative questions as the meaning of life as well as the basic Socratic question of what it meant to be a genuinely good human being. To read Kant merely as the answer to skepticism or the grand synthesis of the warring schools of rationalism and empiricism is to miss what is most important and exciting about him. So, too, to see Hegel as the continuation or "completion" of Kant is to deny what is most fascinating about his philosophy. And to read the *Phenomenology* as if it were only a wordy and difficult introduction to the mature "system" that followed is to miss what is most important and exciting about that book. For the "spirit" of the *Phenomenology* is nothing less than an all-embracing conception of the world, an attempt at synthesis, yes, but nothing so meager as a mere collaboration between (as Schopenhauer called them) "irritated professors."

In the Tübingen seminary or *Stift*, Hegel, Schelling, and Hölderlin had dreamed of a new religion.[10] They despised much of their theological training, dismissing it with those familiar vulgarities with which students have always dismissed the dogmatic studies they were forced to mouth and respect in the classroom.[11] They had deep misgivings about German culture as well, torn between the cosmopolitan clarity and free-thinking of the French and British Enlightenment (represented in Germany by Kant) and the romantic nationalism mixed with mysticism that marked the German romantic reaction to the Enlightenment.[12] The Enlightenment seemed to many Germans to be vulgar, overly concerned with economics, and contemptuous of religion and the "spiritual" aspects of social life.[13] And yet the promises of the Enlightenment seemed so attractive, and the dead weight of feudalism, Lutheran theology, and the medieval church, by comparison, seemed to have philosophy as well as German life pinned down in a decidedly most unenlightened past. Reconciling the cosmopolitan demands of the Enlightenment and their regional pride and piety seemed essential to the young Germans, and the events across the French border made these conflicts very real and very urgent. In the years between his graduation from the seminary and his first university post, Hegel wrote his early essays on the nature of religion.[14] Most of them were hostile to Christianity and held up the spiritual life and the "folk religion" of the ancient Greeks as an attractive alternative.[15] Hegel's early essays were often sarcastic, sometimes clumsy attempts to revise and reconcile Christianity with Greek folk religion, insisting on a "natural" religion rather than one based on authority, and a "subjective" religion – a religion of ritual and social participation – rather than the "objective" religion taught by theology.[16] Religions, Hegel surmised, are and ought to be particular to particular people and a particular time, part of the life of a people and not merely abstract beliefs with no practical manifestations.[17] And yet, it makes sense to speak of "religion" in general, and of certain universal features that all religions and all people share in common.[18]

Hegel here is an evident disciple of Kant. In his *Critique of Practical Reason* and his *Religion within the Limits of Reason Alone*, Kant had insisted on the rational defense of religion and the bond between morality and Christianity.[19] Hegel does find much to criticize in Christian morality, in particular its unworkability in large groups and whole societies. He finds much to criticize in Kant too, notably Kant's neglect of local custom in ethics in favor of universal categorical principles, but he makes it clear nevertheless, in straightforward Kantian terms, that "the aim and essence of all true religion, and our religion included, is human morality."[20] To this end, Hegel tries to revise Christianity as a folk religion concerned first of all with the cultivation of morality, culminating in his awkward but amusing attempt to have Jesus preach the categorical imperative.[21] But as these early unpublished efforts deepen in their thought and their sophistication, Hegel drops much of his hostility and begins to suggest that in all religions one can discern a kind of necessary development of the human spirit.[22] He begins to focus not just on the failings of Christianity but rather on its internal contradictions, "disharmonies," or "alienations" (*Entfrem-dungen*).[23] He finds fault with the idea that God and man are separate and distinct, in which God is infinitely superior and we are mere "slaves."[24] He also finds fault with the distinctions between and separation of reason and the passions, theology and faith, theory and practice. And here we find the seeds of two of the most dramatic and central themes of the *Phenomenology*, the grand conception of Spirit or *Geist* as immanent God incorporating us all, and the all-important place of local customs and affections in ethics. Like so many other thinkers and poets in Germany of the time, Hegel found his inspiration and alternative visions in the fascinating life of the early Greeks. But with the close of the century and the French Revolution in tatters, with German culture in ascendancy and his young friend Schelling already engaged in a very contemporary philosophy that would change the way we think about ourselves, Hegel abandoned his nostalgic posture and moved into the moment. For what he saw happening was just what his youthful essays had been suggesting to him. The world was filled with contradictions and disharmony, but philosophy would make a difference. Only a few years later, ending his lectures at Jena in 1806, the manuscript of the *Phenomenology* in hand, Hegel announced to his classes:

> We find ourselves in an important epoch, in a fermentation, in which Spirit has made a great leap forward, has gone beyond its previous concrete form and acquired a new one. . . . A new emergence of Spirit is at hand; philosophy must be the first to hail its appearance and recognize it.[25]

The concept of Spirit or *Geist* is clearly the key to Hegel's philosophy. It is important not to translate "*Geist*" as "mind," as some early translators have done, not because it is literally incorrect but because it is extremely misleading. "Spirit" has a religious significance which is missing from "mind," and, more important, "spirit" suggests something larger about a person while "mind" suggests something merely internal and private. We typically speak of the spirit of a group or a nation and "team spirit" as a way of indicating unity and fellow-feeling, and we may also note that "spirit" thus indicates passion, whereas "mind" suggests rather only thoughts and intelligence – not, we should quickly add, that the two are or need be opposed. But what Hegel has in mind by Spirit is nothing less than the ultimate unity of the whole of humanity, and of humanity and the world. It is the concept in which he seeks to synthesize or at least embrace the various contradictions and disharmonies of religion and morality and reconcile humanity and nature, science and religion. Hegel rarely talks about God, but it is quite clear as we trace our way through the labyrinth of the *Phenomenology* that it is God, God as Spirit, who is our subject and who is our guide. Not a God within, and certainly not a transcendent God without, but the God who ultimately we are emerges from its pages. Thus Hegel's work has often been touted as a "theodicy," an account of God's revelation on earth, and Heinrich Heine, one of Hegel's less pious students, ironically commented: "I was young and proud, and it pleased my vanity when I learned from Hegel that it was not the dear God who lived in heaven that was my God, as my grandmother supposed, but I myself here on earth."[26]

What makes Heine's comment so outrageous, of course, is his mocking usurpation of the role of God himself, but what is essential to Hegel's concept of Spirit is precisely the loss of individuality and the gain in comprehension that it requires. The realization of Spirit is not the recognition that I am myself God but that we are all God, that Spirit pervades and defines all of us. In this, Hegel's notion is much like Spinoza's pantheism, the realization that we are all one, a claim repeated by Schelling and criticized brutally by Hegel in his Preface with the sarcastic comment "the night in which all cows are black."[27] What Hegel is getting at is the necessity to demonstrate his thesis through reason and by way of a lengthy demonstration of its necessity, not by way of mystical experience or dogmatic insistence. And that is what the *Phenomenology* does or tries to do, to demonstrate by actually guiding us through the emergence of Spirit from its various individualistic guises to the recognition of the necessity of larger, more comprehensive forms.

One can understand here the political as well as ontological imagery which pervades Hegel's philosophy. Hegel is not an individualist. In the *Phenomenology* he comments that much less should be thought of and expected of the individual, and in his later *Philosophy of History* he famously tells us that even the greatest individuals follow unwittingly "the cunning of reason" and find themselves pawns in the hands of a larger fate, a dramatic idea that is embodied in flesh and blood by Tolstoy in his later account of Napoleon's Russian campaign in *War and Peace*. One can imagine Hegel envisioning the great battles of that war, in which hundreds of thousands of undifferentiated "individuals" in identical uniforms moved in waves and slaughtered one another for the sake of larger and dimly understood ideas and loyalties. So viewed, the individual does indeed count for very little, and it is the larger movement of humankind that comes into focus instead. And yet, Hegel is no fascist – whatever ideas or inspiration Mussolini and his kind may have drawn from him. Hegel insists on this larger view of human history but nevertheless insists throughout his work that the ultimate aim and result of that history has been human freedom and respect for the individual. But it is the individual as an aspect of Spirit that impresses us, not the ontologically isolated and autonomous individual of Hegel's liberal predecessors, notably Kant.

There is a more philosophically profound way of making this point, which makes much more sense of the imagery of Spirit than the usual quasi-mystical accounts. Among the many borrowings of Hegel from Kant was the basic orientation of his philosophy, variously described as "subjective" or "Cartesian" or "phenomenological," although all of these characterizations have the potential to be mislead-ing. (For example, both Kant and Hegel found much to criticize in Descartes, so the "Cartesian" designation has to be much qualified.) This orientation, common to the empiricists as well as most other modern philosophers, might simply be described as "the first-person standpoint," or the attempt to understand the world beginning with one's own experience. Thus the familiar questions, entertained by Des-cartes, Locke, Hume, and Kant, such as: How do I know that the world conforms to my experiences? Although Hegel will reject this question, as did Kant, they share this phenomenological approach to philosophy and the world in terms of one's own experiences. But, we must ask, **whose** experiences? Are they the isolated and perhaps eccen-tric experiences of a single individual? Or are they in some sense more general and shared? Kant identifies the subject of all experiences as what he called "the transcendental ego," distinct from the merely empirical ego that we normally refer to as the self, a particular person. The transcendental ego imposes the categories and processes our sen-sory intuitions into our experience of the phenomenal world, but – and this is the crucial point – it does not experience itself through those same categories. In a famous but somewhat obscure chapter of the *Critique of Pure Reason*, Kant argues against the "paralogisms of psychology," in which the self or soul is misinterpreted as a "thing," a potential object of consciousness. But the self, Kant argues, can never be the object of consciousness; it is always the subject. And because it is therefore immune from the application of the various categories of number, substance, and identity, it cannot be specified as "yours" or "mine," but remains **the** transcendental ego, "consciousness in gen-eral." What lies behind this technical move, of course, is Kant's insist-ence that the forms of experience cannot be matters of personal idiosyn-crasy and must be universal and necessary. But Hegel rather easily takes the notion of a "consciousness in general" and converts into a literally general consciousness. That general consciousness is Spirit, the self that pervades and ultimately embraces us all.[28]

The importance of Spirit, however, lies not only in its shared immanence but in its development. The *Phenomenology* is, from begin-ning to end, the phenomenological account of that development. To put it in an expanded way, the *Phenomenology* adds a new dimension to philosophy, and that is the dimension of history. Not that the *Phenomenology* as such is a historical account – although it contains quite a few such accounts, some easily recognizable, some not – but the idea that ideas and movements can be understood only through their development is a bold conjecture, and one rarely appreciated before Hegel (and still too rarely). In his later lectures, this insight becomes the centerpiece of Hegel's philosophy, as he traces the origins and development of the various religions, the course of human history, and the evolution of philosophy itself. Religion, he had recognized toward the end of his early essays, was not abstract dogma but the expression of certain basic human needs and tendencies, and these are not to be found whole in any single religion, nor are they ever entirely absent, but it is in the interplay and development of religions that the ultimate nature of religion emerges – eventually, he suggests, in philosophy. Human history, he will later write, first appears to be a "slaughter-bench," on which whole nations as well as millions of individuals are butchered. But to one who "looks with a rational eye," Hegel argues, "history in turn presents its rational aspect." The history of humanity, brutal as it has been, nevertheless displays an ineluctable sense of progress and increasing freedom.[29] Finally, in philosophy, Hegel teaches us not to see the history of the subject as merely competing answers to the same ill-formed questions but rather as a growth of certain ideas and their importance at certain times into subsequent, improved ideas that have benefited from the conflicts and confrontations of the past. The name of this process or confrontation and improvement, as everyone knows, is **dialectic**, and we shall have more to say about it shortly. But the point to be made here is that the **form** of the *Phenomenology*, its complex organization in terms of some sort of conceptual development, is not just an oddity of Hegel's authorship but, perhaps, the most single important feature of the book.

And yet, the *Phenomenology* is not history, and it is not as such an empirical study of the development of anything, philosophy, humanity, or religion. To be sure, various movements in philosophy are traced in more or less historical order in the first few chapters of the book, and there are bits of actual history spread through the later sections. But one also notes with some consternation that the Greeks are discussed after the moderns and Sophocles after the Stoics, and one would be hard pressed to formulate a historical interpretation that would account for such chronological oddities. What the *Phenomenology* is doing, therefore, is not tracing the actual order of the development of various "forms of consciousness" in history but rather ordering them and playing them against one another in such a way that we see how they fit and how they conflict and how a more adequate way of thinking may emerge. Dialectic is not just development but a mode of argument, and the order of the *Phenomenology* is not just a demolition derby, a process of elimination and the survival of the fittest, but a **teleology**, a genuine progression from less adequate ways of thinking to more adequate and more comprehensive and, finally, to the most comprehensive way of all.

❧ THE *PHENOMENOLOGY*: PREFACE AND ❧ INTRODUCTION

The Preface to the *Phenomenology* is one of the best-known, least-understood documents in modern philosophy. Like most prefaces, it was written after the text as a whole was completed, and what it tries to do is to describe the point and purpose of the entire monstrous manuscript. Or, less sympathetically, the Preface is Hegel's attempt to force an interpretation on his book that the text itself does not easily sustain. It is a rambling, convoluted, grandiose monologue punctuated by some striking passages which do, indeed, give considerable insight into Hegel's whole philosophy. It is there that he argues (or insists, at any rate) that "the truth is the whole," that it is a process and not merely a result, and that philosophy must be systematic, scientific, and developmental in its form. But he also insists that such comments are inappropriate in a preface and that, in any case, their whole meaning must be demonstrated in the text, not simply declared beforehand. It is in the actual "working out" of various one-sided positions and "forms of consciousness" that we come to understand how truth emerges in philosophy and how that truth is the history of philosophy itself. One must see ideas and philosophies and whole stages of history as an organic, developing process. In one of his most striking metaphors, Hegel writes, only somewhat tongue-in-cheek:

> The bud disappears in the bursting-forth of the blossom, and
> one might say that the former is refuted by the latter; similarly
> when the fruit appears, the blossom is shown up in its turn as
> a false manifestation of the plant, and the fruit now emerges
> as the truth of it instead. These forms are not just distinguished
> from one another, they also supplant one another as mutually
> incompatible. Yet at the same time their fluid nature makes them
> moments of an organic unity in which they do not only not
> conflict, but in which each is as necessary as the other, and this
> mutual necessity alone constitutes the life of the whole.
>
> *(PG, 2)*

Hegel also announces in the Preface and in the wake of Napoleon his vision of a "birth-time" and the beginning of a new era, and in philosophy he announces the emergence of what he calls "the concept" (*Begriff*), a holistic comprehension of the world through reason.[30] Indeed, philosophy properly developed should exist wholly in the realm of the concept. But that philosophy would be more in evidence in the works and lectures that followed the publication of the *Phenomenology* rather than in the *Phenomenology* itself.[31]

The Introduction to the *Phenomenology*, by contrast, is short and straightforward. It is indeed an introduction. It sets up the standpoint from which the *Phenomenology* will proceed. The Introduction begins where Kant's first *Critique* ends, with the rejection of skepticism and a declaration of transcendental idealism. The history of modern epistemology from Descartes and Locke through Kant's grand synthesis is very much in evidence there, as it will be in the opening chapters of the *Phenomenology*. What concerns Hegel in the Introduction is a metaphor, or rather, a pair of metaphors, whose consequence is skepticism. The irony is, of course, that the metaphors in question originated with philosophers who could not tolerate skepticism and sought to lay it to rest once and for all. The metaphors concern the seemingly contingent relationship between knowledge and truth. The first and more prominent is the metaphor of knowledge as a tool, through which we "grasp hold" of the truth. The second is the metaphor of knowledge as a medium through which the "light of truth" must pass. Both Locke and Descartes attempted to examine this tool or medium, and the ultimate result was the skepticism of David Hume. Kant was "awakened from his dogmatic slumbers" by Hume but only pursued the metaphor further with his "critique" of reason and the understanding. Hegel's argument, simply stated, is that the metaphor itself is mistaken. Skepticism can be laid to rest, as Kant had tried and seemingly succeeded in doing, only if the contingency of knowledge and the metaphors of knowledge as instrument and medium are rejected from the outset (*PG*, 73).

In Descartes, Leibniz, Locke, and Berkeley, the distinction between our knowledge and "the external world" had made way for Hume's devastating skepticism. Kant had solved the problem, in the eyes of many philosophers of the time, by incorporating the external world into the realm of knowledge itself, constituted by the categories of the understanding and the forms of intuition. But with Kant's further distinction between phenomena and noumena – the world-as-we-know-it and the world-as-it-is-in-itself – it remains impossible for us to know the world as it is in itself. Once the distinction is made between the world-for-us and the world-independent-of-us, there can be no escape from the conclusion that we can know only the world as it is for us. Hegel's pursuit of absolute knowledge begins with the rejection of this distinction.[32]

In the Introduction to the *Phenomenology*, Hegel begins his revision of Kant's theory of knowledge by attacking just this distinction, which he claims is based on unanalyzed and undefended metaphors in which knowledge is considered a "tool with which one masters the Absolute." If knowledge is a tool, there must be a certain necessary distortion due to the operations of knowledge on reality, and therefore we can never know reality (the Absolute) itself but only as it has been manipulated and distorted by the instrument of knowledge. We can, therefore, have only mediated knowledge of the Absolute, and never know the Absolute itself. This is Kant's problem in the first *Critique*, and his solution to it is the critical doctrine that we never know reality independent of the conditions imposed on it by knowledge. The best that can be done by the philosopher is an exploration of the nature of this tool of knowledge and the demonstration of the necessary conditions it imposes on reality. Kant's *Critique*, therefore, abandons the search for absolute reality and simply investigates the tool by which we come to know reality.

But why should we accept this metaphor? Kant never examines or defends this metaphorical starting point, and Hegel turns it against itself:

> If the fear of falling into error sets up a mistrust of Science,
> which in the absence of such scruples gets on with the work itself
> and actually cognizes something, it is hard to see why we should
> not turn around and mistrust this very mistrust.

$$(PG, 74)$$

By beginning with the investigation of the faculties of knowledge, Kant has already determined the critical outcome of his first *Critique*. Once the distinctions between things as known and things in themselves and between reality-for-a-subject and absolute reality are introduced, one must conclude that we cannot have any but conditioned knowledge and that the demands of traditional metaphysics are utterly impossible. Kant, according to Hegel, offers no justification for this starting point and, more importantly, fails to see fatal problems inherent in this approach. First, the metaphor simply plays on the notions 'truth', 'reality,' and 'knowledge,' and, given Kant's distinctions, Hegel argues that what he ought to have concluded was that we can have no knowledge at all, that our cognitive faculties are such that we can never know the truth. Second, Hegel argues that one cannot begin by investigating the faculties of knowledge before one attempts to gain knowledge in philosophy, for the investigation itself already utilizes these faculties and their concepts. Any such analysis is covertly circular, and one might as well try, Hegel suggests, to learn to swim before getting into the water.

Thus Kant, on the basis of the instrument metaphor, distinguishes between two different sorts of knowledge, two different kinds of truth. There is limited or conditional knowledge giving us truth limited by the conditions of our cognitive faculties, and there is absolute or unconditioned knowledge of things as they are in themselves which human consciousness cannot have. But even limited truth is indeed truth only if it is the way things really are. If it is an unconditioned or *a priori* truth that all events must be temporally ordered (for us), then this limited truth is a truth only if all events really are ordered. If events are not really so ordered, but rather ordered by us, then this limited truth is a falsehood, even if it is **necessary for us**. (Thus Nietzsche will argue that **all** of our *a priori* or necessary truths are such 'falsehoods.') Similarly, our conditioned or limited knowledge is really knowledge only if it is in agreement with what is really true. If we have conditional knowledge that there exist objects 'outside' us due to the nature of our cognition, this knowledge is true knowledge only if there truly are such objects. In other words, truth is Absolute Truth; knowledge is Absolute Knowledge. The 'real' world is the world as it is in itself, whether that is the world of our experience or not. But what would it mean to even suggest that it is not?

Hegel's reason for rejecting the dualism between knowledge and reality is not simply its skeptical conclusions; the preliminary investigation of knowledge, which is part and parcel of the "knowledge as tool" metaphor, is logically ill-conceived. Kant argues that philosophy must begin by examining those faculties which purport to give us knowledge, but with what do we examine these faculties? The investigation of cognition must itself be carried out by cognition; thus Kant demands that we examine reason by using reason, but a preliminary investigation of the tool of knowledge is already a use of that tool. Hegel agrees with Kant that philosophy must begin with an investigation of knowledge, but unlike Kant he recognizes that this investigation cannot be independent of the use of the faculties of knowledge. Hegel argues that the investigation of knowledge changes that very knowledge, and that such an investigation can never be preliminary, but constitutes the whole of philosophical investigation. The critique of knowledge is the development of knowledge as well.

Once we appreciate this problem as Hegel perceived it, we are in an excellent position to understand the necessity for the peculiar dialectical structure of his work, particularly of the *Phenomenology*. Knowledge *develops* with our conceptual sophistication. This is not to say merely that as we learn more, our knowledge increases; rather, the **kind** of knowledge changes. Specifically, knowledge changes in kind when we turn to focus on our faculties of knowledge, when we question not so much our knowledge of the world, but ourselves. For

Kant, self-knowledge was either empirical knowledge of ourselves as phenomenal objects or transcendental knowledge which could disclose only the necessary forms of our consciousness, but, according to Kant, we could not have knowledge of ourselves in any other sense (e.g. as moral agent or as immortal soul). Neither could we have knowledge of things-in-themselves. For Hegel, knowledge of objects and transcendental self-knowledge are but two stages in the attainment of further kinds of knowledge, knowledge of oneself and the world as Spirit. The *Phenomenology* is just the demonstration and the development of such knowledge, starting with the lowest forms of knowledge, showing how these are inadequate to other forms, and culminating in Absolute Truth in which all of the problems, paradoxes, and inadequacies of the lower forms disappear.

Philosophy, for Hegel, is the demonstration of the 'becoming' of Absolute Knowledge. Such a becoming need not be the pattern of development of any particular individual consciousness, and the development of knowledge in the system is not the psychological development of an individual. For that matter, it does not faithfully appear in or as the history of philosophy either, although this history is inevitably a close approximation of the development of Absolute Knowledge and Spirit. The "forms of consciousness" or forms of knowledge derived in the *Phenomenology* lead to Absolute Knowledge, that level of conceptual development where traditional conceptual (philosophical) problems disappear, but it is not at all obvious that there is but one route – the way described in the *Phenomenology* – from partial or inadequate knowledge to absolute knowing.[33] At the ultimate stage of knowledge, traditional philosophical dichotomies are eliminated and nature and Spirit find their place together. The Fichtean antitheses of dogmatism and idealism are synthesized. The development of Hegel's system is the "working out" of these various traditional forms of consciousness and ordering them in a hierarchy of more sophisticated forms. The purpose of this ordering is to demonstrate how each level corrects inadequacies of the previous conceptual level and how it is possible to correct all these inadequacies once we adopt an all-encompassing vision of the whole rather than limit ourselves to advocacy of this or that particular position.

CONSCIOUSNESS AND THE DIALECTIC

The *Phenomenology* is divided into three uneven sections, each representing one type of 'form' or 'level of consciousness,' in (more or less) ascending order of sophistication. The first and shortest section is called "Consciousness," which deals with relatively naive epistemological consciousness. It is a critique, among other things, of the narrowly epistemological vision of philosophy that had begun to emerge in the eighteenth century and which still, regrettably, persists today.[34] The second is called "Self-consciousness" and traces the first crude beginnings of the awakening of the consciousness of Spirit in its early form of simple antagonistic recognition of other people and the development of paradigms of dominance and submission ("master and slave") as prototypical forms of self-recognition and awareness. Finally, there is the long, twisting section on "Reason," which traces the ultimate development of a holistic spiritual-rational consciousness from the most simple sense of community to its penultimate realization of Spirit in art and religion before its ultimate realization in Hegel's philosophy.

We can summarize the progression or dialectic of the section on "Consciousness" in three readily identifiable steps, each of them corresponding to a family of "common-sense" claims and philosophical positions. At the beginning is the common-sense notion which Hegel calls "sense-certainty," that we simply know, prior to any verbal description or conceptual understanding, what it is that we experience. Hegel demonstrates that such a conception of knowledge is woefully inadequate. He then brings us from this naive realism through a number of theoretical variations in which can be recognized major insights from Leibniz and some of the empiricists, which he abbreviates as "Perception," to the philosophy of Kant's first *Critique*, in which knowledge is demonstrated to be a form of understanding. In "Understanding," Hegel also tackles the question of the thing-in-itself by way of an extended *reductio ad absurdum* and, following his opening argument in the Introduction, shows us the nonsense of supposing that the true world might be different from the world of our experience.[35]

The first section of the *Phenomenology* develops the role of the understanding in experience, but as an analysis of the entire movement in modern philosophy including such central problems as the nature of substance, the necessity of concepts, and the nature of connections between experiences and the synthesis of objects. In other words, it covers, in a dialectical way, the subject matter of Kant's first *Critique* and the major epistemological work of Locke, Berkeley, and Hume. The stage of consciousness referred to as "sense-certainty" is "knowledge of the *immediate*" (*PG*, 90; Hegel's italics). It is "what is presented before us," "what is given." It is "the richest kind of knowledge, of infinite wealth. . . . It is thought to be pure apprehension without yet any conceptual comprehension, raw experience, without the need of understanding, the experience of a passive sensitive receptacle" (*PG*, 91). But because it involves no understanding, just a pure knowledge of "This," the particular thing in front of me, one might say that this stage is not truly consciousness or knowledge at all, but merely "knowledge implicit." This is the pure data of the senses which so many philosophers, of this century as well as the past, have taken to be the indubitable, secure foundation of human knowledge. It is pure experience, uninterpreted and thus unadulterated by us in any way. Accordingly, sense-certainty also includes the claims of many mystics and intuitive philosophers, including, perhaps, Schelling and Jacobi, who have claimed that the knowledge of the Absolute is not conceptual or rational but strictly intuitive, a pure experience, undistorted by human concepts and categories. Traditional epistemologists have argued that errors in human knowledge, when they arise, must arise after this level. For on this level, our knowledge is certain and becomes fallible only when we attempt to conceptualize or to understand our experiences.

Although this section is among the shortest of the *Phenomenology*, it provides us with some vital clues for understanding the nature of Hegel's dialectic. Hegel's argument against this form of 'knowledge' as certain knowledge, or even as knowledge at all, is clear and to the point. Briefly, Hegel argues that this knowledge, which he describes as a mere "this, here, now," is the very opposite of pure, "authentic" knowledge, knowledge which is complete as opposed to all other knowledge which is abstract and conditioned. It is really "the most abstract and poorest truth" (*PG*, 91). It is what we "mean" only in the sense of pointing (*this*) and thus not really meaning at all. It might be said to be reference, perhaps, but not sense. In fact, it is not even reference. How does one point to a particular without specifying what it is to which one is pointing? Thus Hegel concludes that there can be no knowledge without concepts, and the supposed certainty of sense-certainty seems certain only because it is not knowledge at all. It is, at best, mere presence. The infallibility of sense-certainty, of pure experience, lies in its failure to assert any claim to knowledge which might be shown to be wrong. This knowledge which "is called the unutterable, is nothing else than the untrue, the irrational, what is merely meant" (*PG*, 110).

We can see that Hegel essentially agreed with Kant that there can be no unconceptualized knowledge, that knowledge is essentially a product of the understanding. From this agreement, however, we can also appreciate one of the keys to Hegel's works, that knowledge is essentially an *active* process, that mere experience can never give us knowledge, that synthesis of experience by rules or concepts is necessary. To use a common philosophical term, knowledge necessarily consists of *universals*. This does not mean that it is the same the world over, "for all rational creatures" as Kant would say. It means that all sense and reference relies on concepts, on the recognition of general properties which apply not to this or that particular but to an indefinitely large number of particulars (and possibly to no actual particulars at all). One might note that Hegel's insistence on universality as the essence of knowledge is already a reply to the Schelling–Kierkegaard criticism of Hegel as a "negative" philosopher (who ignores individual existence) which gathers momentum after Hegel's death.

The *Phenomenology* is not a running autobiography of Spirit but rather a retrospective of the development of Spirit, an attempt to understand why some forms of consciousness are inferior to others and force us to search for more adequate, more all-embracing modes of comprehension. The transitions between forms of consciousness represent a demonstration and a development, perhaps an explanation, but there is no mechanism which pushes one stage to the next and Hegel does not claim that each stage necessarily leads to the next. What he does claim is that the process itself is necessary, that consciousness is driven by its own inadequacies to pursue other modes of understanding. Sense certainty is not itself a mode of consciousness but, in more modern terminology, a theory about consciousness, a conception of knowledge. Hegel shows that this conception of knowledge is an inadequate conception, and concludes that no such conception of knowledge can succeed. Sense-certainty is inadequate as knowledge because it is not knowledge at all. Therefore, we move along the dialectic to a more adequate form of consciousness, which is that of *Perception*.

Perception is the first appearance of knowledge, for now we can interpret our experiences by applying concepts. In Hegel's short description, the object of consciousness is now "the thing." As a thing, the object is characterizable and characterized by ascription of properties, in other words, by the application of universally applicable concepts to a particular. Our experience is therefore no longer "pure" experience but experience of a thing defined by its properties. For example, our perception of a tree consists of a certain unity of colors, shapes, tactile sensations, perhaps sounds, and smells. Over and above this, we suppose that there is *the tree*, that which "lies behind" all of these experiences and ties them together. In traditional philosophical terms, there is the tree as *substance* which is responsible for the unity of the tree-perceptions. The problem, familiar from Locke, Hume, and Kant, is what if anything warrants our conclusion that the tree-perception refers to the tree, for any substance 'behind' these perceptions is by its very nature not the object of any possible perception.

In the recent history of philosophy, this line of questioning sent Berkeley to idealism, the view that there are no material substances, only ideas, although idealism does not yet appear as such in the Hegelian hierarchy of knowledge. In Hegel's terms, substance would be an "unconditioned universal," that is, not experienced through the senses. As such, it cannot be an aspect of perception. Thus Locke was forced to some rather *ad hoc* stipulations to explain how we can make the inference to substance and Hume insisted that we could not justifiably make such inferences in philosophy. Moreover, there was the question, unanswered and even unasked by the traditional empiricists, how the various properties perceived were in fact unified as the properties of an object. Since that general view of knowledge which Hegel calls "perception" does not recognize the extraperceptual, that is, anything but conditioned (sensory) universals, if we are to understand the unity of objects and the idea that we actually know objects and not mere clusters of properties we find ourselves moving on to the next stage of consciousness.

The solution to the problem of unity is provided by the understanding. The concept of "understanding" here is clearly taken from Kant's use of the term and refers to the application of concepts to experience. However, as Kant uses the term, there is a special focus on *a priori* or "unconditioned" concepts, which Kant calls the "categories." Among these categories is the category of substance, which is the solution to the problem of unity. The tree-perceptions have a unity of a tree because of our employment of the concept of substance. Similarly, problems such as the coexistence of various objects, the reality of causal interconnections between perceptions, as well as successions of perceptions, all appear at this level of the dialectic, to which one might refer as the Kantian level, for it consists primarily of the conclusions of the Transcendental Analytic of the first *Critique*.[36] Of central interest in this section is Hegel's analysis of the theory of the understanding as culminating in a dual worldview. On the one hand, there is the world as perceived, and the laws intrinsic to that perception. On the other hand, there is the world in itself, which is postulated 'behind' this world to 'explain' it.

In the understanding, we postulate 'unconditioned universals' in our experience to represent objects in themselves. But Hegel does not adopt the traditional notion of 'substance' for those objects. He prefers a more dynamic vision of experience, and so calls them as 'forces' or 'powers,' which are related to the "kingdom of laws" which is Kant's vision of a necessarily unified and ordered (phenomenal) world. But while the chapter called "Force and understanding" is essentially Kantian, it contains a powerful critique of Kant's *Critique* and suggests that the laws of nature are not merely imposed but inherent in the world itself. In other words, Hegel rejects the Kantian insistence that we should not look for "the universal laws of nature in nature" but rather "in the conditions of possibility of experience."[37] According to Hegel, there is no valid distinction to be made here. Indeed, Hegel suggests that scientific explanation might better be understood as a **redescription** of phenomena. Again, Kant's noumenon–phenomenon distinction is fundamentally wrong; if there is any sense to be made of the notion of "thing-in-itself" it must be as part of the thing-as-phenomenon. Indeed, "the Understanding in truth comes to know nothing else but appearance . . . in fact, the understanding experiences only *itself*" (*PG*, 165; Hegel's italics). Noumena are not transcendent to phenomena but immanent in them.

The closing argument of "Force and understanding" and, the "Consciousness" section as a whole consists of one of Hegel's longest and most peculiar counterexamples. He postulates a noumenal world which happens to be an inverted (*verkehrte*) world. According to Kant, the world-in-itself is a necessary supposition of the conditions of knowledge but by its very nature cannot be known. Because knowledge depends on the human faculties of knowledge, and because we cannot know that our knowledge is not therefore some distortion of things as they exist independent of our experience of them, we must, while supposing our knowledge to be valid, resort to *noumenon* which very possibly might have its own principles, different from the world as perceived and known by us. Kant insists that there is nothing more to be known about the world in itself, this unknown "x." But Hegel provocatively goes on to suggest what the world-as-it-is might be like by suggesting that everything in this world is 'unlike' that in our own. "What is there black is here white, what by the first law [of phenomena] is in the case of electricity the oxygen pole becomes in its other supersensible reality the hydrogen pole" (*PG*, 158). The two-worlds doctrine is carried to the realm of morality, where Hegel argues that the two-worlds view destroys the very concept of morality it is invoked by Kant to protect. For, according to Hegel:

> an action which in the world of appearance is a crime would,
> in the inner world, be capable of being really good (a bad
> action be well-intentioned); punishment is punishment only in
> the world of appearance; in itself, or in another world, it may
> be a benefit for the criminal.
>
> (*PG*, 159)

Here we have the first reference to Kant's morality, which begins with the crushing criticism of Kant's *summum bonum* and his entire two-world view. The problem, as stated here, is that the *summum bonum* and Kant's morality in general require man and his actions to be considered as noumenon. A man and his actions are also part of the phenomenal world where they are evaluated, and Hegel is here briefly pointing out the problem in applying the phenomenon–noumenon distinction to a man acting. Why suppose that what we consider punishment to the phenomenal man will have any such effect on man as noumenon. Here, even in this first section, we have a clear indication of the continuing attack of Kant's moral-religious philosophy that will be the core of Hegel's mature writings.

The inverted-world passage is essentially an argument by ridicule, for what becomes evident is that, if we take Kant's notion of noumenon seriously, any sort of nonsense becomes equally intelligible. Either the noumenal world is just like the phenomenal world, or, not only does it not make sense to talk about it, but it does not even make sense to suppose that there might be one. The inadequacy of consciousness, considered in its entirety, is the inadequacy of Kant's philosophy, which Hegel considers the culmination of all modern philosophies before it. The inadequacy of the understanding as such is a signal to a new move in philosophy, a move which is not simply new knowledge or a new progression in conciousness, but which is an entirely new *kind* of knowledge and a new kind of consciousness. Insofar as one wishes to interpret the progress of the *Phenomenology* along philosophical-historical lines, one might say that this new stage was initiated implicitly by Kant and made explicit by Fichte. But the *Phenomenology* is not intended to be just a history of philosophy.

Throughout the *Phenomenology*, Hegel displays similar inadequacies in one form of consciousness after another, and so we are guided from one form to another in an ongoing "dialectic," eventually to reach "absolute knowing," which is the all-encompassing overview of all that has preceded it. The dialectic often proceeds by way of conflict and confrontation, when one form of consciousness contradicts another. But it is a misunderstanding of Hegel to think of the dialectic as a mechanical meeting of "thesis and antithesis," resolved by a "synthesis." That formulation, which comes from Kant, Hegel explicitly criticizes. The dialectic is rather a complex interplay of conceptions, some of which are simply improvements on others, some of which are indeed opposites demanding synthetic resolution, but others simply represent conceptual dead ends, which indicate a need to start over. Indeed, it is not at all clear that Hegel's dialectic is a linear progression from simplicity to the absolute but rather a phenomenological tapestry in which a great many (hardly "all") of the forms of human experience and philosophy jostle against one another and compete for adequacy. Within that tapestry, however, can be found much of the history of Western epistemology and metaphysics, and a great deal of ethics and social history and the history of religion. Whether or not Hegel reaches the absolute, as he states so proudly in his Preface, he gives us an eclectic but systematic philosophy which boldly demonstrates both the complex life of ideas and the role of those ideas in defining human history and consciousness.

◆◆ SELF AND SELF-CONSCIOUSNESS ◆◆

The *Phenomenology* makes what might well seem to be an abrupt turn from consciousness, an essentially epistemological study, to self-consciousness and "the truth of self-certainty" and an obscure discussion of "desire" and "life." But the historical linkage here is provided by Fichte, who had charted the move from the theory of knowledge to the importance of a broad, pragmatic conception of self-knowledge several years before. Consciousness becomes self-consciousness when it understands itself as the source of the understanding. To consider the problems of knowledge alone, without reference to the uses of knowledge and the psychological-social world in which knowledge functions, is futile. Thus any adequate conception of knowledge must begin with an understanding of the living self, which is not first of all epistemic but needy, full of demands and desires.

"Self-certainty," like sense-certainty, begins with a common-sense, cocksure conception of the self – in this case clearly reminiscent of Descartes's "I think, therefore I am." Hegel goes on to show that the self is not certain at all. To the contrary, in the confusion of desire and the urges of life the self is confused and desperately seeking in identity. As in the preceding epistemological chapters, Hegel will bring us from a naive view to a more complex and sophisticated philosophical standpoint, but in contrast to the preceding chapters he will now insist that there is an essentially "practical" dimension to knowledge. But "practical" here means, as in Kant, the self conceived as a true self, not just the self of appearances. Accordingly, what emerges in the section on "Self-consciousness" is a reappearance of the old dichotomy of appearance and reality. But instead of rending the world in two, as in the "upside-down" world, the self is shattered into the most "unhappy" of consciousness.

Following Hegel's brief opening comments on the supposedly self-certain "I" and its relation to desire and life, we find the best-known and most dramatic single chapter in the *Phenomenology*, the parable of the "master and slave." The point is to show that selfhood develops not through introspection but rather through mutual recognition. The self is essentially social or, more accurately, interpersonal, and not merely psychological or epistemological. But Hegel is also concerned to speculate on a certain kind of "natural" relationship between primitive, "stripped-down" human beings. It is an imaginary situation envisioned by many philosophers (notably Hobbes and Rousseau) in their hypotheses about the "state of nature." Their common assumption is that human beings are first of all individuals and only later, by mutual agreement, members of society. Hegel thinks that this assumption is nonsense, for individuality begins to appear only within an interpersonal context.

The confrontation of two consciousnesses is the key to the master–slave relationship, which Marx would later take up as a model for his social theory and Jean-Paul Sartre would borrow as a paradigm for his analysis of "Being-for-others" in *Being and Nothingness*. Hegel tells us that "self-consciousness achieves its satisfaction only in another self-consciousness" (*PG*, 175), and that "Self-consciousness exists in itself and for itself when and by the fact that it so exists for another; that is, it exists only in being acknowledged" (*PG*, 178). These cryptic sentences are the crux of "self-consciousness"; they spell out for us the first appearance of Spirit – the recognition of the existence of a universal consciousness in the primitive form of the recognition of consciousness other than one's own. But Hegel is also arguing a radical thesis about the nature of origin of selfhood. First, there is the suggestion that the concept of "self-consciousness" or "self-identity" can only arise in confrontation with others. Hegel's thesis might thus be construed as the claim that a person has no concept of self, cannot refer to themselves and cannot say things about themselves (for example, ascribe states of consciousness to themselves) until he is shown how to do so by someone else. This thesis has remarkable affinities with Ludwig Wittgenstein's and later P.F. Strawson's claim that psychological predicates can only be learned through learning to apply them to someone else.

Second, there is a more modest thesis that one can only develop self-consciousness, that is, a particular concept of oneself, through confrontation with other people. This weaker thesis does not insist that one cannot have concepts of self-reference before social confrontation but rather that the particular image one has of oneself is acquired socially, not in isolation. It is this sort of thesis which occupies much of Sartre's quasi-psychological efforts in *Being and Nothingness*. The first claim, that concerning the concept of self-reference, is not pursued by Hegel, for he considers self-reference as such to be "merely formal" and "entirely empty," hardly worth the title of "self-consciousness" at all. (Compare his discussion of the "knowledge" of sense-certainty.)[38] The second thesis, however, seems to fit precisely into the overall ambition of the *Phenomenology*, to show how an inadequate conception of oneself is forced into some remarkable and surprising twists and turns.

The first part of the master–slave parable is quite simple and straightforward: two self-consciousnesses encounter each other and struggle to "cancel" each other in order to "prove their certainty of themselves" (their independence and freedom) against the other, who appears as an independent and therefore limiting being.[39] Each self-consciousness originally tries to treat the other as object, but finds that the other does not react as an object. Each demands that the other recognize them as an independent consciousness. But recognizing another as independent limits one's own independence, and each becomes determined to prove their own freedom and independence. Hegel tells us:

> they have not yet exposed themselves to each other in the form of pure being-for-itself, or as self-consciousness. Each is indeed certain of its own self, but not of the other, and therefore its own self-certainty still has no truth.

(*PG*, 186)

Hegel suggests that it is solely by risking one's life that such a truth is established, and, indeed, the two self-consciousnesses fight (almost) to the death. The other must be "cancelled" because their otherness contradicts one's view as self-conscious, free, and independent. However, it becomes clear that the role of the other in this life-and-death struggle is not only that of a threat or purely destructive. The recognition by the other of one's self is at the very crux of the conflict. Thus it is gaining the recognition of the other that is the point of the battle, not the extinction of the other. Hegel says that "trial by death does away with the truth which was supposed to issue from it, and so, too, with the certainty of self generally" (*PG*, 188). Thus Hegel argues that self-consciousness requires the presence of another for one's own self-consciousness. In fighting for recognition, each tries to save their own life, but each tries also, if possible, to preserve the life of their opponent. If one consciousness is victor, and neither loses their life, then one becomes a consciousness "for itself," independent, a master, while the other becomes a consciousness 'for another," a slave whose essence, Hegel comments, is "life," suggesting that all that the slave has salvaged, at least for the moment, is their life.

The lord or master "is the consciousness that *for itself*, which is mediated with itself through another consciousness" (*PG*, 190). But the master, although self-sufficient in the sense of having the slave dependent on him, is also dependent on this dependence. Because the master maintains the power, they are the master, but because they are now self-sufficient only through the industry of the slave, they are also dependent on the slave. Hegel stresses the importance of a Lockean relationship to "the thing" – presumably land, food, or some craft – which the slave has immediately ("he labours upon it") but "the master only mediately, except that he gets the enjoyment of it" (ibid.). In the course of the dialectic, the slave, because of their direct relation to the thing, becomes self-sufficient, while the master, because of their dependence on the slave, becomes wholly dependent. (From this reversal Marx is to take his central theses of class struggle and the ultimate degeneration and self-destruction of the economic master classes.) Furthermore, the problem of the continued need for the recognition of the other breeds a further instability into this relationship. The master, who depends on the slave for the recognition that they are indeed the master, now finds that the slave is a totally dependent creature without an independent will, incapable of giving them the recognition of an independent other. The slave, in other words, becomes a "yes-man," whose recognition is irrelevant precisely because it is coerced.

In the master–slave relationship, we first see the striving for freedom of Spirit, the ultimate truth of self-consciousness. In the master–slave relationship, we see only the inadequacy of the attempt to derive this truth from human relationships which treat persons as independent and opposed. Hegel will go on to argue that the way to freedom, the goal of self-consciousness, lies not in such relationships but in the direction of increased civilization. Rousseau had famously argued that society takes a man and turns him into a citizen. For Hegel, too, individual freedom will be found not in isolated independence but in citizenship. But none of this, the explicit recognition of Spirit, appears in the section on "Self-consciousness." The master–slave relationship rather gives way to the wholesale rejection of the master–slave situation and the mutual dependency it entails, denying all external reality and rejecting all action as meaningless. Here Hegel locates the impressive philosophy of Stoicism, which flourished in the ancient world for more than 600 years. The Stoic rejects both slavery and mastery, and Hegel makes much of the fact that two of the leading Stoics, Epictetus and Marcus Auelius, were a slave and the master of the Roman Empire respectively (PG, 197–203). In an even more extreme form, self-consciousness attempts to get beyond the frustrations of the master–slave relationship by taking everything as meaningless, which Hegel interprets along the lines of the ancient (not the modern) philosophy of Skepticism (PG, 204–5). Ultimately, the contradictions or disharmonies of all possible forms of self-consciousness become explicit in a self-consciousness that is so alienated that it conceives of itself as nothing, or as worse than nothing, in contrast to a holy ideal before which it humbles itself. This unhappy consciousness is the primitive Christian ascetic who believes himself to be both part of this world and essentially divine, but the "creature of the flesh" and the "soul before God" cannot coexist (PG, 206–30). The master–slave relationship, which became an impossible relationship between two people, here becomes internalized in a single schizoid individual. A decade after Hegel's death, Hegel's Danish critic Søren Kierkegaard would return to this disharmonious Christian for his "knight of resignation." Where Kierkegaard will insist that this incomprehensible schizophrenia is a necessary condition for Christianity, however, Hegel insists that we go beyond this internalized master–slave relationship with its self-flagellation and self-denial. At the very end of the discussion of the "unhappy consciousness" and the section on "Self-consciousness," Hegel anticipates a new and happier conception of Christ and Christianity, but not through self-consciousness alone. It is rather in "the idea of *Reason*, of the certainty that, in its particular individuality, it has being absolutely *in itself*, or is all reality" (*PG*, 230; Hegel's italics).

REASON AND SPIRIT

Rational consciousness is the goal of the *Phenomenology*, a final "unification of the diverse elements in its process" and "the consciousness of the certainty of being all truth" (*PG*, 231). Reason resolves by harmonizing and elevating (*autheben*) the disharmonies between self and others, between God and man, between morality and personal inclination, between nature and knowledge. The Spirit of Absolute Knowing is both immanent God and human society. It is also nature, which one might think of as the material aspect of Spirit. There is no separating God from nature or from man and it is folly to separate freedom from nature, reason from passion, or morality from society, as Kant seemed to have done in his philosophy. Reason in the *Phenomenology* marks the synthesis of a number of conflicts that have been introduced in the dialectic of the *Phenomenology* itself, the inadequacies of traditional epistemological thought, the resolution of the master-slave relationship, and interpersonal conflict (including the internalized conflict of the unhappy consciousness); and, most ambitious of all, the *Phenomenology* is Hegel's first attempt to integrate and harmonize all human forms of consciousness and find the proper conceptual place for each of them.

The long section on "Reason" – considerably more than two-thirds of the *Phenomenology* – appears to have no organizing principle or straightforward argument, such as one can discern in the first two sections on "Consciousness" and "Self-consciousness." The first part of the section is a lengthy discourse on the philosophy of nature, including what we would now call the philosophy of science, and it culminates in a particularly peculiar discussion of the oddball sciences of physiognomy and phrenology, the claims that personality and deep psychology can be "read" from certain facial features or the bumps on a person's skull. What occupies Hegel throughout the entire discussion, however, is an attempt to emphasize the nature of the organic, rejecting the familiar Cartesian divisions of mind and body, "inside" and "outside," and the reductionist conceptions of nature. The argument about faces and skulls is not so much a defense of dubious sciences as it is a defense of the integration of our conceptions of psyche and expression, much as he had argued for the organic integrity of nature earlier in the discussion.[40]

Immediately following this discussion we find ourselves suddenly steeped in certain perennial questions of ethics, "the actualization of rational self-consciousness through its own activity" (*PG*, 347ff.). If there is a principle of transition here, apart from the holistic impetus that motivates all of reason, it is not at all easy to discern. In rapid succession, Hegel considers hedonism, what we would call moral self-righteousness, and a certain tragic conception of integrity or "virtue," but the discussion here seems to follow more or less directly from the unhappy resolution of self-consciousness. Indeed, one of the more familiar channels of denial for the unhappy consciousness is the soon jaded road of hedonism. The predictable reaction, a stubborn asceticism and the rejection of "the way of the world," is equally familiar in both literature and life (*PG*, 381). In these short chapters, as so often for the rest of the book, Hegel seems to be incorporating any number of more or less contemporary themes and controversies, rarely identified as such, from the psychology of Rousseau to the world-weary asceticism of the Jansenists. Nevertheless a general theme is perceptible through the details and meanderings, and that is the inadequacy of any conception of ethics that remains restricted to the isolated individual. Thus the emphasis in this discussion is on the phrase "actualization through its [one's own] activity," which leads inevitably to new versions of the frustrated, unhappy, divided consciousness. The discussion culminates in Kant and a discussion of the categorical imperative. This is, perhaps, the most enduring argument of the *Phenomenology*, some aspects of which are routinely trotted out in introductory ethics classes as criticism of Kant without recognizing their source in Hegel. But before we actually get to Kant, Hegel slips in one of the oddest chapters of the entire *Phenomenology*, a covert discussion of university life under the title, "The Spiritual Animal Kingdom and Deceit, or 'the Matter in Hand' itself" (*PG*, 397–418). To explain just the title would take several pages, but the upshot of the chapter is as easy to understand as it is amusing. Professors love to conceive of themselves as independent individuals, but they really are the ultimate conformists, utterly dependent on each other and on their mutual opinions of one another. Whereas the unhappy independent spirits of the "Actualization" chapter erred in their efforts to remain wholly isolated, the rather self-satisfied creatures in the "academic zoo" simply pretend to be isolated and independent, whereas in fact they are nothing of the kind. It is from here we suddenly leap into the ethical thinking of the greatest professor of all academic zoos, Immanuel Kant. For he, too, likes to feign an autonomy that is more imagined than actual.

Ever since Kant, autonomy has been the watchword of ethics. Autonomy is the ability of each of us, as rational creatures, to ascertain for ourselves what is right and, in words drawn from Rousseau, impose the moral law on ourselves. Ethics in general and Kant's categorical imperative in particular concern the recognition of our moral autonomy. Indeed, one of the three formulations of the categorical imperative appeals explicitly to the notion of autonomy.[41] But Hegel criticizes this notion of autonomy, and he does so on two different grounds. The arguments are quite succinct, perhaps because Hegel had already published them at length elsewhere.[42] The primary criticism, still the focus of much critical discussion today, is the illusory nature of Kant's moral self, which is no particular self with no particular properties but simply a confused abstraction from the social life of bourgeois or *bürgerlich* Prussian morality (*PG*, 419f.). Moreover, the basic Kantian distinction between reason and the "inclination" unwisely divides the moral self in two and gives unwarranted precedence to formal laws rather than particular moral contexts (*PG*, 425f.). But those formal laws, Hegel argues (like our best undergraduates today), cannot be so readily applied to our concrete, often ambiguous everyday situations. There is no satisfactory criterion for "testing laws," as Kant had argued; there are only the *ad hoc* stipulations of the "maxim" of one's actions such that the moral law can be made to fit as needed (*PG*, 429–37). But behind these brief hit-and-run attacks on Kant, Hegel has an alternative conception of ethics, which will soon appear. What he really objects to is the bogus individualism and *a priori* universality of Kant's notion of morality (*Moralität*). In its place, he will emphasize the social foundations of ethics, or *Sittlichkeit*, much as he had in his first youthful essay on Greek folk religion over a decade before.

The notion of *Sittlichkeit* stands at the center of Hegel's ethics, and with it we are finally informed that we are now on the home ground of Spirit. The master–slave relation may have in some sense appeared to be a social encounter, if by that one means only the joint appearance of two or more mutually aware creatures, but society and the social are much more than a collection of individuals. They presuppose mutual attachments and dependencies – just those attachments and dependencies that those antagonistic self-consciousnesses denied. They presuppose a sense of community, a shared identity. Ethics, in other words, is based on community values, on shared customs (*Sitte*), not autonomy. And reason, in Hegel's philosophy, refers not to that abstract *a priori* ability to calculate and deliberate so much as the very concrete conception of oneself as part of the whole. Reason is not an individual "faculty" but a social process. And ethics as an exercise of practical reason means not working it out for oneself so much as understanding one's duties and obligations to one's community.

But, of course, there are different communities, with different customs, and sometimes these communities come into conflict. Nothing could have been more evident to Hegel, who as he wrote watched the tragedy of Europe tearing itself apart in the name of competing ideologies, just as Germany had torn itself apart many years before in the name of what would appear from a distance to be a couple of theological nuances.[43] Thus the upshot of Hegel's philosophy and the grand hope of the *Phenomenology*, announced with great fanfare in the Preface, is the birth of a new, international world, in which cultural differences might be preserved but the harmony of the whole would be assured. But this is getting ahead of ourselves. At this point in the *Phenomenology*, *Sittlichkeit* has just appeared, and it is immediately rent apart by tragedy. Within communities, as well as between them, conflict is always possible. And as so often in Hegel's writing, particular conflicts have great philosophical consequences. At this juncture, Hegel chooses to write about Sophocles' tragedy *Antigone*, one of his favorite plays (which he would discuss at length again in his *Philosophy of Right*, fifteen years later). The point of the play is taken to be the clash of two sets of laws, human and divine. The divine law, defended by Antigone, is the law of the primitive tribe, blood law, the ultimate sanctity of the family. The human law, or what would later become civil law, was represented by Creon, the king. In the battle over the burial of Antigone's brother, required by sacred law but prohibited by Creon, the two laws meet in mortal conflict within the individual person Antigone. She is simultaneously embedded in two societies, the "divine" tribal society of her family, in which family duty and honor were all, and civil society in which law and obedience were essential. Her individual case is tragic and unresolvable, but the movement of history and the dialectic provide a resolution to the conflict which was not available for the tragic heroine. With the development of modern civil society, individuals and families are integrated under the law of the land.

Hegel then goes on to speculate on the development of civil society and the concept of culture, as he would again in his *Philosophy of Right*.[44] He discusses the Enlightenment as the embodiment of a false because anti-spiritual effort to build a truly universal society, and he introduces the almost current-events topic of the French Revolution and in particular the Terror of 1793–4 and the character of Robespierre as something of a *reductio ad absurdum* argument against the Enlightenment pretense of pure reason against the more humble security of traditional spirituality and community. And at this point Kant comes back into the dialectic, not Kant of the categorical imperative but the Kant who defended the religious "postulate" of "the moral worldview" and the grand teleology of the third *Critique*. According to Hegel, Kant had earlier argued for the importance of autonomy and his narrowly described notion of morality only at a terrible cost, a one-sided picture of man as separated from nature and his own desires and happiness, concerned only with the imperatives of duty. Hegel now argues (as he had in his earlier writings) that morality and happiness cannot be separated: "enjoyment lies in the very principle of morality." Hegel thus restates what Kant called the *summum bonum* as a necessary condition for morality: "The harmony of morality and nature, or . . . the harmony of morality and happiness, is thought of as necessarily existing" (*PG*, 599). This "harmony of morality and objective nature" Hegel refers to as "the final purpose of the world" (*PG*, 604). Postulation, however, is not proof, and Kant's belief in a divine moral Legislator and the Kingdom of Heaven, his "postulates of practical reason," cannot be left to mere postulation. Thus the dialectical movement fron Kant's ethics to religion is an attempt to broaden the field of ethics and get away from Kant's overly restrictive notion of duty and the ultimately self-defeating distinction between duty and reason on the one hand and the inclinations, including both the moral sentiments and the pursuit of happiness, on the other. In the *Phenomenology*, as in his early writings, Hegel suggests that a more sophisticated and harmonious conception of morality can be found in *Sittlichkeit*, but now expanded to global and even cosmic proportions. After one final, unusually harsh attack on Kant, Hegel resurrects the early Christian ideal of conscience, in which, he argues (following Fichte), the commands of duty and the incentives of the inclinations are synthesized.[45] Conscience acts on implicit principle, yet it is also specific to particular situations. It is individual yet derivative of a person's upbringing in society. Conscience finds its living ideal in the figure that Hegel identifies as the "beautiful soul," a holy figure whose "pure goodness" makes them "lose contact with social reality." One immediately thinks of Dostoevsky's Prince Myshkin (*The Idiot*), or more aptly, it is the conception of the historical Jesus who best characterizes the beautiful soul and the perfect voice of conscience. It is the person of Jesus who moves the dialectic to that penultimate level of consciousness known as religion (*PG*, 632–71).

"The concept of Religion," according to Hegel, "is the consciousness that sees itself as Truth" (*PG*, 677). After a brief excursion through primitive and 'artistic' religious consciousness, Hegel brings us back to Christianity, whose Judaic origins have already promoted the conception of God as Spirit, but an objective or transcendent Spirit, "out there." What Christ represents, according to Hegel, is not a concrete manifestation of God in the form of one man. Christ is rather the symbol of the conception that God and all men are a unity. That spirit is "substance and subject as well" means that the Christian Spirit and we ourselves are the same (*PG*, 18, 748). Here is the resolution of the disharmony between man and God which had caused Hegel to renounce Christianity in his early writings, but it is not to be thought that this is an unambiguous endorsement of traditional Christianity either. Christianity has failed to become Absolute Truth, according to Hegel, because it has become obsessed with figurative thinking in stories and pictures. To become Absolute Truth, Christianity must reject such thinking and become wholly conceptual. Needless to say, this entails a rejection of many of the teachings and most of the ritual storytelling of the Christian church. The Absolute Knowing of the *Phenomenology* can thus be interpreted as a reconceptualization of the basic themes of Christianity. But it is, apart from its trinitarian jargon, a notoriously weak vision of Christianity.[46] The insistence that Christianity become totally conceptual does not mean that it must dispense with any content, but its content is ultimately the content of the *Phenomenology* rather than the theological constructs that Hegel occasionally imitates but just as often lampoons. It has been said that the end and the purpose of the *Phenomenology* and the justification and end of all human activity rest in Hegel's revised Christianity, but, as Kierkegaard bitterly points out, this alleged Christianity is far more Hegelian than Christian. So, too, what Hegel means by "reason" may be no more than nominally related to what most philosophers designate by that term. The tricks and twists of the *Phenomenology*, not to mention its often impossible language, belie the claim that this is a work of, indeed the very embodiment of, reason. Nevertheless, it is a masterpiece of a very different kind, and philosophy would certainly never be the same without it.

⤙ CONCLUSION ⤚

Hegel intended his *Phenomenology* as the "introduction" to a system of philosophy. It was supposed to establish the standpoint of Absolute Knowledge from which the system itself could be formulated. That task occupied Hegel for the rest of his career. The conclusion always seems to be: We do experience Absolute Reality, but we conceive of it in many different ways and these various ways can be contrasted, compared, and fitted into a single, overall system of philosophy. Nietzsche later urged us to "look now through this window and now through that one," but where Nietzsche would insist (against Hegel) on the inevitable conflict and incommensurability of these various forms of experience, it is Hegel's project to show us how they grow from and complement one another as well as conflict. A sufficiently broad, indeed "absolute", perspective will absorb (which is not to say resolve) all of those conflicts as well.

❧ NOTES ❧

1 H. Heine, *German Philosophy and Religion*, in *Werke*, Vol. V, trans. J. Snodgrass (Boston: Beacon, 1959), p. 137.

2 *Hegel's Early Theological Writings*, trans. T.M. Knox (Chicago: University of Chicago Press, 1948). For an excellent treatment of Hegel's early years and philosophical development, see H.S. Harris, *Hegel's Development: Towards the Sunlight 1770–1801* (Oxford: Clarendon Press, 1972).

3 Friedrich Heinrich Jacobi is said to have commented, reading one of Hegel's early unsigned academic essays: "I recognize the bad style." See R.C. Solomon, *In the Spirit of Hegel* (Oxford: Oxford University Press, 1983), pp. 147ff.

4 *The Difference between Fichte's and Schelling's Systems of Philosophy*, or "The Difference Essay," published in the *Critical Journal of Philosophy* in the summer of 1801, English trans. H.S. Harris and W. Cerf (Albany: SUNY Press, 1977).

5 All references to the *Phenomenology* in this essay are based on the A.V. Miller translation of *Die Phänomenologie des Geistes* (Oxford: Oxford University Press, 1977), henceforth referred to as *PG*; citation numbers refer to paragraph numbers, not pages. My account of the *Phenomenology* is based on two earlier treatments in R.C. Solomon, *From Rationalism to Existentialism* (New York: Harper & Row, 1972; Savage, Md: Rowman & Littlefield, 1992), and, at much greater length, *In the Spirit of Hegel*, op. cit.

6 Among the fans of the third *Critique* were the great German poet Goethe, his equally talented playwright friend Friedrich Schiller, author of *Letters on the Aesthetic Education of Mankind* (1795), and many of the young romantics of the day.

7 Fichte, *Wissenschaftslehre*; Schelling, *System of Transcendental Idealism*; see Daniel Breazeale's excellent introduction to these works in Chapter 5, "Fichte and Schelling: the Jena period."

8 The notion of "truth" employed here was obviously not strictly an epistemological notion, but one based on the original German root "*Wahr*" (like "*treowe*" in Old English and "*veritas*" in Latin) which means genuine, not simply "true to the facts." See Hegel's own etymology of "truth" in his *Encyclopedia, Logic*, trans. W. Wallace (Oxford: Oxford University Press, 1892), 24, p. 172, where he distinguishes philosophical truth (*Wahrheit*) from mere "correctness" (*Richtigkeit*); and my analysis in "Hegel: truth and self-satisfaction," in R.C. Solomon, *From Hegel to Existentialism* (Oxford: Oxford University Press, 1987), pp. 37–55.

9 Nietzsche once wrote that "Kant's joke" was the defense of the common man in language that the common man could not possibly comprehend.

10 Harris, op. cit., pp. 258–310; J. Hoffmeister, *Hølderlin und Hegel in Frankfurt* (Tübingen, 1931).

11 See Harris, op. cit., p. 140; and Solomon, *In the Spirit of Hegel*, op. cit., pp. 115–16.

12 Notably, in the work of Johann Herder, F.H. Jacobi, and Kant's close friend, Hamann. See Lewis White Beck's discussion of this period in Chapter 1, "From Leibniz to Kant," esp. his discussion of the Spinoza dispute, pp. 28–32.

13 Hegel defended such a position in the *Phenomenology*, ch. 6B, but evidently held it much earlier. See Harris, op. cit., e.g. pp. 140, 299. Years later, Nietzsche caught the German attitude with a quip against utilitarianism: "Man does not live for pleasure: only the Englishman does."

14 Knox, op. cit., and in Harris, op. cit., pp. 488ff.

15 Notably, "Hegel's Tübingen essay" of 1793, trans. in Harris, op. cit.; and his notoriously hostile "The Positivity of Christianity" (1795), in Knox, op. cit.

16 Harris, op. cit., pp. 504–5. Cf. Kierkegaard, Hegel's posthumous nemesis: "The way of objective reflection makes the subject accidental." *Concluding Unscientific Postscript*, trans. W. Lowrie (Princeton: Princeton University Press, 1941), p. 173.

17 Harris, op. cit., p. 499.

18 Ibid.; also Hegel, "The Spirit of Christianity and its Fate," in Knox, op. cit., pp. 182–301.

19 Hegel, *Critique of Practical Reason; Religion within the Bounds of Reason Alone*.

20 Hegel, "Positivity" essay, op. cit., p. 68.

21 Hegel, "The Life of Jesus," also written in 1795.

22 A theme he clearly borrowed from Lessing's *Education of Mankind*, which he read in 1787 and again in 1793. See W. Kaufmann, *Hegel: A Re-examination* (New York: Doubleday, 1966), pp. 67f. Hegel, "The Spirit of Christianity and its Fate," op. cit., markedly shows this change of temper.

23 See also Hegel's fragment on "Love," in Knox, op. cit., pp. 302–8.

24 Hegel, "Positivity" essay, op. cit., pp. 185–7; Solomon, *In the Spirit of Hegel*, op. cit., pp. 142–3. Cf. Nietzsche's later argument in *On the Genealogy of Morals*, Book I, trans. W. Kaufmann (New York: Random House, 1967).

25 Quoted from Solomon, *In the Spirit of Hegel*, op. cit., pp. viii–ix. See also Leo Rauch's discussion of Hegel on "Spirit" in Chapter 8, "Hegel, Spirit, and Politics."

26 Quoted in Kaufmann, op. cit., p. 366.

27 *PG*, 16. Hegel denied making personal reference to Schelling in that comment and in a crack about "monochromatic" and "schematizing formalism" a bit later (*PG*, 51–2); but compare his only somewhat more diplomatic comments on Schelling in his later *Lectures on the History of Philosophy*: "His defeat is that the idea in general [is] not shown forth and developed through the concept [*Begriff*]," p. 242. He also distinguishes himself from Spinoza's pantheism – a dangerous position to be associated with in those days – in his *Encyclopedia*, op. cit., p. 573.

28 See my "Hegel's Concept of *Geist*," in Solomon, *From Hegel to Existentialism*, op. cit., pp. 3–17.

29 See Leo Rauch, Chapter 8.

30 The "concept" is opposed to "intellectual intuition" and represents an argumentative or "dialectical" conception of philosophy compared to the emphasis on mystical insight that fascinated many of the romantic philosophers. Just after the publication of the *Phenomenology*, Schelling wrote to Hegel: "I confess that I do not comprehend the sense in which you oppose the *concept* to intuition. Surely you do not mean anything else by it than what you and I used to call the idea, whose nature it is to have one side which is concept and one from which it is intuition" (from Munich, 2 November 1807).

31 For Hegel's mature notion of "the self-development of the concept," see Willem deVries's acount in Chapter 7, "Hegel's logic and philosophy of mind."

32 See Daniel Bonevac's discussion of Kant's first *Critique* in Chapter 2, "Kant's Copernican Revolution."

33 I have suggested elsewhere that one could begin the route traced in the *Phenomenology* at any number of different starting points and, presumably, cover much of the same territory and arrive at the same conclusion. Solomon, *In the Spirit of Hegel*, op. cit., ch. 4c, pp. 235ff.

34 One of the most outspoken advocates of this attack on epistemology today is Richard Rorty, who perhaps gives too little credit to Hegel in this regard. Despite his systematic pretensions, Hegel would seem to be a much more palatable ancestor than Heidegger, for example. See Rorty, *Philosophy and the Mirror of Nature* (Princeton: Princeton University Press, 1977).

35 Cf. Nietzsche, "How the 'True World' Finally Became a Fable," in *Twilight of the Idols*, trans. W. Kaufmann, *The Viking Portable Nietzsche* (New York: Viking, 1954), pp. 485f.

36 Again, see Daniel Bonevac's chapter on the first *Critique*, Chapter 2.

37 Kant, *Prolegomena to Any Future Metaphysics* (Indianapolis: Bobbs-Merrill, 1950), p. 66.

38 An extended discussion of this empty self-reference can be found in Part III of the *Encyclopedia*, op. cit.

39 This conception of the individual as essentially independent but limited by others comes to Hegel from Jean-Jacques Rousseau, who influenced Hegel in many ways as much as he influenced Kant.

40 *PG*, 309ff. See A. MacIntyre, "Hegel on Faces and Skulls," in MacIntyre (ed.), *Hegel* (New York: Doubleday, 1972).

41 See Don Becker, Chapter 3, "Kant's moral and political philosophy."

42 In Hegel's essay on "Natural Law" in the 1802–3 volume of the *Critical Journal* and in his *System of Sittlichkeit* based on the lectures of that same period, trans. H.S. Harris and T.M. Knox (Albany: SUNY Press, 1979).

43 Cf. Hölderlin: "I can think of no people as torn apart as the Germans. . . . Is it not like a field of battle where hands and arms and other limbs lie scattered in pieces while the blood of life drains into the soil?" *Hyperion*, trans. W. Trask (New York: Ungar, 1965).

44 See Leo Rauch, Chapter 8, on Hegel's social and political philosophy.

45 *PG*, 625. Cf. Fichte, *Science of Ethics*, pp. 150ff., and his *Vocation of Man*, pp. 136, 154, both in *Science of Logic* (*Wissenschaft*), trans. P. Heath and J. Lachs (New York: Appleton-Century-Crofts, 1970).

46 See my "Secret of Hegel," in Solomon, *In the Spirit of Hegel*, op. cit., ch. 10.

❧ SELECT BIBLIOGRAPHY ❧

Original language editions

6.1 Hegel, G.F.W. *Gesammelte Werke*, ed. Rheinisch-Westfälischen Akademie der Wissenschaften, Hamburg: Meiner, 1968–.

6.2 Hegel, G.F.W. *Sämtliche Werke*, 20 vols, ed. E. Moldenhauer and K.M. Michel, Frankfurt: Suhrkamp, 1970–1.

6.3 Hegel, G.F.W. *Theologische Jugendschriften*, ed. H. Nohl, Tübingen: Mohr, 1907.

English translations

6.4 *Hegel's Early Theological Writings*, trans. T.M. Knox, Chicago: University of Chicago Press, 1948.

6.5 Hegel, G.F.W. *The Difference between Fichte's and Schelling's Systems of Philosophy*, trans. H.S. Harris and W. Cerf, Albany: SUNY Press, 1977.

6.6 Hegel, G.F.W. *The Phenomenology of Spirit*, trans. A.V. Miller, Oxford: Oxford University Press, 1977.

Books on the Phenomenology

6.7 Fackenheim, E. *The Religious Dimension in Hegel's Thought*, Indianapolis: Indiana University Press, 1967.

6.8 Findlay, J. *Hegel: A Re-examination*, London: Allen & Unwin, and New York: Oxford University Press, 1958.

6.9 Gadamer, H.-G. *Hegel's Dialectic*, trans. C. Smith, New Haven: Yale University Press, 1976.

6.10 Harris, H.S. *Hegel's Development: Towards the Sunlight, 1770–1801*, Oxford: Clarendon Press, 1972.

6.11 Hyppolite, J. *Genesis and Structure of Hegel's Phenomenology of Spirit*, Evanston: Northwestern University Press, 1974.

6.12 Inwood, M.J. *Hegel*, London: Routledge & Kegan Paul, 1983.

6.13 Inwood M.J. (ed.) *Hegel*, Oxford Readings in Philosophy, Oxford: Oxford University Press, 1985.

6.14 Kaufmann, W. *Hegel: A Re-examination*, New York: Doubleday, 1966.

6.15 Kojéve, A. *An Introduction to the Reading of Hegel*, New York and London: Basic Books, 1969.

6.16 Lauer, Q. *A Reading of Hegel's Phenomenology of Spirit*, New York: Fordham, 1976.

6.17 MacIntyre, A.C. (ed.) *Hegel: A Collection of Critical Essays*, New York: Doubleday, 1972.

6.18 Marcuse, H. *Reason and Revolution*, New York: Oxford University Press, 1941; Boston: Beacon, 1960.

6.19 Norman, R. *Hegel's Phenomenology: A Philosophical Introduction*, Sussex, 1976.

6.20 Plant, R. *Hegel: An Introduction*, Oxford: Oxford University Press, 1983.
6.21 Robinson, J. *Duty and Hypocrisy in Hegel's Phenomenology of Mind*, Toronto: University of Toronto Press, 1977.
6.22 Rosen, S. *G.W.F. Hegel: An Introduction to the Science of Wisdom*, New Haven: Yale University Press, 1974.
6.23 Schacht, R. *Hegel and After*, Pittsburgh: University of Pittsburgh Press, 1983.
6.24 Singer, P. *Hegel*, Oxford: Oxford University Press, 1983.
6.25 Solomon, R.C. *From Hegel to Existentialism*, Oxford: Oxford University Press, 1987.
6.26 Solomon, R.C. *From Rationalism to Existentialism*, New York: Harper & Row, 1972: Savage, Md: Rowman & Littlefield, 1992.
6.27 Solomon, R.C. *In the Spirit of Hegel*, Oxford: Oxford University Press, 1983.
6.28 Solomon, R.C. *Introducing the German Idealists*, Indianapolis: Hackett, 1981.
6.29 Taylor, C. *Hegel*, Cambridge: Cambridge University Press, 1975.
6.30 Taylor, C. *Hegel and Modern Society*, Cambridge: Cambridge University Press, 1979.

Selected articles on the Phenomenology

6.31 Bernstein, R. "Why Hegel Now?" *Review of Metaphysics*, 31 (1977): 29–60.
6.32 Bossart, W.H. "Hegel on the Inverted World," *Philosophical Forum* (1982).
6.33 Gadamer, H.-G. "Hegel's Dialectic of Self-Consciousness," in Gadamer [6.9].
6.34 Kelly, G.A. "Notes on Hegel's Lordship and Bondage," *Review of Metaphysics*, 19 (1965); repr. in MacIntyre) [6.17].
6.35 Taylor, C. "The Opening Arguments of the *Phenomenology*," in MacIntyre [6.17].
6.36 Zimmerman, R. "Hegel's 'Inverted World' Revisited," *Philosophical Forum* (1982).

CHAPTER 7

Hegel's logic and philosophy of mind

Willem deVries

～ LOGIC AND MIND IN HEGEL'S ～ PHILOSOPHY

～ LOGIC AND MIND IN HEGEL'S ～ PHILOSOPHY

Hegel is above all a systematic philosopher. Awe-inspiring in its scope, his philosophy left no subject untouched. Logic provides the central, unifying framework as well as the general methodology of his system. Understanding Hegel's logic is therefore essential to a comprehensive understanding of any piece of the system and any subject it deals with.

Hegel never slavishly accepted received wisdom in any field and less so in logic than anywhere else. The philosophical revolution began by Kant demanded a thoroughgoing reconception of the purpose, method, and content of logic, Hegel believed, and his expositions of this newly reconstituted discipline in the *Science of Logic* and the *Encyclopedia of the Philosophical Sciences* remain among the most intractable works of the philosophical canon. Hegel's logic breaks radically from the Aristotelian and scholastic logic that had dominated previous philosophical speculation, and it is unrelated to the mathematical logic that began to develop soon after Hegel's demise. The primary focus of this essay will be on what Hegelian logic is about, rather than on the details of its execution.

In the first section the essential problem of Hegel's logic is introduced, viz., that logic, according to Hegel, cannot be a purely formal discipline. The second section summarizes the textual development of Hegel's logic. The third section establishes the parameters constraining the interpretation of Hegel's logic. Because of the obscurity of the texts, it is valuable to state explicitly the conditions that constrain an adequate interpretation. Succeeding sections address these conditions by showing what it means that Hegel's logic is a self-movement of the concept and how this relates to his theory of subjectivity (the fourth section), in what sense logic is a formal science for Hegel (the fifth section), how one begins the enterprise of logic (the sixth section), and why Hegel's logic exhibits such a particular structure (the seventh section).

The paramount importance of logic within Hegel's system cannot be denied. A relatively large proportion (over 30 per cent) of his written work is devoted to logic: Of the four books Hegel published, one (the largest) is solely devoted to logic, and it is that book Hegel wrote in order to make his mark in the philosophical world after his first book, the *Phenomenology of Spirit*, garnered little notice. One-third of the *Encyclopedia* is devoted to logic. More importantly, Hegel's system begins with logic and culminates by returning to the point of departure for logic; logic is the alpha and omega of the system. Logic provides the alphabet for the system as well, for the conceptual analyses provided by logic serve as the patterns for the rest of the system. Logic is also the discipline in which Hegel's methodology is explicitly thematized. The idea that there is a "dialectical method" that can be illuminatingly brought to bear on any subject matter has fascinated post-Hegelian thought. (What this method is, however, has been notoriously difficult to specify.) Hegel's logic remains the primary source for any understanding of dialectics.

Logic plays such an important role in Hegel's philosophy, in part, because of his revolutionary interpretation of the discipline. Traditionally, logic has been understood as the study of the *formal* conditions of truth or as the study of the laws of thought. As the study of the formal conditions of truth, logic pays no attention at all to the *contents* of the items it addresses.[1] But Hegel rejects this interpretation of logic, arguing, in effect, that truth is both the subject and content of logic, and that logic cannot be a purely formal enterprise, for the notion of truth is not and cannot be a purely formal notion. If truth is the agreement of thought (or language) with reality, there is no guarantee that there must be certain conditions that thought or language on their own must satisfy in order to be able to agree with reality.[2] The conditions for the possible agreement between thought and reality or concept and object must depend in part on reality (see e.g. *WL*, I: 25; *SL*, 44–5).[3] But, then, they cannot be purely formal.

Hegel also picks up on the ancient theme that logic is the science of the laws of thought and infers that "as thinking and the rules of thinking are supposed to be the subject matter of logic, these directly constitute its peculiar content; in them, logic has that second constituent, a matter, about the nature of which it is concerned" (*WL*, I: 24; *SL*, 44). Whether the connection to truth or the connection to thought is emphasized in understanding the nature of logic, Hegel concludes that logic cannot be a purely formal enterprise. Since logic concerns the fundamental conditions of truth and thought and these cannot be specified independently of their content, the fundamental structures of reality, logic merges with basic metaphysics in Hegel's system.

The hope to derive metaphysics from logic is not peculiar to Hegel by any means – besides Hegel's predecessors (Leibniz and Kant, in particular), the twentieth-century logical atomists (Russell and early Wittgenstein), who in most other ways were Hegel's antithesis, also sought to read their metaphysics off of their logic. The logic–metaphysics connection acquires still further weight in Hegel's system from his idealism. Idealism is a tricky "ism" because so many different theories have gone by that rubric. Hegel's version, *absolute* idealism, must be distinguished from Berkeleyan subjective idealism (the claim that material bodies do not exist and the only things that do exist are mental substances and their modifications), what Kant calls Cartesian "problematical" idealism (the claim that the only things we know for certain are our own mental states, all other knowledge being a probabilistic inference therefrom), and Kantian transcendental idealism (the claim that our knowledge is restricted to things as they appear to us given our forms of intuition and that things as they are in themselves can never be known). Some versions of idealism thus have metaphysical theses at the core, while others are grounded in epistemological theses.

Absolute idealism is principally a metaphysical position characterizable as the claim that mind and reality share the same categorical structure. The categorical structure of thought ("thinking and the rules of thinking"), which is the subject matter of logic, must also be, according to the absolute idealist, the categorical (read here "ontological") structure of reality, and thus logic *is* metaphysics. Hegel's epistemology, in contrast to his metaphysics, is fundamentally realist and committed to our ability to cognize the objective structure of reality, although it is complicated by a sophisticated understanding of the historical conditions of knowledge.

Without looking in greater detail at the arguments Hegel gives to back up his claims, it is hard to grasp his points fully, but one immediate warning is warranted in this introductory glimpse of his position. Do not confuse mind (spirit) with minds. Hegel's German term *Geist*, formerly translated as "mind" but now increasingly translated as "spirit," can apply to individual minds, in which case Hegel would talk of *subjective* spirit. This is the usage that is most like our contemporary use. Hegel has a specific section of the *Encyclopedia*, called the "Philosophy of subjective spirit," focused on problems in philosophy of psychology. But *Geist* or spirit can also apply more broadly. Hegel generalized the Kantian notion that the self (the transcendental ego) is a principle uniting a disparate manifold of sense impressions into the notion that *Geist* is a principle uniting the disparate manifold of natural and historical events. Schematically:

Kant's transcendental ego : phenomenal world ::
Hegel's absolute spirit : the world

This vast oversimplification leaves at least two important questions: What happens to the Kantian thing-in-itself in Hegel's version? And what is the relation between subjective spirits and absolute spirit for Hegel? Let me briefly address the second question here; we will return to both questions later. Individual minds *embody* spirit; they are necessary to and participate in the development of absolute spirit, but no individual mind is itself essential to spirit's self-realization.

The movement and development of absolute spirit constitutes a higher level of abstraction than the psychological or historical development of individual people or societies. It is at this very high level of abstraction that we can describe pure thought. Logic is therefore not concerned with the thinking of any individual – that would make it psychology – nor with the "rules of thinking" governing any particular culture, period, or discipline.

> Logic is to be understood as the system of pure reason, as the realm of pure thought. This realm is truth as it is without veil and in its own absolute nature. It can therefore be said that this content is the exposition of God as he is in his eternal essence before the creation of nature and a finite mind.
>
> (*WL*, I: 31; *SL*, 50)

❧ DEVELOPMENTAL HISTORY OF HEGEL'S ❧ LOGIC

This essay does not purport to trace the development of Hegel's logic (a study which is yet to be written), but here a few landmarks may help orient one within the somewhat idiosyncratic world of Hegel's thought. Hegel's earliest philosophical speculations center around issues in ethics and the philosophy of religion – in particular Hegel seeks to understand how it might be possible to reconcile the oppositions that he felt characterized modern life: the oppositions, e.g. between reason and faith, society and individual, universal and particular. In his earliest writings (1795–1801), Hegel believes philosophy cannot itself escape the contradictions of such finite oppositions, for it remains trapped within them. Philosophy can at best lead us to see their inadequacy; religion alone can take us beyond them.

In Hegel's Jena period (1800–7) philosophy gains ascendancy over religion as the field in which the sought-for resolution of the tensions and oppositions of the modern world can be found. Nevertheless, during most of this period at least, Hegel thinks of logic and metaphysics as an *introduction* to philosophical speculation, not yet an essential *part* of it. The principal problem governing Hegel's thinking in Jena is that of overcoming the subject–object opposition. Hegel assumes that beneath the apparent opposition there is an underlying unity that takes on different forms in each of the opposed concepts. Speculative philosophy itself is the consideration of this unity and its various forms. Logic and metaphysics are preliminaries: In logic and metaphysics the fixed oppositions in terms of which we normally understand the world are shown to self-destruct. This destruction of the concepts of the understanding should then liberate us from the rigid categories that make resolution of the conflicts of modern life impossible (the task of logic) and, according to Hegel, also establish the Absolute, the unity underlying all oppositions, as the principle of all philosophy (the task of metaphysics). After the ground is cleared by logic and metaphysics, philosophy proper – the philosophy of the object, the philosophy of the subject, and the philosophy of the Absolute – can begin.

Unfortunately, little of the material in which Hegel works out his conception of logic and metaphysics at this time has survived. Yet one of the most important changes in Hegel's development is the shift in his understanding of the nature and place of logic and metaphysics that occurs toward the end of the Jena period (c. 1805–6). During this period Hegel ceases to distinguish between logic, metaphysics, and speculative philosophy. Briefly, Hegel seems to have discovered the idea that the formal structure of self-consciousness provides a model in which the conceptual oppositions of logic as well as the phenomena of nature and the social world can be treated in a unified, meaningful manner. Logic is the science of pure, self-conscious thought, and is therefore an essential part of the new system. In the light of this new conception Hegel adds a new kind of introduction to the system, the massive *Phenomenology of Spirit*, published in 1807, in which he traces the different forms consciousness and self-consciousness may take, culminating in the pure self-consciousness that is both the subject and object of logic.

The *Phenomenology of Spirit* was finished, as the story goes, with the battle of Jena booming in the distance. Subsequent to Napoleon's defeat of the Prussian army at Jena, the university was shut down, and Hegel had to go looking for employment, spending the next year as editor of a newspaper in Bamberg before accepting a post as the rector of a *Gymnasium* (a college-preparatory academy) in Nuremburg.

During his time in Nuremberg the Hegelian system, especially the logic,[4] as we now know it really took shape. The first installment of his *Science of Logic* (the so-called objective logic) was published in two volumes, the Doctrine of Being in 1812 and the Doctrine of Essence in 1813. The second installment (the subjective logic) containing the "Doctrine of the Concept" was published in 1816, the year Hegel was called to a chair at the University of Heidelberg. Hegel needed a text for his students in Heidelberg, so he put together the first edition of his *Encyclopedia of the Philosophical Sciences*. This contained a brief outline of his entire philosophical system and was intended only as an aid to those attending his lectures, orienting them within his system.

Hegel was called to Berlin, the leading university of Prussia, in 1818. He was to become the dominant figure in German philosophy during the subsequent decade. He published his last book, the *Philosophy of Right*, in 1821; he began another on the philosophy of subjective spirit, but never completed it. The second edition of the *Encyclopedia* appeared in 1827. Only a few years later, he revised the *Encyclopedia* yet once more, its third edition appearing in 1831. By 1826 the original copies of the *Science of Logic* were sold out, and the printer suggested reprinting the work. Hegel, however, decided to rework the book. The new version of the Doctrine of Being was given to the printer in 1831, the new preface dated 7 November 1831. A week later, on 14 November 1831, Hegel died of cholera.

After Hegel's death a group of Hegel's students, calling themselves the Society of Friends of the Eternalized, undertook to publish a complete edition of Hegel's philosophy. Their edition of the *Science of Logic* combined the newly revised version of the first third with the older, still unrevised remainder. Thus the first third of the *Science of Logic* as it has come down to us was written almost a decade and a half after the rest of the book. In the posthumous edition of the *Encyclopedia* the editors decided that it was too cryptic in the form Hegel gave it and therefore added supplementary additions (*Zusätze*) drawn from both Hegel's own and students' lecture notes. Most of the original notes have since been lost, so there is some question about the authenticity of some of this additional material, but the *Zusätze* have been a part of the Hegelian corpus since shortly after his death and can provide a valuable perspective on the argument of the text.

In the new, critical edition of Hegel's texts currently in preparation, both versions of the *Science of Logic*'s first part are available, as will be much more reliable editions of the notebook material utilized by Hegel's various editors in compiling *Zusätze* and lectures.

❧ ADEQUACY CONDITIONS ON ❧ INTERPRETATIONS OF HEGEL'S LOGIC

Since the texts of Hegel's logic are among the most difficult in the philosophical corpus, it is not surprising that there is a wide variation in the interpretations that have been offered and that no school of interpretation is currently dominant. The salient aspects of Hegel's logic that any interpretation must account for fall into two categories, the structural and the testimonial. Any adequate interpretation must account for the place of logic within the Hegelian system, the general structure exhibited by Hegel's logic, and the particular transitions found in it. Further, any adequate interpretation of Hegel's logic must also account for Hegel's own pronouncements about its scope, content, and method. An interpretation that gave a detailed, sensible account of the progress of the argument in the logic would be powerful and very valuable – but if it could not be made consistent with Hegel's own testimony, it would always face skepticism. It seems clear, however, that Hegel's practice in the logic does not always coincide with his preaching; every interpretation of Hegel's logic will have to construct a fine balance between the structural and testimonial evidence.

Structural conditions on interpretations

What role does Hegel's logic play in the system? The system consists of three parts: Logic, Philosophy of Nature, and Philosophy of Spirit. Hegel tells us that his system is a "circle of circles," so this is not merely a linear ordering. At the end of the Philosophy of Spirit we are to be in a position to begin again with the logic in some manner. Logic, therefore, is both the antecedent and the product of spirit. Other puzzling questions quickly arise in trying to understand this triad: The Philosophies of Nature and Spirit concern items within our experience that occupy space and time, but logic seems concerned with things of quite a different stripe. Just what is the relation between the logical realm and the realms of nature and spirit?

Next, the internal structure of Hegel's logic must be accounted for by any acceptable interpretation. It is instructive to look at the arrangement of topics in the logic to get a sense of what an interpretation must cope with. Hegel's logic appears to have a very rigid hierarchical organization. An interpretation that accounts for the gross structural organization may have difficulty with the fine structural detail of the system, and two different interpretations may be able to penetrate the fine detail better in different areas of the logic. Appended to this essay is an outline of the system as found in the *Science of Logic* (in the hybrid edition).

Several features of the logic immediately leap to the eye. Virtually everything is grouped in triads. The only exceptions are: (a) there are four groups of judgments at the fourth level under III.A.2 (see Appendix, pp. 246–7), and (b) the Idea of Cognition has only two subheadings, the Ideas of the True (which itself has only two subheadings, Analytic and Synthetic Cognition) and the Good. This triadicity is not a mere artifact of compulsive German orderliness; it is supposed to be a necessary consequence of the method of logic that generates the outline. But why, then, does it have *any* exceptions?

Several of the titles are repeated. Thus, Being is both heading I, heading I.A.1., and heading I.A.1.a; Appearance is both heading II.B and heading II.B.2. How can the same topic or concept appear at several places in the hierarchy? Other than the triad Concept, Judgment, Syllogism under III.A, most of the concepts have apparently very little to do with logic as standardly understood, then or now. Most of them are, however, connected with classical problems of metaphysics.

It is also notable that the relations among the concepts dealt with in each of the three main divisions differ. In the Doctrine of Being the concepts within a triad tend to be contrastive and mutually exclusive; in the Doctrine of Essence they tend to come in coordinate pairs, both of which can be applied to an object; in the Doctrine of the Concept the successor concepts are supposed to retain and contain their predecessors. Or at least Hegel tells us that there are such structural changes within the Logic, and on the whole his assertion seems borne out.

Testimonial conditions on adequacy

Any fully adequate interpretation will have to take account of what Hegel says about his Logic, its purpose, its method, and its achievement. We have already seen some of Hegel's own interpretation: that his logic is about thinking and the rules of thinking, that it constitutes the system of pure reason, truth in its own nature, and, more obscurely, that it is an exposition of "God as he is in his eternal essence."[5] Hegel's logic, while both logic and metaphysics, is a theology as well. According to Hegel religion and philosophy share the same content – the Absolute. In religion this content is couched in an imagistic form that is not fully adequate to the content itself; it is only in philosophy that this content receives a form adequate to itself. Thus we should expect a mapping between the truths developed within logic and the images and stories found in religion such that logic reveals the full message embodied obscurely in the mythology of religion.[6] Christianity may be the highest form of religion, the form in which the content can, given the limitations of the imagistic presentation, most fully express itself, but every religion has at heart the one true content, the Absolute.

Undoubtedly the most difficult problems in interpreting Hegel are generated by his pronouncements about the *method* of the logic. For his method is no method at all: What we have before us in the logic is *the self-movement of the concept*. That is, Hegel rejects the idea that in philosophy there is one thing, a method, that is applied to a separate thing, a content. The logic traces out what is contained in its content, and it does that not by applying some externally definable, content-independent method to produce a result, but by allowing the content to unfold itself. There is no "dialectical method," despite its supposed practice by so many of Hegel's followers. But then just how is the elaborate structure of the logic generated?

While Hegel's logic is not in any normal sense a formal logic, Hegel does claim that it is a formal science in the sense that it is the science *of* form. What does this mean? Hegel attacks the form/content distinction, but he does not simply reject that distinction as either senseless or even necessarily confused: What he objects to is the notion that form and content are absolutely separable and autonomous elements of a whole. No form and no content are *pure*. Instead, Hegel believes form and content are necessarily correlative; some forms are best suited for some contents but not others, and vice versa. Hegel constantly distinguishes the formal aspects of phenomena from their particular contents – that is, in part, what the philosophies of nature and spirit are all about – but what kinds of forms are available and how they relate to each other simply as forms are matters for logical analysis. In the logic as a whole, form *is* its content, and this content dictates its form.

Logic must also be a presuppositionless science, according to Hegel. This is a fundamental distinction between logic and all other scientific disciplines. Other scientific disciplines must presuppose some particular, independent subject matter; to this subject they bring some method or procedure. In neither case is the justification of these presuppositions a problem within that discipline. "Logic, on the contrary, cannot presuppose any of these forms of reflection and laws of thinking, for these constitute part of its own content and have first to be established within the science" (*WL*, I: 23; *SL*, 43).

Let me summarize the set of adequacy conditions for an interpretation of the logic delimited here. These conditions are not exhaustive; the logic is an extremely rich and perplexing text. But an interpretation that can meet these conditions will have a good chance of responding to other challenges as well.

1   Any interpretation must explain the sense in which the logic is the self-movement of the concept and the implications of this for its methodology.

2   Any interpretation must explain how the logic is the science of form.

3   Any interpretation must be able to explain the relation between the Logic and the Philosophies of Nature and Spirit. It should also explain the logic's relation to the *Phenomenology of Spirit*, which was proposed to be an introduction to the logic.

4   Any interpretation must explain the presuppositionlessness of the logic and how such a presuppositionless science can get started.

5   Any interpretation will have to account for the internal structure of the logic:
    (a) Triadicity.
    (b) Repetition of titles.
    (c) Differences between types of concepts in the three parts of the logic.
    (d) A detailed reconstruction of the particular arguments and transitions found in the texts.

6   Any interpretation must explain the relation between logic and God.

❧ THE SELF-MOVEMENT OF THE CONCEPT ❧

The concept

Understanding Hegel's claim that logic is simply the self-movement of the concept requires understanding the particular meanings Hegel gives the terms of that dictum. Hegel has quite a particular notion of a *concept*, which is central to his whole system. Of course, Hegel's notion of a concept is heir to a significant history, and much can be revealed by tracing its roots in the philosophical tradition. While there is little space here for such development, a few allusions may help situate the discussion.

Hegel's logic, like that of his predecessors, is a logic of terms and concepts, not a logic of relations between sentences and operations upon sentences. The modern logician begins by specifying a syntax, that is, a vocabulary and rules of sentence formation. These initial steps are followed by specifying a proof theory and then a semantics. Thus, if the modern logician thinks of the syntax, the vocabulary and formation rules for the system, as the preliminary set-up, the actual beginning would most likely be a set of axioms or fundamental truths. One way in which Hegel differs is that he expects logic to develop a system of relations among concepts, not a system of relations among sentence forms. Aristotelian logic provides very few sentence forms and no system by which to generate arbitrarily complex new forms. What flexibility Aristotelian logic affords, by which it can be applied to a relatively broad range of sentences and arguments, comes from our ability to formulate arbitrarily complex concepts to use within the sparse syntax provided. Hegel therefore focuses his logic on the forms of concepts, not the forms of sentences. So he looks to begin with a fundamental, simple, immediate, unstructured concept – the simplest form a concept can take – and end with the all-inclusive, absolutely self-constituting concept, the Idea. Just as the early Wittgenstein sought the general form of a proposition, Hegel seeks the general form of a concept.

The historical background for Hegel's notion of a concept properly begins with Plato's notion of a separable form (*eidos*), a universal in which any number of sensible things can participate. This notion was then transmuted by Aristotle into a form immanent in the sensible object that shared it and necessarily embodied in an appropriate kind of matter. The most important fact about these classical Greek speculations is that both considered their concept-precursors, the forms, to be *objective* features of the world graspable by human reason. The skeptical attacks of Hellenistic philosophy coupled with the rise of Christian metaphysics forced these objective universals inside the mind; they were saved from complete subjectivity only because they could be located in the mind of God, who created the world in accordance with his divine plan. But the mind of God itself became more and more distant as the Middle Ages wore on, and by the time modern philosophy came on the scene only such patently inadequate ruses as Cartesian innate ideas guaranteed by a beneficent but ultimately unknowable God protected universals from complete entrapment in subjectivity. In the subjective idealism of the empiricists this development reached its sorry nadir.[7]

Kant began the climb out of the subjectivist coal pit when he reasserted the objectivity of certain universal concepts on the grounds that they are necessary constitutive conditions of thought itself. Such concepts are objective because without them thought could have no *object* at all. But Kantian concepts are limited to the material of sensuous intuition; *substance, cause,* and other *a priori* concepts objectively characterize phenomenal objects, but have no application beyond the bounds of sense. Our concepts do not apply to things as they are in themselves.

Kant falls back into a subjectivist skepticism despite his valiant effort to climb out (e.g. *Enz.* [*Encyclopedia*], §§ 40–5). Hegel is quite convinced that any "knowledge" that is not of the object as it is in itself is not *knowledge* at all. Hegelian concepts, like those of the great classical thinkers, must be objective, humanly graspable features of things as they are in themselves (*Enz.*, §§ 19–25). In order to develop and defend his idea of a concept, however, Hegel must demonstrate how finite, sensuous intelligences like ours can grasp such objective features of our world: He must develop both an ontology and an epistemology. The general outlines of both his ontology and his epistemology emerge from Hegel's rejection of the possibility of a purely formal logic together with the constraints he believes ·govern any adequate theory of thinking. As a first step toward climbing out of the subjectivism Hegel thinks besets modern philosophy, let us develop the Hegelian theory of subjectivity, for only an adequate theory of subjectivity can demonstrate that we are not trapped in our own minds with no access to the world.

Logic as a theory of subjectivity

A full theory of subjectivity must account for all the phenomena of mind: sensation, feeling, perceiving, thinking, desiring, willing, etc. It would be a mistake, however, to think that the Hegelian theory of subjectivity is essentially a theory of *human* subjectivity. Human subjectivity is distinguishable from the pure thinking thematized in the logic in that it is still beset with the contingent, variable structures of sensation, feeling, desiring, etc. Pure thinking is abstracted from such contingencies. Here we will reconstruct the theory of pure thinking, for this is also the content of Hegel's logic. There are two constraints that any adequate theory of thinking must observe: First, the Kantian transcendental unity of apperception, the fact that the 'I think' must be able to accompany all my representations.[8]

Kant was always unclear about the exact status of the 'I think' – to this day his commentators wrangle about it – but it is at least clear that the 'I think' that occurs in the principle of the transcendental unity of apperception cannot, on Kantian principles, itself be a piece of objective knowledge. Objective knowledge requires application of a schematized category of thought to the sensuous content of intuition, and the transcendental unity of apperception is an analytic principle not based in any way on sensuous intuition. Kant, therefore, cannot justify his belief that he thinks. Hegel could not accept the notion that our self-reflection is in a substantially worse position than our other knowledge, and is furthermore unwilling to draw the distinctions in kind between, on the one hand, transcendental 'knowledge' of the form of experience and the role of the unity of apperception and, on the other hand, objective knowledge of items within our experience.

The second constraint on the theory of thinking is that the 'I think' expresses an objective cognition. In this sense Hegel reasserts the Cartesian *cogito*.[9] These two constraints jointly require thought to be capable of objective self-reflection.

Hegel's theory of thinking is logic itself. In what sense logic is a theory of thinking, however, needs further clarification, for a thorough-going empiricist such as J.S. Mill might agree with this and conclude that logic must itself be an empirical discipline, though admittedly at a very high level of abstraction. Hegel is certainly not an empiricist, though the extent to which his system accommodates the empirical has generally not been well enough recognized. Nor is Hegel's logic itself psychologized, for it is a mistake to assume that *thinking* is solely an activity of human subjects. Psychology is a particular discipline handled within the system at its appropriate place. But *thinking* is the activity of the universal, the concept itself.

If the psychological process of thinking is not what provides logic with its content, then in what sense is thinking the content of logic? Kant distinguishes between general logic – a formal discipline that concerns the conditions of thought in general, regardless of its object – and *transcendental* logic – the discipline concerned with the *a priori* conditions of thinking about objects of our sensibility (objects located in space and time). General logic must be purely syntactic, but transcendental logic has an irreducible semantic component, for it must deal with the conditions of reference to spatio-temporal objects. Kant's table of categories, the list of those *a priori* concepts he thinks structure our abilities to think and know about the sensible world, is a product of transcendental logic, the analysis of the *a priori* conditions for applying the forms of judgment to spatio-temporal objects.

Hegel maintains, in effect, that the syntax/semantics distinction Kant presupposes to separate general and transcendental logic cannot be sustained.[10] Syntax is always contaminated with semantic content precisely because syntax's role is to subserve a semantic purpose: the embodiment of *truth*. The hope of analyzing out of language or thought a pure logical syntax without any metaphysical implications about the nature of objects is a pipe dream, or worse, a delusion. Even the bare subject/predicate distinction constrains our metaphysics; it is no accident that a traditional definition of 'substance' is the *ultimate subject of predication*. Again, *noun* is usually supposed to be a syntactic category, but its classical definition, "name of a person, place, or thing," is given semantically. In fact it is impossible to give a nontrivial but general, purely syntactic characterization of the nouns, verbs, etc. of any natural language.

For Kant, pure (unschematized) thought has no intrinsic relation to anything; it is, as it were, merely the form of relatedness to an object. Actual relation to objects is the business of another and separate faculty of mind, sensibility. Hegel responds that thought must have, intrinsically, a relation to itself – that, as he sees it, is the point of Kant's transcendental unity of apperception. And this relation is capable of sustaining a knowledge-claim; that is the point of the *cogito*. The *cogito* does not express a piece of sensory knowledge, according to Hegel; neither does it express a direct nonsensory intuition of a thing-like existent. The self or 'I' is itself a *concept* in Hegel's special sense of that term.[11] The *cogito* expresses a recognition and preliminary understanding of that concept, an understanding that *presupposes* a good deal of sensory knowledge, but cannot be *reduced* to such sensory knowledge. Since the 'I think' does not itself *contain* distinctively sensory knowledge, Hegel sees it as purified of such sensory content, as having left the sensory realm behind. Thus, although he rejects the Kantian notion of a pure reason entirely and in principle divorced from sensibility, Hegel recovers a notion of pure reason by postulating a form of thought and knowledge that rises above the sensory to achieve independence of any and all particular sensory contents.

Reason necessarily goes beyond sense, but the *cogito* shows that it does not thereby lose either its object of its objectivity. It therefore cannot be the case that all relation of thought to its object is the business of an entirely separate, nonrational faculty of mind. Since not *all* relation to objects is directly mediated by sensibility, sensibility is no longer the universal limitation on all thought. Thus for Hegel the distinctions Kant relied on to separate general and transcendental logic have evaporated, and the conclusion must be that all logic has a transcendental component and thus merges into metaphysics.

Bluntly put, since thought must be capable of self-relation, the conditions necessary to that self-relation are conditions on all thought. Some objects we may relate to through sensation, but the thinking that relates to them must still belong to a structure of thought capable of pure (nonsensuous), objective self-relation. The *cogito* shows the reality of this self-relation of thought to itself, but the lesson of the *cogito* goes beyond a mere ability of thought to *refer* to itself: It shows that thought must be capable of *knowing* itself. Hegel would *not* claim that the *cogito* itself contains or expresses such self-knowledge of thinking by thinking, but he does believe that he can demonstrate that the self-reference of thought to thought contained in the *cogito* is itself possible only if thought is also capable of complete self-comprehension. (This is a major result of the *Phenomenology of Spirit*.) The reality of the self-related structure of thought demands closure. The self-related structure of thought is the topic for logic.

Thus Hegel's logic is at the same time an implicit theory of subjectivity, of what kind of structure is necessary in order for thinking to comprehend itself.[12] The self-comprehension of thought requires a comprehension of the object of thought and thought's relation to that object, for, as we have seen, thought cannot be characterized in an entirely self-contained, purely syntactic way. In completely characterizing itself, thought must also completely characterize its range of possible objects, and there can be no remainder, no things-in-themselves left over outside the structure of thought. The structures revealed by the self-comprehension of thought include necessarily the structures of all objects of thought as well; an object that is not a possible object of thought is nothing at all. But what the logic does not itself directly consider are the ways in which thought structures are embodied in the world. The rest of Hegel's philosophy deals with this, for thought structures are embodied in nature (thus the philosophy of nature), in social structures (thus the philosophy of objective spirit), in the expressive products of human activity (thus the philosophy of absolute spirit), and, of course, in the psyches of individual organisms. It is the task of the philosophy of subjective spirit to discuss how it is possible for an individual animal organism to embody within itself the structures definitive of thinking. Needless to say, the complex organization requisite to embodying a self-comprehending structure of thought imposes significant constraints on the nature and capacities of such an organism. But for our purposes it is more important to see that Hegel does not believe that the embodiment of the structures constitutive of thought is confined solely to individual animal organisms: The world as a whole also embodies these structures. In order to see why Hegel thinks this is necessary and how he believes it to be possible, we need to look more closely at his ontology.

The active concrete universal[13]

Hegel believes that most of his predecessors chose the wrong paradigm of predication. These philosophers – philosophers trapped in the "attitude of the understanding"[14] according to Hegel – took accidental predications (e.g. "The ball is red") as paradigmatic. In such a case there is no intrinsic connection between the universal and the individual it is predicated of; both the universal and the individual seem quite indifferent to each other. Taking this to be the paradigmatic predication relation, Hegel believes, leads to a metaphysics in which the world is seen as composed of a nexus of bare particulars (in his terminology *abstract individuals*) and ontologically independent universals (he would call these *abstract universals*). Hegel thinks such a metaphysics impossible; to escape being trapped in it one must reject both the abstract individual and the abstract universal.[15]

In the place of accidental predication Hegel substitutes a version of essential predication, for in an essential predication the universal and the individual are intrinsically tied. The essence of something is also seen by Hegel to have some explanatory power; saying of what kind a thing is can be a legitimate explanatory move. In Hegel's view an essence, something's concept, is not a *descriptive* characterization, but a *prescriptive* ideal, and it plays a role in a teleological explanation. Something's concept offers an ideal pattern which the thing strives to realize in the course of its existence, though individual things are never perfect exemplars of their essence. In this respect we can begin to see a rather strange melding of Aristotle's concept of an essence with the Kantian notion of a concept. Kant insisted that "a concept is always, as regards its form, something universal which serves as a rule" (*Critique of Pure Reason*, A 107). Hegel seizes on three aspects of Kant's *a priori* concepts – their unrestricted universality, their prescriptive force, and their conceptual priority over their instances – and transfers these properties to the basically Aristotelian conception of an essence or thing-kind.

Hegel also learned from Kant that concepts are not discrete entities that exist and can be known each independent of any others; neither thinker employs the notion of a *simple* concept. We can say that Hegel took over from Kant a coherence theory of concepts: Even bottom-level basic ideas are to be understood through their interaction with other ideas in basic principles, in contrastive relationships, and so forth. Hegel is committed to a more thoroughgoing holism of concepts than Kant, for he cannot distinguish absolutely between formal and material representations. Perhaps most important, the crucial relationships between concepts need not all be construed as analytic 'inclusions': Kant inaugurated the search for nonanalytic but also nonpsychological, rational connections between concepts, and Hegel willingly followed. Thus, what Hegel calls a *concept* is a prescriptive ideal that is part of a system of such ideals that the world is striving to realize and in terms of which we can make sense of what happens in the world.

However, Hegel takes the rulelike character and implicit systematicity of concepts so seriously that he made a move Kant would never have dreamed of making. Hegel insisted that the being of the 'I' is the being of a concept, for the 'I' is the rule for the unification of all experience. The unity of apperception is the ideal governing all synthetic activity in the mind. Indeed, since the 'I' provides the ultimate rule – all concepts must be unified under the 'I,' including the pure concepts – the 'I,' the self, becomes a superconcept, a concept of concepts, *the* concept (*WL*, II: 220–1; *SL*, 583). Thus the *cogito* becomes the first and immediate expression of the self-directed, self-organizing activity of the concept. The 'I' or self is not a thinglike substance, but a conceptlike self-organizing activity.

Every universal of whatever kind unifies something, but in contrast to abstract universals like 'red,' concrete universals like 'dog' or 'thinker' not only unite various different individuals under some heading but also account for their internal unity. The model for this internal unification is the synthesis of the manifold into the unity of apperception. The manifold is unified, according to the Kantian vision, because I make it mine, constituting myself in that very process. Hegel attributes this kind of self-constituting activity to every concrete universal, to all concepts. Any unity of a manifold that is not thus actively involved in the very nature of the elements, while also constituting its own self in the activity, is to that degree a merely abstract universal. A concrete universal is therefore different from the *abstract* universals that previous thinkers in the classical tradition took to be the objects of thought.

> The universal of the concept is not a mere sum of features
> common to several things, confronted by a particular which
> enjoys an existence on its own. It is, on the contrary, self-
> particularizing or self-specifying, and with undimmed clearness
> finds itself at home in this antithesis.
>
> (*Enz.*, § 163; my translation)

An abstract universal is a tag which can be hung on things otherwise quite indifferent to it in order to sort them out for whatever purposes one may have. A concrete universal, on the other hand, divides nature at the joints; it must reach to the very hearts of things and afford an understanding of their being. An abstract universal is static and unchanging because it is dead, a mere sum of otherwise unrelated features. A concrete universal, a concept, however, is alive, dynamic, and dialectical; it is essentially a part of a self-developing system.[16]

In sum, the foremost characteristic of a concept is that it is *active*. Thus Hegel explains the stability of the world, the fact that the world is not a sheer, unstructured chaos, by the activity of *concrete* universals. The manifold unified by these concepts is not itself entirely separate from them in nature, provided from the outside, but must itself be of some determinate kind and therefore itself already conceptualized. Thus there is a complex structure of interrelated concepts, a structure that is not built up from the outside by some external agency, but develops its own organization from within. Its mode of action is teleological, that is, it is self-realization. The concept is both cause and effect; it is self-developing. Second, a concept is the *truth* of those objects it characterizes and animates. It is their essence, that which explains what they are and why they have the unity they do. Third, a concept is not separable from its instances, but actively manifests itself in and through them. Fourth, concepts have an essence of their own, *the* concept, which realizes itself in the active self-realization of its contributory moments. Concepts are essentially parts of a self-realizing system. What ultimately *is*, according to Hegel, is a universal self-constitutive activity that becomes self-conscious in man's knowledge of it – the Absolute.

The self-movement of the concept

In Hegel's vision this universal self-constitutive activity expresses itself in the world via the articulation of nature into different orders of entities and properties. But the expression of the Absolute in nature is itself static; the movement and change within nature are but a pale reflection of the dynamic self-activity of the Absolute, for nature itself is ahistorical, it does not *develop*, but simply changes endlessly. It is in the realm of spirit that this universal self-constitutive activity expresses itself adequately, both as historical development across the human, spiritual community and as the individual development of a thinker's thought in contemplation.

Subjectivism is no longer a problem, Hegel thinks, because the active concrete universals that structure and inform the world are one and the same as the structures that animate subjective thought (when it has freed itself from the strictures of sense and understanding). One and the same rule system governs both thought and the world. That structure is reason itself, and it is *grasped* by individual minds through their instantiating the structure of rules in a self-conscious way.

All this grand talk of self-constituting activities can still, however, leave one dissatisfied, convinced that the fundamental questions still remain: In the self-movement of the concept, just *what* is moving, and how? We have seen that concepts are items in a complex, self-developing system and that this system is itself supposed to be a concept. It is easy to get the impression that this is a case of pulling oneself up by one's own bootstraps. This is a serious charge against Hegel, and one that is not without merit, but a finer appreciation of his position shows that the situation is at least a good deal more complex.

Concrete universals must be embodied, so Hegel would not take the self-movement of the concept to be something that occurs only in a kind of Platonic heaven, apart from all sensuous, material reality. The movement of the concept must be embodied in a movement of things embodying the concept. Nature embodies the concept in one way, but not a way best suited to showing the concept's own self-movement. It is spirit that embodies the concept in a way capable of exhibiting its self-movement. On the one hand the social structures of humanity embody the concept, and thus the historical development of those social structures is one form of the self-movement of the concept.

But this is not the sense in which the logic is the self-movement of the concept. The other form in which spirit embodies the concept is in thinking itself. In philosophy, pure thinking, we realize the self-movement of the concept by instantiating the self-developing system of concrete universals in a higher and still more adequate form than either nature or social reality finds possible.

Importantly, however, Hegel realizes that even this pure thinking must be embodied, and its embodiment is language, for "we think in names" (*Enz.*, § 462). But if we think in words, then the movement of thought must also be a movement of words, and an investigation of "thinking and the rules of thinking" will result in conclusions that apply indirectly to language as the essential expressive embodiment of thought. This line of thought leads to the notion that Hegel's logic is an attempt to construct an ideal language. What is the Hegelian ideal for language? This is a difficult question, but one desideratum stands out above all others: The ideal language must be its own meta-language. It must contain its own truth concept and be capable of expressing its own relation to the world (and itself) truthfully. Indeed, since Hegel believes thought must *necessarily* know itself as thought, its embodiment, ideal language, must also *necessarily* be expressively complete and capable of demonstrating this expressive completeness. Thus Hegel's logic is an attempt to elaborate a set of conceptual *qua* linguistic structures that are expressively complete and capable of demonstrating this completeness by (a) reconstructing the depth-conceptual and linguistic structures we in fact find around us in ordinary language, in the sciences, and in religion and philosophy, and (b) accounting for its completeness by generating these structures from the very idea of (linguistically embodied) thought.

Hegel takes this project to be implicit in the very existence of language. He regards it as a project to which language users contribute unconsciously as they use language in navigating through the world and consciously as they engage in logic or philosophy. Hegel's logic presents an explicit and self-conscious culmination of this historical development, but not *as* an historical development – that occurs in the philosophy of history and also, in part, in the *Phenomenology*. Hegel's logic presents us with the pure results of this process: an expressively complete and self-reflexive set of linguistic/conceptual structures.

❧ LOGIC AS THE SCIENCE OF FORM ❧

Since everything that can be thought or expressed must utilize one of the conceptual structures/expressive forms elaborated in the logic, it is easily seen how the logic constitutes the science of form. Every possible form is systematically generated in the course of the logic, Hegel claims, and all content, every phenomenon, will find its appropriate form somewhere in the battery of conceptual forms so generated.

It is no objection that this means Hegel intends his logic to be irrefutable and unfalsifiable; anything properly called logic intends to be irrefutable. Usually this is explained in terms of the contentlessness, the pure formality of logic. This explanation is not open to Hegel. His explanation can only be that his logic simply spells out the necessary conditions of thought, and therefore the necessary conditions of the existence of the refutable. It would be self-defeating to reject it because it is irrefutable.

But there is also no guarantee in Hegel's logic that phenomena come with their logic already patent. Although it seems to be a consequence of his interpretation of the form/content distinction that every content will have some form in which it is best expressed and comprehended, given the imperfection of nature, form–content mismatches in which both moments are obscured are only to be expected. In this case a great deal of acumen may be required for proper analysis. Surface structure may conceal logical form.

So-called "dialectical" consideration of nature or society is nothing more than a learned ability to identify the conceptual structures characteristic to the phenomena at stake.[17] This means that one understands the dialectic of X when one has properly diagnosed the kinds of conceptual structures definitive of X's. For instance, the dialectic of the family is controlled by the fact that implicit in the very concept of a family are certain kinds of relationships within the family, certain kinds of relationships between the family unit and the external world, the general function of the family in the ethical life of a community, and the relation of the family, as a social structure, to other forms of social organization such as the commercial marketplace. Not all of these relationships are superficially evident within the concept of the family, however, Dialecticians may start with a superficial understanding of the concept of a family, but as they seek to understand the concept more deeply, they can use the abstract structures plotted out in logic to explore the conceptual space of the family in greater detail. What conceptual tensions are resolved within the family structure? What tensions does it itself generate? Under what higher heading would the family fall? The concept of the family reveals as well the dysfunctional family, for it will then be clear how families can fall short of the concept. The logic provides the theoretical structures within which our comprehension of such phenomena operates; all of these phenomena and their relationships will be instances of the most general kinds of objects of thought as laid out in the logic.

❧ PRESUPPOSITIONLESS BEGINNINGS ❧

Though we have now seen how Hegel thinks his logic compares to the traditional conceptions of logic and metaphysics, the characterization has been very abstract. It is still hard to see how to begin this project and then carry on with it. Let us therefore consider these matters at a more practical level. How does one start doing logic? Since logic is the self-movement of the concept, it seems that there is nothing that one *does* at all. How does one get concepts to move themselves?

Hegel insists that logic can have no presuppositions, even to the point of not having a clear conception of the discipline itself until it is completed. "What logic is cannot be stated beforehand, rather does this knowledge of what it is first emerge as the final outcome and consummation of the whole exposition" (*WL*, I: 23; *SL*, 43). Yet, as we will see, he also knows exactly where to begin: Being. The presuppositionlessness of logic is apparently the guarantee of its purity, its universality, its necessity, its absoluteness, and it is therefore extremely important. Yet Hegel also says that the system is a circle of circles, and that seems clearly to imply that the logic is in some sense generated by, derived from, or entailed by the rest of the system as well; why isn't this a form of presupposition?

Apparently, then, one can begin doing logic without any clear idea of what it is that one is doing or how it is to be done. Nonetheless, despite all the talk about presuppositionlessness, it is not the case that logic is begun absent of all conditions. "The beginning is *logical* in that it is to be made in the element of thought that is free and for itself, in *pure knowing*" (*WL*, I: 53; *SL*, 68). The point seems to be that the essential condition for logic consists in a certain attitude or state on the part of the logician. This state of pure knowledge is reached at the end of the 1807 *Phenomenology of Spirit* by overcoming the subject–object distinction altogether. However one arrives at it (there is no reason to believe it can be reached only via the train of thought contained in the *Phenomenology*),[18] pure knowing is a state in which thinking is directed solely upon thought itself (shades of Aristotle's thought thinking thought!), without constraint from any sensory conditions, prejudices of the understanding, or even preconceptions about thinking. One has, as it were, opened oneself up to the world, which can finally lay itself bare before one, unobscured by merely subjective intrusions. Even this way of describing the situation rings slightly false, for it makes the world seem something distinguished from and therefore opposed to an observing consciousness. But in pure knowing the distinction between knower and known, subject and world, has utterly vanished, or more accurately, there is only a distinction in their forms, for in pure knowing the content of world and thought is identical.[19]

> Now starting from this determination of pure knowledge, all that is needed to ensure that the beginning remains immanent in its scientific development is to consider, or rather, ridding oneself of all other reflections and opinions whatever, simply to take up, *what is there before us.*
>
> Pure knowing as concentrated into this unity has sublated all reference to an other and to mediation; it is without any distinction and as thus distinctionless, ceases itself to be knowledge; what is present is only *simple immediacy.*
>
> (WL, I: 54; SL, 69)

Hegel admits that in this case pure knowing as an outcome of finite (impure) knowing is presupposed, but pure knowing in this sense is not a thesis or claim that is presupposed. It is itself a mode of being, a being in a position to know. It is not itself a cognitive presupposition, but only the presupposition of pure cognition. The circle is complete when this mode of being has itself been reapprehended in knowledge and the identity of thought and being it is predicated upon is vindicated.

> But if no presupposition is to be made and the beginning itself is taken *immediately*, then its only determination is that it is to be the beginning of logic, of thought as such. All that is present is simply the resolve, which can also be regarded as arbitrary, that we propose to consider thought as such.
>
> (WL, I: 54; SL, 70)

The claim here seems even more radical: The honest, even naive resolve to think about thought as such should be sufficient to begin logic, for that honest, if naive, resolve begins from the identity of thought and being. We do not need to know that we are in the state of pure knowledge to begin logic. To require that before we begin doing logic we know that we have achieved a state of pure knowing would introduce a cognitive presupposition again. The possibility of pure knowing – which Hegel equates with the identity of thought and being – means that the honest resolve to think about thought can and eventually will succeed. The vindication of the state of pure knowing achieved by the end of our deliberations suffices to legitimate the entire undertaking. The only things that stand in the way of reaching that consummation are the sedimented preconceptions we have accumulated through our experience of acculturation.

But why should the appropriate beginning be pure being? Hegel tells us that since it is a pure beginning, it must be something immediate, that is, not derived from anything else, not mediated by any other. Further, it must be simple, without any internal structure (or we would have to start with that). He then informs us that "this simple immediacy . . . in its true expression is *pure being*" (*WL*, I: 54; *SL*, 69). Why is this? What makes "being" the correct expression of the beginning point of logic? Here we encounter a general difficulty with Hegel's logic: The concept designations he chooses often seem less than compelling. That the simple, immediate universality with which logic begins should be called "being" is, in fact, more intuitive than many of his other choices. Although we have said that logic is tied to language in that thought must express itself in language, there is no guarantee that the purified structures of thought will map exactly onto the pre-existing vocabulary and manipulation rules of any language. Ordinary language gives us a rich resource refined over millennia of reflection, but the logician must get behind the surface structures of the language to uncover the real logical structures embodied in that language.

> Philosophy has the right to select from the language of common life which is made for the world of pictorial thinking, such expressions as *seem to approximate* to the determinations of the Concept. There cannot be any question of *demonstrating* for a word selected from the language of common life that in common life, too, one associates with it the same concept for which philosophy employs it; for common life has no concepts, but only pictorial thoughts and general ideas, and to recognize the concept in what is else a mere general idea is philosophy itself.
>
> (*WL*, II: 357; *SL*, 708)

The history of philosophy provides a particularly rich resource, for it mirrors (though by no means exactly) the progress of thought itself. Thus, the attempt to think pure immediacy appeared early on in the philosophy of the Eleatics. Parmenides' pronouncement that "Being is and Not-Being is not" is its earliest expression, and surely Hegel is leaning on this phrasing when he says that the beginning point, simple immediacy, is being. The attempt to think pure being turns out to be unstable – it is identical to a thought of pure nothing, even though the two concepts are superficially in absolute opposition. And it is no accident that this conflict generates a concept Hegel expresses as "becoming," the key word in Heraclitus' philosophy.

❦ TRIADS AND DIALECTIC ❦

Hegel is perhaps most renowned for the constant triadic structure of his logic, popularized without much textual basis as "thesis–antithesis –synthesis." But whatever slogan one uses to characterize the triadic structures encountered throughout the logic, Hegel believes this pattern arises necessarily from "the method" of the logic. Since, as we have seen, this method is no method at all, but rather the self-movement of the concept, Hegel believes the triadic structure is inherent in concepts themselves (*Enz.*, § 79). What are these triads, and why does Hegel believe that the conceptual realm is so structured?

Logic is the self-investigation of thought; at its end, thought must comprehend itself. We can therefore think of each concept encountered in the logic as a candidate theory of thought. This is a slightly misleading way to phrase it, for it seems to presuppose that someone, a subjectivity external to and separate from the object of its thinking, is proposing some abstract set of propositions intended to characterize correctly that object of thought. Thus, there would be three relata here: a subject, an object, and a theory. But in logic there is only one presence: self-related thought. We might better think of each concept in the logic as a mode of thought's self-relation. And since thought *is* self-constituting activity, each concept is therefore a mode of thought's existence. The highest mode of thought's existence, the mode without which it could not be the completely self-constituting activity of thought, is the Idea, thought's adequate self-comprehension.

Put another way, the constant content throughout the logic is thought itself; each of the concepts encountered up to the Idea is a less than fully adequate form for that content. Though less than fully adequate, each captures a dimension of thought, a real mode of thought's existence. The form adequate to the content of logic is, in fact, none other than the comprehension of the whole of the series of less than adequate forms, for collectively the concepts embody and enable thought's self-comprehension.

Suppose, then, we begin with the honest resolve to think thought, and that we begin with the immediate, simple universality Hegel calls "being." It is important to be clear about what this beginning point is. It is to be *pure* being, which means that no determinate being is in question here. It is not the kind of being one may talk of in speaking of the *being of a number* or the *being of space* or the *being of consciousness*. Hegel is well aware that this concept is an abstraction, indeed, the absolute abstraction from all determinateness.

As the beginning point of the logic this concept is at once a proto-theory of thought and a mode of thought itself, a way in which thought *is*. As a proto-theory of thought, something a consciousness considers for adoption, there are many inadequacies to this concept: It is highly inarticulate, unable to describe or explain any of the phenomena we normally associate with thought, including its own existence. But as correct as such considerations are, they are irrelevant from Hegel's point of view. They do not exhibit the "self-movement of the concept," for one. They exhibit instead an external reflection upon a subjective reality, according to Hegel. Second, while they may give good reason for rejecting the proto-theory, they fail in two regards: (a) they do not show whether the concept indeed captures something of the nature of thought, and (b) they do not point the way to a better conception.

But consider this concept as itself a mode or determination of thought. For being is as much a way of thinking as an object of thought. Concepts are not simple, given entities, each capable of its existence entirely separately from others. They are essentially and necessarily involved in contrastive relations, in entailment relations, etc. The system of pure thoughts forms a self-realizing structure. No single determination of thought is entirely self-subsistent. The concept of pure being, indeterminate immediacy, however, attempts to be just that – without inner determination, without relation to anything else. In its attempt to purify itself from every determinate content, it divests itself of all content and turns out to be identical to the concept of nothing. In this case the self-movement of these concepts turns out to be the intrinsic connection between the contents (or in this case, lack thereof) of the concepts.

Hegel confronts the question of how these concepts could be self-moving more explicitly in considering Jacobi's critique of Kant's notion of *a priori* synthesis. Jacobi claimed that when he achieved a state of purified, abstract consciousness, no synthetic activity, no "movement" among the concepts was evident at all. Hegel replies:

> But this is found immediately in them. They [the thoughts of pure space, pure time, pure being, and so on] are, as Jacobi profusely describes them, results of abstraction; they are expressly determined as *indeterminate* and this – to go back to its simplest form – is being. But it is this very *indeterminateness* which constitutes its determinateness; for indeterminateness is opposed to determinateness; hence as so opposed it is itself determinate or the negative, and the pure, quite abstract negative. It is this indeterminateness or abstract negation which thus has being present within it, which reflection, both outer and inner, enunciates when it equates it with nothing, declares it to be an empty product of thought, to be nothing. Or it can be expressed thus: because being is devoid of all determination whatsoever, it is not the (affirmative) determinateness which it is; it is not being but nothing.
>
> (*WL*, I: 85; *SL*, 99)

The attempt to think pure, indeterminate being is, in effect, a failure, for its indeterminateness is its determinateness. But thought does not stop here. The failure is not absolute. Thinking of pure being has turned out to be thinking of nothing, but this unity of being and nothing has transformed them both. The lesson is that in all thinking being and nothing are thought together.

> Being and nothing are the same; but in their truth, in their unity, they have vanished as these determinations and are now something else. Being and nothing are the same; *but just because they are the same they are no longer being and nothing*, but now have a different significance. . . . This unity now remains their base from which they do not again emerge in the abstract significance of being and nothing.
>
> (*WL*, I: 95; *SL*, 108)

Everything and everythinking is a union of being and nothing; just how these two are to be unified and what further transformations must occur before a fully stable conceptual scheme is available is the story of the logic.[20]

But Hegel admits that the transaction between being and nothing is not typical: there is no real *transition* to be found, but only an immediate identity.

> In the pure reflection of the beginning as it is made in this logic with being as such, the transition is still concealed; because *being* is posited only as immediate, therefore *nothing* emerges in it only immediately. But all the subsequent determinations, like determinate being which immediately follows, are more concrete; in determinate being there is already *posited* that which contains and produces the contradiction of those abstractions and therefore their transition.
>
> (*WL*, I: 86; *SL*, 99)

Nonetheless, this unity of being and nothing, which is their "truth," is labeled "becoming" by Hegel.

> *Becoming* is the unseparatedness of being and nothing, not the unity which abstracts from being and nothing; but as the unity of *being* and *nothing* it is this *determinate* unity in which there *is* both being and nothing. But in so far as being and nothing, each unseparated from its other, *is*, each *is not*. They *are* therefore in this unity but only as vanishing, sublated moments.
>
> (*WL*, I: 92; *SL*, 105)

Depending on whether one emphasizes being or nothing as the immediate element and the other as related to it, becoming has two forms, coming-to-be and ceasing-to-be. But is "becoming" at all an appropriate label for the unity of being and nothing? It has the historical pedigree of being Heraclitus' response to Parmenidean Being, but it is so loaded down with temporal connotations and so closely associated with the notion of change that it seems at best a highly misleading choice of terms. But it is also hard to see what other term might serve better. Becoming is the third, yet it is not itself stable.

> Being and nothing are in this unity only as vanishing moments; yet becoming as such *is* only through their distinguishedness. Their vanishing, therefore, is the vanishing of becoming of the vanishing of the vanishing itself. Becoming is an unstable unrest which settles into a stable result.
>
> (*WL*, I: 93; *SL*, 106)

The stable result is the concept of determinate being. Being and nothing have been transformed, or rather have revealed their true colors in their unity, becoming, but this very unity cannot retain the character of becoming. "It is . . . inherently self-contradictory, because the determinations it unites within itself are opposed to each other; such a unity destroys itself" (ibid.). Becoming destroys itself, not by negating itself entirely – that would return to mere nothing – but by settling into a stable and once again immediate oneness: determinate being.

The identification of being and nothing seems to be motivated by considerations of the nature of identity and individuation of concepts by their contents and other reasonable considerations in the context of the project of the logic. But the subsequent moves to becoming and thence to determinate being do not seem nearly as intelligibly grounded. It is hard not to think that talk of the vanishing of vanishing and suchlike is mere word play without significant philosophical import. Yet there is also something intuitively right about Hegel's conclusion that the attempts to think pure immediacy must fail in favor of thoughts of determinately qualified forms of being. The text of the logic challenges the interpreter to show how Hegel's principal moves actually trace the "self-movement of the concept" – a movement that is supposed to be the very soul of intelligibility – despite a superficial form as crabbed and obscure as any text ever written.

Numerous authors have attempted overviews of the progress of Hegel's logic, and numerous claims have been made about the general course of the argumentation, but there is still no thoroughgoing commentary on Hegel's logic to place beside the commentaries on other philosophical masters by scholars like Cornford, W.D. Ross, Vaihinger, or Kemp Smith. No one has been able systematically to reconstruct the flow of argumentation in the logic in a thoroughly coherent, detailed, and intelligible manner. In the opinion of this writer, generalizations about the overall pattern of argumentation followed by attempts to show with specific examples how the pattern is instantiated have for so long failed so badly to illuminate this text that a new push to investigate the individual arguments entirely on their own should take precedence. If Hegel's pronouncements about his method are correct and in each case only the self-movement of the concept is involved, each argument should be intelligible in its own right. Indeed, if Hegel's remark that the method of the logic just is the self-movement of the concept is taken more seriously than most of his interpreters have allowed, there may be no higher principles involved throughout the whole course of the logic.[21] The detail work may be all that there is to understanding Hegel's logic.

∞ APPENDIX ∞

I have marked one divergence between the *Science of Logic* and the *Encyclopedia* in the Doctrine of Being, but it should be noted that the *Encyclopedia* includes far less detail than the greater *Logic* and that the arrangement in the Doctrine of Essence differs fairly significantly, enough that it could not be easily marked on this outline.[22]

I. The Doctrine of Being
    A. Determinateness (Quality)
        1. Being
            a. Being
            b. Nothing
            c. Becoming
                (1) Unity of Being and Nothing
                (2) Moments of Becoming: Coming-to-be and Ceasing-to-be
                (3) Sublation of Becoming
        2. Determinate Being
            a. Determinate Being as Such
                (1) Determinate Being in General
                (2) Quality
                (3) Something
            b. Finitude
                (1) Something and Other
                (2) Determination, Constitution, and Limit
                (3) Finitude
                    (a) The Immediacy of Finitude
                    (b) Limitation and the Ought
                    (c) Transition of the Finite into the Infinite
            c. Infinity
                (1) The Infinite in General
                (2) Alternating Determination of the Finite and Infinite

C. The Idea
  1. Life
     a. The Living Individual
     b. The Life Process
     c. The Genus
  2. The Idea of Cognition
     a. The Idea of the True
        (1) Analytic Cognition
        (2) Synthetic Cognition
           (a) Definition
           (b) Division
           (c) The Theorem
     b. The Idea of the Good
  3. The Absolute Idea

❧ NOTES ❧

1 Ideally, the formal properties of items do not depend in any way on their semantic or representational properties, and therefore cannot depend in any way on the nature of the reality they represent. But this is really too simple, since the logician must distinguish logical from nonlogical particles. The whole reason for making the distinction and doing logic in the first place rests on the different kinds of content embodied in the symbols.

2 Traditionally, logic is thought to spell out the conditions for thought's 'agreeing' with itself, assuming that unless it agrees with itself, it cannot agree with reality. But there are substantive (and nonformal) assumptions here about the nature of such internal agreement and about the nature of reality.

3 WL: Hegel, Wissenschaft der Logik, 2 vols, ed. G. Lasson (Leipzig: Meiner, 1923); SL: Hegel's Science of Logic, trans. A.V. Miller (London: Allen & Unwin, 1969).

4 I distinguish between the generic discipline of logic and Hegel's particular treatment of it by calling his treatment the logic. This usage does not distinguish between his treatments in the Science of Logic and the Encyclopedia of the Philosophical Sciences.

5 Note that Hegel explicitly does not say that the logic is an exposition of the ideas or the mind of God, for he would insist that this kind of imagistic and metaphoric way of describing the logic is very inadequate. Rather, it is an exposition of God himself.

6 A good example of this occurs in the Zusätz to § 24 of the Encyclopedia, where the Mosaic legend of the fall of man is read as an "ancient picture of the origin and consequences" of the self-disruption of spirit that makes all knowledge possible to begin with.

7 Actually, Hegel himself would have been more likely to have said that this development bottomed out with Kant, whom in this regard he classifies as an empiricist, simply because the hard-core nominalist empiricists still held onto

the simple faith that thought (in their case their ideas and impressions) and reality match. Only in Kant are we inescapably confined to a realm of thought without direct connection to reality.

8 "It is one of the profoundest and truest insights to be found in the *Critique of Pure Reason* that the *unity* which constitutes the nature of the *Concept* is recognized as the *original synthetic* unity of *apperception*, as unity of the *I think*, or of self-consciousness. . . . Thus we are justified by a cardinal principle of the Kantian philosophy in referring to the nature of the *I* in order to learn what the *Concept* is" (*WL*, II: 221–2; *SL*, 584–5).

9 Hegel does not believe that the *cogito* expresses a direct intuition of a substantial soul. Indeed, just what is at stake in the *cogito* turns out to be very complex and intertwined with a great deal of other knowledge about ourselves and the world around us. Thus, Hegel's interpretation of the *cogito* is highly anti-Cartesian. I have discussed this in greater detail in W.A. deVries, *Hegel's Theory of Mental Activity* (Ithaca: Cornell University Press, 1988), ch. 6.

10 Hegel, of course, never couches his objection to Kant in these terms.

11 See *WL*, II: 220–3; *SL*, 583–5.

12 This aspect of Hegel's logic has been emphasized in K. Düsing, *Das Problem der Subjektivität in Hegels Logik*, Hegel-Studien Beiheft 15 (Bonn: Bouvier, 1976).

13 The following section is derived, in substance, from deVries, op. cit., pp. 171–4.

14 The attitude of the understanding seeks to find and hold on to a set of rigid categories and distinctions that can be brought independently to bear on any material. The pre-Kantian thinkers, both rationalist and empiricist, with their consistent drive to decompose everything into simple atoms, are strong examples of this (pre-)philosophical attitude.

15 See R. Aquila, "Predication and Hegel's Metaphysics," in M.J. Inwood (ed.), *Hegel*, Oxford Readings in Philosophy (Oxford: Oxford University Press, 1985).

16 Cf. the discussion of the active universal and "objective thought" in *Enz.*, §§ 19–25.

17 Hegel seems to assume that with sufficient consideration one conceptual structure will present itself as being *the* structure characteristic of the phenomenon in question. But why could there not be alternative structures, perhaps each revealing something important about the phenomenon, but none with a claim to being *the* privileged structure inherent in the phenomenon? Hegel's own attempts to find the "right" structure for the philosophy of religion, for instance, show that he struggled with different alternatives.

18 Nevertheless, there are some contemporary commentators, e.g. Kenley Dove and William Maker, who seem to hold that retracing the *Phenomenology* is indeed the only way to achieve this state.

19 Although Husserl never thought much of Hegel, Hegel's conception of the attitude of pure knowing bears striking similarities to Husserl's notion of the phenomenological attitude. This may help explain why so many of Husserl's followers, unlike their master, found Hegel fascinating.

20 For any excellent review of the interpretations and criticisms of the opening moves in Hegel's logic, see D. Henrich, "Anfang und Methode der Logik," in

his *Hegel im Kontext* (Frankfurt Main: Suhrkamp, 1967). Unfortunately, this essay – the entire book, for that matter – is not available in English translation.

21 The major argument against this particularist reading of Hegel's logic is that it leaves the systematic triadicity of the system totally unexplained. Surely there is no particular reason to think that each and every concept must have an intrinsic, implicit triadic structure. I am willing to hazard the revisionist guess that the triadicity is an artifact of Hegel's commitment to a logic of terms in which the principal model of logical relation is a three-termed syllogism. But this is not the place to defend such a radical interpretation.

22 Hegel succeeded in revising only the Doctrine of Being before his untimely death. This revision brings it into accord with the logic as contained in the third edition of the *Encyclopedia*. But the Doctrine of Essence remains unrevised in the *Science of Logic*, and it differs in some significant ways from the version contained in the *Encyclopedia*. We must assume that had Hegel lived to revise the Doctrine of Essence in the larger *Logic*, it would have been brought into agreement with the version in the *Encyclopedia*. I am not aware of a thorough-going study of the differences between the two logics. Significantly, the Doctrine of the Concept as contained in the *Science of Logic* and published in 1816, several years after the appearance of the first two parts, accords substantially with the version in the *Encyclopedia*; apparently it would not have needed as extensive revision.

⚬ SELECT BIBLIOGRAPHY ⚬

Original language editions

7.1 Hegel, G.W.F. *Sämtliche Werke*, 20 vols, ed. H. Glockner, *Jubiläumsausgabe*, Stuttgart: Frommann, 1927–30.

7.2 Hegel, G.W.F. *Werke*, 20 vols, ed. E. Moldenhauer and K.M. Michel, Frankfurt/Main: Suhrkamp, 1970–1.

7.3 Hegel, G.W.F. *Gesammelte Werke*, ed. Rheinisch-Westfälischen Akademie der Wissenschaften, Hamburg: Meiner, 1968–.

7.4 Hegel, G.W.F. *Wissenschaft der Logik*, 2 vols, ed. G. Lasson, Leipzig: Meiner, 1923.

English translations

7.5 Hegel, G.W.F. *The Encyclopedia Logic*, trans. T.F. Geraets, W.A. Suchting, and H.S. Harris, Indianapolis: Hackett, 1991.

7.6 *Hegel's Philosophy of Mind*, trans. W. Wallace and A.V. Miller, Oxford: Oxford University Press, 1971.

7.7 *Hegel's Philosophy of Subjective Spirit*, 3 vols, trans. M.J. Petry, Boston: Reidel, 1978.

7.8 *Hegel's Science of Logic*, trans. A.V. Miller, London: Allen & Unwin, 1969.

7.9 *The Logic of Hegel*, 2nd edn, trans. W. Wallace, Oxford: Oxford University Press, 1892.

7.10 Hegel, G.W.F. *The Phenomenology of Spirit*, trans. A.V. Miller, Oxford: Oxford University Press, 1977.

Bibliographies and concordances

7.11 Steinhauer, K. (ed.) *Hegel: An International Bibliography*, Munich: Verlag Dokumentation, 1978.
7.12 *Hegel-Studien*, Bonn: Bouvier, published annually.

Influences

7.13 Beiser, F.C. *The Fate of Reason: German Philosophy from Kant to Fichte*, Cambridge, Mass.: Harvard University Press, 1987.
7.14 Fleischmann, E. "Hegels Umgestaltung der kantischen Logik," *Hegel-Studien*, 3 (1965): 181–208.
7.15 Gray, J.G. *Hegel and Greek Thought*, New York: Harper & Row, 1969.
7.16 Hartmann, N. "Aristoteles und Hegel," in *Kleinere Schriften II*, Berlin: de Gruyter, 1957.
7.17 Heintel, E. "Aristotelismus und Transzendentalismus in 'Begriff' bei Hegel," in W. Biemel (ed.) *Die Welt des Menschen – die Welt der Philosophie*, The Hague: Nijhoff, 1976.
7.18 Hölderlin, F. "Urtheil und Seyn," in M. Frank and G. Kurz (eds) *Materialien zu Schellings Philosophischen Anfängen*, Frankfurt/Main: Suhrkamp, 1975.
7.19 Kroner, R. *Von Kant bis Hegel*, 2 vols, Tübingen: Mohr, 1961.
7.20 Parkinson, G.H.R. "Hegel, Pantheism, and Spinoza," *Journal of the History of Ideas*, 38 (3) (1977): 449–59.
7.21 Priest, S. *Hegel's Critique of Kant*, Oxford: Clarendon Press, 1987.
7.22 Royce, J. *Lectures on Modern Idealism*, New Haven: Yale University Press, 1919.
7.23 Solomon, R.C. *Introducing the German Idealists*, Indianapolis: Hackett, 1981.

Hegel's development

7.24 Harris, H.S. *Hegel's Development: Towards the Sunlight, 1770–1801*, Oxford: Clarendon Press, 1972.
7.25 —— *Hegel's Development: Night Thoughts (Jena (1801–1806)*, Oxford: Clarendon Press, 1983.
7.26 Horstmann, R.-P. "Probleme der Wandlung in Hegel's Jenaer Systemkonzeption," *Philosophische Rundschau* 19 (1972): 87–117.
7.27 Lukács, G. *The Young Hegel*, trans. R. Livingstone, Cambridge, Mass.: MIT Press, and London: Merlin Press, 1975.

The philosophy of Hegel: general surveys

7.28 Findlay, J.N. *Hegel: A Re-examination*, London: Allen & Unwin, and New York: Oxford University Press, 1958.

7.29 Inwood, M.J. *Hegel*, London: Routledge & Kegan Paul, 1983.

7.30 Mure, G.R.G. *An Introduction to Hegel*, Oxford: Clarendon Press, 1939.

7.31 Mure, G.R.G. *The Philosophy of Hegel*, London: Oxford University Press, 1965.

7.32 Pöggeler, Otto (ed.) *Hegel*, Freiburg and Munich: Verlag Karl Alber, 1977.

7.33 Stace, W.T. *The Philosophy of Hegel: A Systematic Exposition*, London: Macmillan, 1924.

7.34 Taylor, C. *Hegel*, Cambridge: Cambridge University Press, 1975.

Hegel's logic and metaphysics

7.35 Aquila, R. "Predication and Hegel's Metaphysics," *Kant-Studien*, 64 (1973): 231–45; rep. in M.J. Inwood (ed.) *Hegel*, Oxford Readings in Philosophy, Oxford: Oxford University Press, 1985.

7.36 Burbidge, J. *On Hegel's Logic: Fragments of a Commentary*, Atlantic Highlands, NJ: Humanities Press, 1981.

7.37 Düsing, K. *Das Problem der Subjektivität in Hegels Logik*, Hegel-Studien Beiheft 15, Bonn: Bouvier, 1976.

7.38 Elder, C. *Appropriating Hegel*, Aberdeen: Aberdeen University Press, 1980.

7.39 Fulda, H.F. *Das Problem einer Einleitung in Hegels Wissenschaft der Logik*, Frankfurt/Main: Klostermann, 1965.

7.40 Fulda, H.F., Horstmann, R.-P., and Theunissen, M. *Kritische Darstellung der Metaphysik. Eine Diskussion der Hegels Logik*, Frankfurt/Main: Suhrkamp, 1980.

7.41 Henrich, D. *Hegel im Kontext*, Frankfurt/Main: Suhrkamp, 1967.

7.42 Henrich, D. "Formen der Negation in Hegels Logik," in W.R. Beyer (ed.) *Hegel-Jahrbuch 1974*, Cologne: Pahl-Rügenstein, 1975.

7.43 Horstmann, R.-P. *Seminar: Dialektik in der Philosophie Hegels*, Frankfurt/Main: Suhrkamp, 1978.

7.44 McTaggart, J.M.E. *A Commentary on Hegel's Logic*, Cambridge: Cambridge University Press, 1910.

7.45 Marcuse, H. *Hegels Ontologie und die Grundlegung einer Theorie der Geschichtlichkeit*, Frankfurt/Main: Klostermann, 1932.

7.46 Mure, G.R.G. *A Study of Hegel's Logic*, Oxford: Clarendon Press, 1939.

7.47 Pinkard, T. *Hegel's Dialectic*, Philadelphia: Temple University Press, 1988.

7.48 Pippen, R.B. *Hegel's Idealism*, Cambridge: Cambridge University Press, 1989.

7.49 Rosen, M. *Hegel's Dialectic and its Criticism*, Cambridge: Cambridge University Press, 1982.

7.50 Soll, I. *An Introduction to Hegel's Metaphysics*, Chicago: University of Chicago Press, 1969.

7.51 Theunissen, M. *Sein und Schein. Die kritische Funktion der Hegelschen Logik*, Frankfurt/Main: Suhrkamp, 1978.

7.52 Trendelenburg, A. *Logische Untersuchungen*, Berlin: Bethge, 1840.

7.53 Wolff, M. *Der Begriff des Widerspruchs: Eine Studie zur Dialektik Kants und Hegels*, Königstein: Hain, 1981.

Hegel's philosophy of mind

7.54 Bodammer, T. *Hegel's Deutung der Sprache*, Hamburg: F. Meiner, 1969.
7.55 deVries, W.A. *Hegel's Theory of Mental Activity*, Ithaca: Cornell University Press, 1988.
7.56 Solomon, R.C. "Hegel's Concept of *Geist*," in A.C. MacIntyre (ed.) *Hegel: A Collection of Critical Essays*, New York; Doubleday, 1972.
7.57 Stepelevich, L.S., and Lamb, D. *Hegel's Philosophy of Action*, Atlantic Highlands, NJ: Humanities Press, 1983.

CHAPTER 8

Hegel, spirit, and politics
Leo Rauch

Hegel's impact on political thought has been immense – giving shape to the major political movements of the modern world. Yet the person of average education is hardly familiar with the name, which is usually identified with a small number of simplistic statements, to the effect that Hegel argued for the supremacy of state power over all else; or that Hegel says individuals must subject themselves completely to the will of the state, and so on. Moreover, Hegel was seen (until recently) as the prophet of German totalitarianism – and the alleged evidence for this is in his characterization of the state as "the divine idea as it exists on earth," "the march of God in the world," etc.

In our century, such views have ominous echoes, especially when we have seen states override the rights of individuals; when state power has more often crushed personal freedom than it has preserved it; when individuals have all too often been forced to cooperate in their own enslavement by the state; and when the areas of state power have been expanding irreversibly. In the light of all this it surely seems that any endorsement of state supremacy is suspect and ought to be rejected out of hand.

Moreover, we may well wonder if there is anything in Hegel's political philosophy that merits our attention. The affirmative answer comes from the fact that so much of what he wrote has been reflected in other political streams, even if these involve distortions of Hegel's thinking. World communism, for example, adopted the dialectical logic of Hegel's worldview, although that dialectic was linked (in communism) to a materialism Hegel had rejected utterly.

There is no question about Hegel's power to fascinate readers with his views of state and history. To understand his views, we must understand his reaction to the eighteenth-century Enlightenment. In an age that placed great emphasis on the concept of a static and unchanging human nature, Hegel chose to emphasize the dynamism of the political theater. He sees the political reality as being historical through and through. But that dynamism also characterizes culture in all its aspects. And if we now regard the law, medicine, science, and the arts as fundamentally dynamic – so that it is by now basic for us to study these in their histories – this perspective is due in no small part to Hegel. But in regard to the dynamism of politics we must ask: If politics presents a scene of change, what is it changing from? what is it changing to?

❧ DYNAMISM AND HISTORY ❧

The dynamic emphasis was not always the norm. Thinkers associated with the Enlightenment believed that there is a fixed human nature, making all historical change unreal. As Voltaire is often thought to have said, "Plus ça change, plus c'est la même chose."[1] And Hume, in his *Enquiry* (VIII: i), tells us that if we wish to know the ancient Greeks and Romans we need merely study the French and English, since humanity stays much the same, and history "informs us of nothing new or strange."

Hegel's approach makes a sharp contrast to all this. Instead of arguing for the unchanging character of human nature, Hegel emphasizes the evolutionary perspective in history: the state, and all else that is human, is seen to be in process and to derive its significance from the process. The Spanish philosopher José Ortega y Gasset said: "Man has no nature, only a history." The very concept of an unchanging human nature seems to have been mocked by history's spectacle of mindless chaos and blind change. Hegel rejects the characterization of history as mindless and blind: History does have an aim, and that aim is rational. If so, what is all this change aimed at? If the fundamental characterization of humanity involves its volatility in the dimension of *time*, in what direction does time take us: to development or decline? And how inevitable is the historical process anyway?

Hegel's way of addressing this complex issue is to make it even more complex. If we agree to see human life as historical in its very essence, the historical dimension must be seen in a global perspective – even in a cosmic perspective whereby human history is regarded as a continuation of the development of the cosmos as a whole. In the terminology of our own time, we may see the cosmos beginning as simple matter composed of undifferentiated particles, but ending as mind and culture subsumed under the heading of what Hegel calls Spirit: i.e. all that has been created by humans using their minds, language, culture, and society. *Geist* has also been seen as a "general consciousness, a single mind common to all men."[2] It is this metaphor that makes it possible for Hegel to look at history as though it were the report of the world's own coming to self-consciousness, like a mind growing up and achieving maturity and freedom.

What about matter and spirit? How did we get from the one pole to the other? In the temporal "distance" between these two poles (matter and spirit), we see an emerging process: it all has tended in the direction of the highly complex and self-conscious beings we are – beings capable of understanding themselves in rational terms and giving shape to their lives accordingly; beings capable of grasping their own history, and of seeing reason at work in it.

Hegel must have been struck by the sheer wonder of it all. But if so, he did more than wonder at it: he organized his wonderment into a comprehensive system of metaphysical speculation. In his *Encyclopaedia of the Philosophical Sciences* (1817), Hegel undertook to demonstrate a very remarkable doctrine (among other remarkable ones): namely that the mere *concept* of Being must eventuate in an existing world, an Ontological Argument for the world's existence. Being – a purely abstract and formal concept in metaphysics – must somehow lead to an eventual materialization of itself as reality, so that the self-enclosed concept must produce a version of itself outside itself, as nature! From there, Hegel went on to show how the world of inorganic nature must produce an organic version of itself, as life. And from there he showed how life as such must lead to consciousness and then to self-consciousness. Moreover, he showed how these separate stages *must* follow from one another, not merely as a haphazard biological/ evolutionary progression but as a matter of *logical* necessity.

The final goal of the process – that is, our rational self-consciousness made real in the world – must be seen as somehow embedded in its very beginning. The omega is entailed in the alpha – so that our modern cultural life, in all its wealth of complexity and detail, is implicitly there in the simple first moments of the life of the universe. (Needless to say, Hegel does not use such a term as "the Big Bang.") If we are now so highly evolved as to be capable of understanding ourselves rationally, this self-consciousness of ours must be the final goal of the entire process, the purpose that gives the cosmos its ultimate meaning. Accordingly, it is Spirit – fully evolved and fully self-conscious – that is the goal of history. And the entire process of cosmic evolution culminates in *freedom* (for in being fully self-conscious we are in a position to act freely, according to our own will, and to shape our lives to meet the standards of our own rationality).

Hegel undertakes to show how such freedom has emerged in time. History is the account of the emergence of freedom (in the fullest sense of that term). Not all cultures have attained such self-directing freedom, and they are therefore in the early or intermediary stages in the evolutionary process of history. Obviously, an authoritarian culture, in which only one person is "free," does not provide the setting wherein the individual participants can regard themselves as fully self-motivating, since they are not in a position to shape their lives according to their own rational precepts. Thus Hegel sees history as the gradual fulfillment of our rational potential, in freedom.

All this must change our view of the violent history of Hegel's time – and ours. History is not a chaotic succession of meaningless and disconnected events. There *is* a meaning that unites it all, Hegel says, a meaning we can see if we approach history with a rational attitude. In his view, then, the unifying meaning is implicit in the omega of history: the fully explicit and self-conscious rationality manifested in a public life of full freedom.

Yet we might ask: Assuming that this genuine goal of full rationality could be realized, would it justify the necessary sacrifices? In our century (perhaps the most horrific of them all), the question of a sacrificial calculus is inescapable. Every point on the horizon has its pile of corpses heaped up in the name of so-called "historical" aims: there are the vast multitudes who died in the prolonged trench warfare of the First World War; the millions who were victims of Stalin's collectivization; the millions who perished in Hitler's "final solution," not to mention the further millions, on all sides, who died in the Second World War as its victims or combatants; then think of Hiroshima; of Mao's "cultural revolution"; of Cambodia and Vietnam; and on and on. Can all this misery be said to have contributed to the developing freedom and rationality of history? And even if such a contribution could be proven, in the long range, could the remote goal justify all the immediate suffering?

Hegel has no illusions about history's violence and its short-range irrationality. He does not see history as filled with sweetness and light. Indeed, he speaks of history as a "slaughter-bench." He lived through the Napoleonic Wars; and although he admired Napoleon when he saw him on horseback, riding through the conquered city of Jena in 1806, Hegel knew that he must come to terms with the destructive side in what Napoleon had done, and keep both eyes open to history's murderous aspect. How, then, could anyone argue for the intrinsic rationality of history, in view of its so obvious irrationality?

For Hegel, the irrational element in history is necessary for the fulfillment of the ultimate aims of cosmic reason. He argues for this view on two levels: He begins by saying that "world-historical individuals" such as Alexander, Caesar, and Napoleon (i.e. the "movers" of history) are merely the unwitting instruments of a higher Spirit working through them, a Spirit which is mysteriously exploiting their very irrationality for the sake of Spirit's rational goals, and achieving (through these individuals) ends *they* never intended, but which were the implicit goals of history all along. This is the "Cunning of Reason" in history.

Then he extends this concept to human action in general. Human actions stem from human passions, needs, and interests; and however irrational these may be, they too are the means whereby the World Spirit fulfills its rational goals. Thus the aims of Spirit are made real through the actions of the human will, revolving around its irrational passions, etc. And thus the rational Idea (i.e. cosmic reason) and the irrational passions of the individual are interwoven as the "warp and woof" of history, Hegel says.

✤ THE DIALECTIC ✤

We have seen that human beings can act irrationally, yet serve the rational goals of cosmic Spirit in so doing. Despite all appearances, therefore, there is an implicit rationality at work in history and in states. Does this entail a contradiction? Could this be a positive feature of states and their history?

Here we must say a few words about the topic of Hegel's dialectic. The term "dialectic" means (in Greek) discourse, debate, logical reasoning. Hegel adopted it as a technical term, to mean "logic" in a special sense. Aristotle's logic avoids contradiction – so that if a conclusion contradicts its premises, you know that the argument is invalid. Hegel incorporates the element of contradiction into his discourse, and makes it play a constructive role there.

Here is how it works: An idea or proposition (*thesis*) will readily suggest its opposite (*antithesis*), and the one will enter into the very definition of the other. (Think of the idea of slavery, and how the idea of freedom enters into its very meaning. Think of Rousseau's ringing sentence: "Man is born free, and yet everywhere he is in chains.") For Aristotle, a thesis and its antithesis cannot *both* be true; you must give up one or the other. Hegel says that two opposed statements *can* be true if each is only a partial truth. Indeed, each leads to its opposite *because* it is true in only a partial manner. When we see the partial nature of such truths, we are led to think of a higher truth which is more comprehensive and includes them both, *as* partial, so that the partial nature of these lower truths is overcome. (Thus we could respond to Rousseau by saying: "Yes, man is by nature free, but he himself freely creates the chains of his enslavement.") This higher truth, bringing thesis and antithesis together, is a *synthesis*. The synthesis, in turn, will generate a further opposite. ("If man is free to create his chains, then he is free to break them. Why, then, does he remain unfree?")

Let us take note of the productivity of thought as it arises out of the clash of its implicit opposites. (It, too, is creating its chains, then breaking them.) The Danish physicist Niels Bohr said: "There are two sorts of truth, small truth and great truth; the opposite of a small truth is a falsehood; the opposite of a great truth is a further truth." This remark is straight out of Hegel, except that Hegel was not content to let such a contradiction remain a contradiction; rather, he would take it to a higher synthesis. He might say: "The great truths and their opposites are in opposition only by virtue of their compatibility."

From this, Hegel goes on to the remarkable view that this dialectical logic works in two separate but parallel areas, i.e. in thought and in history. Thus our thinking process is dialectical in character, creating its own counter-questions and their solutions, leading to further questions, etc. But Hegel goes on to say that history, too, is dialectical in the way it unfolds – for it is marked by conflicts and solutions, then further conflicts, and so on. Thus the process of history has the same implicit logic to it, the dialectic.

Thus the main feature of the dialectic is that it is said to work in two spheres – the formal and the factual, i.e. logic and history. This means that if some events are linked logically, that is also the way they are linked in reality – with the same rigorous necessity characterizing both.

But here we may want to ask: Is there not an antithesis between logic and history, as there is between pure theory and concrete reality? (This antithesis, as well, cries out to be resolved in a higher synthesis.) Thus in the field of pure theory we are confronted by an embarrassing series of dichotomies (e.g. freedom vs determinism, facts vs values, individual rights vs collective expectations, etc.) – and the only way these antitheses can begin to be resolved is by showing that their component "truths" are not final, that they are mere abstractions or merely piecemeal truths, and that they can be brought to unifying syntheses if we see them from a "higher" (unifying) perspective. From that perspective, both thesis and antithesis are "negated" at the same time that they are "lifted up" (as we shall see in the forthcoming example of the classless society).

At all events we must grasp the parallelism of logic and history – an isomorphism that becomes feasible when we realize that the way our minds think things through (when we think in a thorough manner) is actually the way things do and *must* happen – again, because the same necessity is to be found in both spheres. It is this feature that enables us to declare, about any series of connected events, that whatever *has* happened *had* to happen.

We can thereby presume to demonstrate the inevitability of (say) the Communist Revolution of 1917 by showing that it occurred with a logical necessity, both in its initial causes and its ultimate aims: Thus the opposed interests of the bourgeoisie and the proletariat (as thesis vs antithesis) erupted into open conflict wherein class differences were eventually to be eliminated through the creation of a supposedly class-less society (synthesis). So, if Marx and Engels are correct, and all history is the record of class conflict, then the synthesis that is the classless society negates social classes entirely at the same time that it elevates them into a higher synthesis – wherein the individual would see him- or herself as belonging to a higher entity, altogether outside class.

It is an ironic fact about the dialectic process that a synthesis need not be final either, but that it too may create a further opposition in another antithesis, to be followed by yet another synthesis, and on and on. If, however, any historical synthesis *is* final, then it becomes the "end" of history – in the combined sense of its completion and its ultimate purpose (and, indeed, that is how the "classless society" was seen by Marxist theoreticians).

We may conclude, therefore, that what drives history is its internal (i.e. formal) conflicts brought about by the one-sided "partiality" and inconclusiveness of its theses and antitheses, and that all this will come to an end in an all-embracing synthesis wherein the imperfections inherent in the one-sidednesses are altogether overcome.

We must leave to the judgment of history the question as to whether this dialectical vision is for the most part correct. However that may be, the fact that so many historical events do involve conflict of some sort tends to make the dialectical explanation a useful model, though probably a reductive and simplistic one. Moreover, since the dialectical model is most often applied after the events, not predictively, its power to explain is limited because it is so arbitrary. Hegel never uses the dialectical model in this formal and puerile manner, but only for the purpose of arguing in support of the link between logic and history – a link that is somewhat reflected in the powerful statement in the Preface of Hegel's *Philosophy of Right*: "What is rational is actual; what is actual is rational" (p. 10).

❧ HISTORY AND THE COSMIC SPIRIT ❧

With the foregoing statement – important enough for Hegel to utter it in his Preface – the parallelism of thought and reality comes into full view. That link is possible because both belong to the realm of Spirit. The concept of "Spirit" (*Geist*) is so central to Hegel's entire doctrine that if that concept falls, then his entire system falls with it. What can be said for it, or against it?

To begin with, the concept of a World Spirit (*Weltgeist*) is the paradigm case of a "metaphysical" concept if ever there was one. And if we adopt the anti-metaphysical stance so typical of our age, we would have to say that *any* sentence with the word "Spirit" in it (as Hegel uses the term) cannot be verified, and so it must be rejected as a sentence devoid of meaning. Thus if I say, "Spirit acts through the world-historical individuals," I cannot describe just *how* the connection works, or how Spirit makes them act as they do. Further, I cannot specify what observable conditions would make that sentence true or make it false. In the absence of such verifying or falsifying conditions, the sentence must be judged to be literally without meaning! (This is the general criticism leveled by Logical Positivists against all metaphysical utterances.)

Moreover, if we were to adopt the Marxian standpoint, we would have to say that Hegel's doctrine of Spirit (as a doctrine) is nothing but theology in disguise. Like the God of the Bible, Hegel's "Spirit" acts in history, chooses certain nations to bring *its* (Spirit's) message to the world, acts through certain individuals to manifest *its* will – and all the while keeps its (i.e. His) ultimate intentions hidden. ("God works in mysterious ways . . ." The sentence has the same meaning if its subject is "Spirit.") And if Hegel is really talking theology in this metaphysical doctrine of his (as Marxist criticism alleges), and religion is the opium of the people (an opium employed for the purpose of keeping the lower classes in their place), then Hegel's doctrine is on very shaky ground indeed.

Yet there is no denying some important points in favor of Hegel's doctrine of Spirit:

(a) In view of history's dynamic nature, it does seem to be moving toward a goal. Hegel speaks of the process of history as though it were an individual mind growing up and becoming aware of itself, a process of maturation in the world's "mind." We therefore need the concept of a "mind" or "Spirit" to give meaning to the process.

Consider the probable mentality of (say) Neanderthals or other paleolithic primitives who might have come only as far as domesticating fire and the dog, and who might have had only the most rudimentary ideas about their surrounding world. They must have had only the vaguest reasonings regarding their own social organization. Their ability to function in the world, to explain it successfully and make use of its opportunities for providing food, clothing, shelter, health, social order, and security – all these would have been severely limited.

Now contrast the picture (admittedly fanciful) of that crude mentality to that of a Freud, Einstein, Bertrand Russell, and it is obvious that we have come a long way in our mental evolution. Our capacity for handling abstract concepts has grown exponentially. Our ability to think our way through a complex series of issues in a sustained way, then to communicate and record the process – all this has far exceeded anything of which the primitive was capable.

In what does the difference consist? If we say it is a difference in "culture" – what does that term amount to in its comparative/ explanatory power? Frued, Einstein, and Russell were the "products" of their culture – and they would hardly have survived in the Neanderthal world. The Neanderthals, in turn, no doubt had their characteristic ways of relating to the world, of using it and explaining it, etc. But this relativistic approach of ours (placing all "cultures" on an equal footing) gives us little; in and of itself, it does not tell us what the differences amount to.

The difference between "us" and "them" is not simply in what we might call civilization. To account for the contrast, we must observe that the intervening process has been thrusting its way *toward* the goal of a more articulate level of self-consciousness – i.e. a more complex mentality or spirituality active in the world. The historical process makes sense only in the light of that increasing complexity in the mentalization or spiritualization of humanity. Thus we become human to the degree that we can think of ourselves as human. With this, the concept of a developing Spirit is indispensable if we are to understand the process as a whole. Otherwise the process itself (along with the contrast between ourselves and the primitives) remains an unexplored mystery.

(b) Moreover, without that concept there would be an unexplained mystery in connection with cultural boundaries which some civilizations have marked out for themselves: Why do the Elizabethans have such sublime theater, but so little painting? Why do the Florentines produce such magnificent painting, but such negligible theater in comparison to the Elizabethans? How is is that the ancient Hebrews develop such an exalted conception of deity, at a level of thought calling for the most profound wisdom and insight – yet have nothing to say in regard to art as such, or democracy, or science? How could the ancient Greeks, that miraculous people, have had so much to contribute in art, science, and mathematics – and even have invented tragic drama, democracy, and philosophy – yet not have gone so far as the most elementary form of monotheism?

Here, the concept of Spirit has considerable explanatory power. Hegel says that the characteristic differences between cultures can be explained by what he calls the "Spirit of a people" (*Volksgeist*). As he sees it, each people has a distinct contribution to make to the great stream of cultural history. A people will step up upon the stage of world history just once, will say its "lines," and then step down. The Hebraic contribution of ethical monotheism is entirely distinctive in the Hebrews; no other people could have made that contribution to world culture, and that world culture is the richer for it. The Greek contribution of theater, democracy, science, and philosophy is (in its totality) similarly distinctive. Again, no other people could have made that combined contribution, and without it the world would be a bleak place indeed – with no civilization at all but only some form of stunted cultural existence.

These contributions – the "lines" spoken by each of these peoples on the world stage – are not arbitrary or accidental, but are rather the necessary steps in the maturation of the world's "mind." At certain definite moments in time, this or that contribution had to be made – and the world's "mind" chose one people or another to make it. This is precisely what demarcates one people or another. It is the Hebraic *Volksgeist* and the Greek *Volksgeist* that explain what these peoples *are*, thereby dispelling the mystery about their different capacities and characteristic achievements. At this level we are no longer dealing with a mysterious cosmic Spirit or world mind, but with Spirit in a more limited scope, the mind of a people or nation – and perhaps the concept's explanatory force is all the greater for being limited.

(c) There is a further argument to support the concept of Spirit, perhaps the most convincing of all: An inventory of the world's "contents" must include not only all material objects and material particles; it must also include all thoughts, all actions, relations, concepts, meanings, etc. All these latter things must be differentiated from material objects, since their descriptions cannot be equated with material descriptions. They must therefore be consigned to a nonmaterial category, and this is Spirit. (We could just as well call it "Mind," or the "mental," and Hegel would accept these terms as equivalent, since *Geist* includes them all.) Spirit embraces the totality of human significations. And if we are to see that totality in dynamic terms, as evolving in history and historical time, then we must have a dynamic conception of Spirit itself, to comprehend all that is cultural and distinctly human.

We ought to respond to the Marxian objection made earlier – to the effect that Hegel's metaphysical doctrine or history is theology in disguise, that his philosophy is merely a version of religion. Thus Hegel's statements about history should (in the view of Marx) be translatable into theological statements, and these translations should then reflect the true meaning of what Hegel has to say. Hegel, however, maintains the converse: rather than philosophy being religion in another form, religion is actually philosophy in another form. That is to say, religious assertions are trying to say what philosophy says, but they say it crudely, by means of imagery (human figures representing abstract concepts, and so on). Thus religious statements are inadequate expressions of deeper philosophic truth; and it is the philosophic truth (not the religious) which is ultimate – since philosophy is fully articulate and self-critical, while religion must express its insights in nothing better than imperfect verbalizations which must wait to get their truth by way of philosophy.

Marx respected Hegel for his dialectical logic – the logic of conflict and its overcoming. He accepted Hegel's view that history works dialectically (the Marxian class struggle being the best example of dialectical conflict in history). But Marx felt that Hegel was wrong about Spirit being the moving force in history; he believed he had cleared up one of Hegel's errors, replacing Hegel's "idealistic" doctrine with a "materialistic" view of history. (This occasioned Marx's famous remark about his finding Hegel standing on his head, and setting him back on his feet.) It was Plekhanov who in 1891 coined the phrase "dialectical materialism" to characterize Marx's view of history. Yet Marx's "materialistic conception of history" involves a false materialism: the "material forces" which he believes move history are the economic factors embedded in human society; they are the products of human effort, not the effects of physical matter. Hegel calls them Objective Spirit – and they *are* the work of Spirit, after all, not of matter. Despite Marx's never-ending attack on Hegel, the Marxian conception of history is Hegelian through and through.

Thus, if there is any doubt about Hegel's view that "ideas" move history, such doubt is readily dispelled by Marx's own case, since the "material forces" he adduces are themselves the work of the "mental," i.e. people's *ideas* about history – and few "ideas" have moved history more decisively than have Marx's doctrines.

❧ REASON IN THE WORLD ❧

We saw Hegel say, "What is rational is actual; what is actual is rational." Here, again, we see the implicit parallelism of thought and history, united by a parallel dialectic. Elsewhere he says that when we approach the world with our own rationality, the world responds by showing us its rationality in return. (This is from his *Introduction to the Philosophy of History*, p. 14.) The rational aspect he shows us is the world's dialectical structure – which we can comprehend because it parallels the dialectical structure of our thinking.

Here, then, we may see a further side to the puzzling theme of Spirit in history: Instead of seeing "Spirit" as a mysterious metaphysical agency (and most critics of Hegel see him thinking in just this way), we might take "Spirit" to refer merely to the element of active reason in the world, the rational in the actual.

Once we have this in full view, Hegel's "metaphysical" utterances are tamed and demystified. In every way he can, he is trying to account for the existence of reason in the world. After we have acknowledged the obvious truism that the world and the mind are mutually reflective, mutually consistent, we can either marvel at the fact or shrug our shoulders at it. Hegel sees the consistency between world and mind, between the actual and the rational, as the most deeply problematic of truths. Einstein said: "The one incomprehensible fact about the world is that it is comprehensible." For Hegel, that fact is *not* incomprehensible, and his aim is to show this to be so.

He approaches the problem at a number of levels: Not only does he make it a metaphysical issue requiring some very complex lines of argument (as in the grand structure of his *Encyclopaedia*); he also examines the actual workings of reason in such different areas as art, religion, culture in general, history – and political life. Here, then (as I suggest), we see a less-than-metaphysical approach being taken by him. And as soon as we realize that this is so – namely, that not all his explanations are intended as metaphysical assertions but rather as statements closer to the world's everyday ontology – then many of his "metaphysical" utterances (so called) become less daunting.

In the *Introduction to the Philosophy of History* (p. 75), there is the oft-quoted statement: "World history in general is . . . the unfolding of Spirit in *time*, as nature is the unfolding of the Idea in *space*." This statement is far less metaphysical-sounding when we realize that Hegel is merely contrasting the realm of mind and culture with that of physical nature. Each has its source in a rational process, Hegel is saying.

❧ HEGEL'S *PHILOSOPHY OF RIGHT* ❧

Much of the tradition of political thought rests on two tenets that are sometimes made explicit, but are more often left tacit. These are:

> The human being is by nature a social animal.
> The human being is by nature a rational animal.

Political theory, throughout its variegated course, has tried to prove the mutual compatibility of these two statements – although there have been thinkers, such as Nietzsche, who have sought to demonstrate how incompatible these are, so that our social inclination is by no means a rational one. If they are compatible, then we may expect human society to exhibit the same rationality that typifies all other human contrivances and constructions; if they are not compatible, then there is no basis for expecting society (or anything else that is human) to display anything like a rational aspect. The problem goes back to a wider controversy in ancient Greek philosophy, as to whether the laws are the product of nature or of convention: Are social values entirely random, arbitrary – and irrational? For Nietzsche, there is nothing in social life or custom that can be given a fully rational and intellectually satisfying justification. (In one of his examples, he speaks of a culture in which the act of scraping ice off one's boots with a knife is punishable by death – and he seems to be saying that there is no socially sanctioned act anywhere that does any better in its justification.)

On the other hand, we have had a host of thinkers who regard the state as a rational device specifically created (by rational and naturally social creatures) to serve one or more of our basic social purposes: to promote peace and social order; to protect life and property; to determine and secure natural rights; to insure that a people will have a unifying voice; to make possible the transmission of inherited values from one generation to the next; to make it possible for the wisest to rule, etc. Whatever these various theories argue for, they share an emphasis on the purposiveness and rationality of societal life. Is it at all rational and sensible for individuals to enter into social ties with others? Presumably, we enter into contractual arrangements with one another for one rational end or another. Having done so, is it rational and sensible for us to try to give further order to our societal interrelations through the application of reason? Or is all this speculation about the social interactions of ourselves as primordial humans merely an idle exercise?

Of course, like Nietzsche, we may express no confidence at all in the reasonableness of human institutions and arrangements. Where Nietzsche is at the nadir of trust in regard to such institutions, Hegel is at the zenith – as reflected in the motto we have been citing about the rational and the actual. Society, as Aristotle says, begins with the process of satisfying the needs of life, although its ultimate aim is the pursuit of the *good* life. Again, how rational are these as goals, and how rational is the aim of achieving them?

We might go so far as to conceive of certain rights, to which all humans may lay claim; we may even speak of such rights as parts of self-evident truths, i.e. as standing to reason. But it is no secret that the theoretical foundations of these rights have been roundly attacked over the centuries. (Can an attack on what is "self-evident" avoid self-contradiction?) Accordingly, we may state one of the challenges confronting Hegel as follows: to decline the use of "natural rights" as a basis for a theory of statehood; yet to maintain the emphasis on the *rationality* of the state.

There are further challenges: Throughout his Preface, Hegel

argues against the uncritical acceptance of social convention and entrenched values. What is to be decisive is not convention but *truth*. We may or may not wish to go along with him in his search for a basis in objectivity for such truth. As for its other criteria we must reiterate his motto, since it tells us that only what is *fully* rational is actualized in the world, and only the fully actual is transparently rational. All this reminds us that we must avoid convention as a basis for argument, along with the intellectual fashion of the moment, and especially the individual conscience. All these are now seen as impediments in the search for truth, its objectivity and rationality.

All this may well be a sensible goal in, say, logic or mathematics. In political theory, moored as it is in the concrete life of society and its values, we can hardly avoid our individual feelings and points of view. Can we be altogether free of perspectives that have become historically ingrained? Hegel insists that we must somehow put these things behind us if we are to have any hope of attaining truth and rationality.

Hegel goes so far as to suggest that Plato drew his *Republic* from the values implicit in Greek ethical life. What is the status of that "actuality"? In Hegel's motto, the German word that is translated as "actual" is *wirklich*. With this, he does not mean that just any actuality is rational – and certainly not the false and ephemeral "actuality" we encounter in political life. Rather, *wirklich* refers to the union of existence and essence – as when we speak of a "real" athlete, one who fulfills the essence of what it means to *be* an athlete. Accordingly, *wirklich* means "real" (or actual), "true," "genuine," etc.

And therefore Hegel's "science of the state" (i.e. of the rational/actual state) is not a study of this or that example of statehood, but of the state that perfectly fulfills the functioning *ideal*. Up to this point we can hardly have been enlightened as to what all this means. Yet when we do grasp this, the challenge that faces us is "to apprehend in the show of the temporal and transient the substance which is immanent and the eternal which is present" (p. 10).

The state's rationality and its actualization as such emerge together. Thus, a further challenge confronting Hegel is "to apprehend and portray the state as something inherently rational" (p. 11). This sounds as though he is trying to set up an ideal of the state as it *ought* to be (à la Plato). But no, it is the state as it *is* which is to be united with its essence, as the actuality. As he tells us: "To comprehend what is, this is the task of philosophy, because what is, is reason."

To apprehend the eternal in what is transitory. But most emphatically, this does *not* involve setting up a standard of perfection with the purpose of getting us to live up to it. Instead, there is a hint of resignation when Hegel admits that the aim of philosophy is not to change the world, but only to apprehend our own time by way of thought (again, the synthesis of the rational and the actual). As for changing the world, wisdom makes its appearance only at the end of an era, when things can no longer be changed but only understood. As he famously says: "The owl of Minerva takes to flight only in the oncoming dusk."

❧ HEGEL'S *INTRODUCTION*³ ❧

We have been speaking of history as an evolutionary process. That process, however, is not entirely value-neutral. Instead, Hegel sees it as involving (a) the concept of right, and (b) its actualization through time, in a transition from merely "abstract" right to "concrete" right, fully realized. Consider, for example, such concepts as these: "selfhood," "humanity," "property," "obligation," and so on. In some societies these could be mere concepts, with an application that is nothing more than a matter of *form* or ritual; in other societies, these concepts might be more fully articulated, with a *content* that can be given words as well as a concrete expression in societal life.

On a broader scale, we may contrast an arid ideology (powerful though it may be) against a set of political tenets whose meaning is made fully verbal and rational. This transition, then, is what occurs (or should occur) in any society in the course of time. It is a transition to a stage of cultural life wherein mind is consciously applied, a transition to something more fully rational and actual in regard to the element of *right*.

We must not identify this with the values held by any particular society (whose existence is in any case contingent and variable). Nor ought we to link "reason" to any social values expressed as positive law in this or that place. Rather, we must think of a universal, or norm, applied to particular cases in law, but reflecting the essential *Geist* of a people (par. 3). Above all else, it is the essence of right that we are seeking: its basis is Spirit which is given expression as the will of a people. Since the will is free, as Hegel explains, freedom is both the substance of right and its goal. Indeed, "the system of right is the realm of freedom made actual, the world of mind brought forth out of itself like a second nature" (par. 4). Yet although the process is free, it is in search of determination. This is provided by its dialectical counterpart.

The free will, taken to an extreme in politics, ignores all restraints. As a result it rises to pure destructiveness, to eliminate all individuals who might pose some sort of a threat to it, and thus turning to destroy the social order itself. Hegel is obviously thinking of the French

Revolution in this regard; but these words of his are ominous for our own time as well – with all the abundant examples of murderous autocracies operating destructively in the name of "freedom," equality, or whatever (as abstract ideas).

This is one of the most penetrating insights Hegel offers: namely, that the abstract idea is not merely one-sided and empty of content; but that it is necessarily destructive, in that its partiality and one-sidedness – mistaken as the *whole* truth – must become destructive of society as a whole, as a result of the violence inhering in the dialectic itself. There are numerous ways whereby this may occur: The will, being free, is indeterminate; it is the ego that seeks to give itself some determinate content. In so doing, it turns back into itself; it becomes the reflection of itself, by reflecting on its own reflection – and this is its universality, its infinity, its self-determination, and also its absoluteness (par. 7). Above all, its self-relatedness is its freedom. And in that freedom from external factors, it may well become politically autistic and violent; or it may become rational.

We might wonder whether Hegel is thinking here in terms of the will of the individual or the will of a people. Most likely, he is deliberately conflating the two levels of discourse, so that the individual will can be taken as a metaphor for the social will. Once he has engaged that metaphor, he can come to analogous conclusions about a social "mind" – attaining its freedom, self-determination, and maturity on the basis of how an individual undergoes the same process. From here it is an easy step to conclude that just as the individual ego is autonomous, so the social "mind" can claim a similar degree of autonomy, even an absolute authority over its own "selfhood." Hegel often decried the use of analogy in philosophical argument; he preferred direct (non-analogical) discourse, whereby we say exactly what we mean, and nothing else.

Yet the fact is that he himself employs analogies – and he does so in support of his most crucial points (the twofold "mind" being one such analogy, among others), and this must cast much of what he says into doubt, since this "double-speak" is deliberately ambiguous on this score. Thus, while leaving the question open as to whether he is speaking of the will of an individual person or the will of a people, he can say: "It is not until it has itself as its object that the will is for *itself* what it is in itself" (par. 10). Only in its self-awareness does the will, or ego, attain its essence. But just *whose* will is this – that of the individual person or that of society? This question is not addressed, since Hegel prefers to leave the ambiguity in place. Shortly thereafter (par. 13), he speaks of the individual will coming to its resolutions; but as individual it is a will only in form, and is therefore abstract.

It is in the individual will that we see the dialectic of choice and resolution combining to form contradictions in the ego, an ego therefore divided against itself. This is surely a destabilizing factor when it occurs in the social "mind," which sees these differences of will as arbitrary, subjective, and threatening; they are therefore uprooted as much as possible. With this remark, Hegel seems to damn all dissent in society, as well as all diversity (par. 19). We get the same result by extending his metaphor: a psyche divided is unhealthy in the individual, and is made healthy by its integration; in the social "psyche" integration is wholesome, a people speaking with one voice, in a unity of social purpose. Such integration ought therefore to be fostered as the primary social goal.

What is most important is to get the will away from its abstractness, so that it becomes self-relating and self-determining, thereby achieving its freedom, universality, and infinitude (as we have seen). This, then, is its truth (pars 21–3). By turning back into itself, the will is able (in its resulting indeterminacy) to turn outward and project itself into the world, which it shapes according to that will.

This defines the progression in Hegel's *Philosophy of Right:* proceeding from the abstractness of its concepts to their external embodiment, thence back into the will and its freedom, it is then turned outward once more, but now energized by its freedom. Having turned outward, the will is made objective in a shared system of morals, to be followed by what he calls "Ethical Life" (par. 33). This will undergo a dialectic of its own. The book is therefore divided into three main sections: "Abstract Right," "Morality," and "Ethical Life."

❧ ABSTRACT RIGHT ❧

John Locke, in his *Second Treatise of Government*, explains how rights evolve, and he uses the right of property as the paradigm of all other rights: Thus, a man in the "state of nature," wherein no one owns anything, mixes his bodily labor with nature (say, by picking fruit off a tree). The resulting product of this mixture is rightfully his. A similar argument holds for all other rights: they, too, are extensions of one's bodily self, expressions of one's will. In this way, the rights to "life, liberty, and estate" are established. Governments are specifically set up for the purpose of safeguarding those rights.

Here we can think of a variety of philosophic approaches describing the basic formation of the state as a primordial instrument for securing property and personal safety. Obviously, we do not leave it at that – as though, with security achieved, the state has completed its task. Rather, the state persists beyond that task; there are further purposes for it.

Moreover, the right which is secured by the primordial state is merely an "abstract" right – namely, a formal, less-than-real right. This is because there can be no "right" to property *prior* to the establishing of a government and a system of ownership, and therefore no rights which a government is *subsequently* meant to protect. What Hegel must do, therefore, is to show that the "abstract" right is an *inadequate* and incomplete picture of rights and their justifications.

The essence of what it is to be a person involves the notion of self-relatedness. Selfhood is a relation in which a self relates itself to itself. This powerful paradox is derived from Schelling. (It is a paradox because a relation relates one term to another that is pre-existing; and yet, in Schelling's terms, the self does not pre-exist for a self to relate to, but only begins to exist as a *result* of the relation itself.) Hegel reiterates this point by saying: "I am simply and solely self-relation" (par. 35). Only by virtue of my relation to my self, which logically should already exist, do I *then* begin to exist as a self. Hegel needs this paradox, this antithesis, as a basis for his subsequent dialectic. On the other hand, Locke's exposition is straightforward, involving a progression from a state of nature, to labor, to property, to ownership, to a civil state which protects property, etc. Hegel goes much deeper, to the ego which originates labor and which owns; yet that ego is paradoxical, since it is not the originator but the *result* of its acts of will.

Locke's picture is that of the rational primitive who discovers that there are things to be gotten through labor, and that these things must be protected by some human invention; the state is that invention. There is nothing problematic about the insight of this primitive individual. Hegel's dialectic, however, is not driven by anything so straightforward. Rather, Hegel's dialectic is driven by paradoxicality: it is the ego itself, in its self-relatedness, that is the engine of the dialectic. My self-relatedness is what gives me my sense of self, my sense of being complete in myself. It is a loop by means of which I have turned inward; that turn has a dimension of universality, for in turning back into myself I see what all human beings are. I am, therefore, an individual and at the same time a universal. I am, so to say, one of a kind – and one *and* a kind, a unit-class, solo yet complete.

Yet that very sense of self is incomplete, since my self begins to emerge only from my relation to the self which is also the *product* of my self-relation. Thus I would have an abstract right if I were a Lockean manager of my external world. But then my selfhood would still be far from established. My act of establishing it, now, is what propels my thoughts and rights in their paradoxicality. Let us examine the dialectics of this.

Social contract theorists – such as Hobbes and Locke – have

portrayed a "state of nature" with human occupants. Each of these is a fully formed ego, with a will which has all of the attributes of the humans *we* know. Such a primordial ego has a will which is free and universal (universal in the sense of representing all humanity). Hobbes and Locke regard their protagonist as psychologically complete, endowed with the various personal characteristics shared by the rest of us (although Hobbes and Locke differ diametrically in regard to what those "common" characteristics are). Hegel, on the other hand, regards that picture of the primal human as incomplete: Rousseau introduced the notion of that human as but half-human; Hobbes's and Locke's man is someone we would readily recognize; Hegel sees this creature as incomplete since he will only begin to define himself through his encounter(s) with others.

Prior to such encounter(s), therefore, the self is not yet in the process of self-formation, let alone the fully formed and recognizable product of that process. That self is abstract, so far. As Hegel says: "The universality of this consciously free will is abstract universality, the self-conscious but otherwise contentless and simple relation of itself to itself" (par. 35). Thus this is not a fully formed individual, but a case of bare self-relatedness, a purely formal narcissism – an abstraction.

From this perspective, it follows that such "rights" as are based on such an abstraction must be merely abstract rights as well. It may be that "in my finitude I know myself as something infinite, universal, and free," but these are still a "contentless" infinitude, universality, and freedom – i.e. not concretely real, but entirely abstract.

On the other hand, it is the very abstractness of these features that enables me to connect myself to others: for in acknowledging my personhood as the basis of my rights (however abstract that personhood and those rights), I grasp my link to others on the same basis. Thus, Hobbes and Locke see my need for personal security as my reason for entering into social relations; Hegel sees those relations emerging from a recognition of others as beings similar to myself. For this purpose he enunciates something like a Kantian imperative: "Be a person and respect others as persons" (par. 36). That is the basis of universality, to be sure. Yet that personhood is incomplete as long as it does not include my recognition of whatever it is that makes me a particular individual and unique. Over against the background of the universal, therefore, I become particularized. Over against the objectivity of the others who are there, I emerge as subjective (although this contradicts my own universality). Out of this struggle between the universal and the individual, and between the objective and the subjective, my own personality evolves (par. 39).

There are rights which I attach to myself on a subjective (i.e. infantile) basis: The world is *my* world, as Wittgenstein says. When I emerge out of my infantile solipsism, my rights take on an objective character, recognized by me as inherent in my very personhood. When I enter into a contract with another person, I implicitly recognize him or her *qua* person, and I am thus recognized in turn. The transfer of property from one to another serves as the medium of personhood.

Let us note how far we have come: i.e. from the rather primitive picture offered by Hobbes and Locke, of self-interested individuals desirous of securing what they have wrested from nature, to a far more ephemeral image of human beings engaged in the far more subtle activity of self-recognition, and from that recognition giving form to selfhood and ego, both in personal and societal terms.

The ego must turn its attention outward, by externalizing the self in some property. But the paradoxical feature of such a thing is that it is both an extension of the self, yet is separable from the self, both different from the self, yet the same. Moreover, a piece of property may be material and inert, and yet the very vehicle of selfhood. "A person has as this substantive end the right of putting his will into any and every thing . . . thereby making it his," Hegel says (par. 44). We may go even further and say that not only does a piece of property become *his*, it becomes *him*. Man puts himself, his will, into a thing – but, in turn, the thing may come to encompass his very self. Property is thus the *embodiment* of personality, involving not only my possession of property but also the recognition of it, as mine, by others (par. 51). This entails their recognition of my will in it. This is so fundamental a feature of ownership that we may say that the fact that a thing is recognized as mine makes the thing take on a character that is external to it.

There are dialectical elements in all this as well, and these elements, in their very contradictoriness, actually propel the dialectic into creating a social fabric. Thus the fact that a thing is *mine* (dependent on me) and also *it* (an object that is independent of me) can be said to raise difficulties which only a society can be called upon to resolve. This piece of earth is mine, although it exists as something on its own; but the opposite is also true, that its being mine becomes an external feature of the object. (Thus slavery, the ownership of a "living chattel," had to be sanctified by society; but when the time came for the abolition of slavery as an institution, only society could be expected to undertake that task.) Similar contradictions obtain with regard to my body as both mine and it; and the social fabric both sustains and dissolves this contradiction. Such contradictions account for the many-sided ambiguity in the use of terms such as "my body," "my person," "my self." In general, the ambiguities arise in the dialectics of those terms as reflecting the selfhood of the user. (Do I warm my "self" at the fire?)

With property, then, a fabric of recognitions emerges. That is to say, we may see society evolving around the mutual recognition of the property right. We might even say that Hegel regards property as the first step away from "abstract right" and into the creation of a social fabric, with "rights" moving in the direction of concreteness.

In discussing the alienation of property, i.e. giving it into the hands of another person, I can also alienate my time, my creativity or ability, etc. But Hegel points out – as Marx does in the section on alienated labor in his Paris Manuscripts of 1844 – that with this I am also alienating "the substance of my being . . . my personality" (par. 67). My product may cease to be strictly mine if someone copies what I have made, and uses it to express their own personality. We may also wonder whether, having put my will or ego into a thing, I must devalue myself when my product drops in value.

Since property involves a tacit agreement between the owner and all others (i.e. to respect the right of the owner), we may regard that relation as implicitly contractual. Now, whether I hold on to my property (and others respect it as such) or I do alienate it by transferring it to someone else, there is a conjunction of wills (for example, in regard to the sale price). Thus we have a conjunction of wills, but also a separation of wills, since each of us is out to serve our own interest by means of the transaction. Once again, we see property and the property relation leading both to a social configuration and to selfhood.

Although we have made mention of Hobbes and Locke, we are by no means proposing to consider Hegel as another social-contract theorist. Hegel does not speak of a social contract as anything like the formative nexus of society, the way they do. For him, society is based on a fabric of mutual recognition – and this is psychological and self-relating, rather than overtly contractual. A contract is therefore a reflection of such recognition, not the genesis of it. When Hegel does discuss the meaning of a contract, he is speaking quite literally of the way contractual relations actually function *in* a social setting; he is decidedly not speaking in a metaphorical sense of a social "contract" arranged prior to the formation of society and therefore the instrument of its formation. His primary aim is to examine the working of the wills of contracting parties. Thus, in the case of a contract for a sale or exchange, he says, value passes in both directions: the seller alienates their property, while the buyer appropriates it and (say) exchanges value for it. Value, therefore, remains as a constant throughout – always provided that there is a concurrence of wills: the seller asking a certain sum, the buyer agreeing to pay that sum (pars 76, 77).

The agreement of the two parties, the legality of their contract, the very notion of right – all these things are negated when the contract is broken or is fraudulent. Thus there is the appearance of legality and formal rightness – and obviously there could be no appearance of right without the implied background of rightness, legality, etc. This rightness is reasserted if the fraud is challenged as fraud, etc. (pars 82, 83).

What we see here is a further stage in Hegel's dialectic of society: a contract requires the concurrence of wills; one of those wills is now challenged, and the challenger asserts a claim on the basis of implicit right – which now becomes explicit – and thus may lead to a clash of rights. This clash is adjudicated on the basis of right, i.e. in the question as to who has the right to the property at issue. When the right is challenged, even when it is negated altogether, the right is in some way asserted, implicitly or explicitly.

This being so, the criminal must be regarded as acting inside the fabric of right, even when he or she violates the right of another (indeed, especially so). Here, Hegel brings out a strange result of this dialectic: namely, that the penalty which is meted out to the criminal is implicitly *his* will, an embodiment of his freedom, his right, even a right established with the criminal himself, Hegel says, so that the criminal's punishment is *his* act: "his action is the action of a rational being . . . [thus] the criminal has laid down a law which he explicitly recognized in his action and under which he should be brought as under his right" (par. 100). In crime, there is a conflict between a universal law (or universal will) which is implicit and a single will (that of the offender) which is explicitly independent. With punishment, the injury done is negated, the law is asserted, and the offender's freedom is secured (that is, in their having determined the law which asks for their punishment).

❧ MORALITY ❧

We have offered some observations about consciousness becoming self-conscious, turning back into itself. This self-consciousness is the key to a society's freedom and autonomy; and it is therefore the key to its morality as well. We might wish to say, superficially, that morality is the product of a society setting up rules for the behavior of its members. This need not necessarily be a self-conscious process. Indeed, we might compare societies for the degree of self-consciousness involved in their choice of values: some societies have managed to develop a set of mores without involving much thought in the process; others more so. But at its best – when a society is entirely conscious of what it is doing, so that it becomes self-reflecting, and examines its values in the light of other values, deeper ones, in an effort at making such values consistent and coherent – then such a society is closest to being fully in control of itself and of its destiny as it exercises its freedom in choosing the values by which it will live.

Let us recall Hegel saying that the self-consciousness of a culture is the goal of history, and this is its freedom. Thus the maturity associated with such freedom is the product of the will which has turned back into itself. In the individual person, such self-reflection is what makes that person the *subject* of their own will; the same holds true for a culture when it becomes the subject of *its* will (par. 105). It is a striking metaphor – whereby social change is presented as a maturation of the individual – yet it is but a metaphor, and thus it has its characteristic weaknesses. Hegel persists in using it – as when, in his *Philosophy of History*, he speaks of a society as though it were an individual growing up, becoming responsible, and so on.

The metaphor is used to its strongest effect in regard to morality. Now, we are not considering the growth of morality from primitive society to complex ones; nor is Hegel giving us a picture of primitive humans in action (as Hobbes and Locke do). Yet Hegel does concern himself with the intrinsic nature of moral values as such; and therefore he must concern himself with the question of how moral values as such; and therefore he must concern himself with the question of how moral values come into being (*as though* there were human beings engaged in creating values, à la Hobbes and Locke).

The point may be clarified methodologically: The analysis of moral values exposes their component elements; with these elements in view we may see how they fit together – as though someone had actually *put* them together, actually synthesized them. This returns us to the metaphor of the maturing individual, standing for the social mind in *its* development. It is a metaphor that prevails throughout Hegel's writing, even if he does not make that metaphor explicit at all points. Thus we can regard Hegel's account of morality as *genetic*, i.e. concerned with the *origin* of values in society (and in this respect he does resemble Hobbes and Locke, though only in an abstract and formal sense).

A further extension of the metaphor is reflected in Hegel's way of regarding morality as the creation of will: he addresses this concept as though it were the will of an individual person, although it is something like an abstract social will that is meant. This adds a further dimension to the dialectic of all this: namely, in that the will is something *subjective*, within the mentality of the individual, and yet its product is *objective*, in that it is given expression in the outer world of social values. Hegel can speak of the "self-determination of the will" in its subjective character (par. 107), yet he can pit against it the objectivity of the social will (par. 109).

It is the characteristic strategy of Hegel's, after setting up a dichotomy, to show the two sides to be identical. In the case of the subjectivity/objectivity dichotomy, this is precisely what he does when he speaks of the objectification of subjectivity. Each of us absorbs social values in our individual process of enculturation, and each of us makes those values private ones, as though each of us had created them for ourselves. It is in this light that we may say that there is therefore a private and a public will at work; it is my will at work, yet it is identical to the will of others (par. 112).

Further dichotomies are reflected in the fact that the subjectivity/objectivity stand-off is externalized (and thus is resolved) in activity, as well as in the fact that the values of the individual are those of the universal, i.e. the intention behind the action (par. 119). In transactions between individuals, it is the shared meaning of the universal that makes mutual understanding possible. The aim of all action is to produce good, or benefit – again, understood in universal terms. There can be benefit without right, or right without benefit – but neither of these is good (par. 130). Only in their combination is good realized. The subjective will sees its object(s) as good, and this is its prerogative, i.e. to judge its object(s) as being right or wrong, good or ill, legal or illegal, etc. (par. 132). But in all this the process of judging is still rather abstract, as Hegel suggests.

All this has the Kantian caste of universalizability – down to the element of duty (and it would be more Kantian still, if not for the genetic dimension of Hegel's account). Thus the objective side is eventually united with subjective knowing, so that the subjective is given expression in ethical life, where the abstractness of mere contentless morality is overcome (par. 137). At this stage, morality subsists in good intentions alone, and the good heart is taken to justify all (p. 99). Yet the objective good is lacking here. As for the identity of the two terms of the dichotomy, it is the identity of objective good with the subjective will that makes for concreteness. Hegel says that the identity of the two is the "truth" of each, and as such it constitutes the Ethical Life.

⚭ ETHICAL LIFE ⚭

From what we have seen of the Morality discussion, the component values were not yet complete. True, there was the element of universality, i.e. the humanity to which we all belong and which we share as humans. But this was still abstract as a value-element and had not yet been given concreteness in a social form. The thrust of Hegel's discussion, hereafter, will be to show that our *moral* values are a function of our *societal* arrangement, and of the way(s) our societal life is actually run.

Hegel will turn his attention to the most rudimentary form of societal life – the family – to show what values are implicit in it and, further, what values can be expected to emerge from it. Then he will go on to discuss civil society, to show some of the workings of the law and its management of justice. And finally, there will be an extended discussion of the state – as the highest (i.e. the most moral) operation of our shared life.

With Ethical Life, we enter into the institutional aspect of societal life. This may suggest the unconscious organic side; yet in Hegel's view it is that part of societal life reflecting self-conscious knowing and willing – i.e. freedom. There are values made concrete as an "objective ethical order" – with such objectivity transcending both the subjectivity of the individual and the mutability of social mores (par. 144). Indeed, the objectivity of these values exceeds (for the individual) the "authority" of nature.

From the very outset, the individual is in a secondary position vis-à-vis these life-regulating values, "as accidents to a substance" (par. 145). And yet, this ethical "substance" is not something external or alien to us, since it is the very element of our spirituality, amounting to a "second nature." As he says: "It is mind living and present as a world, and the substance of mind thus exists now for the first time as mind" (par. 151). This is objectified in institutions such as the family and the nation. It is here that rights and duties become reciprocal, so that having the one entails having the other.

The family is held together by bonds of love, despite the fact that (as a proto-state) its characteristic function is the exercise of power. In this light, the individual exists not as a totally independent entity but as a *member* (par. 158). This is why we may see the family as a state in embryonic form.

History is a process of the growth of freedom, the story of freedom (as we have seen). Hegel can therefore see each stage as mirroring the whole: just as marriage begins with the physical aspect and proceeds to the affirmation of love, so the cosmic process as a whole involves the transition from nature to Spirit. For Hegel, then, we may say that any and every segment of the historical process is the emblem for the entirety: at first, in the opposition between nature and Spirit; then in the transition from the individuality of the two persons to their unity as one (and in the process overcoming the transiency of love).

Monogamy is the essence of marriage, Hegel says, since it entails the total absorption of the individuals in the ethical bond. Thus the family itself becomes an "individual" – one whose personality is constituted by property (par. 169). This is also the basis for setting up further families in the newer generations. Just as the offspring become independent individuals, so do the new families, making their own transition from particularity to universality (par. 181). This transition culminates in civil society, wherein the ethical life of the family is absorbed in a broader context.

We may wish to find that broader context in the state, and to regard the state in terms of some of its services, such as water supply, the post, etc. For Hegel, all these necessary functions come under the heading of civil society. This is a subordinate classification, which allows Hegel to reserve the state for higher purposes: to serve as the vehicle of history, the medium of Spirit, etc.

In the most basic terms, civil society is a communal arrangement for the mutual satisfaction of our fundamental needs. An interesting question, therefore, asks what social values are implicitly attached to that arrangement: Does it lead us to give conscious acknowledgment to our interdependence, so that we actually come to regard society in that way? If so, then the mere understanding is at work: i.e. we grasp the meaning of civil society in its *particularity*, whereby individuals are concerned with their private interests alone. On the other hand, to grasp the essence of the state, we must appeal to reason, which is in touch with *universality*. In regard to the personal needs satisfied by civil society, mere understanding will suffice, with its focus on subjectivity and particularity. Civil society can therefore be regarded as a system of needs; the state, as we shall see, goes far beyond this.

To illuminate the system of needs (and their satisfaction) Hegel speaks of class organization in civil society: there is the agricultural class, the business class, and the universal class (i.e. the civil servants concerned with the needs of society at large). Through some measure of self-identification with the interests of the community, a morality is built up wherein one's wider responsibility is expressed, but where the closest one comes to a universality of interests is in the right to property.

The abstract right becomes objictified when we become *conscious* of its objictification. It becomes binding in our recognition of it as *law*. Obviously this cannot be enough: there are the ties established by positive law in regard to property in civil society; but there also are the ethical ties of the heart, of love and trust (par. 213). Since these ties touch us at the most private level, morals cannot be a matter of legislation. Laws do comprise a system – and, ideally, we ought to be able to expect such a system to fulfill the requirements of any system, namely, that the totality ought to exhibit consistency, coherence, and completeness. All this would come to a test when the universal principles are applied to particular individuals and cases. Here, too, law becomes objictified in our recognition of its objictification – primarily in regard to property and the infringement of the rights connected to it (par. 218).

When a crime is committed, it is the *universal* that is being injured, and when the law exacts its vengeance it goes beyond vengeance in the personal sense which is subjective and contingent. In punishment, an offense is annulled, the law is reconciled with itself. Accordingly, we may see in this an elevation of values to an objective and universal sense – a further reflection of the historical evolution of Spirit (par. 220).

The fact that the parties to a legal case have certain express rights, and that every legal case is established on the basis of argument and proof, also reflects the evolution of spirituality by way of the introduction of reason into public life. In this way, that public life is increasingly moralized – notwithstanding the fact that the legal process *can* turn into lethal formalities. Above all, the fact that a judge applies a universal standard to a single case reflects the process of the rational moralization of society as a whole (par. 225). (Thus we may say that the development of positive law is what enables us, by its example, to think in universal terms and thus to apply the thinking appropriate to, say, the categorical imperative.)

From all this, we might hastily conclude that all social progress is a moralizing process. We have pointed to some clear examples in this regard. Thus, in pointing to some rudimentary forms of social existence, Hegel speaks of the family as the "first ethical root of the state" (par. 255). The continuity is fundamentally ethical.

Civil society can be seen as largely efficacious in providing for society's basic needs. But Hegel also points to some inevitable weaknesses associated with civil society; and he is not far from Marx in this criticism – except for the difference that Hegel does not trace these weaknesses to capitalist production but to civil society itself. Thus there is poverty, massive unemployment, illiteracy, a disparate distribution of wealth, economic imperialism and the search for foreign markets, colonialism, etc. (pars 244–8) – ills which he includes under the rubric of "this inner dialectic of civil society" (par. 246).

Where Marx, however, would condemn the source (capitalism) for its results, Hegel merely sees them as by-products of the larger framework which is civil society. But where Marx sees that source as dissolvable in revolution – so that an industrial society would be made more moral by the removal of capitalism's antisocial and destructive effects on human beings – Hegel goes back to civil society and its broader perspective of the role of power. The primary purpose of public authority, he says, is "to actualize and maintain the universal contained within the particularity of civil society" (par. 249). A further difference, therefore, is that Marx sees true morality emerging in the negating of capitalism's effects, while Hegel sees morality emerging from the social and legal functioning of civil society itself – in its lawlike effect of universalizing human judgment within a framework of law.

∾ THE STATE ∾

All of Hegel's prior discussion has been leading up to his treatment of the state; and indeed, this is the culmination of his *Philosophy of Right*. But here a caution must be noted: the state is the continuation of civil society, yet it is different from it. (This tactic is consistent with his dialectic, where two adjacent areas form a continuum or identity by virtue of their difference from one another, and differ by virtue of their being identical.) Thus civil society is a collection of atomic individuals, each motivated by a private interest that excludes the interests of others; the state, on the other hand, is a collective entity wherein individuals fulfill their separate interests by merging them into the interests of the whole (much like the ideal of the Greek *polis*).

The libertarian tradition of Anglo-American thinking sees the individual as the most fundamental political entity; with this in mind, the state is seen as a device for serving the interests of individuals – and therefore the main stress is placed on the limits to be imposed on state power. Hegel, on the other hand, comes from a *holistic* tradition wherein state power is irreducible to the interests of individuals. The state is a higher entity – even something approaching the mystical – into which the goals of individual persons are to be dissolved. Let us recall Rousseau, who gives emphasis to a *volonté générale*, a consensus wherein all voices share; the libertarian tradition, on the other hand, must allow for a *dissensus* among its individual citizens.

As for the continuity between civil society and the state, this is to be seen in the different moral purposes to be served by each: i.e. the purposes of the individual as against those of the collective. Both are systems of value, existing tacitly in custom, and explicitly in the ideal of a rational self-consciousness. As Hegel says:

> The state is the actuality of the ethical Idea. It is ethical mind *qua* the substantial will manifested and revealed to itself, knowing and thinking itself, accomplishing what it knows and in so far as it knows it. The state exists immediately in custom, mediately in individual self-consciousness, knowledge, and activity, while self-consciousness – in virtue of its sentiment towards the state – finds in the state, as its essence and the end and product of its activity, its substantive freedom.
>
> (par. 257)

Presumably, since all this is reflective of a process *toward* rationality, such rational self-consciousness is not in the state's present, but only in its idealized future. And only when its implicit aim is fully realized – i.e. as "the actuality of the substantial will which it possesses in the particular self-consciousness once that consciousness has been raised to consciousness of its universality" – only then does the state exercise a supreme right over the individual. In other words, the fully realized aim is the right of the state *qua* Plato's *Republic* (nothing less), i.e. the state as "mind objectified" (par. 258). It is also freedom objectified in self-legislating consciousness, and thus closer to Kant's ethic.

At this point, the question that must present itself is this: How can a Platonic universal or a Kantian imperative, although fully rationalized, necessarily entail any socio-political modes common to a perfect state as such? In an Addition to par. 258, Hegel declares:

> The state in and by itself is the ethical whole, the actualization
> of freedom; and it is an absolute end of reason that freedom
> should be actual. The state is mind on earth . . . consciously
> realizing itself there. . . . Only when it is present in
> consciousness, when it knows itself as a really existent object,
> is it the state. . . . The march of God in the world, that is what
> the state is. The basis of the state is the power of reason
> actualizing itself as will. . . . In considering the Idea of the
> state, we must not have our eyes on particular states. . . . Instead
> we must consider the Idea, this actual God, by itself. . . . The
> state is no ideal work of art, it stands on earth and so in the
> sphere of caprice, chance and error, and bad behaviour may
> disfigure it in many respects. But the ugliest of men, or a
> criminal . . . is still always a living man. The affirmative, life,
> subsists despite his defects.
>
> (Addition, p. 279)

With this, we ought to stress the point that Hegel's Platonic/Kantian dimension is no piece of idle metaphysical theorizing; rather, it calls for a fully concrete realization of the essence of political life.

Up to now, what Hegel has said in regard to the state and its supremacy over all other interests has not seemed to contradict the widespread prejudice concerning his supposed sympathy for the totalitarian state. The point is, however, that Hegel does not leave it at that; instead, he clearly argues in favor of (a) the rule of law, (b) the fulfillment of the individual's goals through the political freedom that is guaranteed to the individual by means of a constitution, and (c) the absorption of particular interests into the universal.

Accordingly, it is in this light – i.e. in the light of an existing constitutional system – that Hegel says: "The state is the actuality of concrete freedom" (par. 260). Indeed, it is only by means of particular interests and actions that the universal is achieved. In civil society, the society stands opposed to the individual (who is usually seen in an adversarial position vis-à-vis society); with the state, we see the completion of the individual, and the fulfillment of their most private concerns in and through the social. Nothing less than this can be regarded as a proper state in Hegel's sense.

We may ask, therefore: How is the individual to find a personal fulfillment in a state? Only in the union of the individual with the universal can this be achieved – a union of public and private interests, such that the public interest is that which is closest to the individual's heart. The *polis* alone provided the framework that made such an identity possible, and thinkers such as Rousseau and Hegel have been searching ever since for ways to make it real.

Accordingly, the two polar elements – namely, the public interest and the private interest – comprise an antithesis that demands resolution in a higher synthesis. It is the state that provides such a synthesis – i.e. by offering the individual their personal fulfillment in the state, as well as that very concern as embodied in the words of Hegel's Preface: "What is rational is actual; what is actual is rational." We can now see this for the tautology that it is: When the term *wirklich* is translated as "real," we have some suggestion of the Platonic realism to which Hegel is sometimes prone, though not fully committed; but when we translate *wirklich* as "actual," we have the Aristotelian *entelechy* to which Hegel is fully committed in his notion of development.

Thus Plato seeks the perfect form of the state in its pure and unchanging permanence; Aristotle's emphasis, on the contrary, is on the dynamism of the historical state in its *becoming*. The state is not a finished entity but a process: its *telos* is its *arche*, its end is in its beginning. If we can see duty and right as a dualism of reciprocal entailment (so that where there is one there is the other), we will have grasped Hegel's concept in a nutshell. He stresses this point as being of vital importance, as the source of the state's "inner strength" (par. 261, p. 162).

In civil society the antithesis (of public vs private) is of a limited nature. But when these are resolved (i.e. absorbed) in a higher synthesis, they become "the firm foundation not only of the state but also of the citizen's trust in it" (par. 265). This involves, further, the unification of the opposed realms of freedom and necessity. Thus my personal interest is both preserved and negated (*aufgehoben*) in the state, and this organic unity is, as Hegel says, "the constitution of the state" (par. 269). It should be pointed out that the term "constitution," here, does not refer to a document, or a set of laws (written or unwritten), but is to be taken as the organizing principle(s) of a state, that by which it is constituted. This organizing principle, then, is the nascent reason inhering in the state. It is in this special light, therefore, that Hegel can say: "The state is the divine will, in the sense that it is mind present on earth, unfolding itself to be the actual shape and organization of a world" (par. 270, p. 166).

The task of civilization, over the centuries, has been the transfer of the inner into the outer, "the building of reason into the real world" (par. 270, p. 167). In the modern world, this manifestation of reason in the political has involved "the development of the state to constitutional monarchy" (par. 273, p. 176). Since all this is happening to *reason*, the diremption of that process has occurred to the universal, the particular, and the individual – not as abstract and empty categories, but as the actual legislature, the executive, and the monarch, respectively.

Hegel points to the development of the state to constitutional monarchy as "the achievement of the modern world," and the "inner deepening of the world mind." There is a greater complexity here, whether in the mind of the individual or even in that of the cosmos. This has the consequence of producing diremption, polarization, conflict, and dialectic. Indeed, it is the developing complexity of mental and political life that actually fuels the engines of change and progress. Without such conflict, nothing much would be happening, and certainly no historical advance.

Hegel suggests that the constitution of the state (i.e. its actual organization) is not to be regarded as "made" by humans, but as *sui generis* or (as he likes to put it) "divine" (par. 273, p. 178). His reasoning is peculiarly Feuerbachian (although Feuerbach published his work two decades after Hegel published his *Philosophy of Right*): Anything regarded as having been made by humans can as easily be regarded as capable of being unmade by humans; only by being seen as "divine" does it retain its measure of authority over humans and beyond change.

This must surely introduce a measure of schizophrenia into the body politic (or the mental equivalent of that metaphor): i.e. the difference between the process of opening our political life to increased rationality and the closing of that rationality for the sake of myth. Political maturity (whether in the individual or in the state) involves a coming-to-self-consciousness; and in the light of this, the deliberate self-delusion that prompts us to see the state as "divine" is a piece of counter-rationality that cannot be expected to thrive. Why is this?

One thinks here of Marx's Feuerbachian Paris Manuscripts: With regard to the institution of monarchy (or, equally, the capitalist system), can one actually "tell" oneself that this is *not* an institution made by humans – and believe it? Rather, to take that step in the direction of demythologization, and to regard any institution as man-made, is to start on the road to dismantling it, denying its superhuman authority.

Yet the Crown embodies the element of subjectivity, although this is condensed into the individual human being. To say, "The state decides," is as much as to say "The Crown decides" – but for the fact that in Hegel the crown has the limited authority of a constitutional monarch. Implicitly, the Crown combines its three component elements: the legislative power embracing the universality of the constitution and its laws; the adjudication which subsumes single cases under the universal through the power of the executive; and the power of ultimate decision by way of the self-determination in which the subjectivity of just such determinations are made (pars 273, 275). Nevertheless, the element of self-delusion (as when we say, with the ritualism of the law court, "The state versus . . ." or "The Crown versus . . .") is all too easily dispelled, once seen – and once this is grasped we can hardly resist the inclination to demythologize all our social myths, everywhere and on all sides.

This leads us into the most troubling – and controversial – part of Hegel's entire political edifice, that of the monarch. There is hardly a philosopher who is more of a rationalist; but while this entails the dissipation of myths, we ought not to overlook Hegel's profound respect for myths and their social purpose. In this respect Hegel is the tool of his own myth-making, and this is reflected in his theorizing on kingship. One might wonder why a monarch should be needed at all in Hegel's state, given Hegel's emphasis on constitutionalism and the rule of law. Further, one might ask why a monarch is needed, as Hegel says, to embody the element of subjectivity in the state, or why that subjectivity should need to be *embodied* at all.

Perhaps this is a result of Hegel's pervasive metaphor in all this: If history can be seen as a process wherein the state (as "mind") comes to self-awareness, to maturity and freedom, then that so-called "mind" would certainly require a subjective dimension for its completion.

But must we stay with that metaphor? (Since the main point of history is that it is to be compared to a mind "growing up," we may call it Hegel's "educational metaphor" of the state.) As a metaphor, it has its uses: the state, immersed in time, is necessarily dynamic in its process – just as human individuals are in their endless movement toward a *telos*. That *telos* holds out the hope of progress in history – i.e. human individuals learning from experience. (As Dewey says, experience doesn't merely exist, it *teaches*.) The state, in its various efforts to reconcile its inner contradictions, is what produces this human thrust into the future. The state thereby fulfills the potentialities embodied in the perennial human condition. (Here is the educational metaphor once again.) In so doing, the state can be said to *learn* through time, to improve on its own enlargement, etc. – in effect, to provide the equivalent of a *secular* salvation.

Yet the ubiquitous metaphor is hardly convincing when Hegel, as we saw, speaks of something as dubious as a World-Spirit (*Weltgeist*) coming to self-awareness. He is stuck with the metaphor; we are not. Here is where the monarch comes in: as a concept, the monarch serves to flesh out the metaphor, yet it does little more than leave it in its abstract form; *in concreto*, however, it provides the subjective aspect that a *Geist* ("mind" or "Spirit") would need in order for us to understand it.

The monarch, then, enables *us* to address the metaphor, to question it and to demand that it explain itself and account for itself. Clearly, the figure of the monarch can (in principle) be addressed in this way, while the state cannot (so that we cannot literally speak of the state's "purposes," etc.) because it is entirely impersonal.

Yet the state, as something mental (i.e. spiritual, non material), is the bearer of a "soul," an identity (Addition to par. 275, p. 287). As such it may be seen as "sovereign" over all its component elements, and containing all differences in itself. As the "soul" can be said to unify its disparate elements, so the sovereign performs a similar function by containing all differences itself. Indeed, without a monarch, Hegel says, a people is but a "formless mass" (par. 279, p. 183). As a totality, the state is an organic whole of which the monarch is the "personality."

But here a further contradiction enters, stemming from Hegel's view of the state as the embodiment of reason – i.e. reason objectified: "The state is mind fully mature and it exhibits its moments in the daylight of consciousness" (p. 283). If so, then objectified reason must reflect the realm of the immutable and be unchanging; yet states do change. If it is "the way of God with the world" that there should be states, can the state be regarded as being the effect of temporal forces? To be sure, the person of the monarch is the effect of natural forces, as *this* individual; but the state itself is a nonnatural entity, designed to serve a higher-then-natural purpose. As such, the "immediate individuality" of the monarch must be irrelevant to the state's inherent rationality. And if individuality is the synthesis of the universal and the particular, cannot the state itself be such an individual in its sovereignty, i.e. without a king?

*

Hegel is one segment of the long tradition of visionary philosophers who (beginning with Plato) have sought to introduce reason into the concept of the political world. What we must realize, with Hegel, is that that vision is to be taken as a totality, in which its prismatic elements combine to form a unity wherein those elements are merely *seen* as individual but are actually unified. As he says:

In the state, self-consciousness finds in an organic development the actuality of its substantive knowing and willing; in religion, it finds the feeling and the representation of this its own truth as an ideal essentiality; while in philosophic science, it finds the free comprehension and knowledge of this truth as one and the same in its mutually complementary manifestations, i.e. in the state, in nature, and in the ideal world.

(par. 360)

❧ NOTES ❧

1 *The Oxford Dictionary of Quotations* ascribes the remark to a certain Alphonse Karr (1808–90) in *Les Guêpes* (Jan. 1849).
2 R.C. Solomon, "Hegel's Concept of *Geist*," *Review of Metaphysics*, 23 (1970): 647; see also R.C. Solomon, *In the Spirit of Hegel* (New York: Oxford University Press, 1983), p. 197.
3 Numbers refer to paragraphs in Hegel's *Philosophy of Right*.

❧ SELECT BIBLIOGRAPHY ❧

Original language editions

8.1 Hegel, G.W.F. *Grundlinien der Philosophie des Rechts*, ed. E. Moldenhauer and K.M. Michel, Frankfurt/Main: Suhrkamp, 1970.
8.2 —— *Phänomenologie des Geistes*, ed. J. Hoffmeister, Hamburg: Meiner, 1952.
8.3 —— *Schriften zur Politik und Rechtsphilosophie*, ed. G. Lasson, Leipzig: Meiner, 1923.
8.4 —— *Gesammelte Werke*, ed. Rheinisch-Westfälischen Akademie der Wissenschaften, Hamburg: Meiner, 1968–.
8.5 —— *Sämtliche Werke*, 20 vols, ed. H. Glockner, *Jubiläumsausgabe*, Stuttgart: Frommann, 1927–40.
8.6 —— *Sämtliche Werke*, ed. J. Hoffmeister, Hamburg: Meiner, 1952–60.

English translations

8.7 *Hegel's Philosophy of Right*, trans. T.M. Knox, Oxford and London: Oxford University Press, 1952, pbk 1967.
8.8 Hegel, G.W.F. *The Philosophy of History*, trans. J. Sibree, New York: Wiley, 1956.
8.9 —— *Introduction to the Philosophy of History*, trans. L. Rauch, Indianapolis: Hackett, 1988.
8.10 —— *The Phenomenology of Spirit*, trans. A.V. Miller, Oxford: Oxford University Press, 1977.
8.11 —— *Encyclopaedia of the Philosophical Sciences*, Part III: *Hegel's Philosophy*

of Mind, trans. W. Wallace and A.V. Miller, Oxford: Clarendon Press, 1971.

8.12 —— *Political Writings*, trans. T.M. Knox, Oxford: Clarendon Press, 1962; see "The German constitution."

Bibliographies

8.13 Steinhauer, K. (ed.) *Hegel: An International Bibliography*, Munich: Verlag Dokumentation, 1978; contains 13,400 entries, from Hegel's first work to publications on him in 1973.

Extensive bibliographies are also to be found in:

8.14 Inwood, M.J. *Hegel*, London: Routledge & Kegan Paul, 1983.
8.15 Taylor, C. *Hegel*, Cambridge: Cambridge University Press, 1975.

Influences

8.16 Harris, H.S. *Hegel's Development*, Vol. I: *Towards the Sunlight, 1770–1801*, Oxford: Clarendon Press, 1972; Vol. II: *Night Thoughts, 1801–1806*, Oxford: Clarendon Press, 1983.
8.17 Hook, S. *From Hegel to Marx*, New York: Humanities Press, 1950.
8.18 G. Lukács, *The Young Hegel*, trans. R. Livingstone, Cambridge, Mass.: MIT Press, and London: Merlin Press, 1975.

General surveys

8.19 Findlay, J.N. *Hegel: A Re-Examination*, London: Allen & Unwin, and New York: Oxford University Press, 1958.
8.20 Haym, R. *Hegel und Seine Zeit*, Hildesheim: Ohm, 1962.
8.21 Kaufmann, W. (ed.) *Hegel's Political Philosophy*, New York: Atherton, 1970.
8.22 Löwith, K. *From Hegel to Nietzsche*, trans. D.E. Green, New York: Holt, Rinehart & Winston, 1964; London: Constable, 1965; Garden City: Doubleday Anchor, 1967.
8.23 Marcuse, H. *Reason and Revolution: Hegel and the Rise of Social Theory*, Boston: Beacon, 1960.
8.24 *The Monist*, 48, 1 (Jan. 1964): Hegel Today issue.
8.25 Mure, G.R.G. *An Introduction to Hegel*, Oxford: Clarendon Press, 1939.
8.26 Reyburn, H.A. *The Ethical Theory of Hegel: A Study of the Philosophy of Right*, Oxford: Clarendon Press, 1967.
8.27 Stace, W.T. *The Philosophy of Hegel*, New York: Dover, 1955.

Specific topics

8.28 Avineri, S. *Hegel's Theory of the Modern State*, Cambridge: Cambridge University Press, 1974.

8.29 Foster, M.B. *The Political Philosophies of Plato and Hegel*, Oxford: Clarendon Press, 1935.

8.30 Hyppolite, J. *Studies on Marx and Hegel*, London: Heinemann, 1969.

8.31 Inwood, M.J. (ed.) *Hegel*, Oxford Readings in Philosophy, Oxford: Oxford University Press, 1985.

8.32 Kelly, G.A. *Idealism, Politics and History*, Cambridge: Cambridge University Press, 1969.

8.33 —— "Notes on Hegel's 'Lordship and Bondage'," *Review of Metaphysics*, XIX, (1966).

8.34 Kojéve, A. *An Introduction to the Readings of Hegel*, New York & London: Basic Books, 1969; a Marxist reading.

8.35 MacIntyre, A.C. (ed.) *Hegel: A Collection of Critical Essays*, New York: Doubleday, 1972.

8.36 O'Brien, G.D. *Hegel on Reason and History*, Chicago and London: University of Chicago Press, 1975.

8.37 Pelczynski, Z.A. (ed.) *Hegel's Political Philosophy: Problems and Perspectives*, Cambridge: Cambridge University Press, 1971; see esp. K. Ilting, "The Structure of Hegel's *Philosophy of Right*," and Z.A. Pelczynski, "The Hegelian Conception of the State."

8.38 —— *The State and Civil Society: Studies in Hegel's Political Philosophy*, Cambridge: Cambridge University Press, 1984.

8.39 Plamenatz, J. *Man and Society*, Vol. 2, London: Longman, 1963.

8.40 Rauch, L. *The Political Animal: Studies in Political Philosophy from Machiavelli to Marx*, Amherst: University of Massachusetts Press, 1981.

8.41 Ritter, J. *Hegel and the French Revolution*, Cambridge, Mass.: MIT Press, 1982.

8.42 Sabine, G.H. and Thorson, T.L. *A History of Political Theory*, Hinsdale, Ill.: Dryden Press, 1973.

8.43 Solomon, R.C. *In the Spirit of Hegel*, Oxford: Oxford University Press, 1983.

8.44 Strauss, L. and Cropsey, J. (eds) *History of Political Philosophy*, Chicago and London: University of Chicago Press, 1963.

8.45 Taylor, C. *Hegel and Modern Society*, Cambridge: Cambridge University Press, 1979.

8.46 Wilkins, B.T. *Hegel's Philosophy of History*, Ithaca: Cornell University Press, 1974.

CHAPTER 9
The Young Hegelians, Feuerbach, and Marx
Robert Nola

Largely through lectures delivered at the University of Berlin, Hegel built up a circle of followers, mainly contemporaries or pupils, who were intent on working out aspects of the philosophical system that their master had suggested but left undeveloped. After Hegel's death in 1831 this circle, later dubbed "the Old Hegelians," became the core of a group of philosophers whose task was to put the finishing touches to the Hegelian philosophical edifice. Though there were during Hegel's lifetime external critics of his philosophy, especially his theology, the work of his close associates was directed toward establishing the unity of his system rather than exposing its inner tensions. True to its dialectical character, Hegel's philosophy did contain contradictory tendencies which if taken too far would transform the apparent unity of his system into a clash of opposites. When "the Young Hegelians" emerged in the mid-1830s, they exploited in various ways these contradictory tendencies, thereby dissolving the unity of Hegel's system and bringing about what Marx called "the putrescence of the absolute spirit."

Though his followers were not united on every aspect of Hegel's philosophy, after his death the differences between them became more marked, first in theology then in political theory. Latent divisions became open disputes when the 27-year-old David Friedrich Strauss published his *The Life of Jesus Critically Examined* in 1835–6, thereby breaking with Hegel over matters to do with religion and philosophy. Strauss (1808–74), who had attended some of Hegel's lectures just before his death, differed markedly from his master over the role which was to be assigned to the Gospels and to the life of Jesus within speculative theology.

While Hegel did not pay much attention to the actual details of the life of Christ and the historicity of the Gospels, he did think that the basic tenets of Christianity, found in the doctrine of the Trinity and expressed in historical events such as the Incarnation, the Ascension, the Creation, and the Fall, could be given an independent philosophical foundation. There would be no need to appeal, for example, to miracles or to historical evidence to establish Christian doctrine. For Hegel the very content of Christianity is identical with the content of Hegelian philosophy, though the form of each is different. The difference in form is the difference between *Vorstellung* (representation) and *Begriff* (concept). In the case of the philosophical *Begriff*, Hegelian philosophy gives us the absolute content of Christianity in the form of pure thought, or as a "deduction" from pure thought. In the case of the *Vorstellung*, popular Christianity with its dogmas deals in pictorial or representational imagery or in figurative thought. These images are not logically particular, as are our sensuous experiences of our mental imagery, but are alleged to be of universal significance; aspects of pure thought contained in such imagery are to be made explicit within Hegelian philosophical theology.

During his time as a vicar in 1830–1 Strauss became acutely aware of this difference of form; the popular religious *Vorstellung* of his parishioners seemed far removed from the religious *Begriff* of the Hegelian philosopher-theologian. While not abandoning the latter, Strauss delved more into the former, particularly the historical genesis of the ideas of Christianity among its earliest devotees. This in turn led to a close study of the life of Jesus and the manner in which this was presented in biblical texts. When *The Life of Jesus* was finally published most of it was devoted to a densely argued critical examination of the historicity of the Gospels – with only a little devoted to philosophy and speculative theology.

The startling result of Strauss's research was that even though there was an historical Christ there was little that we could regard as true of him. Instead most of the biblical stories about him were to be understood as myths, constructed not by individuals but by the earliest Christian communities in response to the teaching of Christ and the Messianic tradition which they had inherited from the Old Testament. For Strauss an "*evangelical mythus* [is] a narrative relating directly or indirectly to Jesus, which may be considered not as the expression of a fact, but as the product of an idea of his earliest followers."[1]

Earlier theologians had accounted for much of the Old Testament in terms of myth. Strauss, who drew on their work, was one of the first to extend the mythical account to much that had previously passed as literal truth in the four Gospels and the rest of the New Testament. Though his mythical account of the Gospels still remains contentious, Strauss's critical work on their historicity stands at the beginning of the modern tradition of scholarly and scientific study of the New

Testament. For Strauss the Hegelian theologian, the important consequence of his research was that there was no longer any identity
between Hegelian philosophy and the Christian religion. Hegel's philosophical theology still remained correct, but if the stories of the Gospels
were no longer historical truths but myths, then there is nothing in
the actual history of Christianity for Hegelian theology to capture and
the theology stands quite independently. As Strauss says in the Preface
to the First German Edition:

> The author is aware that the essence of the Christian faith is
> perfectly independent of his criticism. The supernatural birth of
> Christ, his miracles, his resurrection and ascension, remain
> eternal truths, whatever doubts may be cast on their reality as
> historical facts.[2]

At the end of his book Strauss also made another highly contentious claim: since God and man have the same essence, viz., spirit,
then they are not genuinely distinct, and thus humanity is divine.
Strauss even allowed himself to talk of the God-man as an expression
of this unity.[3] The argument for the identity is a bad one; the Young
Hegelians were not, on the whole, sensitive to the logical faults in their
arguments. However, the rejection of a transcendent God and the
identification of God with man underline the extreme humanism that
characterized not only Strauss's thought but the thought of all the
Young Hegelians.

The conclusion of Strauss's investigations would have been, at the
time of their publication, sensational enough for ordinary believers.
The notoriety of his book was such that Strauss was prevented from
ever obtaining a permanent university position in Germany. The reaction of his fellow Hegelians was also sensational; many rejected his
interpretation of the Bible and came to doubt his Hegelian orthodoxy.
In reply to their criticism in his "Controversial Writings"[4] Strauss
divided the Hegelians into the Right, Center, and Left – his model
being the various political factions in the French National Assembly.
The Right Hegelians, also called "Old Hegelians," tended to conserve
as much of the doctrines of their master as possible, particularly the
old doctrine of the unity of Hegelian philosophy with the historical
truth of Christianity. The Right included such people as the old
defender of Hegel against earlier criticisms, Karl Friedrich Göschel
(1784–1861); the successor to Hegel's chair of philosophy in Berlin,
Georg Andreas Gabler (1786–1853); and, very briefly, the young Bruno
Bauer (1809–82). The Center included people such as Karl Rosenkranz
(1805–79) who accepted most of what Strauss claimed about Christ
and the Gospels but who insisted, contrary to Strauss, that Christ, not
humanity as a whole, was divine. (It was Rosenkranz who published

in 1840 a comic drama about the dissolution of Hegel's School after his death.)[5] Strauss's supporters were on the Left – the Left Hegelians. This division of reactions to Strauss's work persisted even when other Left Hegelians subsequently developed their own critiques of Christianity in ways different from Strauss's mythological explanations.

Karl Ludwig Michelet (1801–93), a Center Hegelian who was in other respects sufficiently orthodox to be one of a panel whose task was to edit the works of Hegel, suggested that there was enough in common between the Center and the Left to make the distinction unnecessary. But this initial attempt to overcome one of the divisions among the Hegelians failed to touch the major division. The differences deepened when the terms "Old (i.e. Right) Hegelians" and "Young (i.e. Left) Hegelians" became a common mode of designation for the two factions in the late 1830s[6] – though such a bipartite division simplifies in many respects the complex relationships that existed among German philosophers in the two decades after Hegel's death. As Karl Löwith says of the Old Hegelians who eschewed any radical philosophical innovation:

> They preserved Hegel's philosophy literally, continuing it in individual historical studies, but they did not reproduce it in a uniform manner beyond the period of Hegel's personal influence. For the historical movement in the nineteenth century they are without significance.[7]

The Young Hegelians were more radical; they dared explore innovatively Hegel's philosophy for their own time, rejecting aspects of it as they saw fit.

The important Young Hegelians, some of whom had attended Hegel's lectures at the University in Berlin, include: Arnold Ruge (1802–80); Ludwig Feuerbach (1804–72); Max Stirner (1806–56); David Strauss (1808–74); Bruno Bauer (1809–82) and his younger brother Edgar Bauer (1820–86); Moses Hess (1812–75); August von Cieszkowski (1814–94); Karl Marx (1818–83); and Friedrich Engels (1820–95). As their dates indicate, they were all born within the first two decades of the nineteenth century, and most, if Engels and Marx are excluded, were born in the first decade. Despite appearances the Old/Young distinction is not based on age since many contemporaries of the Young Hegelians were sufficiently philosophically orthodox to be grouped with the Old Hegelians (e.g. Rosenkranz and Michelet). Nor should it be assumed that the Left/Right distinction carries its standard political connotations. Rosenkranz, who was active in politics, adopted a liberal rather than a reactionary stance despite his identification with the Old Hegelians. In contrast, even though Strauss's views on religion were radical, he was conservative politically, especially in the period leading up to the revolutions of 1848 when he became involved (on the whole unsuccessfully) in practical politics.[8] In fact in the 1840s, even though Strauss's *Life of Jesus* was still an important work for unorthodox Hegelians, he ceased to be a leading Young Hegelian as the focus of the criticism of Hegel shifted from his speculative theology to his social and political theory.

Given the close alliance in the Germany of the time between religion and state, any criticism of religion inevitably brought in its train conflict with the state. For this reason alone none of the Young Hegelians were able to obtain permanent teaching positions in German universities and their work was often subject to the scrutiny of the censor. For many of the Young Hegelians their critique of religion in the late 1830s laid the ground for a critique of the state in the 1840s – though few took the bold approach of Marx and Engels in finally jettisoning much of the Hegelian theory of the state and in supporting revolutionary movements. The political and social changes in Germany in the 1830s and 1840s did shape some of the differences between the Old and the Young Hegelians. Löwith makes a suggestive point when he says that the divisions between Old and Young Hegelians can be traced back to Hegel's dictum that "the real is the rational and the rational is the real."[9] The conservative Old Hegelians put emphasis on the first part of this dictum, thereby supporting the status quo, viz., that the real existing state is also rational. In contrast the more radical Young Hegelians put emphasis on the second half of the dictum, viz., currently existing conditions were irrational and would have to be transformed so that in the future the real would be the rational (a view quickly adopted by Marx and Engels). In respect of this dictum Hegel himself was more of an Old than a Young Hegelian.

The Young Hegelian movement began after the European revolutions of 1830, reached its zenith in the early 1840s, and was over by the 1848 revolutions. Frederick-William IV, who ascended the Prussian throne in 1840, had the support of many of the Young Hegelians who looked forward to the reform of the bureaucratic Prussian state and to greater participation of a broader range of people in public life. Initially the Young Hegelians benefited from the relaxation of censorship and the creation of a freer press which allowed their ideas to gain wider circulation. But this was short-lived for by the end of 1842 the radical press had been suppressed and the monarch began to move Prussia in the direction of a conservative Christian state. For the Young Hegelians who had criticized received conceptions of religion and whose political thought was, in several cases, strongly influenced by the ideals of the French Revolution, this was a move in the opposite direction from the constitutional democracy which many favored.

It is thus not surprising that some of the Young Hegelians turned to a critique of Hegel's political and social theory. Among the first of these critics was Arnold Ruge whose "Hegel's *Philosophy of Right* and the Politics of Our Times" appeared in August 1842 in the *Deutscher Jahrbücher* which he edited. Ruge argued that there was a deep-seated contradiction between the theory of the state which Hegel developed and the actual state in which he existed. As he put the matter: "The abstract inwardness of Protestantism did not free even Hegel from the illusion that one could be theoretically free without being politically free."[10] According to Ruge this raised for Hegel an ethical question which had previously haunted Kant, viz., even though one should not state falsely what one believes, should one create controversy by publicly disclosing all of what one truly believes? In Ruge's view it might have been diplomatic for Hegel not to have publicly aired all that he thought. He commented: "If Hegel had been presented with an opportunity to stand up for his theory, his times would have had to have turned against him, as happened with Kant."[11] Even though during his lifetime Hegel's philosophical theories, including his theory of the state, had the support of the Prussian government, Ruge pointedly observed that Hegel passed over the contradiction between his theory and the actual Prussian state without acknowledgment.

Ruge also complained that

> Hegel undertook to present the hereditary monarch, the majority, the bicameral system, etc., as *logical necessities*, whereas it had to be a matter of establishing all of these as products of history and of explaining and criticizing them as *historical existences*.[12]

In Ruge's view there is a place both for the philosophical discussion of the purposes and aims of the state and for the historical (and social) investigation of any form of government. However, one should not conflate historical and logical categories. Ruge goes to the heart of his difficulty with Hegel's *Philosophy of Right* when he says: "[Hegel] wrenches the state out of history and considers all of its historical forms only under logical categories (thus, right from the start the categories of universality, specificity, and singularity are employed again and again)."[13] Ruge's complaint was to be repeated later by Marx.

In February 1844 Ruge published in the *Deutsch-Französische Jahrbücher* Marx's own critique of German philosophy and the German state in an article entitled "A Contribution to the Critique of Hegel's '*Philosophy of Right*': introduction." This was only part of a much longer paragraph-by-paragraph critique of Hegel's *Philosophy of Right* which Marx had written in the previous year and which he had intended to revise for publication; the surviving sections of this critique first saw the light of day only in 1927.[14] Though the published "Introduction" does not contain any detailed criticism of Hegel of the sort found in the unpublished drafts, Marx does use some Hegelian notions when, for the first time, he proclaims that the proletariat is the class whose revolution will bring about the emancipation of humanity.

For Marx the proletariat is a part of what Hegel had called "civil society"; at the time Marx was writing it was just beginning to emerge in Germany with the rise of industrial development. For Hegel civil society is the sphere of private interest in which each person pursues their own ends often in conflict with others; in contrast the state is that sphere in which the clash of private interests is transcended and there is unity and universality of interest. Whatever defects there may be in actual states, Hegel says in the Preface to his *Philosophy of Right*: "This book, then, containing as it does the science of the state, is to be nothing other than the endeavour to apprehend and portray the state as something inherently rational."[15] In criticizing Hegel, Marx sets out to show: there is no separation of the sort Hegel envisages between civil society and the state; the falsity of Hegel's supposition that in the state there is rationality and unity; and universality of interest masks the fact that in actual states the interests of one particular group dominate within civil society.

Though Hegel recognizes that there are various groups within society, such as civil servants, an agricultural class, an industrial/commercial class, etc., the notion of the proletariat developed in Marx's critique of Hegel is distinctively Marx's own – but without the theoretical depth that his later economic analyses would give the notion. However, the genesis of Marx's notion of the proletariat does have its roots in Hegel's notion of a universal class, i.e. a class whose interests are supposedly those of society as a whole. Marx rejects Hegel's idea that the universal class might be the class of civil servants or the bureaucracy. He also claims that Hegel's attempt to reconcile the differences between civil society and the state is misplaced; instead the historical role of the proletariat is to abolish the very ground which makes these differences possible. In answer to the self-posed question "Where is the positive possibility of a German emancipation?" Marx replies that it lies

> In the formation of a class with *radical chains*, a class of civil society which is not a class of civil society . . . a sphere which has a universal character by its universal suffering . . . a sphere, finally, which cannot emancipate itself without emancipating itself from all other spheres of society and thereby emancipating all other spheres of society, which, in a word, is the *complete loss* of man and hence can win itself only through the *complete*

rewinning of man. This dissolution of society as a particular estate is the *proletariat*.

(*MECW*, 3: 186)[16]

The future evolution of the proletariat is also described in the "Introduction" in terms of Hegel's dialectic – the one prominent feature of Hegelian thought that Marx never abandoned. Marx speaks of the proletariat "demanding *the negation of private property*." For the proletariat private property is "the *secret of its own existence*"; by calling for its abolition the proletariat undermines the very condition that makes its own existence possible. Thus the quite thoroughgoing nature of the social transformation that Marx envisages, viz., "the *dissolution of the hitherto existing world order*" (*MECW*, 3: 187). Marx's notion of the proletariat thus has its origin both in a critique of speculative Hegelian political theory and in Marx's observation of the social changes taking place within Germany at the time. Much later when writing *Capital*, Marx found a more secure basis for his views about the proletariat in his economic theory; they are the means whereby surplus value is created. But, as chapter 32 of *Capital 1* shows, Marx still maintained that the future evolution of the proletariat was best described using the notions of the Hegelian dialectic.

It was through Arnold Ruge's activities as an editor and publisher that many of the ideas of the Young Hegelians found a public outlet. In 1837 he started the highly influential *Hallische Jahrbücher für deutsche Wissenschaft und Kunst*. Owing to the pressure of censorship Ruge shifted to Dresden in 1841 and continued the journal under the new name *Deutsche Jahrbücher für Wissenschaft und Kunst*. However, early in 1843 even this journal was suppressed, along with Marx's daily newspaper *Rheinische Zeitung*. In 1844 a similar fate befell the *Allgemeine Literatur-Zeitung*, started by Bruno and Edgar Bauer in Berlin in the previous year, thus ending the sequence of journals that had been the main public vehicle for Young Hegelian thought. These journals helped give the Young Hegelian movement a semblance of identity. Their end was only partly due to censorship; by 1845 the movement itself had lost whatever unity it might have possessed and much of its impetus.

The Berlin wing of the Young Hegelians, also known as Die Freien, had its origin in the Doktorenklub, a group formed at the University of Berlin in 1837 for the discussion of radical Hegelian ideas (it was in this group that Marx became acquainted with Hegelian philosophy). The leading member of Die Freien was Bruno Bauer. As a student he had attended Hegel's lectures and had been deemed sufficiently orthodox to be asked to defend the Right Hegelian position against Strauss's *Life of Jesus*. Soon after reviewing the book Bauer was converted to its general themes and took an even more radical position than Strauss on Christianity; he became an atheist, arguing in several works that not only was there no historical truth to be found in the Gospels but Christianity was a barrier to progress and it was an irrational doctrine that ought to be opposed.

Bauer's subsequent dismissal from his university position became a *cause célèbre* for the Young Hegelians during the early 1840s. With little to lose Bauer wrote an ironic attack on Hegelian philosophy in an 1841 pamphlet, *The Trumpet of the Last Judgment over Hegel the Atheist and Antichrist: An Ultimatum*, in which Hegel is exposed as a closet atheist and revolutionary. Even the apostasy of Young Hegelians, Bauer claimed, is not original to them, for Hegel too, when unmasked, is revealed to be one of them: "It cannot be believed that they [the Young Hegelians] have not recognized the destructive rage of this [Hegel's] system, for they have taken their principle only from their Master"![17] Thus the true heirs of Hegelian thought were not the Old Hegelians and their ilk (found in university and government circles) but the Young Hegelians, since Hegel himself, when properly interpreted, also espoused their subversive and radical doctrines.

Though Bauer continued his attacks on religion he slowly dissociated himself from Die Freien, whom he dubbed "beer literati"; after the 1848 revolution, which he thought seriously mistaken, he became politically conservative. By the early 1840s Marx, who had been close to Bauer when a student at the University of Berlin, had begun to reject many of Bauer's characteristic views, especially his development of a modified version of Hegel's theory of self-consciousness. The progress of man, Bauer alleged, occurred as the result of the development of successive levels of self-consciousness, criticism being the means whereby the development of self-consciousness took place. The term "criticism" was one of the buzzwords of the Young Hegelian movement, meaning many things to each of them; Bauer and his followers even referred to their own theoretical activity as "Critical Criticism."

Bauer became the object of sustained critical attacks by Marx in both his 1844 article "On the Jewish Question" and his first collaborative work with Engels, *The Holy Family, or Critique of Critical Criticism: Against Bruno Bauer and Company* (first published in February 1845). The "Holy Family" were Bauer and his contributors to the *Allgemeine Literatur-Zeitung*, many of whom wrote in opposition to the Communist movement as it was currently developing. They doubted whether any proletarian movement could ever be the means whereby the appropriate development of self-consciousness, whether personal or social, could be achieved. For example, in September 1844 Bauer wrote in his journal that the crowd (i.e. the masses or the proletariat) were in conflict with Spirit, i.e. with critical self-consciousness. Among others he attacks French communism because if it were to achieve its aims "it would abolish freedom in the smallest things" and give rise to a "despotic condition of subdued atoms." His conclusion is that there is "an inevitable war of the multitude against spirit and self-consciousness, and the significance of this war is found in nothing less than the fact that in it the cause of criticism is set against the genus [human species]."[18] With much hindsight it might be thought that Bauer has anticipated the despotic communism of some recent Communist societies – forms of communism which Marx had already criticized in his unpublished *Economic and Philosophic Manuscripts of 1844*.[19] However, Bauer's article is obscure both in its argument and in its appeal to "spirit and self-consciousness" as opposed to "the crowd."

Marx became increasingly opposed to the use of self-consciousness as a fundamental category of analysis; along with this went his rejection of Bauer's Critical Criticism as the means whereby self-consciousness is to be developed. From Marx's perspective it is evident that Bauer's Critical Criticism applied to self-consciousness would represent a dead end in subjective idealism and even a regressive step away from the objective idealism of Hegel. Also in drafts of the unpublished *Economic and Philosophic Manuscripts of 1844* Marx had written of the need to criticize Bauer's views; Feuerbach, Marx claimed, had shown what was wrong with the mystical transcendental aspect of Hegel's dialectic which Bauer continued to use.[20] More significantly, while in Paris in 1844 Marx had attended meetings of a worker's society called the League of the Just and had closely aligned himself with the French Communist movement; consequently he was at odds with all the contributors to the *Allgemeine Literatur-Zeitung* concerning the role of "the crowd" that Bauer and others had denigrated.

The friendship that had developed between Marx and Engels from August 1844 gave them the opportunity to collaborate in producing *The Holy Family*. Beside the broadsides against the Berlin faction of the Young Hegelians and others, the book contains not only the further development of Marx's theory of the proletariat outlined in his earlier critical work on Hegel, but also the first outlines of what was to become Marx's theory of historical materialism. Unfortunately much of the dated polemics of *The Holy Family* obscures this aspect of the development of Marx's thought. Despite the considerable differences between Marx and Bauer, Marx absorbed much of Bauer's writings; as McLellan shows,[21] Marx uses one of Bauer's metaphors when he famously says that religion is the opium of the people.

One of the final works to be identified with the Young Hegelian movement was *Dir Einzige und sein Eigentum* (1845), written by another member of Die Freien, Max Stirner (his real name being the more prosaic Johann Schmidt). Stirner's fame rests on this one book, known in English as *The Ego and its Own: The Case of the Individual against Authority*. The book, which initially attracted much attention, is in several places merely a collection of notes without an overall structure, as befits it anarchistic theme. However, Marx and Engels thought it sufficiently important to write their own book-length critique of Stirner, whom they dubbed "Saint Max"; this long, sometimes turgid, often insightful polemic remained unpublished during their lifetime.[22] Though Marx adopted none of Stirner's views, McLellan argues that Stirner's criticisms of Feuerbach did play some role in Marx's final rejection of Feuerbach, the one Young Hegelian whose influence Marx acknowledged.[23] Commentators have often linked Stirner with Nietzsche in respect of both style and content, though there is no evidence that Nietzsche ever read him. During this century Stirner has had a strong influence upon many of those of the non-Communist left and anarchists. Two writers who have attested to his influence upon their work are Herbert Read and Albert Camus.[24] On the darker side, Stirner has not been without an influence on Fascist thought.

Stirner's work stands opposed to the abstractions of thought and the tendency to systematization found in Hegel and the Young Hegelians. It is also a plea for the totally unconstrained freedom of the individual person. The short introductory section of his book, whose title "All Things Are Nothing To Me" is a quotation from Goethe, ends with the claim:

> The divine is God's concern; the human, man's. My concern is neither the divine nor the human, not the true, good, just, free, etc., but solely what is *mine*, and it is not a general one, but is unique, as I am unique. Nothing is more to me than myself![25]

Since Stirner's theme is the exaltation of the individual above any abstraction such as God, the state, the party, man or mankind, etc., he presents the main body of his book in two parts, the first called "Man," the second "I" – the unique individual or ego.

From the stance of the unique individual not only is all consideration of pure thought or Spirit to be expunged from philosophy but also all talk of man. Even Feuerbach, who believed that all talk of God is really talk of man and man's essence, is still too abstract for Stirner and becomes the object of much criticism and even undergraduate ridicule. For example, in a section of his book entitled "The Spook" Stirner says: "To know and acknowledge essences alone and nothing but essences, that is religion; its realm is a realm of essences, spooks, and ghosts."[26] Elsewhere he adds: "*Man* is the last evil *spirit* or spook . . . the father of lies."[27] Continuing his criticism, Stirner inverts the entire thrust of Hegelian philosophy when he says:

> Feuerbach . . . is always harping upon *being*. In this he too, with all his antagonism to Hegel and the absolute philosophy, is stuck fast in abstraction; for "being" is abstraction, as is even "the I". Only *I am* not abstraction alone: *I am* all in all, consequently even abstraction or nothing; I am all and nothing; I am not a mere thought, but at the same time I am full of thoughts, a thought-world. Hegel condemns the own, mine – "opinion". "Absolute thinking" is that which forgets that it is *my* thinking, that *I* think, and that it exists only through *me*.[28]

Stirner replaces fantastic Hegelian abstractions with almost common-sense banalities about what is the proper subject of thought, viz., the person. As Stirner implores us to realize when reading Hegelian philosophy: "Man, your head is haunted; you have wheels in your head!"[29] This kind of criticism of Hegel, which Stirner could have found in the earlier work of Feuerbach (and, under Feuerbach's influence, is to be found in Marx's unpublished critique of Hegel), would have a sympathetic response from more nominalistically inclined twentieth-century analytic philosophers.

Even Stirner's Berlin associates of Die Freien are not spared when he criticizes various forms of society in a section called "The Free." He attacks the political liberalism of the bourgeoisie, the social liberalism of the Communists, and the humane liberalism of Bruno Bauer, all of whom had their representatives in the Berlin circles in which Stirner moved. In particular Stirner picks out some features of social (or Communist – Stirner did not distinguish) liberalism that have become all too evident in twentieth-century Communist states. He is deeply suspicious of "the Sunday side" of communism in which each man views the other as brother while masking an illiberal "workday side" in which men are merely laborers. He alleges that for communism it is of our essence to labor (strictly not Marx's view). Further he argues that under communism (as well as other forms of state) our labor takes place under the domination of the all-encompassing state with its regulation of life. From this Stirner draws the conclusion that under communism there will appear a new form of tyranny to dominate the individual: "Society, from which we have everything, is a new master, a new spook, a new 'supreme being', which 'takes us into its service and allegiance'!"[30] As he adds later: "Communism rightly revolts against the pressure that I experience from individual proprietors; but still more horrible is the might that it puts in the hand of the collectivity."[31]

In the second section, "I," Stirner explores his doctrine of the unique individual. What is left of the individual once he or she is liberated from the snares of philosophy, religion, culture, family, morality, the various forms of liberalism, the state, any political party, property – even love, equality, and human rights? Concerning the last of these Stirner says: "Right – is a wheel in the head, put there by a spook; power – that am I myself, I am the powerful one and the owner of power."[32] Here the obscure and somewhat sinister side of Stirner's thought appears with its Nietzschean appeal to the power each individual possesses, its exercise, and the egoistic individual so created. He ends his book with a peroration to the power of the self-creating individual:

> I am *owner* of my might, and I am so when I know myself as
> *unique*. In the *unique one* the owner himself returns into his
> creative nothing, of which he is born. Every higher essence
> above me, be it God, be it man, weakens the feeling of my
> uniqueness, and pales only before the sun of this consciousness.
> If I concern myself for myself, the unique one, then my
> concern rests on its transitory, mortal creator, who consumes
> himself, and I may say: All things are nothing to me.[33]

In speaking of the property that the unique individual owns (viz., his or her own self-creative power), it is as if Stirner never got beyond the opening passages of Hegel's *Philosophy of Right*, summed up in, for example, § 47. There Hegel talks about the right of property which each has in their own person, i.e. in their body, and the will they exercise through their body. The ego and what it owns are both the beginning and end of Stirner's anarchistic political theory.

Even in his discussion of love Stirner adopts a completely egoistic position. Though he claims to love every other person he does so egoistically: "I love them because love makes *me* happy."[34] For an extreme individual egoist such as Stirner all forms of the state are to be resisted – the state, too, is a spook. However, he does feel the need to speak of an association or union of egoists; but it is hard to see what such a union is like for an extreme egoist. We are told: "it is not another State (such as a 'people's State') that men aim at, but their *union*, uniting, this ever-fluid uniting of everything standing."[35] Elsewhere he paints a bleak picture of what this ever-fluid union of egoists might be like:

> For me no one person is to be respected . . . but [each is] an
> *object* in which I take an interest or else do not. . . . And if I
> can use him, I doubtless come to an understanding and make
> myself at one with him, in order, by the agreement, to
> strengthen *my power*, and by combined force to accomplish
> more than individual force could effect. In this combination I

see nothing whatever but a multiplication of my force, and I
retain it only so long as it is *my* multiplied force. But thus it
is a – union.[36]

Stirner may have raised some important critical points concerning
Hegel and his fellow Young Hegelians and to have alerted us to the
dangers in appeals to unanalysed abstractions such as "man" and "the
state." However, he often bases his own positive theory of the freedom
of the individual on a false inference from the need to be free of this
and that particular thing (e.g. a political party, or the family, etc.) to
the need to be free from everything. By combining the idea of absolute
freedom from everything with the idea of the power that the individual
can egoistically exert in making itself, Stirner is led to rather unsavory
views about the kind of relationships people can have. Belatedly, Stirner
recognizes the need for some association of egoists; but his theory of
the union does not get beyond the Hobbesian state of nature. In the
end he espouses views characteristic of twentieth-century right-wing
and Fascistic movements:

> My intercourse with the world, what does it aim at? I want to
> have the enjoyment of it, therefore it must be my property,
> and therefore I want to win it. I do not want the liberty of men,
> nor their equality; I want only *my* power over them, I want
> to make them my property, *material for enjoyment.*[37]

No wonder a recent editor of an abridged version of Stirner's book
thought it appropriate to include it in a general series with the title
"Roots of the Right." Even Mussolini wrote: "Leave the way free for
the elemental power of the individual; for there is no other human
reality than the individual! Why shouldn't *Stirner* become significant
again?"[38]

Marx and Stirner have, at a certain level, common themes; Stirner's
graphic account of alienated labor is paralleled by Marx's own account
of alienation given at the same time in his unpublished *Economic and
Philosophic Manuscripts of 1844*. However, at a deeper theoretical level
of the relationship between the individual and society Marx and Stirner
are poles apart. For Stirner the states of mind of, and the powers
exerted by, the egoistic individual are *sui generis* and are not to be
further explained. In contrast, for Marx, as he developed his materialist
view of history, the states of mind to which Stirner appeals are falsely
treated as ultimate and are themselves things which stand in need of
explanation. As Marx first said in *The German Ideology*: "It is not
consciousness that determines life, but life that determines consciousness,"[39] where "life" is to be understood as people "developing their

material production and their material intercourse" (*MECW*, 5: 37). In particular Marx complains:

> Stirner regards the various stages of life only as "self-discoveries" of the individual, and these "self-discoveries" are moreover always reduced to a definite relation of consciousness. Thus the variety of *consciousness* is here the life of the individual. The physical and social changes which take place in individuals and produce an altered consciousness are, of course, of no conern to Stirner. In Stirner's work, therefore, child, youth and man always find the world ready-made, just as they merely "find" "themselves". . . . But even the relation of *consciousness* is not correctly understood either, but only in its speculative distortion.
>
> (ibid.: 128)

Stirner's egoistic individual cannot merely be a person cultivating their unconditioned power unrelated to any circumstances whatever: "[Stirner] quite consistently abstracts from historical epochs, nationalities, classes, etc., [and] he inflates the *consciousness* predominant in the class nearest to him in his immediate environment into the normal consciousness of 'a man's life'" (ibid.: 129). Thus the unique I does not well up out of itself from nothing, as Stirner claims, but, according to Marx, is the product of circumstances to which the I remains blind.[40]

The only Young Hegelian to have exerted an influence on Marx was Ludwig Feuerbach. The nature and extent of Marx's relationship to the work of Hegel and the Young Hegelians have only been able to be fully assessed since the 1930s when the *MEGA* edition (1927–32) made available all of Marx's and Engels's early writings (i.e. before 1848). Before the 1930s the full range of Marx's thought on Hegel and the Young Hegelians and the extent of Feuerbach's influence were not known.

Marx says in his 1859 Preface to *A Contribution to the Critique of Political Economy* that in 1845 he and Engels had

> decided to set forth together our conception as opposed to the ideological one of German Philosophy, in fact to settle accounts with our former philosophical conscience. The intention was carried out in the form of a critique of post-Hegelian philosophy. The manuscript, two large octavo volumes, had long ago reached the publishers in Westphalia when we were informed that owing to changed circumstances it could not be printed. We abandoned the manuscript to the gnawing criticism of the mice all the more willingly since we had achieved our main purpose – self-clarification.
>
> (*MECW*, 29: 264)

This manuscript, first published in full in 1932, is now known as *The German Ideology*.[41] The manuscript left to the mice was in Engels's hands again in 1886 when he leafed through it in the course of writing a review of a book on Ludwig Feuerbach. The review reappeared in 1888 as a separate pamphlet entitled *Ludwig Feuerbach and the End of Classical German Philosophy*. In the Preface, Engels tells us that he had undertaken the earlier review willingly, since "a full acknowledgement of the influence which Feuerbach, more than any other post-Hegelian philosopher, had upon us during our *Sturm und Drang* period, appeared to me to be an undischarged debt of honour" (*MECW*, 26: 520). In the first section of this work Engels treats us to his own brief version of the history of the development of German philosophy from Hegel until the 1848 revolutions. The crucial turning point for Hegelian philosophy was, according to Engels, the publication of Feuerbach's *The Essence of Christianity* in 1841:

> The spell was broken; the "system" [i.e. Hegel's] was exploded and cast aside, and the contradiction [between the Idea and nature], shown to exist only in our imagination, was dissolved. One must have experienced the liberating effect of this book for oneself to get an idea of it. Enthusiasm was universal: we were all Feuerbacheans for a moment. How enthusiastically Marx greeted the new conception and how much – in spite of all critical reservations – he was influenced by it, one may read in *The Holy Family*.
>
> (*MECW*, 26: 364)

Engels's claim in the last sentence is at variance with the facts, as McLellan points out.[42] In *The Holy Family* Feuerbach's *The Essence of Christianity* is not mentioned, as a glance at the index will show. However the index lists two other works by Feuerbach published in 1843 that are arguably an equal or more important influence on Marx, viz., *Provisional Theses for the Reformation of Philosophy* and *Principles of the Philosophy of the Future*. Engels's 1888 pamphlet is important in another respect. In the Preface he also tells us that "in an old notebook of Marx's I have found the eleven theses on Feuerbach, printed here as an appendix. These are notes hurriedly scribbled down for later elaboration, absolutely not intended for publication" (*MECW*, 26: 520). These, now known as the *Theses on Feuerbach*, along with *The German Ideology*, contain Marx's own critical evaluation of Feuerbach.

Marx had been aware of the work of Feuerbach from the time he wrote his dissertation (1840–1). At the beginning of 1842 he said in an article, comparing Feuerbach with Strauss, that "there is no other road for you to *truth* and *freedom* except that leading *through* the stream of fire [the *Feuer-bach*]. Feuerbach is the *purgatory* of the present times."[43] The significance of Feuerbach's work as a tool for the criticism of Hegel became apparent to Marx with the publication of Feuerbach's two 1843 works in which a program is set out for the future development of philosophy once Hegel's speculative philosophy had been abandoned. However, Marx was aware of one important limitation of these works. He wrote to Ruge on 13 March 1843 concerning the *Provisional Theses*: "Feuerbach's aphorisms seem to me incorrect in only one respect, that he refers too much to nature and too little to politics. That, however, is the only alliance by which present-day philosophy can become truth" (*MECW*, 1: 400). In the unpublished *Economic and Philosophic Manuscripts of 1844* Marx has only praise for the "theoretical revolution" that Feuerbach had wrought. The other Young Hegelians, especially Strauss and Bauer, are singled out for failing to appreciate that these two works have "in principle overthrown the old dialectic and philosophy." For Marx, "*Feuerbach* is the only one who has a *serious, critical* attitude to the Hegelian dialectic and who has made genuine discoveries in this field. He is in fact the true conqueror of the old philosophy."[44] It is only in subsequent, unpublished work that one can find Marx's criticisms of Feuerbach.

Feuerbach, who had met Hegel and attended some of his lectures, devoted much of his philosophical career to the study of religion. He gained notice with the publication of *Thoughts concerning Death and Immortality* (1830) in which he argued that there was no personal immortality and no transcendent God but, instead, only the immortality and transcendence of the human spirit. The reception of his book ended any hopes that he may have held for a permanent university position. With the publication of *Toward a Critique of Hegelian Philosophy* (1839)[45] Feuerbach became firmly identified with the Young Hegelians. This work is an attack on several major themes in Hegel's logic and metaphysics, particularly his idealism.

Among the many points concerning Hegelian philosophy that Feuerbach takes up in the *Critique* are the following. (a) In contrast to the idea that Hegelian philosophy is absolute because it is presuppositionless, he argues that, like all other philosophy, it too has its hidden presuppositions. (b) In contrast to Hegel's abstract notion of thought he claims that all thought involves interpersonal dialogue and that language itself is "the realization of the species." (c) Philosophy is bound up with communication and language and is not to be, as in Hegel, imprisoned and compressed into a system. (d) Even though Hegelian philosophy employs a critical method it fails to notice what Feuerbach calls the "genetico-critical philosophy" in which the causal origins of thought and ideas are traced. (e) Common Hegelian errors are to be rectified by turning the Hegelian subject into a predicate and, conversely, the predicate into a subject. This is the first statement of Feuerbach's famous *inversion principle* that so attracted Marx. (f) The Absolute is "a vague and meaningless predicate" and Hegelian philosophy is "rational mysticism." (g) Hegel's opposition of Being and Nothing is to be rejected (though Feuerbach's own arguments concerning Nothing sometimes fall into logical error).

The work which propelled Feuerbach into fame as the leading Young Hegelian was the publication in 1841 of *The Essence of Christianity*. The enthusiasm with which this work was greeted ranged from Engels's remark that "we were all Feuerbacheans for a moment" to Richard Wagner's claim that he "always regarded Feuerbach as the ideal exponent of the radical release of the individual from the thraldom of accepted notions."[46] While the body of the book illustrates how the genetico-critical method is applied to the analysis of religious belief, the Preface to the second edition tells us more about the manner in which Feuerbach's method differs from the approach of Hegel. Importantly Feuerbach views himself as "a *natural philosopher in the domain of the mind*" in applying his genetico-critical method not only to religious belief but to other sorts of belief as well.

The genetico-critical method is not to be understood in the Humean manner in which *epistemological justifications* of our beliefs (i.e. thoughts) are to be sought by logically basing them in our impressions of experience. The method that Feuerbach employs has its roots more in the continental tradition of the interpretation of Locke. It is *genetic* in that it traces the *causal origin* of our beliefs back to their source in experience (but not in the sense of providing an epistemic justification by means of experience). It is *critical* in that it uncovers what is the real cause, as opposed to the commonly believed but false cause, of some of our beliefs. If a belief cannot be epistemically justified, the Humean response is to reject it as epistemically illegitimate; in contrast, such illegitimate beliefs are of prime concern for the genetico-critical method.

It is in this sense that Feuerbach sees himself as "a natural philosopher of the mind" investigating even the residue of our epistemically illegitimate beliefs. Feuerbach speaks in this context of the genetico-critical method being mainly concerned with "secondary" causes, citing as an example the theological view that comets are the work of God and contrasting this with the astronomer's or the natural philosophical view of their cause.[47] This example suggests that what we commonly take to be the cause of a phenomenon might be quite wrong and that there is some other "secondary" cause of the phenomenon which scientific investigation would reveal. It is Feuerbach's view that when it comes to the phenomenon of belief, particularly religious belief, we can be quite mistaken about what is the proper (i.e. secondary) cause of particular beliefs.

For Feuerbach religion provides a particularly fertile field for beliefs which have a causal origin in something quite distinct from their putative object. On Feuerbach's analysis, beliefs about God do not have their causal origin in God but in something quite different, viz., our human nature. As Feuerbach might say, human nature, not God, is the correct "secondary" cause of our religious beliefs. Elsewhere Feuerbach talks of religious beliefs being *reduced* to beliefs about human essence and that God himself has been *reduced* to the essence of the human species. With hindsight the genetico-critical method can be viewed, in part, as an early exercise in the sociology of knowledge, or, much better, the sociology of belief, in which the origins of beliefs are traced to causes other than their putative objects.

Feuerbach's genetico-critical account of the source of our concept of God is at least as old as Xenophanes, who is reported to have said that if horses, cows, or lions could draw then they would draw their gods like horses, cows, or lions; i.e. we make our god(s) in our own image. For Feuerbach's reductive program every predicate of God is in fact a predicate of the human essence. It is we who then project God as an independently existing object onto the world; at the same time we believe that God created us – thus inverting the true but hidden causal relation.

In presenting his case for this inverted picture Feuerbach begins the first section of chapter 1 of *The Essence of Christianity* by describing the essential nature of man, i.e. those features which distinguish us essentially from other animals. We are told that the essence of man is such that each being "has consciousness in the strict sense"; such consciousness is "present only in a being to whom his species, his essential nature, is an object of thought." Feuerbach even claims that science, which has to do with species or kinds rather than individuals, is only possible for beings who can be conscious of their own species, i.e. their essential nature. Feuerbach continues his account of our essence by saying that such consciousness is also consciousness of the infinite. By means of a rather muddled argument he tells us that this means that "the conscious subject has for his object the infinity of his own nature." At best this cannot be the nature of the individual but of the species as a whole, though it does not strictly follow that even the species as a whole will necessarily have an infinite nature. In the course of this discussion Feuerbach introduces the notion of religion; this is, somewhat question-beggingly and without any accompanying argument, identified with our essence, i.e. "with the consciousness which man has of his nature."

When he comes to say what further properties our essential nature has it transpires that our essence is very Cartesian; the essential properties of the human species are reason, will, and affection. Thus our natures are such that we have the power to think, to act forcefully, and to love – and our power to do so as a species is allegedly infinite. Given that this is our essence, how does Feuerbach get from our essential nature to our concept of God? To ask this is to put the wrong question. Rather one must ask: given some feature alleged to be of God, how is this feature to be causally reduced, using the genetico-critical method, to features of our essence?

To assist in this Feuerbach appeals to his inversion principle, adapted to suit the special case of God: "the object [God] of any subject [man] is nothing else than the subject's own nature taken objectively."[48] That is, all the features we attribute to God, e.g. that God is loving, are nothing but features of our own nature – in this case the power we have of affection or love. We then project onto the world an independently existing object which has the power to love. From this Feuerbach concludes that our knowledge of God is nothing but knowledge of ourselves. However, he is careful to point out that the identity of God with man's essence is not something evident to us, for "ignorance of it [the identity] is fundamental to the peculiar nature of religion."[49] This is in effect Feuerbach's genetico-critical method applied to our beliefs about God. As Feuerbach himself later puts the matter, somewhat obscurely:

> Man – this is the mystery of religion – projects his being into objectivity, and then again makes himself an object to this projected image of himself thus converted into a subject; he thinks of himself is [sic] an object to himself, but as the object of an object, of another being than himself.[50]

At the end of Part I of his book Feuerbach does speak of his program in terms of reduction: "We have reduced the supermundane, supernatural, and superhuman nature of God to the elements of human nature as its fundamental elements."[51]

Feuerbach's attempt to be "a natural philosopher in the domain of the mind," especially for our beliefs about God, is not without its problems – not least of which is the use of the inversion principle to get his reductive account of God launched. Related to this is the alleged identity of God with the human essence. To establish this, what Feuerbach needs to show first is that our concept of God does not hold of any external being. Descartes recognized more clearly than Feuerbach the need to show, by argument, that our idea of God is an idea of some external existent entity (though it is generally recognized that Descartes's use of a version of the ontological argument does not prove this). Since Feuerbach is not fully aware of this Cartesian point he makes heavy weather in § 2 of chapter 1 of *The Essence of Christianity* of the question of whether God exists or not. Sometimes Feuerbach says that a God with features other than those of our human essence is not a God we would recognize, and so would not be a God for us. On other occasions he seems to suggest that where God lacks our human features then it follows that God does not exist, i.e. atheism is established.

Nor is Feuerbach particularly clear about whether, in reducing God to our human essence, he has shown that God is identical to our human essence (somewhat in the style of Strauss) or that God does not exist and that he is a fantastic projection of ours upon the world. Often Feuerbach intends the latter, but sometimes his extreme atheism is tempered with the "divine humanism" of the former – this being the manner in which a number of contemporary theologians attempt to interpret Feuerbach. This is important because even if Feuerbach can show that our beliefs about God can be reduced to those about our human essence, it does not follow that there is no God. Whether or not God exists is left untouched by his genetico-critical method applied to religious concepts. Of course, for an already committed atheist the genetico-critical method might tell us something about why so much false religious belief still traffics its way through people's minds. This point brings out the important difference between the Humean *epistemic justification* of a belief and the genetico-critical method for tracing the *causal origin* of a belief. The justification for God's existence is quite independent of how people are caused to have the beliefs they do about God.

Setting aside these difficulties in his account of God, Feuerbach provides a bold and innovative attempt to employ the genetico-critical method to the case of our religious concepts. As will be seen, Marx did not accept Feuerbach's reductive account of religious belief; instead he put more emphasis on the functional role of our religious beliefs. But he did adapt the general reductive program, illustrated by Feuerbach's analysis of religion, to the concepts Hegel employs in expounding his theory about the state.

Feuerbach's two works published after *The Essence of Christianity* in 1843 exerted an important influence on Marx; these were *Provisional Theses for the Reformation of Philosophy* and *Principles of the Philosophy of the Future*, the latter being a more thoroughgoing treatment of themes of the former. Both works are set out in paragraphs, sometimes quite lengthy, and contain criticisms of Hegelian speculative philosophy while outlining a program for an alternative philosophy. The first paragraph of the *Provisional Theses* says:

The secret of *theology* is *anthropology* but the secret of

> *speculative philosophy* is *theology*, the *speculative* theology.
> Speculative theology distinguishes itself from *ordinary* theology
> by the fact that it transfers the divine essence into this world.
> That is, speculative theology *envisions, determines,* and *realizes*
> in this world the divine essence transported by ordinary
> theology out of fear and ignorance into another world.[52]

This summarizes the project of *The Essence of Christianity* – but with
the additional comment that the projection of God into another world
is due to our ignorance and fear. According to this thesis theology
becomes part of anthropology, understood as the study of man and
man's essence; the reduction of ordinary theology to anthropology is
the province of what Feuerbach calls "speculative theology." Such a
reductive program also contains an important message for Hegelian
speculative philosophy; it, too, can be reduced to anthropology:

> The method of the reformatory critique of *speculative philosophy
> in general* does not differ from the critique already applied in
> the *philosophy of religion*. We only need always make the
> *predicate* into the *subject* and thus, as the subject, into the
> *object* and *principle*. Hence we need only *invert* speculative
> philosophy and then have the unmasked pure, bare, truth.[53]

The *inversion principle* (as we have already called it), in which
predicate and subject are interchanged, is not the most perspicuous
of principles. Yet it is this principle, which some call Feuerbach's
"transformative method," that most attracted Marx. It is unclear how
the principle is to be applied in particular cases because what comprises
the subject and predicate and the manner in which they are to be
inverted are not always clear. Consider the following example of inversion given by Feuerbach in *The Essence of Christianity*:

> For, according to the principles which we have already
> developed, that which in religion is the predicate we must make
> the subject, and that which in religion is a subject we must make
> a predicate, thus inverting the oracles of religion; and by this
> means we arrive at the truth. God suffers – suffering is the
> predicate – but for men, for others, not for himself. What does
> that mean in plain speech? Nothing else than this: to suffer for
> others is divine; he who suffers for others, who lays down his
> life for them, acts divinely, is a God to men.[54]

It is obvious, contrary to what Feuerbach says, that "God suffers (for
others)" does not mean the same as "whoever suffers for others is
divine." However, in a slightly strained sense the subject "God" of
the first sentence has become the predicate "divine" of the second

sentence. Also the predicate "suffers" of the first sentence might be construed as the subject of the second sentence; but we must understand the subject of the second sentence not as Feuerbach expresses it, viz., as people (who suffer for others), but as suffering (which is other-directed). Whichever way we take the inversion we lose all reference to God as a subject of discourse. Instead what we talk of is either people who suffer for others, i.e. sufferers (whose suffering is other-directed), or something slightly more abstract than individual people, viz., suffering, which is other-directed.

Feuerbach's reduction of the first sentence to the second via the inversion principle could be resisted on the grounds of lack of meaning equivalence. However, for those not ontologically committed to God, the reduction given might be acceptable, despite the lack of meaning equivalence. Feuerbach's procedure in this example is akin to those twentieth-century nominalists who eschew certain classes of abstract entity and who logically transform their discourse so that apparent references to undesirable abstracta are removed. While it would be out of place to see Feuerbach's inversion principle as an anticipation of some of the reductive or nominalistic moves of Russell or Quine, his procedure in the above example would not meet with their disapproval. We could without too much strain call Feuerbach's inversion a "nominalistic reduction" in that it relieves us of higher levels of abstract entity in favor of lower-level, more nominalistically acceptable items.

With this example of the inversion principle in mind, now consider the following two theses:

> The essence of theology is the *transcendent* essence of the human being, placed outside human beings. The essence of Hegel's *Logic* is *transcendent* thinking, the thinking of the human being *supposed outside human beings*.[55]

> "To abstract" means to suppose the *essence* of nature *outside nature*, the *essence* of the human being *outside the human being*, the *essence* of thinking *outside the act of thinking*. In that its entire system rests upon these acts of abstraction, Hegelian philosophy has *estranged* the human being *from its very self*.[56]

We have seen already how the inversion principle might work in the case of religious claims about God. It is also supposed to work in the case of thought and thinking; the apparent postulation of thought as a subject of predications becomes, by the inversion principle, a predicate, thinking, of other subjects, viz., people (who think) or thinkers. The reverse of the inversion principle is the process of abstraction, viz., the postulation of thought as a subject in its own right with an existence independent of people who think.

Feuerbach applies his inversion in detail only to religious beliefs but sketches ways in which it might be applied to Hegel's *Logic*. Toward the end of the *Provisional Theses* he suggests that the inversion principle can also be applied in political philosophy:

> All speculation about right, willing, freedom, personality without the human being, i.e. outside of or even beyond the human being, is speculation *without unity, without necessity, without substance, without foundation, and without reality*. The human being is the existence of freedom, the existence of personality, the existence of right.[57]

Feuerbach's programmatic claim that the inversion principle can be used to analyze Hegelian political philosophy attracted Marx when he read the *Provisional Theses*. Though Marx had been studying Hegel's *Philosophy of Right* before this, the *Provisional Theses* gave him a new critical tool with which to approach it. He also took to heart, as will be seen, the message of another thesis: "The beginning of philosophy is not God and the beginning of the absolute is not the absolute, not being as a *predicate* of the idea. The beginning of philosophy is the finite, the determined, the actual."[58]

It is impossible to deal adequately here with Marx's detailed paragraph-by-paragraph critique of Hegel's *Philosophy of Right* found in his Feuerbach-inspired *Critique of Hegel's "Philosophy of Right"*.[59] Instead a few examples must suffice. Marx's surviving manuscript begins with § 262 of Hegel's *Philosophy of Right*:

> The actual Idea is mind, which, sundering itself into the two ideal spheres of its concept, family and civil society, enters upon its final phase, but it does so only in order to rise above its ideality and become explicit as infinite actual mind. It is therefore to these ideal spheres that the actual Idea assigns the material of this its finite actuality, viz., human beings as a mass, in such a way that the function assigned to any given individual is visibly mediated by circumstances, his caprice and his personal choice of his station in life.[60]

Often Marx begins the criticism of a section from Hegel by translating it into ordinary prose, removing its stylistic peculiarities; this section is no exception. Marx notes that the actual Idea (mind as infinite and actual) is taken to be something, a subject, that has its own powers to evolve toward a determinate end; moreover it sunders itself into "two ideal spheres," viz., family and civil society. The Idea, which is distinct from family and civil society, makes these into dependent existences; they are finite determinations of the Idea which arise from the Idea's own processes. This Marx condemns as "logical, pantheistic mysticism."

Both following Feuerbach's directive to begin with the "finite and determined" rather than the Absolute, and using the inversion principle, Marx begins instead with the mass of human beings. It is they who make up families and civil society and these in turn are modes of existence of the state: "family and civil society make *themselves* into a state. They are the active force."[61] Speculative Hegelian philosophy treats this wrongly as an achievement of the Idea-subject, its aim being to "become explicit as infinite actual mind." According to Marx: "The entire mystery of the *Philosophy of Right* and of Hegelian philosophy in general is contained in these paragraphs."[62] Marx demystifies § 262 when he rewrites it as: "The family and civil society are elements of the state. The material of the state is divided amongst them through circumstances, caprice, and personal choice of vocation. The citizens of the state are members of families and of civil society."[63]

It is hard to see in Marx's demystified rendering of Hegel's § 262 the precise application of the inversion principle. The Idea as a self-acting subject does not reappear as a predicate. It has disappeared and in its place are new subjects, viz., the masses of people, the family, civil society; they make up the state and, as Marx says, "are the active force." Rather it seems more accurate to view Marx's alleged use of the inversion principle in this case as a reductive nominalizing move in which mystifying abstracta, such as the actual Idea with its powers, are replaced by more concrete talk of the mass of people, the family, civil society, and their powers. The last item, civil society, may itself be somewhat abstract but it is not as obnoxiously so as the actual Idea. How does Marx's desire to rid social theory of abstracta affect his own social ontology? As is well known, the ontology of Marx's later historical materialism, first set out in *The German Ideology*, came to include not abstracta of the sort just mentioned but relational items such as relations of production, and, in some cases, forces of production. The postulation of such relational items in no way counts against Marx's reductive nominalism when used as a critical tool to demystify Hegel's theory which is populated by obscure abstract entities (or as Stirner would say, by spooks).

Sometimes Marx does not employ the inversion principle in his criticisms of Hegel. Thus he complains, in commenting on § 278, that where Hegel says "The sovereignty of the state is the monarch" the common man would say "The monarch has the sovereign power, or sovereignty." This is a straightforward nominalizing move in which the definite description of the first sentence is eliminated in the less mystifying second sentence said by the common man, thereby making it quite clear where the power lies. However, elsewhere in his lengthy comments on § 278 Marx quite explicitly formulates the inversion principle several times in the course of developing his criticism of Hegel on sovereignty. Thus he cavils at Hegel's reification of sovereignty when he says:

> Accordingly, sovereignty, the essence of the state, is here first conceived to be an independent being; it is objectified. Then, of course, this object must again become subject. However the subject then appears to be a self-incarnation of sovereignty, which is nothing but the objectified spirit of the state's subjects.[64]

And so on for other Hegelian reifications, for example, concerning patriotism or the constitution, that Marx ferrets out of *The Philosophy of Right*.

Marx has criticisms to make of Hegel's political philosophy that do not depend on Feuerbach's inversion principle; but its application does relieve one from much that is mind-numbing in Hegel's theory. As a number of commentators have pointed out,[65] the nominalizing moves leave untouched the empirical content of Hegel's claims. This is obviously the case in the above transformation of what Hegel says about sovereignty into what the common man would say. Even though Marx elsewhere makes empirical objections to Hegel's theory (e.g. about the function of primogeniture), the inversion principle, in leaving untouched empirical matters, exposes only the pseudo-profundity of Hegel's mystifying presentation of these empirical matters. As Feuerbach put it in another thesis:

> To have articulated what is *such as it is*, in other words, to have *truthfully* articulated what truly is, *appears superficial*. To have articulated what is *such as it is not*, in other words, to have *falsely* and *distortedly* articulated what truly is, *appears profound*.[66]

Often Marx and Engels assume in criticizing Hegelian speculative philosophy that they are entitled to drop the epithet "Hegelian speculative" and conclude that all philosophy is similarly flawed. However, all they have shown is that one kind of philosophy, Hegel's, is defective. Marx's reductive nominalizing moves are of a piece with much of the logical critique of language developed in twentieth-century analytic philosophy.

Aspects of Feuerbachian, and even Hegelian, influence can be found in another work that Marx left incomplete and so unpublished in his lifetime, now known as the *Economic and Philosophic Manuscripts of 1844*. This is Marx's most humanistic work, particularly in its exploration of the notion of alienation. But within a year Marx explicitly rejected much of Feuerbach's philosophy, including his account of human essence, his critical analysis of religion, and his version of materialism. In *The German Ideology* (1845–6) Marx became impatient with all attempts to define the essential properties of human beings in terms of consciousness and its forms. Without referring directly to Feuerbach he says:

> Men can be distinguished from animals by consciousness, by religion or anything else you like. They themselves begin to distinguish themselves from animals as soon as they begin to *produce* their means of subsistence, a step which is conditioned by their physical organization.
>
> (*MECW*, 5: 31)

But this is not adequate because it leaves out the possibility of humans living in hunter-gatherer societies in which there is no production of means of subsistence. Nor does it take into account the possibility of either biological attempts to specify the human essence, or biochemical attempts in terms of our DNA structure.

Marx did not entirely abandon all talk of necessary features of humanity even in *Capital*:

> So far therefore as labour is a creator of use-value, is useful labour, it is a necessary condition, independent of all forms of society, for the existence of the human race; it is an eternal nature-imposed necessity, without which there can be no material exchanges between man and Nature, and therefore no life.[67]

In the first sentence Marx speaks only of labor as a necessary condition for our existence, and not as our essence. However, in the second sentence he seems to make a much stronger claim when he talks of labor as "an eternal nature-imposed necessity" upon human beings. But all this means is that, given the way the actual world is, we humans must always labor if we wish to exist. Perhaps there are possible worlds in which nature itself is so bountiful that it produces all that would be needed for human existence without any labor on our part. If so, and if we take an essential property of a species to be one without which the species *cannot* exist, then labor is not an essential property of the human species; rather it is a necessary condition of our existence given that in the *actual* world we must work in order to live. Thus in the absence of a different theory of essence in Marx (and in Feuerbach) the above quotation does not entail that labor is an essential feature of human beings.

Marx makes no mention in the above quotation of consciousness. But elsewhere in *Capital* he does appeal to consciousness as that which differentiates us from the animals. In discussing "the labour process independently of the particular form it assumes under given social conditions" he says, when comparing human labor with spiders as makers of webs or bees as makers of cells: "But what distinguishes the worst architect from the best of bees is this, that the architect raises his structure in imagination before he erects it in reality."[68] However, not every laborer raises the product of their labor in their imagination before they make it. This point aside, Marx claims that what distinguishes humans from animals is imagination – a form of consciousness. Even though the kind of consciousness that Marx appeals to is different from the consciousness Feuerbach alleges is our human essence, their claims have this much in common: there exists an essential feature which differentiates humans from the animals.

The above becomes significant when we consider the sixth and seventh of the *Theses on Feuerbach* (1845):

(6) Feuerbach resolves the essence of religion into the essence of *man*. But the essence of man is no abstraction inherent in each single individual. In its reality it is the ensemble of the social relations. Feuerbach, who did not enter upon a criticism of this real essence, is hence obliged:

1 To abstract from the historical process and to define the religious sentiment by itself, and to presuppose an abstract – *isolated* – human individual.

2 Essence, therefore, can be regarded only as "species", as an inner, mute, general character which unites the many individuals *in a natural way*.

(7) Feuerbach, consequently, does not see that the "religious sentiment" is itself a social product, and that the abstract individual which he analyses belongs to a particular form of society

(*MECW*, 5: 4–5)

Thesis (6) begins with a pithy summary of Feuerbach's view of religion, but then challenges it by denying that there is any Feuerbachean essence and, more strongly, that there is a human essence at all. For Marx there is nothing intrinsic to each person, or to humanity as a whole, which is their individual or species essence. Rather, if Marx is going to admit talk of essences at all, then the "essence" of each person will arise from something external to each. According to Thesis (6) each member of the human species exists in some specific ensemble of social relations, different ensembles of social relations existing at any one time and over time. Individual humans, among other things, are the relata, the items that stand in the relations in the ensemble. Moreover the items related do not retain their important characteristics from one ensemble of relations to another since the ensemble plays an important role in "shaping" the characteristics of the items in the relata. Both the relata and the ensemble of relations must be taken together and cannot be easily separated out into relata and relations. That is, the relations are, in some sense, intrinsic to the relata and not extrinsic. (This raises a problem about the extent to which the relata and the ensemble of relations affect one another, which Marx attempts to address in Thesis (3); it will not be discussed here.)[69]

The views Marx expresses in Thesis (6) are of a piece with the remark already cited from *The German Ideology*: "It is not consciousness that determines life, but life that determines consciousness." It follows that the forms of consciousness that people have are "determined" by the ensemble of social relations of which they are the relata, and the forms of consciousness change with change in the ensemble. Thus on Marx's view there can be no common forms of consciousness to which Feuerbach can appeal as the essence of humankind across all the ensembles of relations in which humans can exist – especially emotional features such as suffering for others which Feuerbach mentions. This is not the place to assess this central claim of Marx's materialist view of history; but it does highlight the reasons why Marx rejects essentialist views of human nature.

The two theses are also important for the light they cast on Marx's view of religion. For Feuerbach the reductive base of religion is the human essence. In contrast there is no such universal reductive base for Marx; so he must reject Feuerbach's genetico-critical analysis of religion. Since the ensemble of relations, i.e. society, is alleged by Marx to determine consciousness, the very features of human beings that Feuerbach alleges to be our human essence, i.e. our forms of consciousness, are not *sui generis* and stand in need of explanation. In effect Marx shifts the reductive base from human essence to the ensemble of relations, i.e. society as a whole. Marx expresses just this in his "Contribution to the Critique of Hegel's *'Philosophy of Right'*: introduction": "This state, this society, produce religion, an *inverted world-consciousness*" (*MECW*, 3: 175). This is, in part, Feuerbach inspired; however, it is in the society that "produces" religion, not our human essence. A little further on Marx talks of religion as "the opium of the people" and of the abolition of religion as "the demand to give up illusions about the existing state of affairs" which in turn is "the demand to give up a state of affairs which needs illusions."

It is now commonplace to look for functional explanations of the role of religious belief in the overall fabric of society. For example, the function of religion might be to provide an illusion, e.g. religious consolation or the postulation of a better afterlife, for a state of affairs that needs an illusion, in this case the suffering that people experience as a result of poverty or war. Or religion might have, as Marx suggests in *The German Ideology*, the function of maintaining a form of the division of labor in a given society:

When the crude form of the division of labour which is to be found among the Indians and the Egyptians calls forth the caste-system in their state and religion, the historian believes that the caste-system is the power which has produced this crude form.

(*MECW*, 5: 55)

It is a long-standing issue of interpretation to reconcile Marx's claim here that, on the one hand, the state of society "produces" or "calls forth" religion, and, on the other, the claim he makes elsewhere that religion (e.g. the religious caste system) can help maintain the state and its relations of production (in this case the division of labor represented in the caste system). Cohen has argued that the tension between "producing" and "maintaining" can be resolved by adopting a functional account of the explanation that social factors can give of religious belief.[70] If this is the case then Marx's functional explanation of religious belief is quite distinct from Feuerbach's account of religion; however, both still hold that religion is a form of illusion.

Marx also rejects Feuerbach's version of materialism. Feuerbach provides an explicit, though muddled, statement of his empiricist materialism in his *Principles of the Philosophy of the Future*, § 32: "The real in its reality or taken as real is the real as an object of the senses; it is sensuous. Truth, reality, and sensation are identical. Only a sensuous being is a true real being."[71] Crudely put, this asserts that something is real if and only if it can be sensed (by us humans). When it comes to the theory of perception Marx understands Feuerbach to hold the simple *tabula rasa* view in which the mind is a passive receptacle for sense impressions produced by objects and by our feelings. Marx criticizes this, along with other "old" versions of materialism in contrast to his "new" version of materialism, in the first of the *Theses on Feuerbach*:

The chief defect of all previous materialism (that of Feuerbach included) is that things, reality, sensuousness are conceived only in the form of the *object, or of contemplation*, but not as *sensuous human activity*, *practice*, not subjectively. Hence, in contradistinction to materialism, the *active* side was set forth *abstractly* by idealism – which, of course, does not know real, sensuous activity as such. Feuerbach wants sensuous objects, really distinct from conceptual objects, but he does not conceive human activity itself as *objective* activity. In *The Essence of Christianity*, he therefore regards the theoretical attitude as the only genuine human attitude, while practice is conceived and defined only in its dirty-Jewish form of appearance. Hence he does not grasp the significance of "revolutionary", of "practical-critical", activity.

(*MECW*, 5: 3)

Much critical ink has been spilt on this thesis.[72] For our purposes we need note only the following. In the second sentence Marx appeals to "idealist" theories of knowledge, such as those advocated by German Idealist philosophy from the time of Kant, in which the knower makes an active contribution to perceptual knowledge; the knower actively synthesizes what the senses passively present to him or her in order that the knower can have knowledge of empirically given objects such as chairs or the moon. In this sense Feuerbach is out of step with the idealist tradition concerning ordinary perceptual knowledge in omitting reference to this activist side of idealist epistemology.

But Marx also adds that both Feuerbach and the idealist tradition miss an important aspect of the way in which human activity "constructs" the objects of which we are sensuously aware; this is a central feature of his materialist view of history. In a section of *The German Ideology* (for which editors of this work usually provide a heading such as "Feuerbach's Contemplative and Inconsistent Materialism"), Marx criticizes Feuerbach for having too "contemplative" or too passive a view of our relationship with the objects that exist in the world. The plain fact, claims Marx, is that even the ordinary chairs and tables commonly appealed to as objects of perception by the epistemologist are human creations. Most of the world in which we live is a human-created world; it is our industry over thousands of years that has produced most of the objects which surround us. Even the common cherry tree is a product of human husbandry, a result of "human activity" or "practical-critical activity" as Marx puts it in Thesis (1). Science is also an important part of this practical-critical activity transforming even more thoroughly and rapidly the world in which we live. This does not mean that there is no external world: "Of course, in all this the priority of external nature is unassailed" (*MECW*, 5: 40); but, adds Marx, perhaps only a few Australian coral islands are untouched by human activity. It is the man–nature interaction, emphasized throughout all of Marx's subsequent writings, that has produced our everyday world. It is this that the old materialists and Feuerbach omit totally and that the idealists treat in a one-sided manner by ignoring *objective* human activity in producing the world in which we live. In summary Marx says: "As far as Feuerbach is a materialist he does not deal with history, and as far as he considers history he is not a materialist" (ibid.: 41).

As important as Marx's point is, it fails to address the traditional philosophical problem about the perception of ordinary objects, even if they are human-made chairs. The traditional epistemological problem was of little interest to Marx. Instead he was interested in our practical interaction with the world, how it "revolutionizes" the world and how this is reflected in our discourse about the world. (This is a reorientation of the traditional epistemological problem taken up in some respects by the later Wittgenstein.) The last two sentences of Thesis (1) emphasize this, but in a curious way. The reference to Feuerbach's *The Essence of Christianity* takes us to Chapter 14 of that work in which a contrast is made between "the Greeks [who] looked at nature with the theoretic sense" and the Israelites who "opened to Nature only the gastric sense." In support of this Feuerbach quotes the Bible passage in which it is said that after Moses and the seventy elders ascended the mountain "they saw God; and when they had seen God they ate and drank." Since the sight of God excites in the Jews the appetite for food, Feuerbach claims that the Jewish religion involves "the most practical principle in the world – namely egoism."[73] Later Feuerbach goes on to praise the theoretical attitude of the Greeks as joyful, happy, and aesthetic, while the practical attitude, exemplified by the Jews, is unaesthetic and "is not pure [*schmutzig* – dirty], it is tainted with egoism."[74] Thus Marx was not making an anti-Semitic remark[75] in talking about practice in "its dirty-Jewish form"; rather he was having a dig at Feuerbach for failing to grasp that much of our relationship with the world is not theoretical but bound up in our practical activity, which may be "dirty" and in which egoism may play a part.

Feuerbach's contemplative epistemology omits any role for human practical activity. In contrast Marx's materialistic view of history puts strong emphasis on the practical activity of humans as they labor to produce their means of existence, activity which Marx calls "revolutionary" in Thesis (1). In the final thesis of his *Principles of the Philosophy of the Future*, Feuerbach's proposals for reform remain entirely within the realm of philosophy:

> So far, the attempts at philosophical reform have differed more
> or less from the old philosophy only in form, but not in
> substance. The indispensable condition of a really new
> philosophy, that is, an independent philosophy corresponding
> to the needs of mankind and of the future, is, however, that it
> will differentiate itself in its essence from the old philosophy.[76]

It is surely this passage that Marx has in mind when in the eleventh of his *Theses on Feuerbach* he rejects reform merely at the level of speculative philosophy and emphasizes not only human practical activity in transforming the world but also the revolutionary character of that activity: "The philosophers have only *interpreted* the world in various ways; the point, however, is to *change* it."[77]

For Marx the Young Hegelians provided a range of theories, many still current, about the individual and society which rivaled his own developing theory of historical materialism. His criticisms of the Young Hegelians, though often buried in now irrelevant polemical points, provide a useful survey of the responses a socialist might make to these rival theories. By 1846 the views of Marx and Engels on history and politics had matured to the point where they could fully distance themselves from not only Hegelian political theory but also the theories of all of the Young Hegelians. Marx declared not only that "the decomposition of the Hegelian system, which began with Strauss, has turned into a universal ferment" but also that the Young Hegelian movement was a "philosophic charlatanry," was "parochial" and "tragicomic" in its pretensions, and represented "the putrescence of the absolute spirit."[78] In his view the Young Hegelians had not comprehensively criticized Hegel's system; they had merely played off one part against another. Moreover they had not fully given up religious conceptions of people and their circumstances. Thus their thought was confined to merely ideological accounts of people and their circumstances:

> Since the Young Hegelians consider conceptions, thoughts, ideas, in fact all the products of consciousness, to which they attribute an independent existence, as the real chains of men (just as the Old Hegelians declare them the true bonds of human society), it is evident that the Young Hegelians have to fight only against these illusions of consciousness. Since, according to their fantasy, the relations of men, all their doings, their fetters and their limitations are products of their consciousness, the Young Hegelians logically put to men the moral postulate of exchanging their present consciousness for human [Feuerbach], critical [Bauer], or egoistic [Stirner] consciousness and thus of removing their limitations.
>
> (*MECW*, 5: 30)

After this Marx continues in a manner not unrelated to his eleventh thesis on Feuerbach: "This demand to change consciousness amounts to a demand to interpret the existing world in a different way, i.e. to recognize it by means of a different interpretation." We are now familiar with such radical changes in the way we understand the world through Kuhn's talk of "paradigm shifts" or through recent French philosophy in which much is made of "epistemological breaks." Marx had undergone a change in his understanding of the connections between human beings and society more radical than any of his contemporary Young Hegelians. The above harsh judgments concerning his contemporaries sprang from the self-clarification he had achieved in setting out for the first time the materialist conception of history as opposed to the ideological conception of history in which he believed Hegel and the Young Hegelians were hopelessly enmeshed.

☙ NOTES ❧

1 D. Strauss, *The Life of Jesus Critically Examined*, trans. G. Eliot (London: Swann Sonnenschein, 1906), p. 86.
2 Ibid., p. xxx; or L.S. Stepelevich (ed.), *The Young Hegelians: An Anthology* (Cambridge: Cambridge University Press, 1983), p. 22.
3 See Strauss, op. cit., § 150, "The speculative Christology"; or Stepelevich, op. cit., pp. 44–6.
4 See D. Strauss, *Streitschriften zur Vertheidigung meiner Shrift über das Leben Jesu und zur Charakteristik der gegenwärtigen Theologie* (Tübingen, 1837).
5 J.E. Toews, *Hegelianism: The Path toward Dialectical Humanism, 1805–1841* (Cambridge: Cambridge University Press, 1980), pp. 203–4.
6 For further discussion of the division of Hegelians into Left, Center, Right, Young, and Old, see: Stepelevich, op. cit., "Introduction"; K. Löwith, *From Hegel to Nietzsche: The Revolution in Nineteenth-Century Thought*, trans. D. E. Green (London: Constable, 1965), pp. 53–71; Toews, op. cit., chs 6 and 7.
7 Löwith, op. cit., p. 54.
8 For an account of Strauss's political activities, see W.J. Brazill, *The Young Hegelians* (New Haven: Yale University Press, 1970), pp. 121–3.
9 Löwith, op. cit., pp. 70–1. A version of Hegel's dictum occurs in the Preface to *Hegel's Philosophy of Right*, trans. T.M. Knox (Oxford: Oxford University Press, 1952), p. 10 and n. 27.
10 A. Ruge, "Hegel's 'Philosophy of Right' and the politics of our times" (1842), in Stepelevich, op. cit., p. 223.
11 Ibid., p. 225.
12 Ibid., p. 228.
13 Ibid., p. 230.
14 This material, which was untitled by Marx, is commonly, but not always, known in English as "Critique of Hegel's 'Philosophy of Right'." It was published by D. Rjazanov in Vol. 1 of *Karl Marx, Friedrich Engels: Historisch-Kritisch Gesamtausgabe* (Frankfurt/Main and Berlin, 1927–32); henceforth referred to as *MEGA*. See also *Karl Marx and Friedrich Engels: Collected Works* (London: Lawrence & Wishart, 1975–), henceforth referred to as *MECW*, Vol. 3, "Contribution to the critique of Hegel's philosophy of law," pp. 3–129. The two Hegel critiques, the one Marx published and the drafts he left unfinished, are collected together, with a useful commentary, in Marx, *Critique of Hegel's "Philosophy of Right"*, ed. J. O'Malley (Cambridge: Cambridge University Press), 1970.
15 *Hegel's Philosophy of Right*, op. cit., p. 11.
16 *MECW: Karl Marx and Friedrich Engels: Collected Works*, op. cit.; citations are by volume and page number.
17 A few extracts from this work are available in English in Stepelevich, op. cit., pp. 177–86; the quotation is from p. 183.
18 B. Bauer, "The genus and the crowd," in ibid., pp. 204–5. The German title of the work is "Die Gattung und die Masse"; the term *"Gattung"* was extensively used by Feuerbach and is often translated into English as "(human) species" rather than "genus."

19 See Marx's distinction between crude communism and other forms of communism in *MECW*, 3, pp. 294–7; see also S. Avineri, *The Social and Political Thought of Karl Marx* (Cambridge: Cambridge University Press, 1968), pp. 220–39.

20 See *MECW*, 3, pp. 231–4, Preface, and the concluding section p. 327.

21 D. McLellan, *The Young Hegelians and Karl Marx* (London: Macmillan, 1969), p. 78.

22 See "Part III: Saint Max" of Marx and Engels, *The German Ideology, MECW*, 5, pp. 117–450. In contrast Marx devotes only pp. 27–93 to a critique of Feuerbach, the Young Hegelian generally held to have had some influence upon him.

23 McLellan, op. cit., pp. 129–36.

24 For an account of Stirner's influence, see the Introduction by J. Carroll to his abridged edition of *Max Stirner: The Ego and Its Own* (London: Cape, 1971); this appeared in a series entitled Roots of the Right under the general editorship of G. Steiner.

25 M. Stirner, *The Ego and his Own* (1844), ed. J. Carroll, trans. S.T. Byington (London: Cape, 1971), p. 5.

26 Ibid., p. 40.

27 Ibid., p. 184.

28 Ibid., p. 339.

29 Ibid., p. 43.

30 Ibid., p. 123.

31 Ibid., p. 257.

32 Ibid., p. 210.

33 Ibid., p. 366.

34 Ibid., p. 291.

35 Ibid., p. 224.

36 Ibid., pp. 311–12.

37 Ibid., p. 318.

38 Quoted in Carroll, Introduction, op. cit., p. 14.

39 See *MECW*, 5, p. 37. The import of this central idea of Marx is obscure. I suggest one way in which it might be criticized toward the end of section II of R. Nola, "The strong programme for the sociology of knowledge, reflexivity and relativism," *Inquiry*, 33 (1990): 273–96.

40 For a useful account of Marx on Stirner, see S. Hook, *From Hegel to Marx: Studies in the Intellectual Development of Karl Marx* (Ann Arbor: Ann Arbor Paperbacks, 1962), ch. 5, part II. For an account more sympathetic to Stirner and critical of Marx, see E. Fleischmann, "The role of the individual in pre-revolutionary society: Stirner, Marx and Hegel," in Z.A. Pelczynski (ed.), *Hegel's Political Philosophy: Problems and Perspectives* (Cambridge: Cambridge University Press, 1971).

41 For a history of the manuscript and its publication, see *MECW*, 5, n. 7, pp. 586–8.

42 McLellan, op. cit., p. 93.

43 Marx, *Writings of the Young Marx on Philosophy and Society*, ed. L.D. Easton and K.H. Guddat (New York: Doubleday, 1967), p. 95.

44 For Marx's praise, see Preface to *Economic and Philosophic Manuscripts of 1844*, *MECW*, 3, pp. 232–3, and the final section, headed "Critique of the Hegelian

dialectic and philosophy as a whole," pp. 327–9. See also the letter which Marx wrote to Feuerbach on 11 August 1844, ibid., pp. 354–7.

45 M.W. Wartofsky, *Feuerbach* (Cambridge: Cambridge University Press, 1977), ch. VII, is an excellent account of this work; a translation can be found in Stepelevich, op. cit.

46 The remark of Wagner is cited in Brazill, op. cit., p. 137.

47 For a few brief comments by Feuerbach on his genetico-critical philosophy, see his *Towards a Critique of Hegel's Philosophy*, in Stepelevich, op. cit., pp. 121 and 127; see also the Introduction by E. Wartenberg to Feuerbach, *Principles of the Philosophy of the Future*, trans. M. Vogel (Indianapolis: Hackett, 1986), pp. xxiii–xxvii.

48 Feuerbach, *The Essence of Christianity*, trans. G. Eliot (New York: Harper Torchbook, 1957), p. 12.

49 Ibid., p. 13.

50 Ibid., pp. 29–30.

51 Ibid., p. 184.

52 Stepelevich, op. cit., p. 156.

53 Ibid., p. 157.

54 Feuerbach, *The Essence of Christianity*, op. cit., p. 60.

55 Stepelevich, op. cit., p. 158.

56 Ibid., p. 159.

57 Ibid., p. 170.

58 Ibid., p. 160.

59 See O'Malley's editorial comments in Marx, *Critique of Hegel's "Philosophy of Right"*, op. cit.; R.N. Berki, "Perspectives in the Marxian critique of Hegel's political philosophy," in Pelczynski, op. cit.; Avineri, op. cit.; L. Dupré, *The Philosophical Foundations of Marxism* (New York: Harcourt, Brace & World, 1966), ch. 4; and D. McLellan, *Marx before Marxism* (London: Macmillan, 1970), ch. 5: all of whom attempt to evaluate Marx's own criticisms of Hegel.

60 Marx, *Critique of Hegel's "Philosophy of Right"*, op. cit., p. 7.

61 Ibid., p. 8.

62 Ibid., p. 9.

63 Ibid., p. 8.

64 Ibid., p. 24.

65 For example, O'Malley in ibid., p. xxxiii.

66 Stepelevich, op. cit., p. 162.

67 Marx, *Capital: Volume 1* (Moscow: Progress Publishers, 1973), p. 50.

68 Ibid., p. 174.

69 For a useful analysis of Marx's *Theses on Feuerbach*, see W.A. Suchting, "Marx's *Theses on Feuerbach*: a new translation and notes towards a commentary," in J. Mepham and D. Ruben (eds), *Issues in Marxist Philosophy*, Vol. 2: *Materialism* (Brighton: Harvester, 1979); and W.A. Suchting, *Marx and Philosophy: Three Studies* (New York: New York State University Press, 1986), ch. 1; see also Hook, op. cit., ch. 8.

70 See G.A. Cohen, *Karl Marx's Theory of History: A Defence* (Oxford: Clarendon Press, 1978), chs VI, IX, and X, for his account of functional explanation in Marx's historical materialism.

71 Feuerbach, *Principles of the Philosophy of the Future*, op. cit., p. 51.

72 For a useful commentary, see Suchting, "Marx's *Theses on Feuerbach* . . . ,"
op. cit., and *Marx and Philosophy: Three Studies*, op. cit., chs 1 and 2.
73 Feuerbach, *The Essence of Christianity*, op. cit., p. 114.
74 Ibid., p. 196.
75 Some commentators – such as Hook, op. cit., p. 278 n. 2 – miss Marx's reference
to Feuerbach writings in the penultimate sentence of Thesis (1). See Suchting,
"Marx's *Theses on Feuerbach* . . . ," op. cit., p. 11 and nn. 18 and 19, for a
useful commentary on this sentence; the remarks in the text above have been
adapted from Suchting.
76 Feuerbach, *Principles of the Philosophy of the Future*, op. cit.
77 Marx, "Theses on Feuerbach," in *Karl Marx: Selected Writings in Sociology
and Social Philosophy*, ed. T.B. Bottomore and M. Rubel (London: C.A. Watts,
1956), p. 69.
78 These scathing comments come from the first few pages of *The German Ideology*, *MECW*, 5, pp. 27–8.

❧ SELECT BIBLIOGRAPHY ❧

Original language editions

9.1 Feuerbach, L. *Ludwig Feuerbach: Sämtliche Werke*, ed. W. Bolin and F. Jodl
(additional volumes ed. H.-M. Sass), Stuttgart: Frommann, 1903–11.
9.2 Feuerbach, L. *Gesammelte Werke*, ed. W. Schuffenhauer, Berlin: Akademie-
Verlag, 1967–.
9.3 Löwith, K. (ed.) *Die Hegelische Linke*, Stuttgart and Bad Cannstatt: Frommann, 1962.
9.4 Lübbe, H. (ed.) *Die Hegelische Rechte*, Stuttgart and Bad Cannstatt: Frommann, 1962.
9.5 Marx, K., and Engels, F. *Karl Marx, Friedrich Engels: Historisch-Kritisch
Gesamtausgabe*, ed. D. Ryazonov and V. Adoratsky, Berlin: Dietz,
1927–32.
9.6 Marx, K., and Engels, F. *Karl Marx, Friedrich Engels: Werke*, Berlin: Dietz
Verlag, 1956–.
9.7 Stirner, M. *Dir Einzige und sein Eigentum* (1845), ed. H. Helms, Leipzig:
1892.
9.8 Strauss, D. *Das Leben Jesu, Kritisch Bearbeitet*, Tübingen, 1835–6.
9.9 Strauss, D. *Streitschriften zur Vertheidigung meiner Schrift über das Leben
Jesu und zur Charakteristik der gegenwärtigen Theologie*, 2nd edn,
Tübingen, 1837, 1841.

English translations

Complete

9.10 Marx, K., and Engels, F. *Karl Marx and Friedrich Engels: Collected Works*,
London: Lawrence & Wishart, 1975–.

Separate works

9.11 Carroll, J. (ed.) *Max Stirner: The Ego and its Own*, London: Cape, 1971; published in the series Roots of the Right, general ed. G. Steiner.

9.12 Feuerbach, L. (1957) *The Essence of Christianity*, trans. G. Eliot in 1854 from the 2nd German edn of 1843, with an introductory essay by K. Barth, New York: Harper Torchbook.

9.13 Feuerbach, L. *The Fiery Brook: Selected Writings of Ludwig Feuerbach*, ed. Zawar Hanfi, New York: Doubleday, 1972.

9.14 Feuerbach, L. "Towards a Critique of Hegelian Philosophy" (1839), in Stepelevich [9.22].

9.15 Feuerbach, L. "Provisional Theses for the Reformation of Philosophy" (1843), in Stepelevich [9.22].

9.16 Feuerbach, L. *Principles of the Philosophy of the Future* (1843), trans. M. Vogel with introduction by T.E. Wartenburg, Indianapolis: Hackett, 1986.

9.17 Hegel, G.W.F. *Hegel's Philosophy of Right*, trans. T.M. Knox, Oxford and London: Oxford University Press, 1952, pbk 1967.

9.18 Marx, K. *Writings of the Young Marx on Philosophy and Society*, ed. L.D. Easton and K.H. Guddat, Garden City: Doubleday Anchor, 1967.

9.19 Marx, K. *Critique of Hegel's "Philosophy of Right"*, ed. J. O'Malley, Cambridge: Cambridge University Press, 1970.

9.20 Marx, K. *Capital*, Vol. 1, Moscow: Progress Publishers, 1973.

9.21 Marx, K. *Karl Marx: Early Texts*, ed. D. McLellan, Oxford: Blackwell, 1971.

9.22 Ruge, A. "Hegel's *'Philosophy of Right'* and the Politics of Our Times" (1842), in Stepelevich [9.22].

9.23 Stepelevich, L.S. (ed.) *The Young Hegelians: An Anthology*, Cambridge: Cambridge University Press, 1983.

9.24 Stirner, M. *The Ego and its Own* (1844), trans. S.T. Byington in 1907, New York: Libertarian Book Club, 1963; ed. J. Carroll as *The Ego and his Own*, London: Cape, 1971.

9.25 Strauss, D. *The Life of Jesus Critically Examined*, trans. from the 4th German edn of 1840 by G. Eliot in 1860, London: Swann Sonnenschein, 1906.

Bibliographies

9.26 Brazill, W.J. "Bibliographical Essay," in Brazill [9.32].

9.27 McLellan, D. "Select Bibliography," in McLellan [9.37].

9.28 Mah, H. "Bibliography," in Mah [9.38].

9.29 Stepelevich, L. (1983) "Young Hegelianism: A Bibliography of General Studies, 1930 to the Present," in Stepelevich [9.22]; this also contains bibliographical material in the editor's introduction preceding each selection.

9.30 Toews, J.E. "Bibliography" (up to 1840), in Toews [9.40].

General surveys

9.31 Berki, R.N. "Perspectives in the Marxian critique of Hegel's political philosophy," in Pelczynski [9.39].

9.32 Brazill, W.J. *The Young Hegelians*, New Haven: Yale University Press, 1970.

9.33 Crites, S.D. "Hegelianism," in P. Edwards (ed.) *The Encyclopedia of Philosophy*, Vol. 3, New York: Macmillan and Free Press, 1967.

9.34 Fleischmann, E. "The role of the individual in pre-revolutionary society: Stirner, Marx and Hegel," in Pelczynski [9.39].

9.35 Hook, S. *From Hegel to Marx: Studies in the Intellectual Development of Karl Marx*, Ann Arbor: Ann Arbor Paperbacks, 1962.

9.36 Löwith, K. *From Hegel to Nietzsche: The Revolution in Nineteenth-Century Thought*, trans. D.E. Green, New York: Holt, Rinehart & Winston, 1964; London: Constable, 1965; Garden City: Doubleday, Anchor, 1967.

9.37 McLellan, D. *The Young Hegelians and Karl Marx*, London: Macmillan, 1969.

9.38 Mah, H. *The End of Philosophy, the Origin of Ideology: Karl Marx and the Crisis of the Young Hegelians*, Berkeley: University of California Press, 1987.

9.39 Pelczynski, Z.A. (ed.) *Hegel's Political Philosophy: Problems and Perspectives*, Cambridge: Cambridge University Press, 1971.

9.40 Toews, J.E. *Hegelianism: The Path toward Dialectical Humanism, 1805–1841*, Cambridge: Cambridge University Press, 1980.

9.41 Wartofsky, M.W., and Sass, H.-M. (eds) *The Philosophical Forum*, 8, 2–4 (1976–7); a special triple issue devoted to works on or by the Young Hegelians.

Books on Feuerbach

9.42 Kamenka, E. *The Philosophy of Ludwig Feuerbach*, London: Routledge & Kegan Paul, 1970.

9.43 Wartofsky, M.W. *Feuerbach*, Cambridge: Cambridge University Press, 1977.

Books and articles on Marx, Engels, and the Young Hegelians

9.44 Althusser, L. *For Marx*, Harmondsworth: Penguin, 1969.

9.45 Avineri, S. *The Social and Political Thought of Karl Marx*, Cambridge: Cambridge University Press, 1968.

9.46 Barth, H. *Truth and Ideology*, Berkeley: University of California Press, 1976.

9.47 Cohen, G.A. *Karl Marx's Theory of History: A Defence*, Oxford: Clarendon Press, 1978.

9.48 Colletti, L. *Marxism and Hegel*, London: New Left Books, 1973.

9.49 Dupré, L. *The Philosophical Foundations of Marxism*, New York: Harcourt, Brace & World, 1966.

9.50 McLellan, D. *Marx before Marxism*, London: Macmillan, 1970.

9.51 Mepham, J. and Ruben, D.H. *Marx and Philosophy: Three Studies*, New York: New York University Press, 1986.

9.52 Suchting, W.A. "Marx's *Theses on Feuerbach*: A new Translation and Notes Towards a Commentary," in J. Mepham and D.H. Ruben (eds) *Issues in Marxist Philosophy*, Vol. 2: *Materialism*, Brighton: Harvester, 1979.

CHAPTER 10

Arthur Schopenhauer

Kathleen M. Higgins

Despite a recent surge of philosophical interest, Arthur Schopenhauer remains one of the most underappreciated philosophers of modern times. He has arguably had a greater influence on subsequent philosophy and intellectual history than any other figure. The richness of Schopenhauer's thought is suggested even by a perusal of the intellectual world's reactions. Friedrich Nietzsche, Ludwig Wittgenstein, Sigmund Freud, Thomas Mann, Thomas Hardy, Richard Wagner, and Woody Allen all claim him as their intellectual and/or spiritual ancestor. Such influential concepts as Wittgenstein's "family resemblance,"[1] Nietzsche's "will to power"[2] and "eternal recurrence,"[3] and Freud's "libido"[4] all develop from ideas originally suggested by Schopenhauer.

Yet Schopenhauer's philosophy has often been dismissed as being of mere historical interest. One explanation is that Schopenhauer is an emphatically systematic thinker. In claiming that his philosophy is an "organic" whole, composed of elements that stand or fall together, Schopenhauer invites the reader who rejects a part of it to reject the theory *in toto*.[5] In light of his insistence on complete resignation, extreme asceticism, and sexual abstinence as the only alternative to a life of futile struggling, many readers understandably balk at embracing his theory wholesale.

Another explanation for Schopenhauer's unpopularity is the reaction of many readers to his personality. Bertrand Russell, who criticizes Schopenhauer's philosophy for "inconsistency and a certain shallowness," seems most indignant about Schopenhauer's character. After complaining about the internal tensions in Schopenhauer's doctrine of resignation, Russell continues:

> Nor is the doctrine sincere, if we may judge by Schopenhauer's life. He habitually dined well, at a good restaurant; he had many trivial love-affairs, which were sensual but not passionate; he

was exceedingly quarrelsome and unusually avaricious. On one occasion he was annoyed by an elderly seamstress who was talking to a friend outside the door of his apartment. He threw her downstairs, causing her permanent injury. She obtained a court order compelling him to pay her a certain sum (15 thalers) every quarter as long as she lived. When at last she died, after twenty years, he noted in his account-book: "Obit anus, abit onus." ["The old woman dies; the burden departs."] It is hard to find in his life evidence of any virtue except kindness to animals, which he carried to the point of objecting to vivisection in the interests of science. In all other respects he was completely selfish.[6]

Russell's sense of virtue is probably quite different from Schopenhauer's. But even if Russell is not entirely fair in his attack, Schopenhauer's biography suggests grounds for *ad hominem* attack. Russell's anecdote alone suggests an impulsive, willful personality, a matter worth comment in one convinced, as is Schopenhauer, that Will is the fundamental metaphysical principle of the world.[7] Schopenhauer's system and, in particular, his denunciation of sex as the focal expression of the will and guarantor of human unhappiness prompt Nietzsche to remind his readers:

> In all questions concerning the Schopenhauerian philosophy, one should, by the bye, never lose sight of the consideration that it is the conception of a youth of twenty-six, so that it participates not only in what is peculiar to Schopenhauer's life, but what is peculiar to that special period of his life.[8]

Whether or not one considers such *ad hominem*s to be legitimate in philosophical argumentation, Schopenhauer's writings present a psychological puzzle.[9] Although misanthropic and barbed in his tone, Schopenhauer advocates an ethic of compassion. Despite his elitism, he insists that all individuals are manifestations of the identical Will. Consistently analyzing the world's phenomena as manifestations of futility, Schopenhauer nonetheless describes them with voluptuous enthusiasm. He displays great wit and insight into human behavior – and yet he shows no sign of self-irony. Perhaps it was this last feature of Schopenhauer's work that moved the youthful Nietzsche to describe him as motivated by the need "for love above everything else."[10]

SCHOPENHAUER'S LIFE AND WORKS

Schopenhauer's biography at least sheds light on his intellectual breadth. Schopenhauer was born in Danzig on 22 February 1788 to a cosmopolitan couple, consisting of Heinrich Floris Schopenhauer, a prominent merchant, and Johanna Henriette Trosiener, a successful novelist. Heinrich's penchant for travel and unconventional views on schooling led to Schopenhauer's receiving a rather nomadic education. He lived in Hamburg from ages 5 to 9, spent the following two years in France, and subsequently spent two more years traveling the world with his parents and sister, briefly attending a British boarding school in Wimbledon. As a result of this globe-trotting lifestyle, Schopenhauer developed fluency in several languages and his own predilection for travel.

Schopenhauer's father died, apparently through suicide, when Schopenhauer was 17. Schopenhauer briefly attempted to fulfill a promise to his father that he would become a merchant; but concluding after two years that this career choice didn't suit him, he abandoned that career for classical studies. He began these at Gotha, but transferred to Weimar, where his mother lived. Schopenhauer and his mother were constant antagonists who could not bear to live in the same house. Indeed, Schopenhauer's misogynist comments, directed in particular at the modern "ladies" of Europe, may stem from this relationship to his mother.[11] Despite his dislike for her, however, Schopenhauer frequently visited her and her salon during this period, which included some of the most celebrated literary figures of the time (Goethe, Schlegel, and the brothers Grimm among them).

When he received his considerable inheritance at the age of 21, Schopenhauer began medical studies at the University of Göttingen. His growing interest in philosophy prompted him to transfer to the University of Berlin, where Fichte was professor. Schopenhauer found the lectures of both Fichte and his colleague Schleiermacher wanting, however, a conclusion reiterated in footnotes to virtually all of his subsequent works.

The proximity of battle during the Napoleonic Wars prompted Schopenhauer's next move, to a small town called Rudolstadt, near Weimar. There he wrote his dissertation, *On the Fourfold Root of the Principle of Sufficient Reason* (1813), which was awarded the doctorate by the University of Jena. Schopenhauer's private printing of the thesis did not win him a large readership. Nevertheless, Goethe read and praised it. In response to their subsequence conversations, Schopenhauer wrote a short book entitled *On Vision and Colors* (1815).

After returning to Weimar and briefly living with his mother, Schopenhauer completely severed his relation with her, never to see her again. He moved to Dresden, where he wrote the central statement of his philosophical theory, *The World as Will and Representation* (1818). The book was by no means a bestseller, but Schopenhauer's publication record was strong enough to gain him a lectureship in philosophy at the University of Berlin. Hegel, object of Schopenhauer's considerable scorn, had inherited Fichte's chair. By scheduling his courses at times when Hegel was also lecturing, Schopenhauer forced his students to choose between himself and Hegel. The predictable result was that the students chose Hegel, with the consequence that Schopenhauer's lectures were canceled. The independently wealthy Schopenhauer never again sought an academic position; indeed, he consistently disparaged academic philosophy in his writings.

The cholera epidemic that killed Hegel in 1831 inspired the somewhat hypochondriacal Schopenhauer to make his final move, this time to Frankfurt. He devoted his remaining years to writing and traveling. His works of this period include "On the Will in Nature" (1836) and "On the Foundation of Morality," which were conjoined in *The Two Fundamental Problems of Ethics* (1841); the second edition of *The World as Will and Representation*, together with a second volume of supplementary essays (1844); a revised and enlarged edition of *On the Fourfold Root of the Principle of Sufficient Reason* (1847); and a collection of essays entitled *Parerga and Paralipomena* ("Supplementary Works and Omitted Material") (1851). Schopenhauer lived to see his works become popular in his waning years. He died on 21 September 1860.

❧ SCHOPENHAUER'S GRAND SYNTHESIS ❧

Schopenhauer's principal statement of his philosophical system is *The World as Will and Representation*, Volume I. Although he added subsequent essays in the years following its publication, these only elaborated on positions he initially stated in that volume. Schopenhauer never disavowed any detail of his initial formulations. As he announced in his Preface to the book's second edition: "I have altered nothing."[12]

Schopenhauer's Preface to the first edition of *The World as Will and Representation* reveals a demanding author. Schopenhauer insists that the book is the development of a single thought, and that the first chapters depend as much on the last as the other way around. Hence, he insists that the reader must read the entire book twice. In addition, since he is presupposing the work he had done in his dissertation, Schopenhauer also requires that his readers be familiar with *On the Fourfold Root of the Principle of Sufficient Reason* (and ideally with *On Vision and Colors* as well). Finally, he requests that the reader have thorough familiarity with the writings of Kant, and preferably with Plato's dialogues and the *Upanishads* as well.

These last requirements give a hint as to what will follow. Schopenhauer's system aims to synthesize the philosophies of Kant, Plato, and India (in particular Buddhistic philosophy). The common denominator of the three is a distinction between the world of everyday appearances and a truer reality, ascertainable by the human mind. In order to accomplish his grand synthesis, Schopenhauer has to modify considerably the works from which he draws inspiration. Nonetheless, it is noteworthy that for all his curmudgeonly complaints about most other human beings, Schopenhauer expresses awe for his heroes.[13] (In fact, he decorated his rather sparse living quarters in Frankfurt with a bust of Kant and a statue of the Buddha.)[14]

The essential moves involved in Schopenhauer's synthesis are as follows. Schopenhauer accepts Kant's distinction between the phenomenal world and the noumenal world. The former is called, in Schopenhauer's idealistic scheme, the **world as representation**, for it is composed of objects constituted by the forms imposed by the conscious mind. The noumenal world, or thing-in-itself, is the reality underlying the world as representation. Schopenhauer disagrees with Kant that the thing-in-itself is inaccessible to us. Instead, he points out that each of us, in our own case, recognizes an immediate reality behind the phenomenal behavior of our own body. This inner reality is "will." Schopenhauer extends this inner reality to all phenomena, concluding that **"Will"** is the thing-in-itself.[15]

Although the entire phenomenal world is a manifestation of "Will," Schopenhauer maintains that the Will manifests itself to various degrees in different types of things. He invokes the Platonic Ideas (or Forms) to account for the different forms of the Will's manifestation. Following Plato, he argues that everyday human awareness usually focuses on particular things, not on their eternal, universal prototypes. However, in aesthetic experience, the individual sees the object as the Platonic Idea, and in the process raises him- or herself to the condition of "the universal subject of knowledge." In aesthetic experience, the willful character of our inner life is silenced. Aesthetic experience, therefore, affords the human being brief moments of inner peace.

Schopenhauer places high value on inner peace, and this valuation prompts him to incorporate insights from Indian philosophy into his system. Although the Will is the fundamental metaphysical principle behind all phenomena, its internal struggling character ensures that its phenomenal manifestations will themselves be characterized by struggle and suffering. Schopenhauer follows Buddhism in concluding that the only way to stop suffering is to stop desiring. Hence, he contends that resignation and the asceticism that arises from it are the only alternative to a life of continuing suffering. Resignation is the outlook attained by the human being who fully grasps that the same Will is the inner reality within all phenomena. When one has fully incorporated this insight, one is no longer capable of competing or struggling with other phenomena. One achieves in this case the ideal that lies at the core of all religions – the ideal of compassion toward all other beings, in the full recognition that all are, in reality, one.

THE WORLD AS REPRESENTATION AND THE PRINCIPLE OF SUFFICIENT REASON

Let us now consider Schopenhauer's system in more detail. Schopenhauer begins *The World as Will and Representation* with a clear statement of his idealism. " 'The world is my representation': this is a truth valid with reference to every living and knowing being, although man alone can bring it into reflective, abstract consciousness."[16] The existence of the world as it appears to us – the world as representation – is entirely contingent on consciousness.

True to his word, Schopenhauer begins his analysis of the world as representation by presupposing the account that he had given in *On the Fourfold Root of the Principle of Sufficient Reason*. Indeed, he asserts the world of representation is entirely governed by **the principle of sufficient reason**, a principle which he simply assumes. This principle, although variously formulated, essentially contends that there is a sufficient reason for every phenomenon. In one formulation Schopenhauer states that the principle holds that "every possible object . . . stands in a necessary relation to other objects, on the one hand as determined, on the other as determining."[17] The principle of sufficient reason establishes that all objects that are represented for the conscious mind stand in a nexus of connection with one another. Thus, every represented object can be entirely explained in terms of its relation to other objects.

In his dissertation Schopenhauer describes the different forms that the principle of sufficient reason takes in relating the four possible types of objects to their grounds. The four types of objects he analyzes are those of **being, becoming, knowing,** and **acting,** a list which he takes to be exhaustive of possible objects. By considering these sequentially, we can observe much about the structure of the Schopenhauerian world as representation.

As representation, the world is subject to the Kantian forms of intuition, **time and space**. These are forms essential to the constitution of all objects by consciousness, and they individuate the world into particular, individual objects. For this reason, Schopenhauer sometimes refers to time and space as the *principium individuationis* (the principle of individuation). He also designates them "the ground of being" because of their fundamental role in securing the possibility of the world that we perceive. When Schopenhauer considers the principle of sufficient reason as it pertains to "being," he has time and space in mind.

The principle of sufficient reason pertains to our intuitions of time and space by establishing that positions within time and space exist in a nexus, mutually determining each other. In other words, the location of objects in time and space can be determined only in relation to other locations. Schopenhauer takes the existence of mathematics to reflect the lawlike interrelation of positions in the time–space continuum. Arithmetic focuses on relationships within time (for Schopenhauer sees it as originating in counting, which deals directly with succession in time). Geometry focuses on relationships within space. Geometric proofs depend on the principle of sufficient reason, for they draw on the fact that certain relationships imply others.

The representations of consciousness include both intuitive and abstract representations. Among the objects that are directly intuited are both objects of perception and the conditions of their possibility. These latter include time and space, and also causality. The **law of causality** is the form that the principle of sufficient reason takes in connection with perceptual objects, whose character Schopenhauer analyzes in terms of "becoming." Causes, for Schopenhauer, have to do with changes of states over time.

In order for change to occur within time, something must undergo the change. Schopenhauer considers the persisting object of change to be **matter**. He even defines matter as "the perceivability of time and space."[18] Matter and causality are conflatable, for "matter is absolutely nothing but causality . . . its being is its acting."[19] The "acting" that concerns Schopenhauer in this connection is the action of perceptual objects on our bodies. By means of these effects, we come to know causes. Causes provide the ground for given states of perceptual objects. Thus they are the form of connection that the principle of sufficient reason provides between representations of this type.

One might ask, at this juncture, how we come to know causes. Schopenhauer, like Kant, contends that perception is intellectual, for it essentially involves the **understanding** as well as sensation.[20] But Schopenhauer's conception of understanding differs from Kant's. Kant considers the understanding to be the faculty that applies principles of judgment to representations. Schopenhauer considers the understanding to be a faculty that leaps from a represented effect to its cause. At times Schopenhauer argues that apprehension of causality is the sole operation of the understanding.[21] Schopenhauer attributes understanding to animals, as well as to human beings, maintaining that the "most sagacious animals" (e.g. dogs, monkeys, elephants, and foxes) give us an accurate picture of what the understanding can achieve without the assistance of reason.[22] Because causality is among the forms that constitute the world as representation, the world as representation exists only insofar as the understanding of at least one animal or human being is in operation.

Reason is the faculty, uniquely possessed by human beings, that enables them to form abstract representations, or concepts, the third possible object of consciousness that Schopenhauer considers. Concepts are "representations of representations." Thus, they are derived from perception. Many particulars (known through perception) can, at least in principle, be thought under a given concept, for concepts are essentially abstract and universal. Any concept can therefore be said to have a range. The faculty of **judgment** determines the relations among the ranges of various concepts.

"**Knowing**" is a matter of determining the truth of given judgments. The principle of sufficient reason ensures that every true judgment can be referred to a ground, and that truth can be established by this means. The particular form of the ground for a judgment depends on the type of judgment being made. Logical truths are grounded in other judgments; material truths are grounded empirically; transcendental truths are grounded in the conditions of the possibility of experience; and metalogical truths are grounded in the formal conditions of thought (the laws of identity, excluded middle, and contradiction, and the principle of sufficient reason).

Despite the fact that Schopenhauer credits judgment with the ability to interrelate concepts in a way that yields knowledge, he has little enthusiasm for the abstract articulation of such relationships in logic. "It is merely knowing in the abstract what everyone knows in the concrete."[23] Logic has no practical use, although Schopenhauer is willing to declare it "perfectly safe."[24] The only useful role of logic, according to Schopenhauer, is to assist philosophers in gaining insight into the nature of reason – and this should be their concern in their logical investigations.

The fourth type of object that Schopenhauer considers to be governed by the principle of sufficient reason, the object of "action," is the self as a willing being. In this case, the ground of action is a **motive**. Motives determine only the external results of willing – actions within the world as representation. The inner reality involved in willing will be discussed in connection with the world as Will.

In every case, the principle of sufficient reason pertains only to objects in the world as representation. It does not govern the thing-in-itself. Schopenhauer utilizes this distinction to dismiss a number of traditional philosophical positions. Among these are all views regarding what Schopenhauer calls "the foolish controversy about the reality of the external world."[25] Because causality operates only within the phenomenal world, i.e. the world as representation, Schopenhauer argues, causality obtains only between objects, not between subject and object. The real object is always a representation of consciousness. Therefore, it is nonsense to seek (as do all who concern themselves with the problem of the external world's existence) a "real" object outside the phenomenal realm.[26]

Schopenhauer dismisses materialism on similar grounds. The materialist attempts to explain consciousness by reference to a prior material ground. But "matter" is, as we have seen, one of the forms fundamental to the thinking subject's capacity for representation. Without the thinking subject and the forms that it uses to constitute its representations, "matter" evaporates. " 'No object without subject,' is the principle that renders all materialism for ever impossible."[27]

❧ THE AMBIVALENCE OF REASON ❧

Reason affords the human being unique possibilities, unavailable to animals. Through reason, human beings can transcend their own understanding. Unlike animals, who are motivated only by what they perceive directly, humans can be motivated by abstract ideas. They are also able to choose among motives because reason can represent several simultaneously. This transcendence enables the human being to have a sense of time, and to plan for the future. The use of words as tokens for concepts, an essential characteristic of rational beings, facilitates the formulation and preservation of knowledge, which in turn can be put to use in actualizing human plans.

Schopenhauer is less enthusiastic about reason, however, than most of his fellow philosophers. Reason introduces error, care, and doubt into human experience. By virtue of reason, human beings can lose touch with their perceptions and behave much more foolishly than animals can act. Along with consciousness of time, reason produces consciousness of death, and the dread that goes with it.

Schopenhauer considers reason's proper role in human experience to be relatively modest. Rational knowledge fixes "in concepts of reason what is known generally in another way."[28] Thus, reason does not, strictly speaking, yield knowledge; instead, it reproduces perceptual knowledge in an alternative form.

The value of reason's alternative mode of formulation is primarily that it enhances the communicability and preservation of knowledge. The price, however, is a sacrifice of some of the fineness of perceptual knowledge, such as that which an expert billiard player or musician can employ in practice. The concepts of reason are also insufficient to produce art, which depends on the artist's perceptual acumen. Even in behavior, the concepts of reason are deceptively clear, lacking the fine-grained character of perceptual knowledge.

Schopenhauer concludes that reason, while essential and useful in human life, must never gain the upper hand over perception. In this, he opposes not only the philosophical commonplace that reason is the pride of humanity. He also opposes the common ethical view that reason should be entrusted with control of one's behavior.

Reason is so far from being a trustworthy guide in behavior that Schopenhauer considers it to be an essential presupposition of folly. He analyzes the ludicrous, the ground of all humor, as arising from the incongruity of reason's concepts in relation to real objects. Behavioral foolishness, like other forms of humor, occurs when one interprets an object in terms of a single concept, but suddenly perceives that the object has one or more characteristics that are incompatible with that concept. Thus, to appropriate a joke from Kant's *Critique of Judgment*, the man who complained about the mourners at his loved one's funeral, on the grounds that they kept looking happier the more he paid them to look sad, makes a conceptual error. He interprets the mourners' expressions as being the services for which he pays them, and he ignores the fact that their expressions might literally "express" their pleasure at being paid.[29] Building on this analysis, Schopenhauer labels "foolish" those principled moralists who see reason as the appropriate ethical guide:

> Pedantry . . . arises from a man's having little confidence in his own understanding, and therefore not liking to leave things to its discretion, to recognize directly what is right in the particular case. Accordingly, he puts his understanding entirely under the guardianship of his reason, and makes use therefore on all occasion; in other words, he wants always to start from general concepts, rules, and maxims, and to stick strictly to these in life, in art, and even in ethical good conduct. . . . The incongruity between the concept and reality soon shows itself, as the former never descends to the particular case, and its universality and rigid definiteness can never accurately apply to reality's fine shades of difference and its innumerable modifications. Therefore the pedant with his general maxims almost always comes off badly in life, and shows himself foolish, absurd, and incompetent.

Even Kant, whom Schopenhauer largely admires, is convicted by this analysis:

We cannot entirely exonerate Kant from the reproach of causing moral pedantry, in so far as he makes it a condition of the moral worth of an action that it be done from purely rational abstract maxims without any inclination or momentary emotion.[30]

Schopenhauer's insistence on the primacy of perception over reason extends to his analysis of science. Science aims at complete knowledge in the abstract of some particular species of objects. It is concerned with the form of knowledge, for it aims at facilitating and completing (i.e. systematically connecting and hierarchizing) what is known about its objects. Perception, however, being the ultimate source of knowledge, is also the basis of science. All scientific evidence derives ultimately from intuitive perception.

As a systematic employment of reason, science is subject to the limitations inherent to abstract thought. Frequently, science makes use of proofs, which involve the deduction of new consequences from previously accepted propositions. Proofs do not establish the certainty of their conclusions, for the truth of a conclusion depends on the truth of the premises. The conclusion of an abstract chain of reasoning, moreover, is never really new knowledge; it is only an exposition of what the premises already imply. "Proofs are generally less for those who want to learn than for those who want to dispute."

Schopenhauer is so thoroughly convinced that reason is subordinate to perception that he believes that every truth ascertained through proof or syllogism is, in principle, recognizable through direct perception as well.[31] He recommends a strategy of teaching geometric truths through direct observation of geometrical figures. This he prefers to Euclid's method of proof from axioms, "a very brilliant piece of perversity." Schopenhauer likens Euclid's approach to "a conjuring trick" that brings truth in "almost always . . . by the back door, since it follows *per accidens* from some minor circumstance."[32] Through direct perception we can see both *that* something is so and *why* it is so, according to Schopenhauer, while with Euclid's method, we see only the former.

Science, insofar as it aims to explain things, is concerned ultimately with the principle of sufficient reason. Explanation establishes the relations of phenomena with one another, a relation always determined by the principle of sufficient reason. In every case, however, the systematic pursuit of explanation stops, confronted either with the necessary truths fundamental to our basic forms of knowledge or with "an accepted *qualitas occulta* ('occult quality'), which is entirely obscure."[33] Primary concepts of science, such as weight, cohesion, and chemical properties, as well as the inner nature of a human being, are all *qualita-*

tes occultae. Such occult qualities establish the limits of every science. Schopenhauer sees these as indications of the thing-in-itself, which appears in them. The thing-in-itself is the inner reality that science cannot explain. It is thus the absolute limit that science cannot penetrate.

❧ THE WILL AS THING-IN-ITSELF, THE ❧ INNER LIFE OF OBJECTS

Schopenhauer's account of the world as representation presupposes a third-person point of view. But what is the real significance of the world as representation? Schopenhauer observes, regarding the world's phenomena, that "these pictures or images do not march past us strange and meaningless ... but speak to us directly, are understood, and acquire an interest that engrosses our whole nature."[34] Yet if we restrict our attention to what Schopenhauer considers in his account of the world as representation, our interest in these phenomena is mysterious. Our own position seems a bit like that of

> a man who, without knowing how, is brought into a company
> quite unknown to him, each member of which in turn presents
> to him another as his friend and cousin, and thus makes them
> sufficiently acquainted. The man himself, however, while
> assuring each person introduced of his pleasure at meeting him,
> always has on his lips the question: "But how the deuce do I
> stand to the whole company?"[35]

The key to resolving this question regarding our relationship to phenomena is the status of our own bodies. Each of us is not merely the consciousness for whom the world as representation exists. We are not only consciousness, but embodied. The body to which each consciousness is attached has an odd relationship to the world as representation. On the one hand, the body is itself a representation, which behaves much like other representations. On the other hand, the body seems to be moved by an inner mechanism. This inner mechanism, according to Schopenhauer, is aptly designated "will."

Schopenhauer takes sexual desire to be a paradigmatic manifestation of this inner will.[36] The will is demanding, persistent, discontented, and perpetually goal-oriented. Insofar as one has desires, one has will, according to Schopenhauer. The will connects us to the world as representation; it gives us "interests." We take an interest in our world because it provides objects, instruments, and obstructions in connection with our various desires and projects.

The individual's direct knowledge of his or her body has two aspects. The individual experiences inner acts of will; yet these acts of will are simultaneously acts of the body. Schopenhauer concludes that the body is "nothing but the objectified will, i.e. will that has become representation." From the point of view of the world as representation, it is "the immediate object," but from the point of view afforded by one's inner awareness, it is "the objectivity of the will."[37]

Schopenhauer indicates several corollaries to his principle that the will and the body are one. First, willing and acting are one and the same. "Only the carrying out stamps the resolve; till then, it is always a mere intention that can be altered; it exists only in reason, in the abstract."[38] Second, pleasure and pain are not representations, but impressions of the will through the body. Such impressions are pleasure when they accord with the will, pain when they contradict the will. Third, every emotion, which Schopenhauer defines as a "vehement and excessive movement of the will," directly "agitates the body and its inner workings," thereby disturbing its vital functions.[39] Fourth, one cannot separate one's knowledge of the will from one's knowledge of the body and its individual acts in time. Thus, one cannot observe one's will as a whole, in its timeless reality.[40]

Schopenhauer considers the individual's direct knowledge of the will within the body to be knowledge of what the body is in itself. In this respect, our bodies afford access to the thing-in-itself, the realm that Kant denies to knowledge. Schopenhauer's approach here raises a conceptual problem. He accepts Kant's claim that the thing-in-itself does not admit of plurality. Yet in appealing to each individual's insight into the inner mechanism of his or her own body, Schopenhauer seems to have indicated an "inner reality" that still admits of plurality. He goes on to argue that the inner life that each individual recognizes in the body is a single life common to all. But how do we get from the plurality of inner "wills" to the unified thing-in-itself? Schopenhauer's statements regarding the relationship of particulars to the Will are not particularly illuminating: "only the will is thing-in-itself. . . . It is the innermost essence, the kernel, of every particular thing and also of the whole."[41]

Schopenhauer's argument for extending the concept of "will" to refer to the inner reality of all phenomena is similarly problematic. He defends this move by arguing that one has only two options. Either one can account for one's unique access to the inner life of one's own body by claiming that it is the *only* object that is both will and representation. This course would amount to solipsism, or theoretical egoism, the conviction that one's own being is the only real being. Or the individual can assume that all objects have a similar inner reality, and that while one's *relationship* to one's body is unique, the body itself is not. Serious theoretical egoism being a form of insanity, Schopenhauer dismisses the former alternative as a view that requires "not so much a refutation as a cure."[42] He concludes that one is warranted in granting to every other phenomenal object a reality comparable to that of one's own body.

Thus, Schopenhauer exends the term "will," which seems apt for the inner life of our own bodies, to refer to the inner nature of all objects. Schopenhauer's primary defense of this extension is that we have no better alternative. He believes that we naturally tend to anthropomorphize our world because anthropomorphic metaphors convey the most to us. "Will," accordingly, conveys more to us than any other term we could use.

"Force" might be thought a viable alternative. But we have no insight into the basic forces of nature at all, Schopenhauer insists. They are *qualitates occultae*, completely unfathomable to us. By contrast, the word "will" refers to the most distinct form in which the reality underlying all phenomena appears to us. Thus, "will" is the most meaningful term we could use to name the inner reality of all things.

Schopenhauer considers the inner reality of other phenomena to be thoroughly comparable with our own. "Spinoza (*Epist.* 62) says that if a stone projected through the air had consciousness, it would imagine it was flying of its own will. I add merely that the stone would be right."[43] Schopenhauer points out, however, that in calling the inner nature of all objects, including inanimate ones, "Will," he does not mean to attribute sentience and conscious motives to all of them. Will operates differently in different types of objects. Only in humans and animals does it employ motives determined by knowledge. The stimuli that prompt most organic processes and the causes that occasion inorganic ones are mechanisms that do not involve knowledge. Nevertheless, despite the differences among these forms of causation, the Will is operative through all of them.

❧ NO FREE WILL ❧

Because he believes that motives determine the will in human beings, Schopenhauer denies that human beings have free will. An individual's actions are completely determined by motives in conjunction with his or her character. Schopenhauer follows Kant in distinguishing the **empirical character**, the character of the individual as it appears in phenomenon, from the **intelligible character**, the character as it is in itself, outside of time and space. Schopenhauer considers the latter to be a timeless, unalterable act of the Will, which is manifest in empirical behavior over time. The empirical character accurately objectifies the intelligible character: "the man . . . will always will in the particular what he wills on the whole."⁴⁴ But it does this gradually; and the precise forms through which it manifests the intelligible character are in part determined by the entirely contingent features of circumstances.

Given that the empirical character, motives, and one's actions are all among the objects of representation, causality obtains among them. Hence, in principle, a causal account can be given to explain any of an individual's actions. However, in practice such accounts are limited. In the first place, human beings possess more striking individuality than do any other kind of beings. The range of human characters is considerable. Hence, one needs considerable knowledge of a particular person's character, in addition to knowledge of the motive, in order to predict what that person will do in a given case.

Moreover, the knowledge that one can have is knowledge of the empirical character, which is not the character of the individual in itself, but only the appearance of the latter over time. In the case of those whom we have known well for a long time, we may be fairly competent predictors of behavior. But we come to know the empirical character only through its actions. after the fact; thus, our knowledge is limited. This is as true of one's own character as of any other individual's. Knowledge even of one's own character is a considerable achievement. Schopenhauer labels such gradually accumulated knowledge of what one wills and what one can do "**acquired character.**" Such knowledge enables one to direct one's actions consistently and effectively toward satisfaction of one's will, for it allows one to recognize in advance what courses of action are worth attempting, given one's own limitations.

Our ignorance, even of our own characters, leads many to believe that human beings have free will. Because we lack sufficient information to predict our own and others' behavior accurately, we cannot see that it follows absolutely from the interaction of character and motive. Moreover, because we engage in deliberation, the abstract contemplation of multiple motives, each of which recommends a different course of action, we tend to feel as though the ensuing action is in suspension until we choose. "But," claims Schopenhauer,

> this is just the same as if we were to say in the case of a vertical
> pole, thrown off its balance and hesitating which way to fall, that
> "it can topple over to the right or to the left" . . . this "*can*"
> has only a subjective significance, and really means "in view
> of the data known to us." For objectively, the direction of the
> fall is necessarily determined as soon as the hesitation takes
> place. Accordingly, the decision of one's own will is
> undetermined only for its spectator, one's own intellect, and
> therefore only relatively and subjectively. . . . In itself and

objectively, on the other hand, the decision is at once determined and necessary in the case of every choice presented to it.[45]

The true situation is reflected by our own attitudes regarding freedom. Schopenhauer observes that

> everyone considers himself to be *a priori* quite free, even in his individual actions, and imagines he can at any moment enter upon a different way of life, which is equivalent to saying that he can become a different person. But *a posteriori* through experience, he finds to his astonishment that he is not free, but liable to necessity; that notwithstanding all his resolutions and reflections he does not change his conduct, and that from the beginning to the end of his life he must bear the same character that he himself condemns, and, as it were, must play to the end the part he has taken upon himself.[46]

The explanation lies in the fact that as individuals our actions are completely determined by our characters and a motive. However, because our own inner reality is the Will, which is not constrained by causality, we feel the Will's freedom within ourselves and mistakenly associate it with our own individuality. What the Will freely does, however, is to assign to each of us a character, which we have no power to alter. We are also incapable of explaining why an individual has the particular character he or she does, for the Will is not subject to causality, and thus is not constrained by anything in its selection of this character.

Thus, no explanation can be provided as to why an individual is motivated by the particular motive he or she is. Our account of human behavior is necessarily limited. In this respect, human behavior is akin to the behavior of everything else in the phenomenal world. All rests on *qualitates occultae* which cannot be further illuminated.

❦ PLATONIC IDEAS ❦

We have already observed that Schopenhauer's account of the unity of the thing-in-itself does not square easily with the plural points of departure we are told to use to infer it. Schopenhauer touches on the problem of bridging the noumenal and phenomenal realms in his appeal to the Platonic theory of the Forms, or "Platonic Ideas."

Schopenhauer attempts to clarify the Will's relationship to its plural manifestations by arguing that it does not make sense to say that "more" will is in the human being than in the stone. "More" and "less" depend on the spatial form in which the representation appears and have to do only with the will's objectification, not with the Will itself. The inner life of each thing is "present whole and undivided" within it.[47] However, it is appropriate to say that the Will is objectified to a higher degree in the human being than in the stone. The Platonic Ideas are the immediate objectivity of the Will at particular grades, or degrees.

The Platonic Ideas are for Schopenhauer, as for Plato, the unchanging eternal patterns, or Forms, in which the innumerable, transient particulars of the phenomenal world participate. Every particular Idea, in Schopenhauer's usage, is a definite "grade of the will's objectification . . . related to individual things as their eternal forms, or as their prototypes."[48] These are, according to Schopenhauer, intuitively graspable by perception, not mediated by the abstractions of reason.

The "location" of the Platonic Ideas in relation to the noumenal and phenomenal worlds (i.e. the world as Will and the world as representation) is a bit confusing. The Platonic Ideas are outside time and space, and hence not in the world as representation. On the other hand, they are multiple, while the Will is not. Perhaps the best way to understand the Ideas' "bridging" of the world as Will and the world as representation is to envision the Ideas as windows through which the Will has access to the world as representation. Of course, the world as representation is entirely a manifestation of the Will, according to Schopenhauer. Thus, the window image is misleading, in that it makes the world as Will and the world as representation seem more distinct than they are in Schopenhauer's scheme.

Although the Platonic Ideas and the thing-in-itself are not identical, Schopenhauer considers them "very closely related," being two "paths leading to one goal."[49] He concludes that the most paradoxical concepts in the thought of Plato and Kant – the Forms and the thing-in-itself – are thus reflections of essentially the same insight:

> the inner meaning of both doctrines is wholly the same; that both declare the visible world to be a phenomenon which in itself is void and empty, and which has meaning and borrowed reality only through the thing that expresses itself in it (the thing-in-itself in the one case, the Idea in the other).[50]

The unity of the Platonic Idea in all its phenomena is, according to Schopenhauer, what is meant by "a law of nature." Laws of nature relate the Idea to the forms of representation. Because both the Idea and the conditions of its representability are constant, a law of nature holds for all the phenomena it governs, without exception. What acts in any such case is an inexplicable natural force. The "cause" involved determines only when and where a particular natural force has the occasion to exhibit itself in a particular piece of matter.

The Platonic Ideas, according to Schopenhauer, comprise a hierarchy of discrete levels. The "lowest" grades of the Will's objectification are the universal forces of nature. Among these are gravity and impenetrability, which govern all matter. Schopenhauer also includes "rigidity, fluidity, elasticity, electricity, magnetism, chemical properties, and qualities of every kind," forces that govern some pieces of matter but not others.[51]

Individuality is a function of the hierarchy of the Platonic Ideas, such that the higher grades of the Will's objectification exhibit more individuality than the lower ones. Accordingly, higher animals have more individuality than lower ones. In the lower animals, one sees no trace of individuality, but only the general character and physiognomy of the species. Plants have little individual character, according to Schopenhauer, while inorganic objects have virtually none.

Human beings have more individuality than anything else in nature. Individuality is so extreme in human beings that every person can "to a certain extent" be described in terms of a particular idea. Schopenhauer identifies this "Idea" of the individual as the individual's intelligible character, the result of a unique act of the Will outside time. Nonetheless, Schopenhauer insists that human beings manifest a common form of humanity. Perhaps the best way of integrating these two claims is to see the "special" Ideas of each individual human to be facets of the more encompassing Idea of humanity. Indeed, Schopenhauer indicates that individuality in general amounts to partial expression of "the whole of the Idea."[52]

Because the same Will manifests itself in all Ideas, all phenomena manifesting the Ideas have an inner relationship with one another. One consequence is that the forms of the various plants and animals all bear a kind of analogy with one another. A family likeness prevails even between the Ideas of inorganic phenomena. Schopenhauer points to the analogies that can be observed between electricity and magnetism, and between chemical attraction and gravitation.

The levels of the Will's manifestation are also mutually dependent upon one another. The Ideas form a pyramid, with the Idea of humanity as its culmination. The manifestations of the higher Ideas, accordingly, presuppose the manifestations of the lower in external nature. Hence, the human being depends on animals; animals depend on other animals and plants; the plants need soil, water, sun, etc.; and all of nature depends on the inert mass of the planet. Every phenomenon adapts itself to its environment, while its environment similarly adapts itself to each phenomenon. This interdependence of all phenomena in nature reflects the fact that "the will must live in itself, since nothing exists besides it, and it is a hungry will."[53]

Despite such analogies, however, Schopenhauer insists that the Ideas should not be conflated with one another. Indeed, phenomena of different Ideas can be seen as essentially at war with one another. Throughout the organic world, one organism eats or somehow assimilates another: "every animal can maintain its own existence only by the incessant elimination of another's."[54] The struggle among the various kinds of phenomenon assimilated in the organic body exemplifies a more basic struggle, that inherent to the nature of the Will. The Will, as Schopenhauer conceives it, is fundamentally at "variance with itself."[55] Even matter exists by virtue of a struggle among forces of attraction and repulsion, manifested as gravitation and impenetrability. Although the unity and oneness of the Will are manifest in the mutual adaptation of all natural phenomena, the harmony goes only so far as is necessary for "the continuance of the world,"[56] which requires only the continuance of species, not that of particular individuals.

The essential struggle among all phenomena corresponds to the fact that the Will operating within them is blind. Even in beings that have knowledge, knowledge is originally and fundamentally an expedient of the will. Only rarely, in aesthetic experience and ethical insight, does human knowledge do anything but assist the fulfillment of the will's demands. Thus, humans, too, with rare exceptions, struggle endlessly with other phenomena.

Although the Will struggles continually, we are not in a position to say why the Will wills. Even to ask the question is to confuse the Will with the phenomenon, for it amounts to asking what causes the Will's willing. Nothing can cause the Will's willing, for the Will is not determined by causality, which is only a form of the Will's objectification in the world as representation. As thing-in-itself, the Will is groundless. Schopenhauer concludes that the Will is aimless, and that aimless, endless striving is also characteristic of its manifestations.

❧ AESTHETIC EXPERIENCE ❧

Aesthetic experience provides, for most individuals, the sole respite from "the penal servitude of willing."[57] According to Schopenhauer, aesthetic experience involves direct knowledge of the Platonic Ideas. Because these Ideas are not subject to the principle of sufficient reason, they are not objects of knowledge in the phenomenal world. The individual is manifest as an individual only within the phenomenal world, however. Schopenhauer concludes that the Ideas can only become objects of knowledge "by abolishing individuality in the knowing subject."[58] This is what aesthetic experience accomplishes.

Schopenhauer describes aesthetic experience by means of a contrast with everyday experience. In everyday experience, the individual experiences his or her body as existing in a world of other objects that stand in various relations to it, and by means of it, to the individual's will. The other objects of the phenomenal world are conceived by the individual as either potential means or potential obstacles to the fulfillment of the will's desires. These objects are known, in fact, only in terms of their relations to other manifestations of the will – for accounts in terms of the principle of sufficient reason are essentially relational accounts.

Aesthetic experience alters the individual's perception of objects and the individual's awareness of self. The individual ceases to be "merely individual" and becomes "a pure will-less subject of knowledge."[59] In aesthetic experience, the subject is no longer concerned with relations between his or her body and other objects, but instead restfully contemplates the object alone, outside of all relations. This contemplation is not mediated by abstract concepts; instead, one devotes one's mind entirely to perception of what is present. The distinction of subject and object drops away in this state of absorption; one does not differentiate the perceiver from the perception. In aesthetic experience, we are appropriately said to "lose ourselves."[60]

The "knowledge" involved in aesthetic experience does not involve knowledge of an object's relations. What is known, instead, is the Idea of the object. The object is rendered universal in this experience, for it becomes, for the perceiver, the eternal form of the will's objectivity at its grade. The subject, at the same time, also becomes universal as the "*pure* will-less, painless, timeless subject of knowledge."[61] Both subject and object have passed beyond the forms of the principle of sufficient reason. The timeless Idea that is the object's prototype becomes present to the observer as a timeless intellect, no longer engaged in projects of the will.

In arguing that aesthetic experience undermines desire, Schopenhauer accepts Kant's claim that aesthetic experience is essentially disinterested. Nietzsche indicates the controversial nature of this claim in his caricature of Schopenhauer's aesthetics:

> Schopenhauer speaks of *beauty* with a melancholy fervor. . . .
> Beauty is for him a momentary redemption from the "will" –
> a lure to eternal redemption. Particularly, he praises beauty as
> the redeemer from "the focal point of the will," from sexuality
> – in beauty he sees the negation of the drive toward procreation.

Queer saint! Somebody seems to be contradicting you; I fear it is nature.[62]

Nietzsche rejects Kant and Schopenhauer's characterization of beauty as inspiring contemplation that is "disinterested," arguing that nothing is of greater interest to human beings.

Although Schopenhauer follows Kant in his analysis of aesthetic disinterestedness, he breaks from Kant in his analysis of the difference between **the beautiful** and **the sublime**. According to Kant, appreciation of the beautiful and appreciation of the sublime involve different mental operations and even different faculties. Schopenhauer, by contrast, insists that the beautiful and the sublime differ rather slightly. Both aim, in his view, at contemplation of the Idea within phenomena.

The difference between the beautiful and the sublime lies only in the contemplated object's usual relationship to the will. In the case of the beautiful, the object contemplated seems almost designed for willless contemplation; its form is so well suited to the human senses that it invites tranquil observation. In the case of the sublime, however, the contemplated object has, by its very nature, a hostile relationship to the observer's will, and the observer is consequently aware of some inner aversion to it. One can achieve aesthetic contemplation of the sublime, therefore, only by means of forcibly subduing the will's aversion. In the case of the beautiful, on the other hand, the object itself soothes the will, and no effort is required to silence it.

Schopenhauer concludes that the beautiful and the sublime are two ends of the same continuum. Besides paradigm cases of each, certain cases fall in between. These Schopenhauer considers relatively sublime. For example, even the aesthetic appreciation of radiant sunlight on a snowy landscape is somewhat sublime; one must forcibly resist dwelling upon the inhospitable temperature of the snow in order to enjoy the visual spectacle.

Like experience of the beautiful and of the sublime, in Schopenhauer's analysis, aesthetic experiences of nature and art are essentially kindred. **Art** is "the work of **genius**."[63] Genius is a pre-eminent talent for engaging in aesthetic contemplation. The genius is able to "grasp the Idea of each thing, not its relation to other things."[64] Because this process involves forgetting one's own personal concerns, Schopenhauer describes genius as "the most complete objectivity, i.e. the objective tendency of the mind."[65]

The genius's talent is possessed in some measure by all human beings. According to Schopenhauer, this is why the average individual is able to enjoy art. In art the genius communicates his or her own recognition of Ideas. Aesthetic pleasure is always a matter of grasping the Idea, whether the phenomenon contemplated is a natural object or an artwork. For most individuals, however, "the Idea comes . . . more easily from the work of art." This is because "the artist, who knew only the Idea and not reality, clearly repeated in his work only the Idea, separated it out from reality, and omitted all disturbing contingencies."[66]

Through this analysis of the artwork, Schopenhauer suggests criteria for evaluating art. Good art is produced when the artist works from direct perception of the Idea, not from conceptual recipes. The success of an artwork also depends on the artist's technical skill at communicating this direct perception to the audience.

Like many aestheticians of his own and the previous century, Schopenhauer hierarchically classifies the types of art. His criterion for classification is the significance of the Platonic Ideas that are focal within a given medium. Thus, the arts that invite contemplation of the lower Ideas are ranked lower than those that invite contemplation of the higher Ideas.

Architecture is assigned the lowest place in Schopenhauer's hierarchy, because it brings "to clearer perceptiveness some of those Ideas that are the lowest grades of the will's objectivity." Among these, he includes "gravity, cohesion, rigidity, hardness," and also "light, which is in many respects their opposite."[67] Architecture reveals the way in which these basic forces oppose one another. Thus, rigidity opposes gravity in certain constructions. Schopenhauer classifies "artistic arrangements of water" on the same level as architecture, for fountains bring into prominence the Ideas of fluidity and gravity, again Ideas at the lowest grades of the Will's objectivity.

Landscape gardening and landscape painting comprise the level above architecture and fountain art in Schopenhauer's scheme, for these reveal the Ideas of the vegetative world. The next level includes animal painting and animal sculpture, which reveal the Ideas of animal life. Historical painting and sculpture reveal the Idea of the human being, and hence these occupy a still higher level. But a fuller revelation of the Idea of the human being occurs in poetry, where the principal object is the human being "in so far as he expresses himself not through the mere form and expression of his features and countenance, but through a chain of actions and of the accompanying thought and emotions."[68]

Schopenhauer believes that the most profound insight into humanity involves awareness that the same Will wars against itself in the conflicts among human beings. Presumably, this is why he classifies tragedy as "the summit of poetic art." Tragedy aims at "the description of the terrible side of life," and it reveals the profound insight "that what the hero atones for is not his own particular sins, but original sin, in other words, the guilt of existence itself."[69] Optimally, tragedy can bring home to its audience the true character of our interactions with one another. In the best type of tragedy,

> characters as they usually are in a moral regard in circumstances
> that frequently occur, are so situated with regard to one
> another that their position forces them, knowingly and with
> their eyes open, to do one another the greatest injury, without
> any one of them being entirely in the wrong.[70]

Thus far, no mention has been made of music. Schopenhauer sees music as being entirely unlike the other arts. All other arts aim to facilitate perception of the Ideas, on his account; but music copies the Will directly. As a consequence, "the effect of music is so very much more powerful and penetrating than is that of the other arts."[71] Not at all concerned to represent specific phenomena, as do the visual arts, music transcends particularity even in emotional expression:

> Therefore music does not express this or that particular and
> definite pleasure, this or that affliction, pain, sorrow, horror,
> gaiety, merriment, or peace of mind, but joy, pain, sorrow,
> horror, gaiety, merriment, peace of mind *themselves*, to a
> certain extent in the abstract, their essential nature, without any
> accessories, and so also without the motives for them.[72]

Because the world as representation itself, taken as a whole, is an objectification of the Will, music and the world have a parallel relationship to the Will. Thus, Schopenhauer concludes that a complete philosophy of music would "also be at once a sufficient repetition and explanation of the world in concepts, or one wholly corresponding thereto, and hence, the true philosophy."[73]

Schopenhauer elaborates on this suggestion by indicating points of analogy between features of music and characteristics of the world. These depend, to a certain extent, on the structure of the music with which Schopenhauer was contingently familiar. Thus, he compares the relatively hierarchical relationships among voices common in Western music of the eighteenth and nineteenth centuries to the hierarchical relationships among Ideas. The low voices, like the lowest Ideas, provide the ground on which all the others depend. Schopenhauer compares the melody to "the intellectual life and endeavor of man," for unlike the inner voices in his analogy (which he compares to animal and vegetable life), "*melody* alone has significant and intentional connexion from beginning to end."[74]

Despite Schopenhauer's analysis of music as a copy of the Will, he believes that music, like the other arts, affords escape from everyday awareness, which is constantly driven by will. This is because music expresses the nature of willing in universal form, without concern for particular phenomena. In this respect, the insight that music affords resembles that which Schopenhauer sees essential to ethics, the insight that the phenomenal world, with its apparently separate objects and individuals, is an illusion that veils the transcendent nature of the world.

❧ LIFE IS SUFFERING ❧

Because all individuals, and indeed all living phenomena, are objectifications of the Will, their essential tendency is to will. Striving continually, living beings gain one objective only to strive anew for another. Dissatisfaction of one sort or another characterizes life from beginning to end. The life of all humans and animals "swings like a pendulum to and fro between pain and boredom, and these two are in fact its ultimate constituents."[75]

Analyzing all striving as essentially "need, lack, and hence pain," Schopenhauer concludes that life is essentially suffering:

> The life of the great majority is only a constant struggle for this same existence, with the certainty of ultimately losing it. What enables them to endure this wearisome battle is not so much the love of life as the fear of death.[76]

Schopenhauer contends that fear of death is irrational. Only the human being as phenomenon is transient; as thing-in-itself the human being is eternal. Nevertheless, this is rarely consoling to the individual, who most often takes individual existence (understood through the forms of the world as representation) extremely seriously. Thus, the life of the individual human being is for the most part perverse and pointless:

> The life of every individual, viewed as a whole and in general, and when only its most significant features are emphasized, is really a tragedy; but gone through in detail it has the character of a comedy. For the doings and worries of the day, the restless mockeries of the moment, the desires and fears of the week, the mishaps of every hour, are all brought about by chance that is always bent on some mischievous trick; they are nothing but scenes from a comedy. The never-fulfilled wishes, the frustrated mistakes of the whole life, with increasing suffering and death at the end, always give us a tragedy. Thus, as if fate wished to add mockery to the misery of our existence, our life must contain all the woes of tragedy, and yet we cannot even assert the dignity of tragic characters, but, in the broad detail of life, are inevitably the foolish characters of a comedy.[77]

Sexuality, which most pointedly displays the Will in human

beings, exemplifies this connection between desire and suffering. The Will deludes the individual into imagining that gaining the beloved will result in happiness. In fact, however, the Will is only concerned with the preservation of the species, not with the happiness of the individual. Thus, while human sexual desire is extremely individualized, it is motivated only by the Will's concern that the species propagate a new generation of healthy children with relatively standard traits.[78] Schopenhauer concludes that the embarrassment surrounding sexuality stems from guilt at renewing the world's suffering by contributing to a new generation.

> If . . . we . . . contemplate the bustle and turmoil of life, we see everyone concerned with its cares and troubles, exerting all his strength to satisfy infinite needs and to ward off suffering in many forms, yet without daring to hope for anything else in place of it except just the preservation of this tormented existence for a short span of time. In between, however, we see in the midst of the tumult the glances of two lovers meet longingly; yet why so secretly, nervously, and furtively? Because these lovers are the traitors who secretly strive to perpetuate the whole trouble and toil that would otherwise rapidly come to an end. Such an end they try to frustrate, as others like them have frustrated it previously.[79]

❧ SALVATION AND MORAL GOODNESS ❧

The affirmation of the Will-to-live, which is fundamental to all living beings, necessarily results in a life of suffering. The only salvation from suffering, according to Schopenhauer, is the denial of the Will-to-live. This is possible only for human beings, for human beings alone are capable of inner knowledge into the reality behind phenomenon. In rare individuals this knowledge becomes so completely absorbed that particular phenomena come to seem merely illusory. In such a case, these phenomena no longer provide motives for the will. When this happens, the will is quieted, "and thus the will freely abolishes itself."[80] The suffering Will itself, in such an individual, attains peace. The saintly individual, therefore, fulfills the ultimate aim of the Will (the cessation of struggle), but precisely by denying the will within.

Although Schopenhauer's formulations of such ascetic salvation sound negative, the insight motivating the holy life is essentially the same insight that motivates all virtuous behavior. The basic knowledge fundamental to both is the knowledge that the Will driving all phenomena is essentially one.

When one perceives this truth, one is no longer motivated to do **wrong**, which Schopenhauer describes as being the denial of the will in another individual. Egoism, the source of all wrongdoing, arises from the delusion that one's individual, phenomenal existence is tremendously important. Perception of the truth – that the same will is manifest in all beings – dispels this delusion.

Such perception, however, admits of degrees. Even the **bad** person, who is so little in control of the will within that he or she chooses to violate the will in other individuals, has a pained awareness that such action is wrong. This is because every individual dimly grasps that such action violates one's own true being. The person who recognizes the Will's oneness to a somewhat greater degree is **just**. Such a person refrains from affirming his or her own will at the expense of any other individual's right to a similar affirmation.

Moral goodness, in Schopenhauer's analysis, stems directly from knowledge and its quieting effect on the will. Schopenhauer denies that universal moral principles have any value, for virtue is achieved individually by means of insight. One might wonder how beings without free will can achieve moral transformation by means of insight. Schopenhauer's answer is that while motive and character together determine action, change of knowledge produces a change of motive, which in turn affects the action that results. All **repentance** arises from a change of knowledge, not from a change of will. When one recognizes that one has used an inappropriate means for obtaining one's object, for instance, this knowledge results in a change of behavior. In the case of radical transformation toward virtue, Schopenhauer would argue that one has recognized that no action directed against another's will could possibly enhance one's life. Hence, any such action is no longer seen as a viable means to achieve one's ends, so one comes to avoid such actions.

The **good** person goes further than the just person and is moved to **compassion** for all sentient beings by the recognition that they are all phenomena of the same will. A truly noble person "makes less distinction than is usually made between himself and others," and thus displays concern for others of the same degree as that concern directed toward the self.[81] Such individuals have penetrated the *principium individuationis*, which creates the illusion of individual separateness.

The ultimate penetration of the *principium individuationis* is achieved by the saint. A saint has seen through the delusions of the phenomenal world and responded with so much compassion that he or she no longer wants to have any part in inflicting suffering. This self-abolition of the will is the course taken by mystics of all traditions, according to Schopenhauer. No longer motivated by phenomena, these holy individuals abandon the usual expressions of will in human life.

Thus, they abstain from sex, adopt voluntary poverty, fast, and in general mortify the body, which is objectified affirmation of the Will. Their entire existence is characterized by **renunciation of the will**, and their lives are models of **resignation**.

True salvation stems from this complete denial of the will.[82] At its extreme point, the result is the extinction of character, for no motive still stimulates willful action on the part of the saint. The saint's will evaporates. But in addition, with the evaporation of the will, the entire world as representation, with its inherent distinctions among objects and individuals, vanishes. What remains is "empty *nothingness*," which the Buddhists have labeled *nirvana*.[83]

This nothingness is not, however, absolute. Indeed, the saints and mystics of the ages have described their state as full and blissful. Schopenhauer observes that we conceive of their condition as nothing only because our world of suffering and struggle complete absorbs us:

> we have to banish the dark impression of that nothingness,
> which as the final goal hovers behind all virtue and holiness,
> and which we fear as children fear darkness. . . . On the contrary,
> we freely acknowledge that what remains after the complete
> abolition of the will is, for all who are still full of the will,
> assuredly nothing. But also conversely, to those in whom the
> will has turned and denied itself, this very real world of ours
> with all its suns and galaxies is – nothing.[84]

❧ SCHOPENHAUER'S INTELLECTUAL ❧ LEGACY

Schopenhauer did not really expect his theory of resignation and denial of the will to inspire enthusiasts. Indeed, he prided himself on his renunciation of popularity with his contemporaries.[85] Nevertheless, Schopenhauer would presumably be gratified by the extent to which his ideas have assumed prominence.

Most strikingly, Schopenhauer's conviction that knowledge is subordinate to will – as well as his suggestive remarks on the unconscious – have taken root in contemporary psychological theory. In these respects, as well as in his focus on the body as a philosophical starting point, he reverses Cartesianism and influences much twentieth-century thought. Schopenhauer is also pioneering in developing a systematic philosophy that is completely disconcerned with theology. His pessimistic theories offer a critical response to German romanticism within its own century. Schopenhauer is also closer to the following century in valuing and engaging in comparative studies of the philosophical traditions of the East and the West. Finally, although the ethical claims that he would endorse are relatively traditional, Schopenhauer's denial of the efficacy of moral maxims and universal principles precurses later radical critiques of morality in general.

Ironically, given his doctrine of renunciation of the will, Schopenhauer's writings reveal an insatiable zest for life. Impatient with virtually all of his contemporaries, Schopenhauer seems nevertheless to delight in description and to take pains to move others through his prose. Perhaps his clarity of insight into phenomena is Schopenhauer's greatest philosophical legacy. Schopenhauer lends us his own perceptions of the world. Fittingly, in one who elevates perception over reason, Schopenhauer's perceptions continue to provoke and inspire many who reject every detail of his philosophical system. Although his system is "ingeniously elaborated,"[86] his perceptions are brilliant.

⚬⚬ NOTES ⚬⚬

1 See Schopenhauer, *The World as Will and Representation*, 2 vols, trans. E.F.J. Payne, Vol. I (New York: Dover, 1969), hereafter referred to as *WWR*, I, pp. 96–7, 154.

2 See ibid., pp. 326f.

3 Ibid., pp. 280, 283–4, 324.

4 See ibid., p. 330.

5 Ibid., p. xii.

6 B. Russell, *A History of Western Philosophy* (New York: Simon & Schuster, 1945), p. 758.

7 The German word *"Wille,"* like all German nouns, is consistently capitalized. Payne, in his translations of Schopenhauer, consistently translates this term as "will," with the "w" in lower-case type. I shall adopt the convention of using "Will" to refer to Schopenhauer's metaphysical principle and "will" to refer to the individual will in my own discussion. In citations from Payne's translations, however, I shall follow his usage.

8 F. Nietzsche, *The Genealogy of Morals*, in *The Complete Works of Friedrich Nietzsche*, ed. O. Levy, Vol. 13, trans. H.B. Samuel (Edinburgh: T.N. Foulis, 1910), p. 132.

9 For a sympathetic discussion of the tensions within Schopenhauer's personality, see T. Mann, Introduction to *The Works of Schopenhauer*, ed. W. Durant (New York: Frederick Ungar, 1928), pp. xvii–xxi.

10 F. Nietzsche, *Schopenhauer as Educator*, trans. W. Arrowsmith, in *Unmodern Observations*, ed. W. Arrowsmith (New Haven: Yale University Press, 1990), p. 176.

11 See Schopenhauer, "On Women," in *Parerga and Paralipomena: Short Philosophical Essays*, 2 vols, trans. E.F.J. Payne, Vol. II (Oxford: Clarendon Press, 1974), hereafter referred to as *PP*, pp. 614–26. There, after insisting that women have no talent for the arts, Schopenhauer compares contemporary "ladies" to

"the sacred apes at Benares who, conscious of their sanctity and invulnerability, think that they are at liberty to do anything and everything" (p. 622). He also contends that unlike men, who feel rivalry only for other members of their profession, women feel hostility for all other women. The explanation he offers for this alleged phenomenon is that "with women" professional jealousy "embraces the whole sex since they all have only one line of business" (p. 619). Copleston observes that Schopenhauer's experience of women other than his mother was also "of a character hardly calculated to generate a real respect for and appreciation of the other sex." See F. Copleston SJ, *Arthur Schopenhauer: Philosopher of Pessimism*, Bellarmine Series, XI, ed. E.F. Sutcliffe SJ (London: Burns, Oates & Washbourne, 1947), pp. 39–40.

12 *WWR*, I, p. xxii.

13 This is reflected by his choosing to open his Appendix to *WWR*, I, entitled "Criticism of the Kantian Philosophy," with Voltaire's comment: "It is the privilege of true genius, and especially of the genius who opens up a new path, to make great mistakes with impunity" (p. 413). This sentiment contrasts markedly with Schopenhauer's assessments of virtually every other philosopher in the Western tradition, with the exception of Plato. Consider, for example, his remarks on Aristotle in "Fragments for the History of Philosophy": "The fundamental characteristic of Aristotle might be said to be the greatest shrewdness and sagacity combined with circumspection, power of observation, versatility, and want of depth. His view of the world is shallow, although ingeniously elaborated." *PP*, I, p. 47.

14 P. Gardiner, *Schopenhauer* (Harmondsworth: Penguin, 1963), p. 21.

15 Julian Young has recently taken issue with the standard reading of Schopenhauer, which interprets the Will as the thing-in-itself. According to Young, the Will is another aspect of the thing-in-itself's appearance, but not the thing-in-itself. See J. Young, *Willing and Unwilling: A Study in the Philosophy of Arthur Schopenhauer* (Dordrecht: Nijhoff, 1987), pp. ix, 32ff.

16 *WWR*, I, p. 3.

17 Ibid., p. 6.

18 Ibid., p. 8.

19 Ibid., p. 8.

20 Kant also claims that perception involves imagination as well as understanding. Schopenhauer focuses exclusively on understanding when he considers the role of the intellect in perception.

21 See *WWR*, I, p. 11. For an analysis of the many additional operations that Schopenhauer implicitly assigns to the understanding, as well as a comparison of Schopenhauer's analysis of perception with Kant's, see D.W. Hamlyn, *Schopenhauer*, Arguments of the Philosophers Series, ed. T. Honderich (London: Routledge & Kegan Paul, 1980), pp. 18–22.

22 *WWR*, I, p. 23.

23 Ibid., p. 45.

24 Ibid., p. 46.

25 Ibid., p. 13.

26 Schopenhauer does, as we shall see, believe that a thing-in-itself exists over and above representation. But the thing-in-itself, independent of the principle of sufficient reason, does not admit of duality. Hence, we cannot construe the

thing-in-itself to be the realm of "real" objects that are only represented in the phenomenal world.

27 *WWR*, I, pp. 29–30.
28 Ibid., p. 51.
29 See I. Kant, *Critique of Judgment*, trans. J.C. Meredith (Oxford: Clarendon Press, 1952), pp. 199–201.
30 *WWR*, I, p. 60.
31 See ibid., p. 65.
32 Ibid., p. 70.
33 Ibid., p. 80.
34 Ibid., p. 95.
35 Ibid., p. 98.
36 Ibid., p. 330.
37 Ibid., p. 100.
38 Ibid., p. 100.
39 Ibid., p. 101.
40 Schopenhauer also considers the validity of physiognomy to be a corollary to the principle that the body and the will are one. See *WWR*, I, p. 225, and Schopenhauer, *The World as Will and Representation*, trans. E.F.J. Payne, Vol. II (New York: Dover, 1958), hereafter referred to as *WWR*, II, pp. 421, 598–9. See also Schopenhauer, "On Physiognomy," *PP*, II, pp. 634–41.
41 *WWR*, I, p. 110.
42 Ibid., p. 104.
43 Ibid., p. 126.
44 Ibid., p. 292.
45 Ibid., pp. 290–1.
46 Ibid., pp. 113–14.
47 Ibid., p. 129.
48 Ibid., p. 130.
49 Ibid., p. 170.
50 Ibid., p. 172.
51 Ibid., p. 130.
52 Ibid., p. 132.
53 Ibid., p. 154.
54 Ibid., p. 147.
55 Ibid., p. 147.
56 Ibid., p. 161.
57 Ibid., p. 196.
58 Ibid., p. 169.
59 Ibid., p. 178.
60 Ibid., p. 178.
61 Ibid., p. 179.
62 F. Nietzsche, *Twilight of the Idols*, in *The Portable Nietzsche*, trans. and ed. W. Kaufmann (New York: Viking, 1968), pp. 527–8.
63 *WWR*, I, p. 184.
64 Ibid., p. 188.
65 Ibid., p. 185.
66 Ibid., p. 195.

67 Ibid., p. 214.

68 Ibid., p. 244.

69 Ibid., pp. 252, 254.

70 Ibid., p. 254.

71 Ibid., p. 257.

72 Ibid., p. 261.

73 Ibid., p. 264.

74 Ibid., p. 259.

75 Ibid., p. 312.

76 Ibid., pp. 312–13.

77 Ibid., p. 322.

78 Schopenhauer elaborates a theory of sexual attraction based on the principle that opposites attract. Opposites attract, according to Schopenhauer, because the Will aims to produce children that correspond more or less to the Idea of humanity. Thus, it tries to prevent individuals who are too similar from mating, lest they reproduce offspring who are too extreme in certain characteristics. See "The Metaphysics of Sexual Love," *WWR*, II, pp. 531–60.

79 *WWR*, II, p. 560.

80 *WWR*, I, p. 285.

81 Ibid., p. 372.

82 Schopenhauer sharply distinguishes denial of the will from suicide. Suicide, in his view, is an extreme expression of affirmation of the will and no salvation at all. See *WWR*, I, pp. 366, 398–9. See also Schopenhauer, "On Suicide," *PP*, II, pp. 306–11.

83 Schopenhauer's assessments that life is suffering, and that only an end to desire would put an end to suffering, are directly taken from Buddhist thought. For some of Schopenhauer's remarks on Buddhism, see *WWR*, I, p. 356, and II, pp. 169, 463, 508, 607f.

84 *WWR*, I, pp. 411–12.

85 See ibid., p. xxi.

86 See *PP*, I, p. 47. See also n. 13 above.

❧ SELECT BIBLIOGRAPHY ❧

Original language editions

10.1 *Schopenhauers samtliche Werke*, 5 vols, ed. W.F. von Lohneysen, Stuttgart and Frankfurt: Cotta/Insel, 1960–5.

English translations

10.2 *On the Basis of Morality*, trans. E.F.J. Payne, New York: Bobbs-Merrill, 1965.

10.3 *On the Freedom of the Will*, trans. K. Kolenda, New York: Bobbs-Merrill, 1960.

10.4 *The Fourfold Root of the Principle of Sufficient Reason*, together with *On*

Seeing and Colors, ch. 1, trans. E.F.J. Payne, La Salle, Ill.: Open Court, 1974.

10.5 Parerga and Paralipomena: Short Philosophical Essays, 2 vols, trans. E.F.J. Payne, Oxford: Clarendon Press, 1974.

10.6 The World as Will and Representation, 2 vols, trans. E.F.J. Payne, New York: Dover, Vol. I 1969, Vol. II 1958.

10.7 The Works of Schopenhauer, ed. W. Durant, New York: Frederick Ungar, 1928.

Bibliographies

10.8 Hubscher, A. Schopenhauer-Bibliographie, Stuttgart: Fromman-Holzboog, 1981.

10.9 Schopenhauer-Jahrbuch, Frankfurt/Main: Waldemar Kramer, 1912–.

Influences

10.10 Kant, I. Critique of Judgment, trans. J.C. Meredith, Oxford: Clarendon Press, 1952.

10.11 Kant, I. Critique of Judgment, trans. W.S. Pluhar, Indianapolis: Hackett, 1987.

10.12 Kant, I. Critique of Practical Reason, trans. L.W. Beck, New York: Bobbs-Merrill, 1956.

10.13 Kant, I. Critique of Pure Reason, trans. N. Kemp-Smith, London: Macmillan, 1964.

10.14 Kant, I. Foundations of the Metaphysics of Morals, trans. L. W. Beck, New York: Bobbs-Merrill, 1959.

10.15 Kants gesammelte Schriften, 29 vols, ed. Deutschen (formerly Königlich Preussische) Akademie der Wissenschaften, Berlin: de Gruyter (and predecessors), 1902–.

General surveys

10.16 Copleston SJ, F. Arthur Schopenhauer: Philosopher of Pessimism, Bellarmine Series, XI, ed. E.F. Sutcliffe SJ, London: Burns, Oates & Washbourne, 1947.

10.17 Fox, M. (ed.) Schopenhauer: His Philosophical Achievement, Totowa, NJ: Barnes & Noble, 1980.

10.18 Gardiner, P. Schopenhauer, Harmondsworth: Penguin, 1963.

10.19 Hamlyn, D.W. Schopenhauer, Arguments of the Philosophers Series, ed. T. Honderich, London: Routledge & Kegan Paul, 1980.

10.20 Hubscher, A. The Philosophy of Schopenhauer in its Intellectual Context: Thinker against the Tide, trans. J.T. Baer and D.E. Cartwright, Lewiston, NY: E. Mellen, 1989.

10.21 McGill, V.J. Schopenhauer: Pessimist and Pagan, New York: Haskell, 1971.

10.22 Safranski, R. *Schopenhauer and the Wild Years of Philosophy*, Cambridge, Mass.: Harvard University Press, 1990.

10.23 Salaquarda, J. *Schopenhauer*, Darmstadt: Wissenschaftliche Buchgesellschaft, 1985.

10.24 Simmel, G. *Schopenhauer and Nietzsche*, trans. H. Lorskandl, Amherst: University of Massachusetts Press, 1986.

10.25 Von der Luft, E. *Schopenhauer: New Essays in Honor of his Two-Hundredth Birthday*, Studies in German Thought and History, 10, Lewiston, NY: E. Meller, 1988.

10.26 Young, J. *Willing and Unwilling: A Study in the Philosophy of Arthur Schopenhauer*, Dordrecht: Nijhoff, 1987.

Specific topics

10.27 Armstrong, L.W. *Schelling, Hegel, Schopenhauer, and the Philosophy of the Absolute*, Albuquerque: American Classical College Press, 1987.

10.28 Atwell, J.E. *Schopenhauer: The Human Character*, Philadelphia: Temple University Press, 1990.

10.29 Bridgwater, P. *Arthur Schopenhauer's English Schooling*, London, Routledge, 1988.

10.30 Bykhovskii, B.E. *Schopenhauer and the Ground of Existence*, Amsterdam, B.R. Gruner, 1984.

10.31 Dauer, D.W. *Schopenhauer as Transmitter of Buddhist Ideas*, New York: Peter Lang, 1969.

10.32 Janaway, C. *Self and World in Schopenhauer's Philosophy*, New York: Oxford University Press, 1989.

10.33 Kishan, B.V. *Schopenhauer's Conception of Salvation*, Waltair: Andhra University Press, 1978.

10.34 Laban, F. *Schopenhauer – Literature*, New York: Lenox Hill, 1970.

10.35 Miller, B.R. *The Philosophy of Schopenhauer in Dramatic Representational Expressions*, Albuquerque: American Classical College Press, 1981.

10.36 Nietzsche, F. *Schopenhauer as Educator*, trans. W. Arrowsmith, in *Unmodern Observations*, ed. W. Arrowsmith, New Haven: Yale University Press, 1990.

10.37 Simpson, D. (ed.) *German Aesthetic and Literary Criticism: Kant, Fichte, Schelling, Schopenhauer, and Hegel*, Cambridge: Cambridge University Press, 1984.

CHAPTER 11

Kierkegaard's speculative despair

Judith Butler

> Every movement of infinity is carried out through passion, and
> no reflection can produce a movement. This is the continual
> leap in existence that explains the movement, whereas mediation
> is a chimera, which in Hegel is supposed to explain everything
> and which is also the only thing he never has tried to explain.
> (Kierkegaard, *Fear and Trembling*, p. 42)

Kierkegaard's critique of Hegel concerns primarily the failure of a
philosophy of reflection to take account of that which exceeds reflection
itself: passion, existence, faith. The irony in Kierkegaard's challenge
to Hegelianism is, however, minimally twofold. On the one hand,
Kierkegaard will ask, where is it that Hegel, the existing individual,
stands in relation to the systematic totality that Hegel elucidates? If
Hegel the individual is outside the complete system, then there is an
"outside" to that system, which is to say that the system is not as
exhaustively descriptive and explanatory as it claims to be. Paradoxically, the very existence of Hegel, the existing philosopher, effectively
– one might say *rhetorically* – undermines what appears to be the most
important claim in that philosophy, the claim to provide a comprehensive account of knowledge and reality. On the other hand, Kierkegaard's counter to Hegel consists in the valorization of passion and
existence over reflection and, finally, language. It is in relation to this
criticism that a different sort of irony emerges, one which Kierkegaard
appears not to know, but which attends his various claims to be writing
on behalf of that which is beyond speculation, reflection, and language.
If Kierkegaard is right that Hegel omits the existing individual from
his system, that does not mean that Kierkegaard maintains an unsystem-
atic or nonspeculative view of the existing individual. Although Kierke-

gaard sometimes uses the speculative terminology of Hegelianism, he appears to parody that discourse in order to reveal its constitutive contradictions. And yet, in Kierkegaard's descriptions of despair in *Sickness unto Death* (1849), his use of Hegelian language works not only to displace the authority of Hegel, but also to make use of Hegelianism for an anlaysis that both extends and exceeds the properly Hegelian purview. In this sense, Kierkegaard *opposes* himself to Hegel, but this is a vital opposition, a determining opposition, one might almost say 'an Hegelian opposition,' even if it is one that Hegel himself could not have fully anticipated. If Hegel's individual is implicated in the very existence that he seeks to overcome through rationality, Kierkegaard constructs his notion of the individual at the very limits of the speculative discourse that he seeks to oppose. This appears to be one ironic way, then, that Kierkegaard's own philosophical exercise is implicated in the tradition of German Idealism.

∾ DESPAIR AND THE FAILURE TO ACHIEVE ∾ IDENTITY

In the following, I will try to make clear why *despair* is a category or, in Kierkegaard's terms, a sickness and a passion, whose analysis is crucial to both the extension and critique of Hegel in Kierkegaard's work. Insofar as despair characterizes the failure of a self fully to know or to become itself, a failure to become self-identical, an interrupted relation, then despair is precisely that which thwarts the possibility of a fully mediated subject in Hegel's sense. That subject is documented in Hegel's *Phenomenology of Spirit* as an emerging set of syntheses, the subject as one who mediates and, hence, overcomes that which initially appears as *different from itself*. The success of this mediating activity confirms the capacity of the subject to achieve self-identity, that is, to know itself, to become at home in otherness, to discover that in a less than obvious and simple way it *is* that which it incessantly encounters as outside of itself.

Hegel narrates in *The Phenomenology of Spirit* the various ways in which this mediating relation can fail, but insofar as Hegel claims that subject is substance, he defends the ideal possibility of articulating the *successful mediation* of each and every subject with its countervailing world. The various failures to mediate that relation effectively are only and always instructive; they furnish knowledge that leads to more effective proposals for how to mediate that apparent difference. Each time the subject in *The Phenomenology of Spirit* claims to discover the condition by which the mediating relation works, it fails to take into account some crucial dimension of itself or of the world which it seeks to bind together in a synthetic unity. That which it fails to comprehend returns to haunt and undermine the mediating relation it has just articulated. But that which remained outside the relation is always recuperated by the subject's synthesizing project: there is no final or constitutive failure to mediate. Every failure delineates a new and more synthetic task for the emerging subject of reflection. In a sense, Kierkegaard enters Hegel's system at the end of the *Phenomenology*: if Hegel thought that the subject of the *Phenomenology* had taken account of everything along the way which turned out to be outside the terms to be mediated, understanding *what* needed to be synthesized as well as how that synthesis could take place, then the last laugh is on Hegel's subject. In its mania for synthesis, the subject has forgotten to include that which can never be systematized, that which thwarts and resists reflection, namely, its very existence and its constitutive and mutually exclusive passions: faith and despair.

In Kierkegaard's view, despair is precisely that passion that can never be 'synthesized' by the Hegelian subject.[1] In fact, despair is defined by Kierkegaard as "a misrelation" (*SUD*, 14),[2] one which confirms the failure of any final mediation and, therefore, signals the decisive limit to the comprehensive claims of the philosophy of reflection. Despair not only disrupts that subject's efforts to become at home with itself in the world, but it confirms the fundamental impossibility of ever achieving the self's sense of belonging to its world. The Hegelian project is not only thwarted by despair, but it is *articulated in despair ("the category of totality inheres in and belongs to the despairing person": SUD*, 60). As we shall see, one form of despair is marked by the effort to become the ground or origin of one's own existence and the synthetic relation to alterity. A kind of arrogance or hubris, this conceit of the Hegelian project suffers a humiliation at Kierkegaard's hands. To posture as a radically self-generated being, to be the author of one's will and knowledge, is to deny that one is constituted in and by that which is infinitely larger than the human individual. Kierkegaard will call this larger-than-human source of all things human "God" or "the infinite." To deny that one is constituted in that which is larger than oneself is, for Kierkegaard, to be in a kind of despair. Toward the end of this essay, we will consider just how crucial this form of despair is for Kierkegaard's own authorship. Indeed, it may turn out that the despair that Kierkegaard diagnoses in *Sickness unto Death*, and which, in part, he attributes to Hegel, conditions essentially the very writing whose object it is to denounce and overcome despair.

So despair is a "misrelation," a failure to mediate, but what are the terms to be mediated? And if Hegel fails to understand (his own) despair in the system he articulates, is it also true that Kierkegaard fails to understand the speculative conceptualization that inheres in the very notion of despair by which he counters speculation?

The opening page of *Sickness unto Death* appears to be a properly Hegelian exegesis populated with familiar terminology: 'self,' 'spirit,' 'mediation,' 'relation.' And yet, as the first paragraph proceeds it becomes clear that Kierkegaard is parodying Hegel's language; significantly, however, this is a parody that does not entail a thorough rejection of Hegel. On the contrary, through parodying Hegel, Kierkegaard both recirculates or preserves some aspects of Hegel's system and jettisons some others. Parody functions like the Hegelian operation of *Aufhebung*, set into motion this time, ironically, by Kierkegaard to preserve, cancel, and also transcend the Hegelian corpus itself. The crucial dimension of *synthesis* is, of course, absent from this Kierkegaardian redeployment of Hegel. Parody functions for Kierkegaard as an *Aufhebung* that leads not to synthesis between his position and Hegel's, but to a decisive break. Kierkegaard does not lay out his arguments against Hegel in propositional form. He re-enacts those arguments through the rhetorical construction of his text. If the issues he has with Hegel could be *rationally* decided, then Hegel would have won from the start. Kierkegaard's texts counter Hegel most effectively at the level of style, for part of what he wants to communicate is the limits of language to comprehend that which constitutes the individual. Let us, then, consider the way in which this argument is performed through the parodic reiteration of Hegel at the outset of *Sickness unto Death*.

Kierkegaard begins Part One of this text with a set of assertions and counter-assertions, splitting his own philosophical voice into dialogic interlocutors, miming the dialectical style which dates back to Socrates: "A human being is spirit. But what is spirit? Spirit is the self. But what is the self?" (*SUD*, 13). Then comes a ponderous sentence which one might expect to encounter at the hilarious limits of rationality in a Woody Allen film: "The self is a relation that relates itself to itself or is the relation's relating itself to itself in the relation; the self is not the relation but is the relation's relating itself to itself." The first part of the sentence is a disjunction, but it is unclear whether the disjunctive "or" operates to separate alternative definitions or whether it implies that the definitions that it separates are essentially equivalent to one another. Prior to the semicolon, there appear to be two definitions: one, the self is a reflexive relation (the self is that which takes itself as its own object), and two, the self is *the activity* of its own reflexivity (it is that process of taking itself as its object, incessantly self-referential). If this is an Hegelian exposition, then one expects that this self will achieve harmony with itself, but here it seems that the more the possibility of a synthesis is elaborated, the less likely that synthesis appears.

In the above quotation, then, we might ask: can the self both be the relation and the activity of *relating*? Can the differently tensed definitions be reconciled? Is the first a static conception, and the second, a dynamic and temporalized one which is incompatible with the second? Or will we learn, Hegelian style, that the static notion is *aufgehoben* in the second, that the temporalized version of the reflexive self presupposes, transforms, and transcends the static one? After the semicolon, the sentence appears to contradict the definition of the self as static relation and to affirm the temporalized version of the self, thereby undermining the possibility of an emerging synthesis between the two versions: "the self is not the relation but is the relation's relating itself to the self." The original ambiguity over whether the "or" functions to set up a mutually exclusive set of alternatives or a set of appositional and equivalent definitions appears temporarily to be resolved into the first alternative.

The development of the sentence echoes the narrative logic of Hegel's *Phenomenology*, but in that text it is more often the case that mutually exclusive alternatives are *first* laid out only then to be synthesized as part of a larger unity. Already in Kierkegaard's style of exposition, we see how the expectation of an Hegelian logic is both produced and undermined. Indeed, as the paragraph proceeds, that failure to conform to Hegelian logic turns into a full-blown illogic, a kind of high philosophical comedy. The rest of the paragraph reads as follows:

> A human being is a synthesis of the infinite and the finite, of the temporal and the eternal, of freedom and necessity, in short, a synthesis. A synthesis is a relation between two. Considered in this way, a human being is still not a self.

Here the development of what appears to be an argument takes several illogical turns and seems by the propelling force of rationality to be spiraling into irrationality. By the end of the first sentence, we have concluded (a) that the self is temporalized, (b) that it is the *activity* of relating, and (c) that it is *not* a static relation. The possibility of a synthesis is therefore negated. This next sentence, however, poses as a logical consequence, but only to make a mockery of logical transition. Here we have the sudden and unwarranted shift from a discussion of the "self" to that of the "human being," and the announcement that the human being is a synthesis. Moreover, the terms of which that synthesis is composed are in no way implied by the static/temporal opposition that preoccupied the preceding sentence. Instead, we find wild generalizations asserted at once in the mode of a conclusion and a premise. As a conclusion that follows from the earlier sentence, this second sentence makes no sense. As a premise, it is equally absurd:

the synthesis is asserted and described, and then the appearance of a conclusion emerges, "in short, a synthesis," which can be read only as a flagrant and laughable redundancy.[3] A didactic sentence follows, which is itself nothing other than a repetition of the obvious: "a synthesis is a relation between two." And then a most curious sentence concludes the paragraph in which Kierkegaard appears to take distance from the Hegelian voice that he has both assumed and mocked. "Considered in this way," the sentence begins, suggesting that there might be another way, Kierkegaard's way, "a human being is still not a self." Here Kierkegaard offers a distinction to suggest that what is called "the human being" is not the same as the self. But interestingly, we are also recalled to the problem of the temporality and tense of the self. What is described as the human being is "still not a self," not yet a self, a self that has not yet been articulated, or, rather, cannot be articulated within the language of synthesis.

Kierkegaard proceeds to take issue with this self which seems never to coincide with itself. He remarks that any synthesis requires a third term. The second and third paragraphs proceed in a note of tentative seriousness, making use of an Hegelian schematic precisely in order to show the way beyond it. The second paragraph begins: "In the relation between two, the relation is the third as a negative unity, and the two relate to the relation and in the relation to the relation." The examples of the terms to be related are the "psychical and the physical" in this textual instance. Kierkegaard argues that if the self is a synthesis of psychical and physical dimensions, and if it is *also* the activity of relating its psychical aspect to its physical aspect, then that very act of relating will have to be composed of one of those aspects. Here he assumes that the activity of "relating," a term that seems to have been kept purposefully abstract in the previous discussion, calls now to be specified as a psychical activity. This more specific determination of that relating activity will become even more significant as Kierkegaard's text proceeds to distinguish between *reflection*, the Hegelian way of understanding that constitutive relation, and *faith*, Kierkegaard's preferred way. As this semi-Hegelian exposition proceeds, Kierkegaard will show what is concretely at stake for the existing individual in this abstract logic.

Kierkegaard begins here to confound the distinction between the self as a static relation and the self as a temporal or active one. The two dimensions of the self to be related must already in some sense *be* the very relation, which is to say that psychical and the physical, as parts of the relation, are definitionally related, that is, presupposed as related, and are constantly in the activity of becoming relating. These two dimensions of that relation cannot be captured by a logic of noncontradiction. The reflexivity of this relation is what marks the relation as a self. For it is the distinguishing feature of a self to endeavor to become itself, constantly and paradoxically to be in the process of becoming what it already is. For one can always refuse to 'relate' to oneself, to endeavor to become a self, but even then that very refusal will still be a way of relating to the self. To deny that one has a self, to refuse to become one: these are not only modes of reflexivity, but specific forms of despair.

This paradoxical view of the self, as that which incessantly becomes that which it already is, coincides partially with Hegel's view of the subject. Hegel argues that the subject of the *Phenomenology* will develop and become increasingly synthetic, including all that it discovers outside itself in and as the world. And this subject, which successively appears to be identified as life, consciousness, self-consciousness, Spirit, Reason, and Absolute Knowledge, discovers finally that *implicitly* it has always been what it has become. The *becoming* of the Hegelian subject is the process of articulating or rendering explicit the implicit relations which constitute that subject. In this sense, the Hegelian subject is successively discovering what it has always already been, but has not known that it has been. The development of constitution of the Hegelian subject is the process of coming to know what it is that that subject already is.

For Kierkegaard, however, this view of the subject is only partially true. For Hegel, the subject is every aspect of this relation: the subject is itself, the activity of relating, and that to which it relates (since the world, or Substance, turns out to be synthetically unified with the subject). It is precisely this circle of immanence, however, that Kierkegaard tries to break; he performs this break, however, by working Hegel's own logic to its own breaking point. A new paragraph following the above exposition graphically enacts the break with the Hegelian argument. Kierkegaard states an either/or question that cannot be asked within the Hegelian framework: "Such a relation that relates itself to itself, a self, must either have established itself or have been established by another." Here Kierkegaard raises the question of the genesis of this relation. It is not enough to know what the relation constitutes, nor to know that in some way it constitutes itself. The question remains: What has constituted this relation as a self-constituting relation? What put this circular relation into motion? Kierkegaard infers that there must be a relation that is temporally prior to the self-constituting self, that this prior relation must be reflexive and constituting as well, and that the self must be one constituted product of that prior relation. This prior relation appears to be God, although Kierkegaard almost never supplies a definition of God.

❧ PASSIONATE SELVES AND THE ❧ AFFIRMATION OF FAITH

In *Concluding Unscientific Postscript* (1846), Kierkegaard makes clear that he is not interested in proving rationally that God exists, but only in the question of how to achieve faith as it arises for the existing individual: how do I become a Christian, what relation can I have to faith?[4]

If that which constitutes the self remains part of that self, then the self whose task it is to take itself as its own object will of necessity take that prior ground of its own existence as its object as well.[5] It is in this sense that for Kierkegaard the self which takes itself as its own object will of necessity take "another" as its object as well. In Hegel, this same formulation applies, but the "other" who constitutes the self will be the social other, the community of other subjects who collectively supply the common social and historical world from which the particular subject is derived. That move, however, is for Kierkegaard symptomatic of a refusal to see that which transcends the social and human world, namely, the transcendent or the infinite from which the social world in its concreteness is derived.

The task of the self, for Kierkegaard, is indissolubly twofold: self-constituting yet derived, the self is "a relation that relates itself to itself and in relating itself to itself relates itself to another" (*SUD*, 13–14). Insofar as "another" is infinite, and this prior infinity constitutes the self, the self partakes of infinity as well. But the self is also determined, embodied, and hence finite, which means that every particular self is both infinite and finite, and that it lives this paradox without resolution. Faith will be described by Kierkegaard as infinite inwardness, the unceasing and passionate affirmation of the infinite, and in this sense faith will be an occasion for infinity to emerge within the self: "that which unites all human life is passion, and faith is a passion" (*FT*, 67).[6] In yet another sense, that self, however capable of infinite faith, will never be equivalent to the infinity that is prior to the individual, which Kierkegaard calls "God," but which is sometimes figured in terms of infinite possibility.[7] However infinite in its passion and faith, the self is still *existing* and, hence, finite. Strictly speaking, the infinity prior to the self, the infinity from which the self emerges, does not *exist*. For unactualized and infinite possibility to exist, it would have to become actualized, which is to become finite and, hence, no longer to be definable as infinite possibility. This infinite possibility, this ground or God, cannot be known or affirmed as a finite object, but can only be affirmed by a passionate faith that emerges at the very limits of what is knowable.

This is an affirmation that cannot take place through rationality, language, or speculation; it emerges as a passion and a possibility only on the condition that reflection has failed. In Kierkegaard's *Philosophical Fragments* (1844), he refers to this crisis in speculative thought as "the passion of Reason" and "the passion in all thinking" (*PF*, 46).[8] Here passion carries the meaning of suffering and longing, and Kierkegaard appears to imply that passion is generated precisely at the moment in which thought fails to grasp its object. Because part of what is meant by comprehending an object is comprehending its origin, and because that origin or ground is the infinity of God, every act of knowing is haunted by the problem of faith and, hence, also by passion. Kierkegaard commentator Niels Thulstrup describes this passion as "something which reason cannot comprehend and which leads reason to founder in its passion, the passion which wills the collision, which strives to discover that which cannot be thought and cannot be comprehended in the categories of human thought."[9] In the face of the infinite, thought can only supply a finite concept or a word, but both of these are finitizing instruments which can only misconstrue and, indeed, *negate* that which they seek to affirm. This is, of course, also the problem with Hegel's reliance on the concept to grasp infinity.[10]

One might be tempted here to think that Kierkegaard proposes that the self overcome its finitude in order to affirm through passionate inwardness the infinity from which that self emerges. But that is, for Kierkegaard, an impossibility. And here is where he appears to take Hegel seriously, even as he finally disputes him: the self is inevitably both finitude and infinitude which the self lives, not as a synthesis, and not as the transcendence of the one over the other, but as a perpetual paradox. Inasmuch as the self is self-constituting, that is, has as its task the becoming of itself, it is finite: it is *this* self, and not some other. Inasmuch as the self is derived, a possibility actualized from an infinite source of possibility, and retains that infinity within itself as the passionate inwardness of faith, then that self is infinite. But to reconcile existence and faith, that is, to be an existing individual who, in its finitude, can sustain itself in infinite faith, that is the paradox of existence, one which can only be lived but never overcome. As Kierkegaard puts it with characteristic irony: "to be in existence is always a somewhat embarrassing situation" (*CUP*, 404).

Let us return then to the sentence from *Sickness unto Death* which suggests that the Hegelian subject, reconceived as a self (with the capacity for inwardness), and understood as derived from an infinite source, is both self-constituting and derived, "a relation that relates itself to itself and in relating itself to itself relates itself to another." This sentence, which appears logical and to some extent implicitly theological, leads to the introduction of despair as a psychological category:

This is why there can be two forms of despair in the strict sense. If a human self had established itself, then there could be only one form: not to will to be oneself, to will to do away with oneself, but there could not be the form: in despair to will to be oneself.

(SUD, 14)

Despair is the result of the effort to overcome or solve the paradox of human existence. If one seeks to be grounded in the infinite and to deny that one exists and is, therefore, finite, one falls into the despair of the infinite, willing not to be the particular self that one is. But if one denies the infinite and seeks to take full responsibility for one's own existence, viewing all of one's self as one's own radical creation, that is the despair of the finite.[11] It is this second form of despair, the despair of willing to be oneself, that is, to be the ground or sole source of one's own existence, that is more fundamental than the first. This second form constitutes a refusal to be grounded in that which is more infinite than the human self and so constitutes a defiance of God. The primary way in which human selves fall into despair is through the repudiation of their infinite origins. This despair is marked by a certain hubris or arrogance and, at its limit, becomes demonic, understood as a willful defiance of the divine. We will consider that demonic extreme of despair toward the end of our remarks when we consider Kierkegaard's ambivalent relationship to his own authorship.

What this means, of course, is that if one knows one is in despair and seeks *by one's own means* to extricate oneself from despair, one will only become more fully steeped in that despair. That self is still trying to refuse its groundedness in that which is greater than itself. Paradoxically, the self that refuses the infinite must enact that refusal *infinitely*, thereby recapitulating and reaffirming the infinite in a negative way in the very gesture of disbelief. If Hegel thought that the subject might be a synthesis of finite and infinite, he failed to consider that that subject, reconceived as a self with inwardness, can never mediate the absolutely qualitative difference between what is finite in that self and what is infinite. This failure of mediation is what underscores the paradoxical character of existence; the passionate and non-rational affirmation of that paradox, an affirmation that must be infinitely repeated, *is faith*; the effort pre-emptively to resolve this paradox is the feat of despair. In this sense, despair marks the limit of dialectical mediation or, rather, every effort at mediation will be read by Kierkegaard as symptomatic of despair. Every synthesis presumes and institutes a *repudiation* of that which cannot be comprehended by thought; infinity is precisely that which eludes conceptualization. That refused infinity returns, however, as the infinite movement of despair in the existing individual who seeks to resolve the paradox of existence through thought. Through the invocation of despair, Kierkegaard marks out the limits of the Hegelian ideal of synthesis: "Despair is the misrelation in the relation of a synthesis that relates itself to itself" (*SUD*, 15).

The Hegelian ideal of becoming at one with oneself is achieved through one's social relations and through one's relation to everything that is outside the self. For Hegel, the subject discovers that other human beings and objects are part of its own identity, that in *relating* to others and to objects, the human subject enacts (or actualizes) some of its own most fundamental capacities. Hence, the subject achieves a certain oneness with itself through relating to that which is different from itself. This oneness, however, is not a possibility for the Kierkegaardian self. As much as that self might want to affirm itself as the ground or origin of its own relations with others, it is bound to fail. This self can take responsibility for its own capacities by denying that it is itself produced by that which is greater than itself. That is one kind of despair, the despair of willing to be oneself. On the other hand, if that self tries to relinquish all responsibility for itself by claiming that some greater and infinite reality, God, has produced everything about that self, then that self is in a different kind of despair, the despair of willing not to be oneself. There is no escape from this paradox. Hence, to be a self means either to be in one of these two forms of despair or to have faith. But in both despair and faith, this paradox is never resolved. In despair, one lives one side of the paradox and then another (one takes radical responsibility for oneself or not at all), but in faith, one affirms the paradox, taking responsibility for oneself at the same time affirming that one is not the origin of one's existence.

One might ask, is one always either in despair or faith? The answer for Kierkegaard is yes. For the most part, human beings live in despair, and they do not even know that they are in despair. In fact, this not knowing that one is in despair is a symptom of despair. The person who does not know that there is a task, a struggle to affirm oneself in this paradoxical way, makes some set of presumptions about the solidity of its own existence which remain unquestioned and, hence, outside the difficulty of faith. And there appears to be no way to faith except through despair. But faith for Kierkegaard does not provide a solution for the paradox of the self. Indeed, nothing provides such a solution. The self is an alternation, a constant pitching to and fro, a lived paradox, and faith does not halt or resolve that alternation into a harmonious or synthetic whole; on the contrary, faith is precisely the affirmation that *there can be no resolution*. And insofar as 'synthesis' represents the rational resolution of the paradox, and the paradox cannot be resolved, then it follows that faith emerges precisely at the moment at which 'synthesis' shows itself to be a false solution. This is, as it were, Kierkegaard's last laugh on Hegel. Whereas Hegel argues that the failure of any given synthesis points the way to a greater and more inclusive synthesis, Kierkegaard tries to show that synthesis itself, no matter how inclusive, cannot resolve the paradox of the self. Concretely, this difference between Hegel and Kierkegaard implies that the self will ultimately have a very different experience of and in the world. For Hegel, the subject will eventually find a unified and harmonious relation with what appears at first to be outside itself, so that it can, ideally, find itself at home in the world, 'of' the world that it is 'in.' But for Kierkegaard, that which is 'outside' the finite self, namely, the infinite, is also 'within' the self as freedom and the dual possibility of despair and faith (all of which are 'infinite' passions, passions that can have no end); further, the infinite that persists as the ground of the finite self or within the self as its own passion will never fully belong to the finite self or the finite world in which it nevertheless exists in some less than apparent way. Hence, for Kierkegaard, the infinity that is the source of the self and which persists in the self as its passion will never fully be 'of' the world in which it dwells. The self, for Kierkegaard, will be perpetually estranged not only from itself, but from its origins and from the world in which it finds itself.

One might imagine an Hegelian rejoinder to Kierkegaard's affirmation of the paradoxical self. Hegel might argue that if there is something in the self which is infinite, that infinity must nevertheless *appear* in some way in order to be *known*. In Hegelian language, one might say that for the infinite to become actual and, hence, knowable, it must become determinate or appear in some form. And Hegel imagined that certain kinds of concepts could be both finite (particular, determinate, specific) and infinite (nonspecific, indeterminate, unbounded). Hegel wanted to arrive at a concept, understood as a kind of speculative thought, in which the finite and the infinite would not only coexist, but be essentially dependent on one another. Imagine a thought which would be *your* thought, specifically yours, and therefore determined and specific, but which would *at the same time* be a thought of that which is infinite and, hence, not bound to you at all, indeed, not bounded or limited by anything. Hegel imagined that the thought of the infinite depends on the determinate thinker, the place and existence of that thinker, at the same time that that infinite thought exceeds that determinate place and thinker. In this sense, the infinite thought depends on the finite thinker in order to be thought, in order to have its occasion and its form; and the finite thinker is no thinker, that is, is not really thinking, thinking thought through to its infinite possibility, unless that finite thinker is able to think the infinite. Hence, for

Hegel, a mutual dependency exists between that which is finite and that which is infinite in the human subject, where both the finite and the infinite form the project of thinking.

Kierkegaard's rejoinder is firm. If one tries to *think* the infinite, one has *already* made the infinite finite. There can be no thinking of the infinite, for the infinite is precisely that not only which cannot be thought, but which insistently forces a crisis in thought itself; the infinite is the limit of thinking, and not a possible content of any thought. To the Hegelian claim that the infinite must first *appear* before it can be known, Kierkegaard would have to respond that the infinite can neither appear nor be known. Hence, it is to some extent *against* Hegel that Kierkegaard formulates his notion of the infinite and, therefore, also of faith: the infinite eludes the dialectic, the infinite cannot be grasped or 'understood' by any rational effort of thought or synthesis. The infinite can be affirmed nonrationally and, hence, passionately, at the limits of thought, that is, at the limits of Hegelianism.

❧ FEAR, TREMBLING, AND OTHER INWARD ❧ PASSIONS

This opposition to Hegel puts Kierkegaard in a bind, for Kierkegaard is *a writer*; he puts his opposition to Hegel into words, and he produces concrete and determinate texts, finite things, which house his claims about that which is infinite. How do we understand Kierkegaard, the finite man or 'existing individual,' in relation to this notion of the infinite that can never fully be expressed by any finite or determinate statement or text. As finite expressions, Kierkegaard's own texts, the *Sickness unto Death* itself or *Fear and Trembling* (1843), can only *fail* to express the very notion of infinity that they seek to communicate. Whereas an Hegelian might argue that Kierkegaard's writing of the infinite is itself essential to the infinite that it expresses, Kierkegaard's response will be that if there is an infinite that can never be resolved with the finite, then Kierkegaard's own texts will always *fail* to communicate the infinite. Indeed, Kierkegaard's response will be: 'My texts *must* fail to express the infinite, and it will be by virtue of that *failure* that the infinite will be affirmed. Moreover, that affirming of the infinite will not take the form of a thought; it will take place at the limits of thought itself; it will force a crisis in thought, the advent of passion.'

So, for Kierkegaard to set about to write a book against Hegel, against synthesis, and in favor of passion and faith, he must write a book that fails to communicate directly the very passion and faith he seeks to defend. An author cannot embody or express the infinite, for that 'expression' would inadvertently render finite that which must remain infinite. Indeed, the words "passion" and "faith" cannot express or communicate passion and faith; they can only *fail* to communicate, and in failing, *point the way* to an affirmation that is fundamentally beyond language. Aware of this paradoxical task of trying to write about that which cannot be delivered in language, Kierkegaard insists upon the necessity of indirect communication, a kind of communication that knows its own limitations, and by enacting those limits, indirectly points the way to that which cannot be communicated.

Evidence of Kierkegaard's views on indirect communication can be found in the fact that he often wrote and published under a pseudonym. *Sickness unto Death* was published with "Anti-Climacus" as its author. *Fear and Trembling* was written by "Johannes de Silentio," and *Philosophical Fragments* by "Johannes Climacus," also the author of *Concluding Unscientific Postscript*. Other pseudonyms include "Constantin Constantius" (*Repetition*, 1843) and "Victor Eremita" (*Either/Or*, 1843). The use of a pseudonym raises the question of who is the author behind the author? Why is Kierkegaard hiding? What is it that is concealed in this writing, and what is it that is revealed? Does the author mean to say what he says, or does the pseudonymous author allow the 'real' author to write what he would not write under his own name. What does it mean to write under the name of another? I do not want to suggest that pseudonymous authorship always works in the same way or for the same reasons in Kierkegaard's work. But it does seem directly related to the problem of writing the infinite that we mentioned above. The false name suggests that whatever is written under that name does not exhaust the full range of what the author, Kierkegaard, might be. Something is not being uttered or expressed or made known. Minimally, it is Kierkegaard the man who to some degree hides behind the fictional author under whose name he writes. On an existential level, however, there is something in every self which *cannot be expressed* by any act of writing. There is that in every self which is silent, and Kierkegaard is clear that in the end faith, and passion more generally, is not a matter of writing or speaking, but of remaining silent.

If Kierkegaard's texts, then, are to be works of faith, they must not only be a labor of language, but a labor of silence as well. This is suggested by the pseudonym "Johannes de Silentio," the 'author' of *Fear and Trembling*. And in that text, we encounter the figure of Abraham whose silence cannot be understood by the author. Indeed, Abraham stands for faith; he is called "a knight of faith," and yet he does not speak and leaves us no clues by which we might be able to find reason in his faith. The author tries repeatedly to understand Abraham's faith, but fails.

What is the story of Abraham, and what is the nature of Abraham's faith? Abraham receives a sign from God that he is to take his son to the top of a mountain, Mount Moriah, and there to slay his son as an act of faith. According to the Bible, Abraham does not tell Isaac, his son, what he is about to do, and neither does he tell Sarah, his wife. Through the pseudonym of Johannes de Silentio, Kierkegaard opens *Fear and Trembling* by telling the story of Abraham several times. Each effort to narrate what happened with Abraham is also an effort to fathom how it is that Abraham could prepare himself to act in such a way. If Abraham were willing to slay his son, he risks becoming a murderer according to conventional ethical norms; he destroys his own son, his own family, breaking the most cherished of *human* bonds. Johannes de Silentio tries to fathom how it could be that Abraham, who loved his son, was nevertheless willing to defy, resist, or suspend that love as well as one of the most fundamental laws of ethics in order to perform his faith. What kind of faith has God exacted from Abraham such that he must prepare himself to sacrifice that worldly connection that is most important to him. Is this a cruel God, one to be disobeyed? And why does Abraham persist in his course, silently bringing Isaac to the top of Mount Moriah, and draw his hand only *then* to have his hand stayed by God?

The example is, of course, a shocking one, but Kierkegaard rehearses that scene of Abraham climbing Mount Moriah, drawing the sword, and he tries to understand how any human being could turn against that which is most important to him in the world. Abraham supplies no explanation, and Kierkegaard leads us to the point of understanding that there can be no explanation in words. In the name of what? For what higher good? For Johannes de Silentio, the answer never comes, but the questions repeat themselves insistently, exhausting language and opening out into the silent void of faith.

Kierkegaard imagines how it would be for Abraham to feel the full force of his love for Isaac and at the same time follow the dictate of a faith that requires the sacrifice of Isaac. This is surely a paradox, and in the story of Abraham we receive from Kierkegaard something like an allegory of the paradoxical self. There is no way to reconcile the profoundly finite and worldly love of a father for his son with a notion of faith which is infinite, 'in' the world but not 'of' it. This is precisely the kind of paradox that cannot be thought, cannot be resolved into some harmonious solution, but which wrecks thought, forces an exposure of thought itself. In Kierkegaard's indirect words: "I cannot think myself into Abraham" (*FT*, 33); "For my part, I presumably can describe the movements of faith, but I cannot make them" (*FT*, 37); "faith begins precisely where thought stops" (*FT*, 53).

But Kierkegaard is not only horrified by the sacrifice that faith has exacted from Abraham. He is also appalled by the fact that

Abraham appears to get Isaac back, that God not only asks for a sacrifice, but returns what has been lost, and all this *without reason*. Furthermore, it appears that Abraham does not turn against the God who has, it seemed, played so cruelly with the most precious object of Abraham's human love:

> to be able to lose one's understanding and along with it everything finite, for which it is the stockbroker, and then to win the very same finitude again by virtue of the absurd – this appalls me, but that does not make me say it [faith] is something inferior, since, on the contrary, it is the one and only marvel.

On the one hand, Kierkegaard is appalled by the *arbitrariness* and whimsical character of the way in which God is figured here as giving and taking away. On the other hand, Abraham's faith is a marvel, since it does not waver in the face of the alternating beneficence and cruelty of this ultimate authority. Abraham is not shrewd with respect to God. Abraham does not figure that if he only acts as if he is willing to sacrifice Isaac, God will stay his hand: "he had faith by virtue of the absurd, for all human calculation ceased long ago" (*FT*, 36). If faith designates the limit of thought, if faith emerges precisely when thought fails to comprehend what is before it, then Abraham climbs the mountain and draws the sword *without knowing* that God will return Isaac to him. What is awesome in Abraham is that he sustains his faith *without knowing* that he will receive Isaac back. Faith is not a bargain; it is that affirmation that emerges when all bargaining has failed. This is what Kierkegaard means when he claims that Abraham has faith by virtue of the absurd. And if faith is a leap, it is a leap beyond thought, beyond calculation, a leap made from and with *passion* that can be neither comprehended by thought nor communicated through language.

In *Fear and Trembling*, Kierkegaard claims that he cannot yet make this leap, but that he can only trace its steps and applaud that movement as a marvelous thing. He knows enough to recognize that Abraham must have been in anxiety at the moment in which he drew that sword. And whereas there are those who would defy God and return to the ethical world, refuse to draw the sword, and allay their anxiety in that way, Abraham is not one of them. And whereas there are those who would turn against their love for Isaac and deny the importance of that bond, Abraham is not one of them. He turns against neither the finite (Isaac) nor the infinite (God), but prepares for the paradoxical affirmation of both. In preparing to sacrifice Isaac, however, Abraham performs "the teleological suspension of the ethical" (*FT*, 54). This is not the denial of ethics, but the suspension or postponement of the ethical domain in the name of that which is higher, namely, the infinite or the divine. The human and finite world is grounded in that which is larger than itself, namely, the infinite, and there are occasions in which the affirmation of that infinity takes priority over the affirmation of that finite and ethical domain which is the product of that infinity. But this suspension of the ethical entails anxiety, and faith does not resolve anxiety, but exists with it. Any finite individual can have faith only by contracting anxiety, for all faith involves some loss or weakening of worldly connections, including the worldly connection to one's own finite, bodily self. There is in faith a dying away of the finite self, this body, this name, these worldly connections to family, friends, lovers, this belonging to a time and a landscape, a home, a city. Faith underscores that all those finite things in which we are invested are perishable, and that there is no necessary reason or assurance that they will remain as we know them or survive at all.

If the story of Abraham is an allegory of faith, and if Abraham himself is a figure for faith, then we can read the story for its more general philosophical implications. Aristotle once claimed that philosophy begins with a sense of wonder, the wonder that there are things rather than no things. Aristotle's 'wonder' is not so different from Kierkegaard's sense of the marvelous in his encounter with Abraham's faith. For Aristotle, wonder emerges over the fact *that* there are things, not over *how* things came about – although that interested him, too – but that things came about at all. Kierkegaard writes of "the emotion which is the passionate sense for coming into existence: wonder" (*PF*, 99). In Kierkegaard's terms, it is, on the one hand, a marvel that these specific finite beings, humans, the elements, objects of all kinds, came into the world rather than some other set of beings. On the other hand, it is terrifying that all that exists appears to come into the world for no necessary reason at all. For if there is no necessary reason that things came into the world, there is no necessary reason that sustains those very things in the world, and there is no necessary reason that keeps those things from passing out of the finite world. If these finite beings came into the world from a set of infinite possibilities, then why is it that, of all the myriad and countless beings that came into the world, *these* came into being? There appears to be no necessity that *these* beings came into existence, and that others did not, if we consider that the source or origin of all things is infinite possibility, another name for God. But the wonder or marvel is provoked by another realization as well. If that which exists in the finite realm is the actualization of a set of possibilities, and this set of possibilities is only a subset of the infinite possibilities that are not actualized in the existing world, then how do we account for which possibilities made the *passage* from infinite possibility into that which exists in the finite world? No reason can be supplied: there is no necessity for what exists to exist. In fact, not only is there no necessity for the infinite, God, to create the finite, the human world, but it is perfectly absurd that he did at all.

The finite is grounded in the infinite: we know this from Kierkegaard's analysis of despair. But the finite never fully expresses the infinite which is its origin. Precisely to the extent that an existing individual, for instance, is finite, that is, limited, mortal, located in space and time, and bodily, that individual is clearly not infinite and, hence, does not fully express the infinity out of which he or she (absurdly) arises. This passage from the infinite to the finite cannot be thought; it is wondrous and a marvel, but also quite terrifying, for there is no necessary reason for anything to exist or, for that matter, to persist in its existence, that is, to stay alive. Whatever God is for Kierkegaard, 'he' (Kierkegaard tends not to personify God) is not that which supplies a reason or a necessity for that which exists. On the contrary, the postulation of the Kierkegaardian God underscores that existence itself is absurd.

The story of Abraham suggests that whatever exists in this world does so by virtue of a kind of grace, an arbitrary and irrational act. Existence can be understood as a kind of unexpected gift, one which comes just as easily as it is taken away. To have faith means to affirm this contingency, this absurd coming-into-being of existence, regardless of the suffering that recognition of absurdity causes. To transform the terror produced by the recognition of existence in its absurdity is no easy task. Indeed, the aesthete and the ethicist cannot find relief from this terror; they are in despair to the extent that they are run by this terror and involved in sensuous or ethical endeavors which seek to quell the anxiety produced by the fact of human contingency. The Knight of Resignation in *Fear and Trembling* can be understood as a figure at the limit of the ethical domain, tracing the movements of faith, but not able to make the necessary leap. As a consequence, he is *horrified* by the prospect of Abraham's 'sacrifice' of his own son; indeed, the Knight of Infinite Resignation can understand Abraham's intended act as a murder – and not a sacrifice or offering to God.

We might then understand the movement from the ethical domain to that of faith as the transformation of terror into a sense of grace. The difficulty with making this movement, however, is that the prospect of losing one's worldly attachments, indeed, one's own finite existence for no necessary reason, is not easy to face with anything other than terror. Kierkegaard understood that the task of faith would be especially difficult to accomplish by those who lived according to the romantic impulse to invest existing individuals with such enormous value that they cannot imagine themselves continuing to exist in a world without them. This was the anguished predicament of the young man in *Repetition*, and there is good evidence to support the view that Kierkegaard himself felt just this way about Regine Olsen with whom he broke off an engagement to be married. This broken engagement can be understood as Kierkegaard's own 'sacrifice' which, from an ethical point of view, appeared to be the emotional equivalent of murder.

In the midst of Kierkegaard's discussion of Abraham's faith in *Fear and Trembling*, he remarks with due irony that if Hegel's philosophy were right, then Abraham would, indeed, be a murderer. For Kierkegaard, Hegel represents the ethical domain, for in Hegel's *Phenomenology of Spirit* and *Philosophy of Right*, he argues that the individual realizes his or her true and proper purpose in a community bound by *ethical* laws. Indeed, Hegel argues that if an individual holds him- or herself to be above the ethical law, that individual is sinful. Kierkegaard objects to Hegel's characterization of the assertion of individuality as sin. According to Kierkegaard, Hegel fails to understand that the individual is higher than the universal ethical norm, that there are times when ethical laws must be 'suspended' or 'surrendered' so that a higher value can be affirmed, namely, the value of faith – which, of course, for Kierkegaard, is always an *individual* affair. The relation to God cannot be mediated (this belief aligns Kierkegaard with Luther). Hegel would believe that God is present in the ethical law, and that individuals, by submitting to the ethical law, come into a mediated relationship to God. This happy reconciliation of the ethical (called 'the universal') and the religious (called 'the absolute') is one that Kierkegaard firmly rejects. The middle term, the ethical or 'universal,' which Hegel understands to mediate between the individual, on the one hand, and the divine, on the other, is, for Kierkegaard, precisely that which must be subordinated and suspended for the absolute and immediate relation of faith to take place between the individual and God: "this position cannot be mediated, for all mediation takes place only by virtue of the universal; it is and as such remains for all eternity a paradox, impervious to thought" (*FT*, 56).

In Kierkegaard's view, Hegel's ethical community requires the sacrifice of the individual to an anonymous law. As law-abiding citizens, we are interchangeable with one another; each of us expresses our true and proper self through the same acts by which we conform to a law which applies to all human beings regardless of our differences. In this sense, none of us are individuals before the law or, rather, each of us is treated by the law as an anonymous subject. Insofar as Abraham takes distance from the ethical law which prohibits murder, he becomes an individual, and the more he refuses to honor the authority of that law over his own existence, the more individuated he becomes. This act of putting into question the ethical law as a final authority over one's life engages Abraham in anxiety, for in questioning the law, Abraham encounters his own being apart from the ethical community in which he stands.

Opposing himself to Hegel's notion of individuality as sin, Kierkegaard values this anxiety as human freedom, the demand to make a decision whether or not to comply with the law or whether to follow a higher authority. Although Hegel appears to worry about such a moment in which the individual stands apart from the ethical community, suspending the power of its laws to govern his or her life, Hegel also appreciates fear and trembling as necessary moments in the development of the human subject.[12] Significantly, Kierkegaard does not acknowledge that moment in Hegel in which fear and trembling are considered to be necessary experiences in the acquisition of human freedom. We can find that moment at the end of Hegel's well-known chapter in the *Phenomenology* entitled "Lordship and Bondage." There the bondsman who has been the property of the lord has cut himself loose from his own enslavement. What we might expect is the jubilant celebration of freedom, but what we encounter in the emerging bondsman instead is a shattering fear. Consider the following description of the emancipated bondsman from Hegel's *Phenomenology of Spirit* as an example of the fear and trembling produced by the experience of human freedom temporarily untethered by authority. The bondsman labors on objects, and for the first time *recognizes* his own labor in that which he makes. In the recognition of *himself* in the object of his making, he is struck with fear:

> the formative activity . . . has the negative significance of *fear*. For, in fashioning the thing, the bondsman's own negativity [his freedom] becomes an object for him . . . this objective *negative* moment is none other than the alien being before which it has trembled.

> (*PS*, 118)[13]

Whereas the bondsman has been afraid of the lord, he is now frightened of his own freedom now that that freedom has become that which 'lords' over his own existence. A few lines later, Hegel continues with a passage that further links the expression of freedom through work with the experience of fear:

> Without the formative activity, fear remains inward and mute, and consciousness does not become explicitly *for itself*. If consciousness fashions the thing without that initial absolute fear, it is only an empty self-centred attitude. . . . If it has not experienced absolute fear but only some lesser dread, the

negative being has remained for it something external [its freedom still appears to belong to another and is not yet its own], its substance has not been infected by it through and through.

(*PS*, 119)

Hegel goes on to remark that if the bondsman has not been shaken by fear in the very fiber of its being, it will remain "a freedom enmeshed in servitude."

We can begin to see here that Kierkegaard's characterization of Hegel is not always fair. Hegel is clearly not in favor of the enslavement of the individual to the ethical law, for the fear and trembling associated with the moment of emancipation will inform the individual as he or she enters ethical life in the following chapter in the *Phenomenology*. Indeed, one might well ask the question of whether Kierkegaard's very language of "fear and trembling" is not derived from Hegel's description of the emerging bondsman in *The Phenomenology of Spirit*. How far is the bondsman's trembling at the sight of his own freedom from Abraham's anxiety in the face of his own potential act? How do these 'tremblings' differ?

Whereas Hegel's bondsman trembles before that which he has created, the external confirmation of his own power to create, Abraham trembles (inwardly) before that which he is compelled by God to sacrifice and destroy. Whereas the bondsman is frightened of his own capacity to create, a capacity which in its apparent limitlessness makes the bondsman into a figure with enormous responsibility and power, Abraham is compelled to act according to a divine demand that he cannot understand. In this sense, Abraham's freedom is not guided by reason, but by that which is irrational, beyond reason, and which requires an obedience to that irrationality over any human law. The bondsman, on the other hand, appears to legislate a law for itself, expressed in its own 'formative activity' or labor. The bondsman appears to be temporarily without an authority, a 'lord,' who is other to himself. But Abraham, he is enthralled to a Lord who is so radically different from himself that he cannot understand him at all. That the bondsman is compelled to be free without the guidance of a supervening authority is an unbearable situation which leads to the development, in the following chapter on the "Unhappy consciousness," of a *conscience*, the self-imposition of an ethical law, what Hegel himself understands as a form of self-enslavement. Hence, Hegel's bondsman retreats from the fearful prospect of his own freedom through enslaving himself to ethical projects and practicing various rituals of self-denial. Abraham, on the other hand, must bind himself to an authority whose demands are incomprehensible, an act which leaves him frighteningly detached from the ethical community and from his own rational capacities. Kierkegaard tells us that it is through this persistence in fear and trembling that Abraham comes to the full and gracious experience of faith.

The task of faith is to continue to affirm infinite possibility in the face of events which appear to make existence itself a radically impossible venture. What astonished Kierkegaard about the Abraham story is that Abraham faced the prospect of losing what was most precious to him in the world, and he still did not lose faith and curse God: he maintained his faith not only in the face of that loss, but in the face of having to make the sacrifice himself.[14] Abraham loves Isaac, but that human bond cannot be the most important passion of his life, for what merely exists can come and go, and that transience can never be the object of faith. If in the throes of romantic love or in the complicated emotional ties of family life, we say that our existence is meaningless without some existing individual, that is a symptom that we are in despair. For Kierkegaard, if any existing individual becomes the fundamental reason to live, that individual must be sacrificed so that faith can return to its proper object: the infinite.

In *Repetition*, published simultaneously with *Fear and Trembling*, Kierkegaard relates the story of how a young man, a thinly veiled substitute for Kierkegaard himself, breaks off an engagement with a girl he loves. The sacrifice appears absurd, for he has not fallen out of love with her. And yet, if the girl has become the ultimate reason for living, the source of all affirmation, then the young man has transferred and invested the boundlessness of his passion onto an existing individual: this is, for Kierkegaard, a kind of despair and a failure of faith. Precisely because she has become an object he is not willing to lose, he must demonstrate his willingness to lose her altogether. His sacrifice is not unlike Abraham's, except that Abraham, being a "Knight of Faith," receives Isaac back again, whereas the young man, a veritable "Knight of Resignation," appears to orchestrate and suffer an irreversible loss. He knows how to sacrifice finite things, and to avoid the despair that characterizes the life of the aesthete as well as the ethicist, but he does not know how to affirm that infinity which appears to make existence utterly absurd.

What does it mean that whereas Abraham receives Isaac back, the young man in *Repetition* fails to have his love returned? To have faith means no longer to invest absolute meaning in what is finite, whether it is an individual person, a set of objects or possessions, a homeland, a job, a family. All of these sites of investment are finite and perishable, and when we transfer religious passion onto those things, according to Kierkegaard, we turn away from God and invest the things of this world with a displaced religious meaning and, hence, fall into despair.

If one makes the leap of faith, then one invests absolute passion and meaning in the infinite; this entails a suspension not only of the ethical, but of the finite realm altogether, for any finite object of passion will now be understood as emerging as a gift from the infinite and passing back eventually into the infinite. For Kierkegaard, it is only once we affirm the transience and contingency (nonnecessity) of that which we love in this world that we are free to love it at all. If Abraham gets Isaac back, it is because he has suspended his attachments to that which is finite, affirmed the infinite, and so understood that nothing that exists in this world can sustain an absolute passion. It is in this sense that Isaac was *always* a gift from God; one's own existence is a gift, and that of every other existing thing.

Of course, to recognize that there is no necessary reason that some beings exist and other possible beings do not produces not only a sense of wonder, but a sense of terror as well. The thought of an existing life as a contingency, as an arbitrary event which just as well *could not* have happened, or which could without reason pass away, this is a thought that, strictly speaking, cannot be maintained; it is a thought which founders on itself, for how can a thought think the contingency of the thinker who thinks it? But it is this thought that leads to the anxiety over existence that leads to the question of faith. To witness the existing world this way, as a terrifying and wondrous gift, is to know that one is not the author of that world, that the father, strictly speaking, is not the 'origin' of the son, and that not only do all things originate – absurdly, wondrously – in the infinite, but all existing things return there as well.

For Kierkegaard, this problem of the contingency of existence has implications for human love, a passion that verges on faith, but which becomes despair when it becomes too much like faith, an absolute or infinite passion. To love that which exists without at the same time knowing the fragile and contingent nature of existence is to be in despair; if one tries to love a human object as if it were absolute, one projects a religious passion onto a human object. The result, for Kierkegaard, is to become wracked with displaced passion and a constant sense of loss. Kierkegaard describes this problem at some length in the first volume of *Either/Or*. Considered to be part of Kierkegaard's early writings, *Either/Or* is composed of two volumes. The first offers writings that enact and explore the *aesthetic* point of view; the second volume offers sermons and treatises in the *ethical* point of view. Neither of these perspectives is the same as faith, but Kierkegaard, in unmistakenly Hegelian fashion, suggests that these two spheres, these two ways of approaching the world, have to be experienced in order to understand the limits of each and the superiority of faith. There is no writing in the perspective of faith in either of these volumes, but it is unclear that such a writing could exist; faith is nevertheless there in the writings as the path not chosen, the way to affirm the paradox that emerges between the aesthetic and ethical perspectives.

The vain effort to make of a human being an object of absolute and infinite passion is the fateful predicament of the aesthete in *Either/ Or*. The alternative in that text is to become a purely *ethical* being, one who makes no attachments to anything finite, but acts in accordance with a universal law, a law that applies to everyone, and which makes of its obedient subject an anonymous and impersonal subject. The aesthete, on the other hand, values what is most immediate and finite as if it were absolute; the ethical person (also termed the "Knight of Infinite Resignation") treats the human law as if it were absolute, and invests his or her full passion into the application of that law. The one in faith, however, lives fully in the finite world, but affirms its contingency at the same time. This is the marvel that Kierkegaard claims he cannot perform, to love that which exists and to affirm that it might be lost, that it cannot serve as the ultimate object of passion, that for which one lives. Human love requires the knowledge of grace, that what is given for us to love is not ours, and that its loss refers us to that which is the origin of all things finite, including ourselves. This means that for the one who has faith, love is always an anxious and ironic affair, and there is no way to see directly how that infinite faith in that which is infinite lives alongside the finite love of that which exists. In Kierkegaard's terms, "absolutely to express the sublime in the pedestrian – only that the knight [of faith] can do it, and this is the one and only marvel" (*FT*, 41).

One implication of Kierkegaard's paradoxical view of faith is that it is *not* a form of asceticism. Kierkegaard does not advise a turning away from the finite world. On the contrary, he imagines that the Knight of Faith will be one who dwells among the ordinary world of things, a "tax collector" he suggests in *Fear and Trembling*. One would not be able to see from the outside that this individual has faith, for faith, by virtue of its radical inwardness, is inexpressible. The entirety of the finite realm would be 'returned' to such an individual for the paradoxical reason that, through faith, he or she no longer fears the loss of what exists; in faith, the individual affirms the absurdity and arbitrariness by which the existing world comes into being and passes out again. That affirmation is not a kind of wisdom or knowledge, but an irrational passion that emerges at the limits of all thinking.

❧ THE PARADOXICAL LANGUAGE OF FAITH ❧

Although it is clear that Kierkegaard writes in favor of faith, there are at least two remaining questions that trouble any reader of his works. The first question concerns the 'what' of faith: in what does Kierkegaard have faith? What is this God which appears to be the infinite or, more specifically, infinite possibility? The second question is intimately related to the first: how could we have received an answer to the question 'in what does Kierkegaard have faith?' if we expect the answer to arrive *in language*? After all, we have already learned that faith cannot be expressed in language, that it is the infinite passion of the inwardness of the self. But what is the status of Kierkegaard's own texts, if we understand the purpose of these texts to be an incitement to faith? How do these texts work? How do they achieve their purpose, if from the start we know that they can never express faith or, if they claim to have expressed faith, they have failed in that very task?

Kierkegaard's God is in-finite which means that this God can never be identified with one of his products. This God is said to be the origin of the existing world, but this is not a God who, in a personified form, at some point in history – or prior to history – said 'Let there be light' and light suddenly there was. And it is not that Kierkegaard disputes the truth of the Bible, but he insists that the truth of the Bible is not to be found in the language of the text. In this sense, Kierkegaard is against a literal reading of the Bible, one which takes every word printed there to be the transmitted word of God. On the contrary, the 'truth' of the Bible is not, properly speaking, *in* the text, but is to be found *in the reader*, in the various acts by which the various injunctions to faith are *appropriated* and taken up by those who read the text. The truth of the Bible is to be found in the faith of those who read the Bible. The text is a *condition* by which a certain kind of instruction in faith takes place, but faith can never be achieved by learning what the Bible says, only by finally turning away from that text and turning inward to discover the infinite passion that emerges from the demand to affirm contingency. In *Philosophical Fragments*, the Bible and biblical scholarship are treated with irony: these texts can deliver no *historical* truth of interest to the person interested in faith, for no historical documentation regarding the existence or teachings of Jesus Christ can ever convince a person into faith. Faith does not arrive as the result of a persuasive argument; faith (along with its alternative, despair) is precisely what has the chance to emerge when all argumentation and historical proof fail.[15]

But there is a further difficulty with an historical approach to faith. Some Christian scholars argue that it can be proven that Jesus Christ lived, that he came into the world, and that he was the son of

God. The proof 'that' he existed is, however, not enough for Kierkegaard. That assertion simply prompts him to ask a series of philosophical questions which the historical enquiry cannot answer: what does it mean for anything to 'come into existence'? If something can be said to 'come into existence,' then at some early point in time, it did not exist at all. How, then, can something which is nonbeing become transformed into being? This is, of course, the question that preoccupied us above when we considered how philosophical wonder focuses on the apparent absurdity that some things exist rather than not, that certain possibilities become actual or finite, whereas other possibilities remain merely possible. Possibility and actuality are mutually exclusive states, that is, a thing is either possible or actual, but it would make no sense to say that it is both at once. Therefore, to say that a given thing has come into existence implies that it has moved from a state of possibility to one of actuality. This transition cannot be 'thought,' says Kierkegaard, but is a contradiction, one that accompanies all 'coming into being.'

In *Philosophical Fragments*, Kierkegaard considers the highly significant paradox that in the person of the Savior (whose historical status remains uncertain or, at least, irrelevant), it appears that what is Eternal has come into time, and that what is infinite has appeared in finite form. Whereas Hegel would claim that the finite appearance in this consequential instance expresses and actualizes the infinite, that this person in time, aging and mortal, expressed that which can never die; Kierkegaard takes issue with such a notion, arguing that this occurrence is utterly paradoxical, that the human and divine aspects of the figure of Christ can never be reconciled; insofar as he is infinite, he cannot appear in finite form, without losing his status as infinite; and insofar as he is finite, he cannot become infinite, for finitude implies mortality.

What is striking about Kierkegaard's writing in *Philosophical Fragments* is that the so-called miracle of God coming into existence recurs at every moment that some finite thing 'comes into being.' Christ is no exception to this paradoxical movement, but neither is he singular. After all, every human self emerges from a set of infinite possibilities and so moves from the infinite (which is nonbeing, that which is not yet finite and does not yet have a specified kind of being) to the finite (or being). Indeed, anything that comes into existence is miraculous for the very reasons we set out above in our discussion of wonder. In making this move, Kierkegaard appears to be taking an almost arrogant distance from the church authorities, the Scriptures, and the religious authorities whose task it is to settle historical details about Christ's sojourn on earth. Indeed, Kierkegaard goes so far as to subject the key concepts of Christianity to a new set of definitions, ones that are devised by him. Kierkegaard is not interested in testing his interpretations against the Bible or against earlier interpretations; he devises and sets forth his own. Throughout the introductory chapter of *Philosophical Fragments*, Kierkegaard appears to take over the power to name that properly belonged to God in the book of Genesis. In Genesis, God spoke and said, 'Let there be . . . light, man, woman, beasts, etc.,' and the very power of his voice was sufficient to bring these entities into being. Kierkegaard appears to appropriate this power of naming for himself, but the entities he brings into existence through his writings are Christian concepts. As a result, he *names* these concepts and, in the naming, revises their meaning according to his own interpretive scheme: "What now shall we call such a Teacher, who restores the lost condition and gives the learner the Truth? Let us call him *Saviour* . . . let us call him *Redeemer*" (*PF*, 21). Further definitions are offered for "conversion," "repentance," "New Birth," and more (*PF*, 22–3).

What are we to make of this Kierkegaardian willingness to fabricate new meanings for the orthodox terms of Christianity? Is it not a kind of arrogance or pride to offer new interpretations for such words? By what right does Kierkegaard proceed with such obvious enthusiasm to create new meanings for old words? Is this creative way with words related to Kierkegaard's enigmatic career as an author?

What is the authority of the author? For Kierkegaard, faith cannot be communicated, so that any effort to write a book that communicates faith will, by definition, have to fail. In this way, then, Kierkegaard must write a book which constantly fails to communicate faith, a book which insistently renounces its own authority to state what faith is, a text which turns back upon itself and effectively wills its own failure. If the reader of his book knows that the book cannot offer knowledge of faith, then that reader will be seduced by the promise of that knowledge only to be disappointed in an instructive way. Kierkegaard's language must, then, perform the paradoxical task of enacting the limits of language itself. The author who wishes to point the way to faith must resist every effort to communicate faith directly; in other words, that author must will the failure of his own book, and in that very failure, know its success.

In *Sickness unto Death*, Kierkegaard considers the peculiar kind of despair that afflicts "poets" and makers of fiction. We can read in this diagnosis a thinly veiled autobiographical confession. Consider that Kierkegaard is a kind of poet,[16] one who produces a fictional narrator for most of his early texts through the construction of various pseudonyms. He then produces "examples" of faith and despair, fabricating "types" of individuals, embellishing on biblical and classical characters: Abraham, Don Juan, etc. And now consider Kierkegaard's diagnosis of the person who suffers from defiant despair, the will to be oneself, that is, the will to be the sole ground and power of one's own existence and, therefore, to take the place of God:

> this is the self that a person in despair wills to be, severing the self from any relation to a power that has established it, or severing it from the idea that there is such a power . . . the self in despair wants to be master of itself or to create itself.
>
> (*SUD*, 68)

Kierkegaard then explains that this kind of despairing individual regularly fantasizes that he or she is all kinds of things that they are not: "the self in despair . . . constantly relates to itself only by way of imaginary constructions" (*SUD*, 68). This fiction-producing self can make itself into "an imaginatively constructed God," but this self is for that reason "always building castles in the sky . . . only shadowboxing" (*SUD*, 69). At an extreme, this defiant form of despair becomes *demonic* despair, and here the will to fabricate and fictionalize asserts itself in clear defiance, even hatred, of God. Is there, for Kierkegaard, a stark opposition between the life of faith and that of fiction-making? And can Kierkegaard himself give up his imaginary constructions in order to live the life of faith, one which we know, from the consideration of Abraham, is a life of silence?

Demonic despair, which Kierkegaard calls the most intensive form of despair, is rooted in "a hatred of existence": "not even in defiance or defiantly does it will to be itself, but for spite" (*SUD*, 69). And what evidence does such a person have against existence? The one in demonic despair is himself the evidence that justifies his hatred of existence. This appears to imply that the one in demonic despair, that incessant maker of fictions, *hates himself* for producing an imaginary construction of himself, but nevertheless persists in this self-fabrication. This is a self which, through fiction-making, postures as the creator of its own existence, thus denying the place of God as the true author of human existence. But this demonic self must also despise itself for trying to take over the power of God. This self in demonic despair alternates between self-fabrication and self-hatred. Inasmuch as this demonic one is an author, and is Kierkegaard himself, he produces a fiction only then to tear down the construction he has just made. The one in demonic despair can acknowledge the divine authorship that enables his own fiction, his pseudonymous work, only by admitting that what he has produced is a necessary fraud.

At the end of Part One of *Sickness unto Death*, Kierkegaard appears to begin this disavowal of his own production, clearing the way for an appreciation of God as the only 'first-rate author' in town, acknowledging that Kierkegaard's own work must always be understood as derived from the power that constitutes him, a power that precedes and enables his own imaginary production:

> Figuratively speaking, it is as if an error slipped into an author's writing and the error became conscious of itself as an error – perhaps it actually was not a mistake but in a much higher sense an essential part of the whole production – and now this error wants to mutiny against the author, out of hatred toward him, forbidding him to correct it and in maniacal defiance saying to him: No, I refuse to be erased; I will stand as a witness against you, a witness that you are a second-rate author.
>
> (*SUD*, 74)

Written thus in 1848 and published in 1849, we can see here the fruition of Kierkegaard's intention to resist the seduction of authorship. Two years earlier, he wrote in his journal: "My idea is to give up being an author (which I can only be altogether or not at all) and prepare myself to be a pastor."[17] It appears that Kierkegaard gave up his career as a literary and philosophical author after *Sickness unto Death*, and persevered in writing purely religious tracts. Had he achieved faith? Did he overcome despair? Was his writing as compelling after the leap or did it turn out to require the very despair he sought to overcome?

❧ NOTES ❧

1 It would be interesting to compare this claim with Freud's efforts to address the question of 'anxiety' through analysis.

2 *SUD: Sickness unto Death*, ed. and trans. H.V. Hong and E.H. Hong (Princeton: Princeton University Press, 1983).

3 "Hegel and Hegelianism constitute an essay in the comical." *Concluding Unscientific Postscript*, trans. D. Swenson and W. Lowrie (Princeton: Princeton University Press, 1974), henceforth referred to as *CUP*, p. 34.

4 "In order to avoid confusion, it is at once necessary to recall that our treatment of the problem does not raise the question of the truth of Christianity. It merely deals with the problem of the individual's relationship to Christianity. It has nothing whatever to do with the systematic zeal of the personally indifferent individual to arrange the truths of Christianity in paragraphs; it deals with the concern of the infinitely interested individual for his own relationship to such a doctrine." Ibid., p. 18.

5 Descartes, Fifth Meditation. God is perfect and can only make that which is equally perfect or less perfect than him-/her-/itself, for nothing can be more perfect than God. If there is something which has some degree of perfection in it, that thing must be produced by that which is at least as perfect or more perfect than the thing itself. There is nothing in the world that is more perfect

than human beings even though human beings are imperfect in some ways (they sin, they are ignorant). This implies that human beings must be created by that which is equally or more perfect than themselves. And it is perfect being that is called God.

6 *FT: Fear and Trembling/Repetition*, ed. and trans. H.V. Hong and E.H. Hong (Princeton: Princeton University Press, 1983).

7 See Kierkegaard's discussion of Abraham, ibid.

8 *PF: Philosophical Fragments*, ed. N. Thulstrop, trans. D. Swenson and H.V. Hong (Princeton: Princeton University Press, 1962).

9 "Commentator's introduction," *PF*, p. lxxv.

10 See Kierkegaard's discussion of the limits of speculative thought in *CUP*, ch. 2, "The speculative point of view."

11 This is a view which is falsely attributed to existential philosophy generally, but which we can see ought not to be ascribed to Kierkegaard.

12 It is interesting to note that Kierkegaard takes the phrase "fear and trembling" from the New Testament, Philippians 2: 12–14, but applies it to an Old Testament figure, Abraham. Hegel's placement of "fear and trembling" in relation to work is perhaps slightly closer to the meaning of the New Testament use: "Wherefore, my beloved, as ye have always obeyed, not as in my presence only, but now much more in my absence, work out your own salvation with fear and trembling: For it is God which worketh in you both to will and to do of his good pleasure." *The Dartmouth Bible*, ed. R.B. Chamberlin and H. Feldman (Boston: Houghton Mifflin, 1961).

13 *PS*: Hegel, *The Phenomenology of Spirit*, trans. A.V. Miller (New York: Oxford University Press, 1977).

14 Imagine if Hegel's bondsman were to have created a son with a woman, and that he was then compelled to sacrifice that son, how would Hegel's analysis have to change in order to take account of Abraham's anguish?

15 Note Kierkegaard's ironic tone in his writing against the historical efforts to supply a proof of God's existence: "And how does the God's existence emerge from the proof? Does it follow straightway, without any breach of continuity? . . . As long as I keep my hold on the proof, i.e. continue to demonstrate, the existence does not come out, if for no other reason than that I am engaged in proving it; but when I let the proof go, the existence is there. But this act of letting go is surely also something; it is indeed a contribution of mine. Must not this also be taken into account, this little moment, brief as it may be – it need not be long, for it is a *leap*. However brief this moment, if only an instantaneous now, this 'now' must be included in the reckoning." *PF*, p. 53.

Kierkegaard here plays on the double meaning of the act of letting go being "a contribution of mine." On the one hand, this is his philosophical contribution to the critique of rationalism, and "the leap" is a concept he introduced into philosophical and religious discourse. On the other hand, he is suggesting that no person, including himself, can arrive at faith without making a contribution of him- or herself. And this contribution, being one of passion, has to come from the inwardness of the self, and be directed toward a faith which no 'proof' can automatically produce.

16 See L. Mackey, *Kierkegaard: A Kind of Poet* (Philadelphia: University of Pennsylvania Press, 1971).

17 Quoted in the Introduction to *CUP*, p. xiii.

❧ SELECT BIBLIOGRAPHY ❧

Original language editions

11.1 Kierkegaard, S. *Samlede Vaerker*, 20 vols, ed. P. Rohde, Copenhagen: Gyldendalske Boghandel, 1962–3.

English translations

Works cited

(Dates of original publication in Danish are given with the first reference to the work in the text.)

11.2 Kierkegaard, S. *Concluding Unscientific Postscript*, trans. D. Swenson and W. Lowrie, Princeton: Princeton University Press, 1974.

11.3 Kierkegaard, S. *Either/Or*, 2 vols, trans. D. Swenson and L.M. Swenson, Princeton: Princeton University Press, 1971.

11.4 Kierkegaard, S. *Fear and Trembling/Repetition*, ed. and trans. H.V. Hong and E.H. Hong, Princeton: Princeton University Press, 1983.

11.5 Kierkegaard, S. *Philosophical Fragments* ed. N. Thulstrup, trans. D. Swenson and H.V. Hong, Princeton: Princeton University Press, 1962.

11.6 Kierkegaard, S. *Sickness unto Death*, ed. and trans. H.V. Hong and E.H. Hong, Princeton: Princeton University Press, 1983.

Works not cited

11.7 Kierkegaard, S. *Attack upon "Christendom"*, trans. W. Lowrie, Princeton: Princeton University Press, 1940.

11.8 Kierkegaard, S. *The Concept of Dread*, trans. W. Lowrie, Princeton: Princeton University Press, 1957.

11.9 Kierkegaard, S. *The Concept of Irony*, trans. L.M. Capel, New York: Harper & Row, 1965.

11.10 Kierkegaard, S. *Edifying Discourses: A Selection*, trans. D.F. Swenson and L.M. Swenson, New York: Harper & Row, 1958.

11.11 Kierkegaard, S. *For Self-Examination and Judge for Yourselves!*, trans. W. Lowrie, Princeton: Princeton University Press, 1974.

11.12 Kierkegaard, S. *The Point of View for my Work as an Author*, trans. W. Lowrie, New York: Harper & Row, 1962.

11.13 Kierkegaard, S. *Purity of Heart*, trans. D.V. Steere, New York: Harper & Row, 1956.

11.14 Kierkegaard, S. *Stages on Life's Way*, trans. W. Lowrie, Princeton: Princeton University Press, 1940.

11.15 Kierkegaard, S. *Training in Christianity*, trans. W. Lowrie, Princeton: Princeton University Press, 1944.

11.16 Kierkegaard, S. *The Works of Love*, trans. H.V. Hong and E.H. Hong, New York: Harper & Row, 1964.

11.17 *Soren Kierkegaard's Journals and Papers*, 4 vols, ed. and trans. H.V. Hong and E.H. Hong, assisted by G. Melantschuk, Bloomington: Indiana University Press, 1967–75.

Bibliographies

11.18 Himmelstrup, J. *Soren Kierkegaard International Bibliografi*, Copenhagen: Nyt Nordisk Forlag Arnold Busck, 1962.

11.19 Jorgensen, A. *Soren Kierkegaard-litteratur, 1961–1970*, Aarhus: Akademisk Boghandel, 1971; also *Soren Kierkegaard-litteratur, 1971–1980*, Aarhus: privately printed, 1983.

11.20 Lapointe, F. *Soren Kierkegaard and his Critics: An International Bibliography of Criticism*, Westport: Greenwood Press, 1980.

11.21 McKinnon, A. *The Kierkegaard Indices*, 4 vols, Leiden: E.J. Brill, 1970.

11.22 Thompson, J. (ed.) *Kierkegaard: A Collection of Critical Essays*, New York: Doubleday Anchor, 1972.

Influences

11.23 Crites, S. *In the Twilight of Christendom: Hegel vs Kierkegaard on Faith and History*, AAR Studies in Religion, 2, Chambersburg, Pa.: American Academy of Religion, 1972.

11.24 Dupré, L. *A Dubious Heritage: Studies in the Philosophy of Religion after Kant*, New York: Paulist Press, 1977.

11.25 Heiss, R. *Hegel, Kierkegaard, Marx: Three Great Philosophers whose Ideas Changed the Course of Civilization*, trans. E.B. Garside, New York: Delta, 1975.

11.26 Kroner, R. "Kierkegaard or Hegel?" *Revue International de Philosophie* 6, 1 (1952): 79–96.

11.27 Löwith, K. *From Hegel to Nietzsche: The Revolution in Nineteenth-Century Thought*, trans. D. Green, New York: Holt, Rinehart & Winston, 1964; London: Constable, 1965; Garden City: Doubleday Anchor, 1967.

11.28 Taylor, M.C. *Journeys to Selfhood: Hegel and Kierkegaard*, Berkeley: University of California Press, 1980.

11.29 Theunissen, M. *The Other*, Boston: MIT Press, 1987.

11.30 Thulstrup, N. *Kierkegaard's Relation to Hegel*, trans. G.L. Strengen, Princeton: Princeton University Press, 1980.

11.31 Wahl, J. *Etudes kierkegardiennes*, 4th edn, Paris: J. Vrin, 1974.

General surveys

11.32 Adorno, T. *Kierkegaard: Constructions of the Aesthetic*, trans. R. Hullot-Kentor, Minneapolis: University of Minnesota Press, 1989.

11.33 Agacinski, S. *Aparté: Conceptions and Deaths of Soren Kierkegaard*, trans. K. Newmark, Gainesville: University of Florida Press, 1988.

11.34 Collins, J. *The Mind of Kierkegaard*, Chicago: Henry Regnery, 1953.

11.35 Holmer, P.L. *The Grammar of Faith*, San Francisco: Harper & Row, 1978.

11.36 Lebowitz, N. *Kierkegaard: A Life of Allegory*, Baton Rouge: Louisiana State University Press, 1985.

11.37 Mackey, L. *Kierkegaard: A Kind of Poet*, Philadelphia: University of Pennsylvania Press, 1971.

11.38 Malanfschok, G. *Kierkegaard's Thought*, Princeton: Princeton University Press, 1971.

11.39 Perkins, R.L. (ed.) *Kierkegaard's "Fear and Trembling": Critical Appraisals*, Birmingham, Ala.: University of Alabama Press, 1981.

11.40 Smith, J.K. (ed.) *Kierkegaard's Truth: The Disclosure of Self*, Psychiatry and the Humanities Series, 5, New Haven: Yale University Press, 1981.

11.41 Thompson, J. (ed.) *Kierkegaard: A Collection of Critical Essays*, Garden City: Doubleday Anchor, 1972.

11.42 Thompson, J. *The Lonely Labyrinth: Kierkegaard's Pseudonymous Works*, Carbondale: Southern Illinois University Press, 1967.

11.43 Wyschogrod, M. *Kierkegaard and Heidegger*, The Hague: Nijhoff, 1976.

Glossary

a priori – In the early eighteenth century, knowledge was called *a priori* if it was acquired by reason, not observation, or by deduction, not induction. Opposite: *a posteriori*. Kant introduced a new meaning, described under "*a priori* knowledge."

a priori **knowledge** – what can be known independently of any (particular) experience.

Absolute – the complete, all-encompassing whole of reality. In Hegel's philosophy, the term refers to knowable reality.

absolute idealism – the metaphysical position that mind and reality share the same categorical structure, and thus that understanding the nature and fundamental structures of thought is the same enterprise as understanding the nature and fundamental structures of the world. To be distinguished from epistemological idealisms of any kind.

absolute knowledge – unbiased, undistorted knowledge, without inconsistencies. In Hegel's philosophy, this term does not refer to knowing every detail, but to having an adequate understanding of knowlege and the Absolute, and to recognizing that knowledge and the Absolute are not epistemologically separate.

abstract – in Hegel's philosophy, that which is empty and devoid of content. Abstract knowledge focuses on certain aspects of a thing at the expense of other aspects and the thing's context.

acquired character – in Schopenhauer's philosophy, the gradually accumulated knowlege of what one wills and of one's abilities. Such knowledge has transformative impact on behavior, for it provides new motives to the individual's will.

analytic judgment – a judgment or assertion the predicate of which is implicit in the concept of the subject. Example: a bachelor is an unmarried man.

ars characteristica – a form of symbolic logic invented by Leibniz, in which numbers replace concepts of things, and combinatorial arithmetic is applied to the numbers. Leibniz believed that in this way a universal language could be established.

atheism controversy (*Atheismusstreit*) – a famous public dispute over the relationship between philosophy and religion, provoked by Fichte's assertion that what is truly divine is the moral world order itself and that there is no need to posit a "moral law-giver" or personal God as the creator of this moral order.

Aufheben, Aufhebung – a German word variously translated as "to supersede," "to sublate," "to sublimate," or, more colloquially, "to pick something up." In Hegel's *Phenomenology of Spirit*, the term is used to refer to history moving forward while preserving what has come before. The term also implies improvement, so that the original is "lifted" into something better.

autonomy (positive freedom) – the ability to determine for oneself the principles in accord with which one determines one's will.

principle of autonomy – the categorical imperative.

check (*Anstoß*) – in Fichte's philosophy, the name for the inexplicable thwarting of the outwardly directed, practical activity of the I, in consequence of which one becomes conscious of a "feeling."

cogito – "I think," supposed by Descartes to be a sort of direct intuition of self, by Kant to express the unity of apperception.

compassion – according to Schopenhauer, the orientation that proceeds from the recognition that all beings are manifestations of the same will. A person who fully recognizes this no longer feels any inclination to assert his or her will against those of others and is, accordingly, a saint.

concept – an objective, though often implicit, humanly graspable ideal unity of a "many-ness." A prescriptive ideal that is part of a system of such ideals that the world is striving to realize and in terms of which what happens in the world can be made sense of.

concrete – in Hegel's philosophy, the whole, the thing-in-itself. Knowledge of an entity is concrete to the extent that it comprehends the entity in its entirety.

concrete universal – See "concept."

Critical philosophy, the – another name for transcendental idealism or Kantianism.

dialectic – development through apparently contradictory sequential stages. In Hegel's philosophy, this is the way in which the human Spirit has evolved through history. It is the means by which human beings attain an adequate conception of the world, drawing and carrying forward the conclusions of various conceptions of the world characteristic of the stages sequentially achieved through history.

dogmatism – Fichte's name for philosophical realism, understood as an attempt to derive consciousness from things in themselves.

duty – how one ought to act.

perfect duty -a duty with which one's every act ought to accord.

imperfect duty – a duty with which one ought to adopt a principle of acting in accord, but for which the individual has latitude in deciding exactly when the principle ought be acted upon.

ethical duty – all of one's duties comprehended as ways that one ought to act exactly because they are duties, i.e. because they follow from the categorical imperative. The only incentive for acting in accord with one's duties, so comprehended, is the internal incentive that follows merely from the recognition that they are duties.

juridical duty – those duties that one can be coerced to fulfill through external incentives.

elementary philosophy – the name given by K.L. Reinhold to his own systematic revision of Kantianism.

empirical character – the individual's character as it appears phenomenally.

end of nature – nature's purpose.

> **ultimate end of nature** – the most comprehensive purpose that can be realized within nature and in accord with its laws. Kant thinks that this is human culture, by which he means the development of aptitude of human beings to accomplish their chosen ends.

> **final end of nature** – that purpose for which the entire system of nature functions as an enabling condition, but which cannot be realized within nature. Kant thinks that this is the development of humanity toward moral perfection.

entelechy – an Aristotelian conception concerned with completion. Entelechy is a thing's actuality when it is fully complete, no longer possessing any potentiality. Entelechy is also the directing agent of a thing's natural activity toward the fulfillment of its natural end.

extended – spatial, as in "bodies are extended."

extension – space.

extra mentem – existing outside (independent) of the mind.

faculty – an ability of the mind; for example, "Human beings have an imaginative ability, or faculty."

form of consciousness (*Gestalt des Bewusstseins*) – a self-sufficient conceptual framework. In Hegel's philosophy, a stage of the human Spirit's development.

freedom

> **positive** – See "autonomy."

> **negative** – independence from determination through the laws of nature.

> **internal** – freedom with respect to the determination of one's will.

> **external** – freedom with respect to one's ability to effectuate one's will, especially thought of as independence from constraints that come from the will of other rational beings.

> **innate right to external freedom** – the right that all rational beings have, by virtue of their nature as rational being, to so much external freedom as is compatible with the same for others.

genius – in Schopenhauer's philosophy, an exceptional talent for heightened perception (specifically aesthetic experience) and for communicating this state to others.

Grundbegriff – a simple concept which admits no further analysis. For example: substance, cause.

historical materialism – From 1845 Marx developed the view that the driving force of history was the growth of the productive forces at the disposal of humans and the productive relations into which humans entered. This "economic base," he maintains, "shapes" other aspects of society such as the state and our forms of consciousness. Such a theory of history Marx called "materialist" in opposition to other theories, called "idealist" or "ideological," in which the economic base either was ignored or played hardly any role.

Identity Philosophy (or "System of Identity") – Schelling's name for a system which embraces both transcendental idealism and speculative *Naturphilosophie* and is based upon the idea of "the Absolute," understood as sheer identity, that is, as the undifferentiated unity of the ideal and the real (also called "objective idealism" or "absolute idealism").

imperative – the formula that expresses a command that constrains the will of a rational being whose will is influenced by both pure reason and material incentives.

> **hypothetical imperative** – presents an action as the necessary means to some particular end.

> **categorical imperative** – presents an action as of itself necessary, without regard to any other end. Kant thinks that the categorical imperative is best formulated as "Act only according to that maxim by which you can at the same time will that it become a universal law."

indifference, point of – the first principle or starting point of Schelling's Identity Philosophy; another name for "the Absolute."

intellectual intuition – (a) in Kant, the name for a nonexistent faculty of knowledge, through which one would have direct experience of an object; (b) for Fichte, another name for the original self-positing (or *Tathandlung*) of the I, an act within which the I as an object is directly present to itself as a subject; (c) for Schelling, a higher faculty of direct, nonsensible knowledge of reality, hence a special "faculty of truth" employed by artists and philosophers.

intelligible character – the individual's character as it is, outside time and space. In Schopenhauer's philosophy, the intelligible character is akin to a Platonic Idea for the individual.

justice – the aggregate of those conditions in which everyone's will is completely compatible in accordance with universal law. The condition of justice is identical to the universal realization of the innate right to external freedom.

leap of faith – the nondialectical act of will by which an individual leaves his or her previous stage of experience and achieves the highest stage possible for human beings, the stage of religious faith.

maxim – the general principle according to which an individual acts (e.g. "When I'm hungry, I'll eat").

meta-language – a language used to discuss a language. A meta-language is often a theoretical language. The language being discussed through a meta-language is called, by contrast, "the object language."

moment – a partial but essential aspect, a stage.

monad – in Leibniz's philosophy, a simple spiritual substance whose activities are representation and appetition.

monadology – Leibniz's theory that the world consists of monads.

natural right (*Naturrecht*) or theory of right (*Rechstslehre*) – that portion of Fichte's *Wissenschaftslehre* which examines the ways in which individual freedom must be limited in consequence of (and, at the same time, as a condition of) the recognition of the freedom of the others. The "theory of right" is equivalent to social and political philosophy and is, according to Fichte, entirely independent of ethics.

Naturphilosophie ("philosophy of nature") – Schelling's name for that branch of philosophy which interprets nature as a single, hierarchically organized, and self-developing whole, and thus, not as the opposite, but rather as the complement or "analogon" of the realm of spirit and consciousness; whereas transcendental idealism proceeds from subjectivity to objectivity, Schelling's philosophy of nature begins with objectivity and proceeds toward subjectivity.

negative philosophy – the name by which Schelling, during his final period, designated the transcendental philosophy of Kant and Fichte, as well as his own earlier philosophy.

nominalism – the position that words do not refer to the essences of things (for essences do not exist); instead, they are simply names that we assign to things. On this view, abstractions are all fictions (albeit useful ones). Only particular things exist.

odium theologicum – a special kind of hatred sometimes said to be characteristic of theologians who do not agree.

ontology – the division of metaphysics which deals with the most necessary and universal concepts of being, like Aristotle's enquiry into "being as being." Also called "first philosophy" and "general metaphysics."

pantheism – the doctrine that the world (i.e. the physical universe) is God or a mode of God's being. A Christian heresy which, in the eighteenth century, was usually ascribed to Spinoza.

particular – an entity that is definite and locatable with space and time. This term may refer to an individual person, as well as a thing.

Platonic Ideas – Plato's Forms. In Schopenhauer's philosophy, Platonic Ideas are grades of the will's objectivity. The universal prototypes of phenomenal objects accounting for natural kinds. As the universal forms that are instantiated in particulars, Platonic Ideas are the objects beheld in aesthetic experience.

positive philosophy – Schelling's name for the philosophy of revelation and mythology which he developed during his final period, a philosophy which, he believed, was genuinely capable of dealing with the mystery of existence.

powers, or potencies (*Potenzen*) – Schelling's term for the various levels of systematic organization exhibited within nature, as well as for the various levels of expression of the indifferent absolute.

practical philosophy – that division of transcendental idealism which is concerned with freedom and the will, and hence with "what ought to be" rather than with "what is."

practical philosophy, primacy of – For Fichte, this Kantian maxim implies that theoretical cognition must be grounded in willing and that freedom is thus a determining principle of all experience.

practical reason – reason employed with respect to action, i.e. with respect to bringing about conditions in the world.

pre-established harmony – In Leibniz's philosophy, the apparent causal connections between changes in different monads is denied, and it is asserted that these changes are pre-established (by God) so as to make a harmonious whole.

principium individuationis – principle of individuation. In Schopenhauer's philosophy, the *principium individuationis* is equivalent to time and space, the essential forms through which individuation becomes apparent in the phenomenal world.

pure will-less subject of knowledge – the condition of the individual during aesthetic experience, according to Schopenhauer. The individual becomes, as it were, the universal subject, contemplating the universal forms (or Platonic Ideas) evident in the object observed.

rationalism – a philosophical orientation which considered *a priori* reason capable of ascertaining significant truths about the world, and which considered natural science to be primarily a rational, deductive system only secondarily concerned with sense experience. In this sense, Kant is a rationalist. However, the term is principally associated with Descartes, Spinoza, and Leibniz, who are known as "the Rationalists." Rationalism is frequently contrasted with empiricism, which takes sense perception to be the fundamental basis for knowledge.

reductio ad absurdum – a mode of argument in which one shows that a thesis held by one's opponent, however reasonable it may seem to be, implies an absurdity and is therefore itself absurd.

repentance – According to Schopenhauer, repentance amounts to change of knowledge (and consequently motive), with the result that behavior is transformed.

resignation – in Schopenhauer's philosophy, the renunciation of the will that is characteristic of the saint. This renunciation results from full recognition that the entire phenomenal world, and every object in it, is a manifestation of a single will. In Kierkegaard's philosophy, the condition of being reconciled to tragedy in one's situation, without yet being capable of faith. The person in this condition is Kierkegaard's "Knight of Infinite Resignation," in contrast to the "Knight of Faith."

right in oneself – the right to have others not exercise any control over one's body, i.e. to not be assaulted in any manner.

rightful possession – possession that is consistent with justice.

semantics – the interpretation of a symbolic system.

Sittenlehre (**"theory of ethics"**) – The specifically "practical" portion of Fichte's *Wissenschaftslehre*, the "theory of ethics" provides an account of both the form and the content of the highest principle of morality (the categorical imperative) and derives specific duties from one's general obligation to posit one's own freedom.

social contract theory – the theory that people are subject to political obligations because they have contracted with others to subject themselves to such obligations (presumably because of some benefit that they thereby expect to receive).

solipsism – the theory that "I alone exist." This theory has probably never been held by a sane philosopher, but it is conceptually interesting as a *reductio ad absurdum* of some forms of idealism.

speculative – In the eighteenth century, "speculative" often meant "theoretical." Thus "speculative philosophy" did not mean speculative in the sense of fanciful dreaming, but theoretical as opposed to practical (moral) philosophy.

Spirit (*Geist*) – the subject in a universal sense. In Hegel's philosophy, the Spirit includes every individual and every object of human experience. It amounts to the human world, conceived as self-conscious and a comprehensible unity.

stages – in Kierkegaard's philosophy, a particular orientation or lifestyle that characterizes an individual's pursuits. Kierkegaard describes three distinct stages: the aesthetic, the ethical, and the religious stage. These stages do not automatically or dialectically give way to one another. Instead, an individual must "leap" from one to another by means of an inner response to his or her situation. Such a move is usually precipitated by the individual's recognition that he or she is in despair.

sufficient reason, principle of – the principle that there is a sufficient reason (or cause) of everything that exists or happens. According to Schopenhauer, this principle applies only to phenomenal objects. Each such object stands in a necessary, mutually determining relationship to all other phenomenal objects.

summons (*Aufforderung*) – in Fichte's *Wissenschaftslehre*, the term designating one's inner awareness of the freedom of others, as a consequence of which one is called upon to limit one's own freedom.

syntax – a purely formal specification of the legal strings of a symbolic system.

synthetic judgment – a judgment or assertion which is not analytic.

system – an interconnected set of propositions, demonstrably related. In the eighteenth century, the term referred to a deductive system, a set of first principles and theorems deducible from them.

***Tathandlung* ("fact/act" or more literally, "deed/act")** – a term coined by Fichte to designate the original, self-positing act of the I, an act which is postulated by the philosopher as underlying the experienced separation between the subject and object of consciousness.

teleological suspension of the ethical – in Kierkegaard's philosophy, a condition in which the ethical law, which is universally applicable to human individuals, is suspended in a particular individual's case because that person's religious vocation places more specific demands upon him or her.

theoretical philosophy – that branch of transcendental idealism which accounts for human cognition, that is, for our experience of "representations accompanied by a feeling of necessity."

transcendent, transcendental – These words were used loosely in the eighteenth century before Kant to refer to metaphysical concepts common to all the branches of special metaphysics. For example, "Cause is a transcendent concept." Kant gave specific technical meanings to these words. (See "transcendental argument.")

transcendental argument – according to Kant, an argument in support of one claim, because the truth of this claim can be shown to be a necessary condition of the truth of another claim that is (necessarily) recognized as true.

transcendental unity of apperception – Kant's principle that, necessarily, any conscious state must be so unified with the other states of that consciousness as to make it possibly self-conscious.

transformative method (also called "the inversion principle") – Feuerbach proposed that God was merely a projection of idealized human qualities onto the world in the form of an allegedly independently existing being who is then believed to have the power to create us. As a consequence of this, Feuerbach proposed to trace all our talk of God back to some human quality or qualities. We may say that God is a "reification" of idealized human qualities. Marx adopted Feuerbach's method in political theory to criticize Hegel's reification of features of the state and society above the human relations of production. He transforms the Hegelian reifications into more concrete talk of humans and their productive relations.

universal – what is nonparticular, not specifically located in time and space, and logically accessible to every individual. In Hegel's philosophy, Spirit is universal; it includes all possible particulars, including every individual human being.

veil of Maya – the Vedantic "veil of illusion," a term that Schopenhauer appropriates as descriptive of the phenomenal world.

will – (according to Schopenhauer) the thing-in-itself, the reality that underlies phenomenal appearances.

***Wissenschaftslehre* (literally "theory of science" or "doctrine of scientific knowledge")** – Fichte's name for his entire system of philosophy; not to be confused with any particular book or presentation of this system, and, especially, not to be confused with the presentation of the mere "foundations" of this system (as presented, for example, in *The Foundations of the Entire Wissenschaftslehre*).

world as representation – (for Schopenhauer) the world as it appears as a consequence of the forms imposed by our minds; the phenomenal world.

world as will – (for Schopenhauer) the world as it is in itself; the noumenal world.

Index